Texts and Studies in Ancient Judaism

Texte und Studien zum Antiken Judentum

Edited by
Martin Hengel and Peter Schäfer

85

Hayim Lapin

Economy, Geography, and Provincial History in Later Roman Palestine

Mohr Siebeck

Hayim Lapin (BA, MA The Jewish Theological Seminary; BA, PhD Columbia University) is an Associate Professor at the University of Maryland, with a joint appointment in History and Jewish Studies.

Die Deutsche Bibliothek – CIP-Einheitsaufnahme

Lapin, Hayim:
Economy, geography, and provincial history in later roman palestine / Hayim Lapin. – Tübingen : Mohr Siebeck, 2001
(Texts and studies in ancient Judaism ; 85)
ISBN 3-16-147588-7

The book was printed by Gulde-Druck in Tübingen on non-aging paper and bound by Heinr. Koch in Tübingen.

ISSN 0721-8753

Preface

This study began some time ago in conversations with Steven Rubenstein (now of the University of Ohio, but then a fellow graduate student at Columbia University) who suggested it as a "quick" paper. Other projects, teaching, and occasional administrative responsibilities have intervened between those initial conversations and the present, and these in part account for the number of years that it took for the completion of this project. But the work of data collection and entry have also played a substantial role in postponing completion. In the interval, I have benefited from support from an Iwry Summer Fellowship from the Joseph and Rebecca Meyerhoff Center at the University of Maryland (1995), a Memorial Foundation for Jewish Culture Fellowship (1996–1997), an NEH Fellowship at the Albright Institute for Archaeological Research (1996–1997), a General Research Board Fellowship from the Graduate School of the University of Maryland (Spring 1999), and generous additional research, editorial, and production support from the Meyerhoff Center and from the Kaplan Fund. During a semester leave from Maryland in 1999, the Department of Religious Studies at the University of North Carolina at Greensboro gave me an academic home. In addition to the libraries of the institutions with which I have been affiliated during the writing of this project (the University of Maryland, UNCG, and the Albright Institute), I have also made ample use of the libraries of the Hebrew University (especially the Institute for Archaeology Library) and Duke University.

A number of people have read or heard all or part of the manuscript as it took shape, and to them I am especially grateful: Steven Rubenstein (who was kind enough to read chapters of the finished product), as well as Roger Bagnall, Cynthia Baker, James Brooks, Kenneth Holum, Derek Krueger, Eric Meyers, Jonathan Reed, Michael Satlow, and Seth Schwartz, and the 1996–1997 Fellows of the Albright Institute. Mordechai Avi'am, of the Israel Antiquities Authority, generously took me to several Galilean sites. Professor Martin Hengel, one of the editors of this series, was gracious and encouraging in his acceptance of this manuscript. This is a fitting opportunity to thank Professor Peter Schäfer, the other editor of this series, not only for offering the manuscript a publication home, but also for his support of my work over a number of years. A preliminary version of the argument was presented at the Association of Ancient Historians Annual

Meeting (1999) and I am grateful for the discussion that resulted from that presentation, as well as the comments from the members of a graduate seminar on ethnicity, indigeneity and nationalism at the University of Maryland. It is not merely a pious commonplace on my part to insist that errors or conceptual problems that remain in this book are my own and not theirs. The same is true of the contribution of two other people without whom the manuscript would not be in its present form: Ronda Angel, who provided editing for the manuscript, and Laurence J. Aurbach II, who drew the maps to my (changing) specifications.

Immeasurable thanks are due, finally, to Maxine L. Grossman for her multiple readings, extended discussions and criticism, and long-standing patience and encouragement. It is to her that this book is dedicated.

Table of Contents

Tables, Figures, and Maps

A. Tables

B. Figures

C. Maps

Note on Abbreviations and Citations

In general, abbreviations of the titles of both ancient texts and modern works have followed standard guides (in most cases approximating *The SBL Handbook of Style*, P. H. Alexander *et alii* eds. [Atlanta: Society of Biblical Literature, 1999]). Bibliographical abbreviations used in the notes are filled out in the Bibliography. Citations from the Mishnah, Talmud Yerushalmi, and Talmud Babli are given according to the standard printed editions, the Venice *editio princeps*, and the Vilna editions respectively. The Tosepta is cited by tractate, chapter, and *halākâ* according to the Lieberman edition, and where this is not available, from the Zuckermandel edition. For most other texts citations include page references to modern editions (listed in the Bibliography by editor). A similar citation style is used for texts in Greek and Latin, although editions and page numbers have generally been omitted for texts available in the *Loeb Classical Library*.

Introduction

The cultural and social historiography of later Roman Palestine must be rebuilt from the ground up. By this I mean not only the writing of history "from below" (a project against which both ancient literary evidence and contemporary practices of archaeology generally conspire), but also, quite literally, that a primary starting point for any reconsideration of the history of Palestine is the question of where and how people lived on the ground, and how their living spaces their inhabited landscapes were organized. Such a reconsideration requires a fundamental rethinking of household, local, and regional economies, of power within imperial and provincial political economies, and, ultimately, of such seemingly "primordial" cultural or social ties as kinship, religion, or ethnicity that framed the moral economies of historical agents.

That all of these aspects of the history of later Roman Palestine, and their mutual connections, require rethinking may be illustrated through an examination of two quotations from recent works on ancient Palestine. Neither work is a full-fledged treatment of the Palestinian economic or social landscape in antiquity as such, but, precisely for this reason, they illustrate the dichotomous historiographical use of two rather standard views of the Palestinian economy. They therefore further demonstrate how assumptions about the economy are implicated in a series of judgments about the identity, culture, and history of the people whose economy they describe. The first of these quotations comes from Yizhar Hirschfeld's study of rural settlements in Byzantine Palestine:

> Another, more significant, example of the [typical or generalized] village's lack of planning is the absence of public market squares. Among the many villages known to us, none contains a space that can be interpreted as a market square. This phenomenon corresponds well with the fact that the villages had no rows of shops. It appears, therefore, that the commercial activity reported in the rabbinic sources may have taken place in shops located in private dwellings as at Khirbet Susiya.... Another means of maintaining commercial relations between the cities and the villages was traveling salesmen, or peddlers, who are mentioned several times in rabbinic literature ....[1]

The second is from an attempt on the part of Richard Horsley to place Roman period Palestine within an imperial political economy in which relations of power are exploitative, and where agricultural production is "traditional":

---

[1] Hirschfeld 1997: 63–64.

> Virtually nothing indicates that towns and villages had established stores or even small markets. No buildings have been found in rural settlements that could be associated with stores or markets. No texts attest the appointment of an *agoranomos* (market inspector or supply officer) in villages. Rabbinic passages adduced for "market days" refer instead to "days of assembly" and court.... There would have been no need for a local village market since there was apparently little division of labor in village communities based on agricultural production.... As in agricultural production proper, so in the production of clothing and other crafts, the household members undertook most or all the stages themselves. The rabbinic ideals of a self-sufficient household and hostility to commerce simply reflect the traditional practices of peasant households attached to their ancestral lands. In this regard peasants in Galilee were no different from those elsewhere in the Roman empire. If there was a surplus or if craft-production was for sale, the producers apparently did most of the selling or bartering themselves.... At times the house functioned not only as "workshop," but as "store" as well.... "Most transactions in the village [sphere] were between local householders." Far from the village being a market economy, it appears that most village communities as well as their constituent households were relatively self sufficient.[2]

It is only a slight rhetorical exaggeration to state that, in this refraction of the formalist/substantivist debate, for Hirschfeld village marketing exists because it does, while for Horsley it does not exist because it does not. It is striking that despite their differing conclusions, both authors actually make similar claims, at least about material remains: the evidence for rural market *places* is lacking (do we know what these would have looked like?[3]) and the locus of rural production may have been in, or attached to, domestic spaces.

Underlying these two disparate readings of the Palestinian economy is a whole series of assumptions or questions that need revisiting, of which I will highlight here only a very few. One set of problems has to do with how literary texts are mined for meaningful or useful analytical concepts ("market" or "assembly"?) or for what "people" actually did (where did textually attested marketing, apparently largely invisible in the archaeological remains of the built environment, take place?). Another set, rather surprisingly (especially since Hirschfeld is particularly interested in the typologies of rural settlement[4]), is raised by the apparent willingness on the part of both authors to treat "villages" as a fairly autonomous and undifferentiated field. Yet, need all (or typical) villages have "maintain[ed] commercial relations with cities" (Hirschfeld) in the same ways, or, for that matter, at all? And why must we assume that villages in Palestine, let alone in the entire Roman world, typically were organized around the farming of "ancestral land" (Horsley)? This last expression implies stability of both kinship structures and the distribution of property, and with them a mode

---

2 Horsley 1996: 74–75; I have omitted parenthetical citations. The sentence in quotation marks is from Safrai 1994: 231.

3 Cf. Hirschfeld 1997: 63 n. 118.

4 Cf. Hirschfeld 1997: esp. 37–39.

of production (village and household autarky), lasting generations. Yet the extent to which agricultural land changed ownership in Palestine in late antiquity is in fact unknown, and evidence from tax registers from the Hermopolite nome in Egypt has been taken to suggest a fair amount of turnover through sale.[5] Furthermore, as I will argue in Chapter 2, there were substantial demographic shifts over the long period covered by the "Roman" and "Byzantine" periods, which saw the growth in the raw number of settlements throughout the region (and in some, perhaps, a later decline). Such shifts might plausibly be expected to have affected patterns of cultivation (including the bringing of new sub-regions under cultivation), and (although this is of necessity invisible to us) may well have impacted competition for agrarian resources and their expression at the regional, village, and household levels.

In both cases, too, the respective views of villages carry with them assumptions about religious and ethnic culture and how these are manifested. For Horsley, villages are said to be structurally like villages throughout the Roman empire; but they are also presumed, in their particular northern Palestinian setting, to link back in a meaningful way to an Israelite (i.e., not a Judaean/Jewish) historical identity.[6] For Hirschfeld, settlement patterns in "Jewish" eastern Galilee and the Golan, and in "Samaritan" Samaria, with few or no rural farmsteads, reflect cultural needs of Jews and Samaritans for communal institutions (synagogues) that regulated their religious and ethnic lives.[7] There are specific problems associated with these views. For instance, Horsley's links between Roman-period Galileans and Iron-Age northern "Israel," for instance, are elusive at best.[8] And synagogues themselves emerged for the first time as distinctive buildings in the period that Hirschfeld is surveying, so that the phenomenon of synagogues might equally be described as the product of regional settlement patterns and rural economic structure and not their determining cause.[9] For present purposes, however, it is more important that neither author takes sufficient account of ethnicity as a changing, historically constructed, phenomenon. The relations that bind villagers to one another and to other villages, and that bind non-elites to elites – whether in cities or villages – are among the

---

[5] Bagnall 1993: 72; Bowman 1985 on the Hermopolite Nome in the fourth century; cf. Rowlandson 1996: 178; 192–98 on the Oxyrhynchite.

[6] Cf., e.g., Horsley 1995: 172–75.

[7] Hirschfeld 1997: 42–43, 67; see also Pastor 1997, critiquing Hirschfeld 1996.

[8] See, e.g., Reed 1999; 2000: 23–61.

[9] See, e.g., Magness 2000 for the late dating of Palestinian synagogues. It may also be worth pointing out that the phenomenon of "gathering day" (discussed below in connection with *m. Meg.* 1:1–2), even as an idealizing construct of rural religious interactions by rabbis, may presuppose the role of central villages serving the religious and cultural needs of a wider rural population that gathers there on a periodic basis.

processes that need further elucidation if we are to develop a historically sensitive approach to Palestinian ethnicities in antiquity. These processes, in turn, are economic: they include, for instance, market-mediated ties where these exist, the distribution of landownership, and, with these, patterns of local or regional patronage. They are also inevitably spatial in that they span geographical space, and extend beyond the confines of the individual dwelling, farmstead, or village.

Finally, the place of political economy in all of this needs reconsideration. For Hirschfeld's treatment here it appears to play no particular role (except to the extent that the Roman suppression of two revolts is thought to have played a role in the demography and settlement pattern of Jews in Palestine). For Horsley, however, since the rural economy is subsumed under a regime of "traditional practices of peasant households and villages" and their relationship, marked by exploitation, with cities and elites, political economy is all-important but under-examined. Exploitation, for instance, can take many forms and need not be limited to the direct exaction of tribute.[10] How might particularly Roman and late-antique modalities of imperial rule have transformed the practices of labor, residence, and competition throughout the landscape? Might cities, for instance, have played a transformative role through their own peculiar consumption needs, including not only subsistence and luxury goods for consumption, redistribution, and display, but also labor for building and maintaining the urban agglomerations themselves, or for working the lands that provided the consumption or trade goods?

This book cannot, of course, offer definitive answers to all these questions. Rather, it offers a kind of exploratory exercise: to sift through literary and archaeological evidence and to ask how we might begin to lay the groundwork for a different kind of historiography. In doing so, I have made use of central-place theory, a set of models of geographical interaction, as a way of collecting and organizing material for further study. The pages that follow examine archaeological evidence for the distribution of sites of various kinds and sizes, some of the material evidence for economic activity in those sites, and literary evidence for the organization of economic activities across the northern Palestinian landscape. In this

---

[10] Cf. Wolf 1957, arguing that "closed corporate communities" of the kind Horsley appears to be envisioning (as merely "traditional") are the product of particular histories of exploitation. (Carlsen 1997: 47–50 discusses responses to Wolf, locating the closed corporate character of Mayan villages in pre-Columbian Mesoamerica, rather than in the aftermath of the Spanish conquest as Wolf had argued, but even so, there is no need to assume that all "traditional" villages everywhere are organized in this way.) Wolf 1966: 37–48 surveys a number of types of engagement of "peasants" with markets. See also the comments on Wolf in Roseberry 1989: 117–118; Cancian 1989: 134–137, 158 n. 8; and compare the marketing systems elaborated for China in Skinner 1964, 1965.

context I have asked, first, whether these remains from antiquity fit with ideal central-place landscapes, and second, whether the fit (and its failures) might contribute to reframing the way we understand the regional and economic history of later Roman Palestine.

The book as a whole is organized as follows. Chapter 1 describes one of the standard formulations of central-place theory and some of its implications for the study of a regional economy in later Roman Palestine. The archaeological material assembled for this study is reviewed in Chapter 2, with particular attention to five *Archaeological Survey of Israel* surveys. In addition, I have pointed out areas where archaeological material, as it is reported and published, poses interpretive problems for historians.

Chapter 3 offers hypothetical constructions of central-place models for northern Palestine. Chapter 4 deals with geographically specific literary traditions about marketing, and with texts dealing with marketing and commercialization more generally. Initially the goal of this study was the construction and comparison of detailed central-place "maps" of northern Palestine based on archaeological and literary evidence respectively for the distribution of economic and other institutions. As I argue in Chapters 3 and 4, below the level of the very largest sites such maps are beyond the limits of the evidence available. However, the theoretical framework discussed in Chapter 1 remains useful for thinking through the spatial aspects of the organization of the late-antique Palestinian economy. In general I believe that central-place considerations support a view of the regional economy in which the organization of a commercialized sector of the economy centered on cities may have structured rural production and exchange, but not necessarily or entirely through market mechanisms. Thus, although my general assessment is close to the view of an "embedded" economy, associated among ancient historians particularly with Moses Finley,[11] I have also been interested in the way that markets may have participated in the making of particular patterns of embeddedness. Finally, Chapter 5 reconsiders the history of northern Palestine in late antiquity based on the results of the preceding chapters.

The discussion of archaeological material is based on a database of more than 900 records compiled from published surveys and archaelogical reports. The database covers roughly the Galilee, the Bet Shean valley, and the Golan. Initially, the study was to focus on Galilee alone, but for reasons both practical (most notably, the regions best covered by published archaeological surveys) and analytical (the question of the history of regions in relation to one another), it quickly became clear that I needed to expand my research to adjacent areas. For present purposes (particularly for the

[11] Finley 1985. The characterization of premodern economies as "embedded" goes back to Polanyi 1944: 57.

production of exensive archaeological surveys) those areas fell largely within the borders of the modern State of Israel or territory controlled by it – but did not entirely correspond to late Roman organizations of territory. In this way the politics of contemporary nation-states (and the practices of archaeology within their territorial borders) have shaped my work, a feature whose significance was again underscored only late in the process of revision, when I was evaluating the possibility that what became the fifth-century province of Palaestina Secunda, largely split between present-day Jordan and Israel, could be construed as the unit of regional economic integration (see Chapter 2).

The ancient literary texts that I have drawn upon, preserved in Hebrew, Aramaic, Greek, and Latin, were largely, although by no means exclusively, written or compiled by Jews and Christians working as such. As noted above, the initial plan was to draw a map based on literary evidence, that might be compared in detail to a map based on published archaeological evidence. Although it subsequently became clear the various literary corpora were too spotty in their coverage (or, to put it another way, too rooted in their own specific, and frequently urban and elite, concerns) to allow for such a comparison, this initial goal constrained the way material to be discussed in Chapter 4 was collected, and that chapter therefore is focused primarily on texts (descriptions, anecdotes, rulings, and so on) that specifically localized certain kinds of economic activity in a particular city or village. In this regard, as in many others, given the geographical areas covered by this study, rabbinic texts were by far the richest body of material.

Central-place theory was developed in the early part of this century to describe the distribution of production, exchange, and markets over a geographical space, and like all analytical models starts with "unreal" assumptions, most notably the hypothesis of a flat featureless plain. Standard paradigms are based on assumptions about modern retail trade or production, precisely notions about whose relevance to the ancient economy historians are apt to disagree. Rather than simply provide normative or ideal models, therefore, I have spelled out in Chapter 1 my understanding of the "classical" derivation of central-place theory[12] and some of its implications for thinking through problems of economic history in Palestine. However, two particular features have made central-place theory useful for this study, and bear stressing here.

The first is that despite the ideal assumptions that theorists might make in laying out a model landscape, it is primarily a tool for describing the distribution of individual places over a geographical space and the different kinds of hierarchical relationships places may have to one another. It

[12] Based primarily on Christaller 1966, with Skinner 1964; 1965; C. A. Smith 1976b.

therefore has been useful for proposing possible analytical frameworks for discussing archaeological materials that are typically excavated, published, and interpreted first in connection with a given site, and where it is all too easy to elide the differences between artifacts (for instance, coins, imported pottery, or the presence or absence of pig bones) and the social formations such as trade or ethnicity that might account for their distribution. Slippages between individual examples and "the world" are possible in the case of literary material as well. A case in point is the insistence on the part of some scholars on describing in terms of regional specializations in market crops or in terms of market oriented trade, an episode that Josephus narrates about John of Gischala and the sale of oil to Jews in "Syria" under specific circumstances.[13]

The second feature (although one that will surely raise the hackles of some readers) is precisely the fact that central-place theory neither derives from the disciplines that specialize in the study of ancient Palestine, nor was it developed with the geography of Palestine in mind. It has, however, been used productively to analyze the spatial organization of agrarian economies in both contemporary and historical settings, and to link other questions of social organization to regional economic patterns. Hence in "applying" central-place theory to late antique Palestine, one is constrained to articulate historical questions in terms that are somewhat more abstract, and therefore more readily comparable to other examples across historical and geographical divides, than the terms of a particular geography, a particular political, ethnic, or religious historiography, or particular bodies of textual evidence in which such questions usually are posed.

No amount of theorizing can replace the contextualized study of the data that are available, with all their vagaries, lacunae, and problems. Part of the burden of this book has been to address some of the textual and material data, and I have also attempted to show in the last section of Chapter 1 the extent to which some literary passages are readily interpretable in economic and geographical terms derived from central-place theory and related fields. However, it is primarily the disciplining effects of working with an explicitly theoretical and generalizing framework, rather than pretending to no theoretical presuppositions and letting the "evidence" "speak for itself," that I have found most productive for reexamining some of the conventions of the historiography of later Roman Palestine. Central-place theory has been useful for disentangling the dichotomous terms in which the history of Palestine is frequently discussed – between archaeological and textual scholarship or evidence,[14] between "historical" and "literary"

[13] Josephus *BJ* 2.591–92; *Vita* 74–76. See below, Chapter 4.

[14] See, e.g., the contributions to Edwards, McCollough, eds. 1997. Ma'oz 1997 is a peculiar contribution, written by an archaeologist but insisting on the primacy of literary evidence. See also Reed 2000: 1–22.

understandings of texts,[15] between formalist and substantivist understandings of the ancient Palestinian economy (or in the somewhat cruder terms in which economic history in Roman Palestine is discussed, between assumptions of a free market and the firm knowledge of its absence[16]), not to mention such naturalized dichotomies as that between "Jew" and "gentile" – and hopefully for setting them aside. Perhaps unwisely, given a complex of academic fields that resist "theory" – whether in the form of "positivist" social-science modeling or of "postmodern" notions of indeterminacy, overdeterminedness, or multiplicity of meaning, as coming from outside the "evidence" – this study invokes one such social science model only to insist that the resulting reconstruction of a late antique landscape is at once fictive and at the same time productive for a regional history of later Roman northern Palestine.

The effects of this exploratory exercise – manifested textually in the kinds of arguments about evidence and models made below, and graphically in occasional calculations, diagrams, graphs, or tables – should not be confused with false claims to rigorous proof of historiographical hypotheses. The fit between "model" and "evidence" is never more than approximate or impressionistic. Moreover, it is a certainty (barring accidental resemblance) that no areas of later Roman northern Palestine matched in detail one of the models proposed in Chapter 3. However, the process of asking, for instance, what a maximal distribution of markets might look like, starting with certain kinds of base assumptions (Chapter 3), in turn has led to strategies for rereading texts that are frequently mobilized for discussions of the Palestinian economy, but with more explicit attention to regional contexts in which marketing and commercialization may be differentially distributed across the landscape (Chapter 4), and for placing both "commercial" patterns and "cultural" history within a regional political economy (Chapter 5). In focusing on a somewhat constraining set of analytical problems, I have thus tried to draw attention to the ways we go about asking the discursively powerful questions that make up the historiography of later Roman Palestine (itself a highly ideologically charged field), by bringing to bear on the conventional corpus of evidence a supplementary ("external") set of questions.

The chronological scope of this study is, nominally, the fourth century. This "nominality" bears some discussion since it reflects both my understanding of the evidence and my methodological decisions about how best to address it. The fourth-century present is the result of a somewhat

---

15 Cf. Lapin 1995: 1–36. See also Hayes 1997: 1–30; 1998.

16 The conventional terms of the discussion in recent years are given in the published debate: Horsley 1995a; Meyers 1995; Horsley 1995b. For a capsule description of the formalist-substantivist debate see Hodges 1988.

artificial assignment of a variety of kinds of evidence to a period of apparent convergence. By the fourth century the distribution of *poleis* (juridically recognized cities) and roads was more or less fixed, although there were later adjustments. The period of densest settlement and richest archaeological attestation in the areas covered by this study frequently is dated as simply "Byzantine," by which archaeologists working on Palestine typically mean a period that begins in the early fourth century and extends to the early seventh century, although there are alternative periodizations (see Chapter 2). The fourth century also saw substantial overlap between a developing Palestinian Christian literature relating to the history of Palestine and "amoraic" rabbinic texts. Christian texts with a distinct Palestinian connection began in the third century particularly with Origen but, in terms of the quantity and variety of material that has been preserved, intensify with Eusebius, whose writings straddle the period before and after the triumph of Constantine. "Amoraic" rabbinic texts, that is, texts whose primary named tradents fall between the early third century and the middle fourth century, were compiled and edited no earlier than the end of the fourth century.

If the fourth century setting is thus artificial (and if, in addition, this study makes regular use of material both predating and postdating that century), the effort to locate the historical present of this study in what is by the general standards of Roman and late-antique Palestinian historiography, a fairly circumscribed chronological framework, is significant for what it tries not to do. There is one tendency among some scholars to assume a slow pace of social change and long periods of cultural continuity, and consequently to ascribe to literary texts and archaeological evidence relevance for elucidating extended chronological periods. Groh, for instance, has called upon scholars interested in the first century to work creatively backward from later, more richly documented periods.[17] Safrai's study of Jewish community structures in Palestine explicitly argues that institutions described in some detail in rabbinic texts may be read back on periods centuries earlier.[18] Although they may yield valuable results, such approaches are also fundamentally at odds with the view taken here in that they risk assuming precisely the naturalness, or at least the stability, of "primordialities" such as ethnicity, kinship, or religious affiliation, or of modes of social interactions, such as village organization or trade, that need to be further historicized. Instead, I have attempted to theorize a historical "moment" at which discrete bodies of material can be brought to bear on one another, while striving to be sensitive to patterns of both continuity and change. My approach has its own idealizing and leveling tendencies,

[17] Groh 1997: 33–34. Cf. Taylor 1993.

[18] Safrai 1995.

and can offer no more than a fictive construction of a history (as any "historical" work, at least on late-antique Palestine, ultimately must be), but it is presented as one that may help to recast the terms in which we understand that history and the sources upon which we base it.

In part, this book is intended to lay preliminary groundwork for a reconsideration of the history of Roman Palestine as a history of provincialization.[19] The chapters that follow do not do justice to this area of inquiry, but their geographical focus offers a point of entry. I have tried to show in what follows, and particularly in Chapter 5, that in aggregate, and over an extended period of time, Roman imperial administrative decisions – the initial incorporation of territory into a province or its separation as part of a client kingdom; the placement or removal of soldiers; the elevation or reduction in status of particular sites – transformed the human landscape of northern Palestine. The point is not to argue that Roman administrators systematically set about a coherent and systematic policy of provincial transformation. "Urbanization" may serve as an example of the kind of process I am referring to, in the sense that it is difficult if not impossible to demonstrate an actual imperial policy of building cities,[20] yet cities were tied to imperial Roman administrative strategies on a number of different levels. Nor, in pointing to a *process* of provincialization, do I mean to suggest a series of inevitable stages that the territory went through. The point, instead, is to stress the consequences of imperial power – manifested, on the ground, in which people were given or took upon themselves certain prerogatives; in where and how they lived; and, in a literal sense, in what and how much was planted, and, of that, where and how and by whom it ultimately was consumed – in structuring the historical agencies of both the "rulers" and the "provincials" (neither forming a coherent or uniform group)[21] and in organizing the structures of everyday life.

The approach suggested here foregrounds broad structural problems, such as long-term demographic changes or urbanization. This is, in part, making a virtue of necessity. Given the nature, paucity, and distribution of the literary and archaeological evidence that can be mobilized for a history of Roman Palestine it is much easier to speak in telescoped periodizations of generations or centuries, and of general historical trends that mark such periods. For northern Palestine, where so much depends on rabbinic literature, some scholars still attempt to draw out the intentionalities of agents

---

[19] My thinking on provincialization has been influenced by Mitchell 1993; Alcock 1993; Woolf 1998.

[20] Isaac 1992: 333–371.

[21] My thinking on power (imperial and local) and historical agency has been shaped by Wolf 1982; O'Hanlon 1988; Asad 1993: 1–24; Comaroff, Comaroff 1997: 1–62; Guha 1988; 1997.

whose actions or decisions are narrated in rabbinic texts.[22] However, by and large, scholarly convention has come to emphasize how texts, rather than agents, relate to historiographical problems or questions, rather than to lived events. This generalization on my part encompasses in its sweep practitioners as diverse in their respective methodological (and political) approaches as Daniel Boyarin's study of sex and gender and more recently of martyrdom in rabbinic culture, Catherine Hezser's application of network theory to the history of the rabbinic movement, Lee I. Levine's work on the rabbinic "class" and on the history of the Palestinian patriarchate, and Zeev Safrai's works on economy or on Jewish community, or Richard Kalmin's comparison of Palestinian and Babylonian rabbinic culture.[23]

One consequence of foregrounding long-term developments, and particularly of thinking in terms of provincialization as an organizing problem and framing the discussion of that problem in regional terms, is a historiographical framework in which subject populations do not so much autonomously "make their own history" as come to terms with a political economy that is only ever partly of their own making. In addition to my conviction that such factors as material relations, imperial rule, and ecology do in fact constrain both the day-to-day life of "subalterns" and how this is understood or imagined, in the present instance such a limiting view of subaltern autonomy serves a specific purpose as well. In the case of ancient Palestine, where the autonomy and naturalness of ancient Jews and Judaism as historical entities, as well as the presence of both on the landscape, are too easily taken for granted, a focus on ways in which ethnicity and territoriality are the products of a history and not its motors is a desideratum. In fact, even the notion of a history of Palestine, or of the land of Israel, or of the Holy Land, or of Eretz Israel, is already embedded in a series of competing claims on the identity of a geographical territory, as the variety of names by which one may name that territory illustrates. All of these locutions – regardless of the antiquity of their formulation, their connections with contemporary sensibilities, or the conscious or unconscious ideological (religious or political) commitments of those who insist upon or refuse one or another of the names, or even who dismiss the significance of the debate over terminology – in a sense assume the stability of "the land" as the stage for the unfolding of the drama of history.

Yet "the land" was far from stable, and it has been remade again and again through a history of human use, exploitation, and abandonment. The

---

22 Recent examples, on related issues, include Habas 1996; Oppenheimer 1996: 214–18.

23 Boyarin 1993; 1999; Hezser 1997; Levine 1979; 1987; 1996; Safrai 1994; 1995; Kalmin 1999.

terracing of hillsides, the subdivisions of land into plots, the draining of valley floors, the diverting of water whether to feed (and wastefully) the urban populations or for irrigation, and the introduction or intensification of the production of crops, the quarrying of building stone, and the building or quarrying of agricultural installations in the countryside are some indications of the role that humans in Roman and late-antique Palestine have had in shaping the ecological landscape. One line of historiography running from A. H. M. Jones through Avi-Yonah, to, in their different ways, Z. Safrai and Tsafrir makes note of the administrative aspects of that making and remaking through tracing the history of administrative subdivisions of territory and through the history of urbanization.[24] Perhaps less frequently explicitly addressed is the fact that there is no single, unambiguous set of boundaries for northern Palestine in the Roman and Byzantine periods. Galilee could be ruled from Jerusalem, Caesarea, or Scythopolis, or under Herod Antipas, perhaps locally. Under Herod's sons Galilee was ruled separately from the Golan, while part of the territories under study here (at least the cities of Hippos and Scythopolis each, presumably, with a rural hinterland) were assigned to the province of Syria; and by the late first century Agrippa II, who ruled the present-day Golan as well as territories further to the East, was assigned at least some portion of eastern Lower Galilee. Within that territory, administrative strategies might shift – perhaps most notably after the late first century from a system of toparchies in a royal territory to a provincial territory ruled through urban elites – and might therefore differentially favor certain sites within the region as concentrations of local power or wealth. Such shifts at the local or the broader territorial levels have left their most obvious traces in "the land" in the form of monumental city architecture and in the form of roads. However, to the extent that monumentalized cities were also centers of consumption, and that roads served not only trade between cities but at least in part the needs of a tax collecting provincial administration as well, the administrative history of northern Palestine was played out in generally (from our vantage point) imperceptible ways in the rural hinterland as well. "The land," far from simply a historical constant, is thus in many ways the product of its multiple and dialectical histories linking together the direct use or non-use of land, the groups of humans living on or working it, themselves shaped by complex patterns of cooperation, competition, and exploitation, and the wider political economies that have shaped the patterns of social organization, land use, and social integration on both a local and a broader regional level.

Beyond problematizing the way that we treat land in the history of Palestine in late antiquity, the goal here is to make use of a focus on human

---

[24] Jones 1931; 1971; Safrai 1980a; 1980b; Tsafrir 1986; *TIR*, Introduction.

geography as an aspect of provincial history in order to problematize still other aspects of the historiography of later Roman northern Palestine. Most notably, contemporary histories of northern Palestine conventionally are elided into the history of Jews, and that, in turn, into the history of rabbis. To be sure, there are good reasons for this, primarily the fact that Palestinian rabbinic literature is both quite rich and also provides almost the only literary sources for reconstructing the history of the region, and thus inevitably skews our perspective. What a focus on provincialization may help to highlight, however, is the complexities of the social and cultural history of northern Palestine, including its Jews. Thus, for instance, S. Schwartz argues that in the second and third centuries, following the suppression of the Judaean revolts against Rome, "Judaism" failed as a collective ideology of Palestinian "Jews" and was replaced by a fairly conventional Roman paganism, at least among elites, only to be revived in late antiquity.[25] The very picture we can derive of Jewish ethnicity in later Roman Palestine, seemingly so stable, may in fact be the result of a long history of social and demographic change shaped in part by imperial administration of the province.

Eric Meyers, who first raised the question of Galilean regionalism that the present study attempts to address, continues to argue for "calling the Upper Galilee, and parts of the Golan, conservative, Semitic and overwhelmingly Jewish, and rural," although he has revised the details of this view a number of times since he first proposed it.[26] Yet, the ruralness of these two areas – and in context Meyers seems to understand "rural" as the absence of juridically recognized cities – is an administrative feature, tied, no doubt, to the settlement history and relative ruggedness of the terrain, but certainly not inevitable. The long period to which Meyers refers saw sufficient changes throughout northern Palestine, at least in the number of settlements, to suggest substantial demographic transformations (see Chapter 2). At least in the Golan, Ma'oz has argued for late (i.e., fourth or fifth century) resettlement of the "Jewish" areas.[27] If both that claim and Meyers's characterization are correct, the "conservatism" of the Golan, far from reflecting simply the persistence of ancestral practice by the native populations, may be the product of late settlers in an economic periphery tied to the "urbanized" provincial core. There is, in addition, a certain irony in Meyers's characterization of upper Galilee, since it is a site in upper Galilee that yielded a Greek inscription from the very end of the second century in honor of the imperial family with the involvement of "the Jews" (in fulfillment of a vow?), discovered in a building that some have

[25] Schwartz forthcoming.

[26] E. M. Meyers 1997: 58–59. See also E. M. Meyers 1979; 1985; 1987; 1995.

[27] Ma'oz 1986: 96–101.

identified as a temple.[28] But if Meyers's characterization remains basically correct for upper Galilee in the fourth century and later (and this requires reconsideration), the more interesting question is how such modes of religious acknowledgment of the imperial family, possibly expressed through participation in the building of rural temples, "worked" in the lives of Palestinian Jews who identified themselves as *Ioudaioi*, and whether (and if so, when) they ceased to do so. In other words, provincialization not only may have promoted a kind of obvious "romanization" or "hellenization" (measured in the incidence of Greek inscriptions, architectural conventions, and so on) but also may have been productive of local, seemingly "indigenous" and "conservative," cultures as well. In fact, the very dichotomy between such poles of cultural conformity may miss the construction of both "hellenized" and "conservative" as aspects of a provincial culture.[29]

The immediate project of the chapters that follow is not to study the cultural and social history of provincialization as such, but rather to provide a framework for further examining its geographical dimensions. The "Jewishness" of upper Galilee and portions of the Golan offers an example, since here we may potentially have the intersection between the administrative history of the region including the subdivision of the province into urban territories – the differential economic development of some regions as "core" and others as "periphery" – and their correlation with a history of rural ethnicity as this emerges primarily on the basis of late antique synagogues and their distribution. So too do both the question of "Christianization" in Tiberias and Sepphoris, and the emergence of the rabbinic movement in Palestine with particular connections to cities. But more than this, and somewhat paradoxically given the present insistence upon "theory," the goal of the present study – with its attention to the distribution of villages and towns, and to the articulation of agriculture, exchange, and marketing with respect to that distribution – is to ground a future study of social and cultural history in later Roman Palestine in the everyday lives of provincials.

---

28 *CIJ* 972; literature in *TIR* 209, *s.v.* Qision. Identification as a temple: Kohl, Watzinger 1916: 209; Kitchener in Conder, Kitchener: 1881: 241. Schwartz forthcoming.

29 Cf. Roseberry, O'Brien 1991.

Chapter 1

Central Places in Theory and Practice

In its earliest formulations, and in its conventional applications, central-place theory deals primarily with patterns of distribution of marketing over space. Limited evidence for rural marketing in ancient Palestine can be found in literary texts (see Chapter 4), and the general diffusion of at least some goods (e.g., imported finewares) through trade seems reasonable, although the scale of such trade and its social distribution within villages remains unknown. In addition, a fair amount of material (literary and archaeological) can be marshaled in favor of an argument for at least some intra- and interurban marketing. However, the general absence of detailed evidence (beyond occasional, anecdotal notices) for how urban marketing or trade may have overlaid patterns of rural production or exchange makes it difficult to assess patterns of regional economic integration or striation. Central-place theory, with its attention precisely to such patterns, is useful for theorizing (i.e., for discerning possible "facts of," in light of "evidence for") the structure of the later Roman period economy in northern Palestine. Moreover, in treatments of varieties of rural distribution of markets, central-place theory offers a point of entry for a discussion about modalities of orientation to marketing in agrarian societies, and about the connections between these modalities and structures of social praxis and political power.

A detailed, if hypotetical, reconstruction of central-place models in northern Palestine is postponed until Chapter 3. In this chapter, the focus is on some of the implications of this theoretical framing of geographical space for rethinking aspects of the economy of later Roman Palestine in more general terms. In anticipation of criticism that the use of central-place theory is merely "imposed" upon the "evidence," the chapter concludes with a review of a few examples drawn from rabbinic texts (which almost certainly have a Galilean provenance) that can be read fairly easily in terms of the general theoretical claims of central-place theory.

A. Description of Central-Place Models

Developed independently by two scholars, Christaller and Lösch, in the 1930s,[1] central-place theory attempts to analyze the spatial dimensions of the distribution of markets. Although it had something of a vogue in the 1960s and 1970s outside the discipline of Geography, the theoretical framework has yet to be brought to bear on the history of Palestine in late antiquity in any detail.[2] The following brief description of the geographical and geometrical claims of the theory, is based on the model proposed by Christaller.[3] The starting assumption – clearly one that will not to be confirmed in any empirical context – is that all interactions take place on a flat unbounded plain with an even distribution of resources and population. This means that production costs for the same product at the same scale of production are everywhere the same, and that transportation costs for any given goods are the same in every direction.

Under these circumstances we are able to imagine what usually are referred to as the range and threshold for producers or sellers of any given good. The effective cost for a purchaser of any good produced or sold in a location is the price plus the added costs of acquiring the good, most notably the outlay for transportation, but also opportunity costs such as the loss of work time. The greater the distance, time, or effort involved in finding or transporting the good, the higher that cost. For any given potential buyer, there is a point (a distance from the point of sale) at which the costs associated with acquiring a good will make it too expensive to be bought. A circle marking the distance at which, for a region as a whole, a commodity ceases to be marketable from a given point of production or sale is the absolute (Christaller referred to it as "ideal"[4]) *range* of the good, the maximal area from which a seller might be able to draw customers. Because competing sellers might be expected to cut into each other's territory, Christaller's model recognizes that in practice goods may have rather smaller effective ("real") ranges.

The *threshold* is a circle that encloses the minimum number of sales necessary to make the production or sale of a product viable. Like the range, the size of the threshold is a function of such factors as consumer density (in turn dependent upon population density), price of the good, and

---

[1] Christaller 1966; Lösch 1954, originally published in 1933 and 1939 respectively.

[2] Safrai 1994, and earlier articles upon which that book is based, cites some of the standard literature; see also the rather brief treatment in I. W. J. Hopkins 1980; and Roll, Ayalon 1989: 233–37. Villeneuve 1985: 80 gestures toward central-place theory in connection with the Hauran.

[3] For a more detailed discussion see, in addition to Christaller, Berry 1967; C. A. Smith 1976b; Hodges 1988; and especially Skinner 1964, 1965, 1977b.

[4] Christaller 1966: 57.

transportation costs. With higher consumer density the threshold is smaller (the large number of customers located nearby means that the seller can make more sales in a smaller area). The more expensive or less in demand a good is, the larger the threshold it is likely to require. Thus, in contrast to, say, bakers, who are described, in a passage discussed later in this chapter, as operating even in small villages (*kĕparîm*), such goods or services as expensive luxury textiles or skilled, literate ritual specialists such as amulet writers (reasonable candidates for higher-threshold goods in late-antique Palestine[5]) might be expected to require a sizable threshold: while providers might need to make fewer transactions to break even, the demand is smaller and hence providers may have to draw buyers from a wider area. Where the effective range of a good is smaller than its threshold (where a seller requires purchases from a wider area in order to break even than she or he can actually draw upon) it cannot be sold.

Using the notions of threshold and range, Christaller worked out a hierarchically organized distribution of markets structured according to what he referred to as the "market" principle, where as a result of market competition sellers will attempt to cover the landscape as densely as possible, while at the same time maximizing their distance from one another. Presentations of central-place theory usually include two additional model landscapes based on what Christaller described as the "transportation" and "separation" (or "administration") principles.[6] For simplicity, the following description of all three below uses a four-level hierarchy of sites labeled A through D, where A is the highest-level market center, offering goods with the highest threshold, and D represents sites that do not bear a market (see Figure. 1.1; note that only a few sample D-level sites are marked).

On the most general level, in all three model landscapes the hierarchy is a result of the expectation that goods with a high threshold (requiring a large marketing area) will be offered at fewer places at greater distances from one another than goods with a low threshold (requiring a small market area). Christaller's description focused on the spread of retail providers of "central" goods for which there is fairly elastic demand (his examples, as

---

[5] See, e.g., *y. ʿAb. Zar.* 1:2 (39c): travel to a fair at Scythopolis to purchase special thread; *V. Euthy.* 57, ed. E. Schwartz 1939: 78: travel to a local city to hire a magician.

[6] See Christaller 1966: 72–80. Although the "transportation" and "separation" principles are discussed by Christaller, and the standard landscapes (dubbed $K = 4$ and $K = 7$ by central-place theorists, see below) are usually referred to as "Christaller's" (as early as Lösch 1954: 131–3, n. 16), they are not articulated as such in *Central Places in Southern Germany*. In fact, Christaller's discussion there focuses on the variety of ways a landscape based on the market principle might be distorted by the transport or administration principles, not on the single landscape that exemplifies each of these principles (see especially Christaller's Figures 4 [p. 74] and 6 [p. 79]).

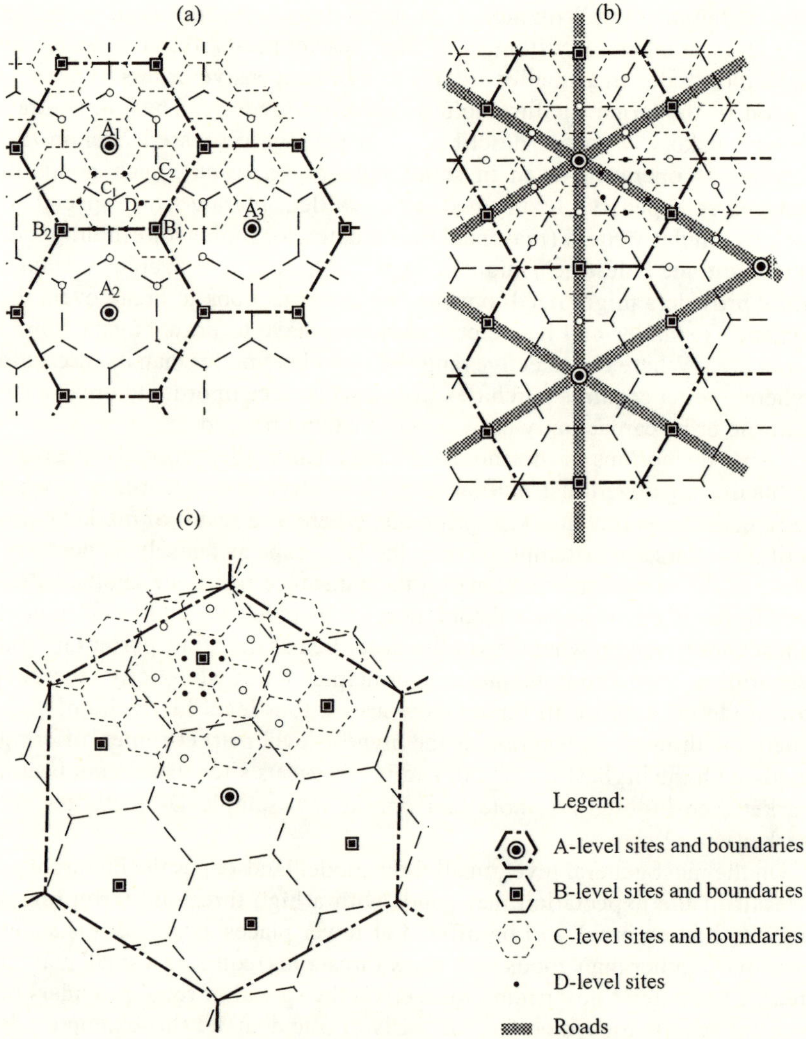

Figure 1.1: THREE CENTRAL-PLACE MODELS
(a) "Market" ($K = 3$); (b) "Transportation" ($K = 4$); (c) "Administration" ($K = 7$)

Smith noted, typically involve visits to a doctor or to a cinema) with respect to potential consumers, and a cash-based economy. One could, especially given the ways in which central-place theory will be invoked below, work from other directions as well (e.g., modeling the location of wholesale traders interested in bulking agricultural surplus production for transfer to central markets). However, Christaller's account is conceptually simple and illustrates well the spatial aspects of location in marketing.

All three model landscapes assume an unbounded, featureless plain, and also that sites are evenly distributed across the landscape. The densest packing of sites occurs if they are positioned on a hexagonal net, and most central-place models are built on this distribution.[7] Because markets are part of this pattern of sites, markets, too, at each level (C, B, and A) are distributed on a hexagonal plan. In addition, markets are arranged so that higher-level markets are superimposed on lower-level markets: each A-level site is also a B-level site for a smaller area, and each B-level site (including the A-level sites) is also a C-level site.[8] To use the examples suggested above, high-level market sites are expected to have bakers serving much the same functions locally as bakers in small villages, but also to have sellers of expensive textiles not found in villages and drawing on customers from a wider area (e.g., visitors from the countryside) than

---

[7] Central-place models can be worked out with any geometrical shapes that will fully cover the surface of the imagined plain: Lösch discusses squares and equilateral triangles (Lösch 1954: 110–114, 133–134), and Johnson 1970: 771–773 (and Fig. 2) makes use of a rhomboidal model.

[8] It is precisely here that Lösch differs from Christaller. Lösch used a somewhat different procedure (Lösch 1954: 116–30): beginning with a background of locations, not all of which are markets, arranged on a hexagonal web he proceeded to draw hexagonal thresholds that were integral multiples of the initial hexagons that also superimposed in a regular way upon lower level thresholds. Thus if we imagine a landscape settled with sites about 1.7 km apart (surrounded by a hexagonal territories of about 4 km^2; for these figures see further below), the first level of markets would have a threshold of approximately 1.5 and would be approximately 2.9 km apart ($K = 3$). However, the next market threshold would be 1.7 km, with sites at 3.4 km apart ($K = 4$), and the one after that at 2.25 km, and 4.5 km apart ($K = 7$), and thresholds of $K = 9$, 11, 12, and still higher values of K would be still further spaced. Thus, unlike Christaller's model, Lösch did not envision discrete levels of sites at each of which essentially the same marketing functions applied, but rather, a more variegated system in which two sites with the same number of superimposed centers might do different things, and in which one of the features of a fully worked out landscape is an internal differentiation between subregions better and more poorly served by roads and markets. My reasons for following Christaller in this regard are as follows. (1) While Lösch's model may lend itself more to the variable locational requirements of industrial production, Christaller's model seems well-suited to agrarian production and exchange, particularly, as in ancient Palestine, more or less the same range of products is likely to have been both produced and consumed in the region. (2) There are examples of the kind of market hierarchy proposed by Christaller in agrarian societies (see C. A. Smith 1976b: 23–28 for discussion). (3) It is precisely the rather strict (artificial) constraints of Christaller-type models that make them good analytical tools for examining the data from late-antique Palestine (where, as we shall see in the next chapter, well quantified measurements are difficult to come by). (4) The most useful applications of central-place theory in agrarian contexts that I have found apply a Christaller-like central-place model (C. A. Smith 1976b, 1976b, and especially Skinner 1964, 1965, 1977b). Hence there is more room for argument both from analogy and by contrast.

do bakers. What distinguishes the three model landscapes ("market," "transportation," and "administration") from one another is how, at each level, market sites are distributed with respect to sites one level lower (C with respect to D; B to C; A to B) or higher (D to C; C to B; B to A).

The first of these models, the so-called "market" landscape, is mapped out in Figure 1.1 (a). In this drawing every lower-level site is located between three higher-level sites. Thus, the point marked D in that figure, which does not bear a market, is equidistant from C_1 and C_2, as well as from B_1 (which also serves as a C-level market). C_1, in turn, is equidistant from B-level markets at A_1, B_1, and B_2; and B_1 from A_1, A_2, and A_3. As a result, in this configuration the hexagon around any upper-level site will enclose an area three times the size of the hexagon associated with a site one level lower.[9] For this reason, this landscape conventionally is referred to as $K = 3$.

The underlying logic of this model landscape can be understood better if we briefly try to "build" it from the top down. Such a procedure, not unrealistically, gives priority to already existing high-level marketing sites in the process of the development and distribution of regional marketing.[10] Imagine a landscape with sites evenly distributed as in Figure 1.1 (a), but where there are only A-level markets, offering the whole gamut of available goods, from highest to lowest threshold. Assuming competitive

---

[9] In Figure 1.1, the A-level boundary of A_1 overlaps with one third of the B-level hexagon around B_1, B_2, and of each of the four other B-level sites on the perimeter of the area around A_1, or two B-level areas. A_1 also serves as a B-level site (hence it too is surrounded by a B-level hexagon), so the entire area within the A-level hexagon around A_1 equals three B-level hexagons.

[10] The model can also be constructed from the bottom up (cf. Table 1.1 below), which emphasizes the pressure to fill the landscape as fully as possible. On the simplest, but also least realistic, level, one can start with the assumption of a landscape fully settled with sites that cannot by themselves support markets (D-level) sites. Marketing might arise at a given site if traders could attract the custom of the six nearest sites (i.e., what central-place theorists call $K = 7$; see below). However, the densest concentration will result if traders rely on only part of the custom of those sites and locate at every third site. Under these circumstances, if a trader of lowest order goods is located in one site, the nearest available sites for market location are the nearest six *non*-adjacent sites. These become C-level sites, organized on a hexagonal plan. If upper-level market sites are assumed to coincide with lower level sites, then if one C-level site should offer still higher-level (B-level) goods, the nearest available sites for similar B-level marketing are the C-level sites on the ring *beyond* the closest C-level sites; and so on for the formation of A-level sites. In this way, the initial distribution of sites and the initial modality of marketing constrains later development. However, the preceding sketch, although useful for understanding the geometry of central-place marketing, certainly does not do justice to the dynamic processes underlying settlement distribution or of village growth or fission, or to marketing as a function of settlement density or intensification, for which see Skinner 1965: 196–206.

marketing, for the highest-order goods the territories separating the existing markets should correspond to something like their minimum threshold.[11] That is to say, sellers of highest-order goods have filled the landscape as densely as possible for those goods. Traders also can offer goods in sites between the existing A-level sites, but only for goods with thresholds low enough to not prevent the marketing of the same goods at the A-level sites, which already offer them. By locating at points equidistant from three A-level sites (i.e., the B-level sites in Figure 1.1 (a)), sellers of B-level goods get as far as possible from existing competition, thus maximizing their effective range, and allowing them to offer goods with as high a minimum threshold as they can. As a result, here, as in the two models to be discussed presently, the A-level sites also serve as B- and C-level sites. (Note that in the drawings in Fig. 1.1, each A-level site is also bounded by smaller B- and C-level hexagons). Depending upon the depth of the model one is constructing, this process of new market location may in theory be reproduced indefinitely for still lower-level sites.

The next standard central-place landscape commonly is referred to as based on the "transportation" principle (Fig. 1.1 (b)). Here the market assumptions are more or less the same, but they are modified by the additional assumption that roads connect major sites and that the placement of lower-level sites is constrained by the course of roads. Each B-level site now occurs along a roadway, midway between two, not three, A-level sites. In this configuration the hexagon marking the boundary of a site is four times that of the sites at the next level down.[12] In central-place theory parlance this is referred to as $K = 4$. In order to fill out lower levels of the system consistently, one must assume that a secondary network of roads (narrower, perhaps, or unpaved, impassable in bad weather conditions, or not suitable for carts or animals) connects B-level sites, at the midpoints of which C-level sites are located; and that a tertiary road system, in turn, connects C-level sites and constrains the placement of D-level sites.[13]

Finally, the third standard landscape commonly is described as based on the "administration" or "separation" principle (see Fig. 1.1 (c)). In this case

---

[11] Lösch 1954: 109–10; Christaller 1966: 60–61.

[12] Thus in Fig. 1.1 (b), each A-level site encloses four B-level hexagons: the B-level boundary surrounding itself the A-level site itself, plus one half the area bounding each of the six surrounding B-level sites.

[13] Again, this description of the "transportation" ($K = 4$) landscape builds downward rather than upward. In terms of the geometry one certainly could have done this, but it seems that if the $K = 4$ network in fact crystallizes a "traffic" principle across an extensive landscape, one should begin with major, if not already existing, roads. However, note once again the developmental model in Skinner 1965: 196–206 that begins at the village level and that assumes the development of both a settlement and market system and a road network more or less concurrently.

each-lower level site is associated with only one upper-level site. Within the constraints we are working with, the densest version of such a pattern occurs if the market territory of one site overlaps with that of the six adjacent lower level sites. As a result, the area of the hexagon bounding an upper-level site is seven times that of a lower-level site, hence the designation $K = 7$. In the previous two model landscapes, "market" considerations (the greatest distribution of goods from the point of view of the consumer; the attempt to fill all possible niches while maximizing distance from other market centers from the point of view of traders) had lower-level markets located at sites equidistant from two or three upper-level sites. Thus, in the two previous models even if a B-level site (a "town") were administratively part of the territory of an A-level site (a "city"), to or through which it paid taxes or to which its officials were answerable, in terms of its market relationships, that town would be equally well-positioned with respect to one or two other cities. By contrast in the "separation" or "administration" ($K = 7$) landscape, market boundaries can be made directly to coincide with administrative boundaries.

For the most part, the preceding sketch of the three primary central-place configurations started from high-level sites ("cities") and worked downward. This draws attention to the differences between the configurations in terms of the extent to which they allow traders to maximize their effective range. For each A-level site there are more B-level markets in a "transportation" landscape than in a "market" landscape, and more still in an "administration" landscape. Although for simplicity these are marked as "B-level" sites in each landscape, clearly, had we begun with equally spaced A-level sites in all three cases, the distance between B-level sites, and consequently the effective range and the minimum threshold of the highest-level goods available there (more or less represented by the size of the B-level hexagon) would get smaller as we move from $K = 3$ to $K = 4$ to $K = 7$.[14]

Some initial implications of this for understanding a "real" economic landscape may be seen by a brief examination of Table 1.1. For purposes of illustration, that table constructs the three standard landscapes from the bottom up, assuming in each case that the distance between non-market sites is the same. Since, in Chapter 3, I will offer the working assumption that at least in lower Galilee settlement density may have been as high as 40 per 100 km^2, or 2.5 km^2 per settlement (see Chapter 2 for discussion of settlement densities), that assumption provided the basis for distances in Table 1.1. With a hexagonal arrangment this settlement density yields an

---

[14] Cf. Skinner 1965: 197–200, who associates his Model A ($K = 4$) with rougher terrain, and assumes that it implies longer absolute distances between sites than his Model B ($K = 3$).

average distance between sites of 1.7 km.[15] Beginning with this distribution the table incoporates additional levels based on values of K until the distance between sites reached something like the scale of distances between cities in later Roman northern Palestine (again, see Chapter 3).

Table 1.1: COMPARISON OF THREE STANDARD CENTRAL PLACE LANDSCAPES

	"Market" ($K = 3$)		"Transportation" ($K = 4$)		"Administration" ($K = 7$)	
Level	*no. of sites*	*distance*	*no. of sites*	*distance*	*no. of sites*	*distance*
F	162	1.7				
E	54	2.9	192	1.7		
D	18	5.1	48	3.4	294	1.7
C	6	8.8	12	6.8	42	4.5
B	2	15.2	3	13.6	6	11.9
A ("City")	1	26.4	1	27.2	1	31.5
Total no. of sites:	243		256		343	

It is worth pointing out that with the bottom-up construction of Table 1.1, distances between B-level sites are greatest for the "market" landscape ($K = 3$) and progressively smaller for the "transportation" ($K = 4$) and "adminstration" ($K = 7$) landscapes, while the distance between A-level sites ("cities") is actually smallest for the "market" landscape and gets larger for the other two models. In other words, relative to higher-level sites, second-level sites (B-level with respect to A, C with respect to B, and so on) are more widely spaced for a "market" landscape. One consequence of this is that a "market" landscape allows for not only relatively more markets over space (one site in three is market-bearing, as opposed to one in four for $K = 4$ or one in seven for $K = 7$), but also a more finely graded hierarchy of markets more closely attuned to the distribution of demand. In contrast to a "market" landscape, an "administration" landscape actually loses two levels of markets despite the larger geographical area covered.

B. Some Implications of Theoretical Landscapes

For a discussion of the regional economy of later Roman Palestine and for a reconstruction of levels and complexities of regional integration (or their

---

[15] Each site is surrounded by an area (A) of 2.5 km^2. Assuming even distribution, the distance (D) between sites is twice that of the distance (h) between the site and the mid-point of the bounding hexagon, or:

$$D = 2h = 2\sqrt{\frac{A}{2\sqrt{3}}}$$

And since A = 2.5 km^2, D = 1.699 km.

absence), one significance of a comparison of these three standard central-place landscapes is that it helps to focus attention on how the pattern of distribution of markets (and not necessarily the presence or absence of markets as such) may relate to rural commercialization. Carol Smith, for instance, has argued that an "administration" landscape is likely to coordinate with low levels of rural commercialization.[16] It is not only that there are fewer markets overall (one market site to six non market sites, as opposed to one to two or three for the other two landscapes). The "administration" landscape also is organized as a pyramid of market sites with potentially monopolistic control over their hinterlands. In terms of distance, consumers – even low-level purchasers from non-market-bearing sites – are always closer to one market site than to another, and as the level of the market rises (and the distance between markets rises, see Table 1.1), the economic implications of that distance rise as well. Recall too that in a $K = 7$ landscape, market boundaries can be made to correspond to administrative boundaries (as, by definition, they cannot for $K = 3$ or $K = 4$). As rural purchasers of commercial goods, inhabitants of non-market sites face markets controlled by comparatively fewer, and potentially centrally organized, people in a position conducive to monopoly, hence higher prices. As sellers of rural produce they are in competition with one another to sell to marketers in those same market sites who may be able to set their own (low) prices. Within such a setting, a low level of rural commercialization and "irrational" strategies of household or village self-sufficiency are a reasonable response.[17] At the extreme limit, the engagement of rural producers in a market may be limited to acquiring those few things that cannot be made or found locally, or to get coin for tax purposes. Indeed, the requirement to pay at least some taxes in coin may in theory be analyzed as a strategy to force rural producers to enter the market so as to "voluntarily" provide goods required by elites in the market centers.[18]

By contrast, a "market" or "transportation" landscape may be conducive to higher levels of rural commercialization. Again, it is not the absolute number of markets that is critical (although there are more in these two models), but their relationship to one another and to non-market sites. As a consequence of the position of lower-level markets between two or three upper-level markets (for $K = 4$ and $K = 3$ respectively), each upper-level market is in competition with all the surrounding markets at the same level for business with the sites one level down.[19] Such an arrangement in theory

---

[16] C. A. Smith 1976b; 1976b.

[17] See, e.g., C. A. Smith 1976c: 336, 341–3.

[18] Compare, e.g., Comaroff, Comaroff 1997: 199–200 on the (not entirely successful) "hut tax" to force people into the wage-labor economy.

[19] In Fig. 1.1 (a), for example, because a producer at the site marked D can attend markets at B_1, C_1, or C_2, traders there are in competition with one another for customers or

works against the ability of colluding marketers or market administrators to control the flow of information about market conditions or of goods and facilitates a higher degree of rural commercialization.[20] In fact, Smith considered landscapes organized on these principles "fully" commercialized.[21]

These analytical concerns offer a corrective to a tendency of the conventional historiography of the Palestinian economy to tabulate literary references to sites of agricultural or craft production scattered through the region, or to list passages that suggest some form of product specialization on the part of a given village or region as evidence of economic development.[22] No doubt such specialization existed, as the work of Adan-Bayewitz shows,[23] but by itself such information does not tell us about the structure of the rural economy. What central-place theory may offer is a framework for assessing the way the very limited evidence that we do have is distributed within a wider geographical and structural framework. In the case of specialized production, we should like to know, for instance, something about the scale of production (for which literary texts are no better than problematic, but for which archaeological remains may sometimes be more forthcoming), how such production was distributed across the landscape (e.g., in relation to cities or roads, something that might at least be teased carefully from texts as well as archaeological remains), and whether that production was actually by independent freeholders or tenants for trade or was the result of some other production mode (such as estate production for urban consumption, thereby bypassing *rural* commercialization[24]), before characterizing the degree and kind of rural integration into a regional commercial economy.

Just as problematic, however, is the assumption that a relatively high level of rural commercialization – with rural producers sacrificing a measure of the security gained by producing all subsistence necessities in-house, in favor of producing a measure of market-oriented products, and relying on the marketplace to provide some subsistence goods – means the transformation of a "peasant" producer into a rationalist "farmer."[25] This is a matter of some concern, since Chapter 3 will argue that at least for the

---

produce from D. Since each of the C-level sites also competes for other D-level sites, the aggregate effect is that each C-level is in competition with the surrounding C-level sites in interlocking rings.

20 See C. A. Smith 1976b: 14; see also 1978: 578–579.

21 C. A. Smith 1976c: 320 and n. 12.

22 See, e.g., Strange 1997: 41–42; see also Schürer, Vermes, *et al.*, 1973–87: 69–72 (a catalog of terminology, not necessarily trade, see pp. 68–69); see also Safrai 1994: 365–369; 380–96 on items of trade and regional (not necessarily local) specialization.

23 Adan-Bayewitz 1993, 1995; Adan-Bayewitz, Perlman 1990.

24 See, e.g., Whittaker 1988.

25 Weber 1906 [1946]: 363–365.

very largest sites in northern Palestine the distribution roughly matches that of a "transportation" ($K = 4$) landscape (although for still smaller settlements the distribution of markets may have been more like $K = 7$, or even rarer). However, rather than necessarily offering a model of entrepreneurial, proto-modern, market-oriented farming, a "pure" $K = 4$ landscape may instead allow us to think through how the demand generated by "consumer" cities of Roman Palestine may have shaped the regional distribution of settlements, production, and consumption.[26]

Consider a "transportation" landscape from the point of view of the non-market-bearing sites (see Figure 1.1 (b)). These are always located between two low-level markets (C-level in the drawing). However, with respect to still higher-level markets D-level sites are always (in relation to B-level sites) or mostly (in relation to A-level sites – and the exceptions are precisely in highly disadvantaged positions, furthest from any market) entirely within the territory of the one higher-level market. With respect to higher-order goods, non-market-bearing sites are therefore potentially in much the same relationship with market centers as in the "administration" landscape. Higher-level markets may compete with others at the same level to get customers from sites one level lower, and may require business from non-market sites in their hinterland for high-threshold goods, but they need not necessarily compete intensively with other high-level markets to attract purchasers from those non-market sites. Even on the basis of a highly schematic "transportation" ($K = 4$) model, it is possible to envision how a "commercialized" system of rural production may sector the landscape into a hierarchy of consumption, where rural producers produce for the market primarily to the extent of acquiring those low-level goods most accessible to them, while much that is available in high-level markets – although deriving directly or indirectly (e.g., after processing in towns) from

26 Because of the argument in Chapter 3 this discussion focuses on a $K = 4$ landscape; however, similar arguments could be made for a $K = 3$ configuration. For ancient "consumer cities" see Finley 1985; Whittaker 1988, 1990, 1993; Garnsey, Saller 1987: 48–49; see also K. Hopkins 1980, whose connection between taxes and trade might be reproduced on the local level of cities and their rural hinterland. The differentiation between ancient "consumer" cities and medieval "producer" cities often is attributed to Weber, who, it should be noted, assumed that markets, commercialization, and trade nevertheless played an important role in the making of ancient cities (Weber [1896] 1976: 391–92). Among the notions that need adjusting, particularly for the later Roman Near East, is Weber's sharp dichotomy drawn between the commercialized cities on the coast and the "natural economy of the primitive peasants" of the interior, tied also to his assumption of slave-labor based estates. Note also Braudel's discussion of the role of the consumption needs of early modern London and the transformation of the economy of rural England, Braudel 1982: 40–42.

commercialized rural production – might well be targeted primarily to the inhabitants of market-towns and cities.

Even the rigid artificiality of central-place theory and the simplifying assumptions that are used to generate theoretical landscapes,[27] then, are useful for thinking through questions that are critical to the social and economic history of later Roman Palestine. However, since much of this book will attempt to draw conclusions about a historical landscape with reference to central-place theory, it is worth considering some areas of discontinuity between theoretical conventions and historical data or historiographical practice. Thus, for instance, while the notions of threshold and range make good intuitive sense, it is impossible to evaluate these in practice for ancient Palestine. In the first place, the information available for how actual goods circulated, what goods might have had a high or low threshold, or a high or low range, is quite limited. Second, it is difficult to know how to measure the cost of distance for rural producers. Based on Diocletian's price edict, the monetary cost of transportation (some 3.7% to 7.3% of the official price for ten Roman miles per wagon load of wheat; perhaps somewhat lower for camel and (probably) donkey loads) may have been fairly modest as long as distances were quite short.[28] However, these prices reflect the ability to take advantage of economies of scale (persons able and needing to hire wagons, animals, etc.).[29] For retail purchases of the kind that Christaller invoked, choices may be limited by what the buyers and members of their household could carry and how far they could walk, but the actual monetary cost of transport might be negligible (to the extent that thinking in terms of quantifiable costs makes sense in the agrarian society under discussion here). The time and other opportunity costs are similarly difficult to evaluate. For independent farmers or tenants who were not constrained by wage-labor relations, the time available for marketing might vary seasonally, but so might availability of goods or the money to spend on them.[30] Persons dependent upon wages might have less

---

[27] For a theoretical attempt to allow for greater flexibility within the framework of classical models see, e.g., Parr 1980. For other modifications to the standard theory, with an eye to modeling "real" landscapes, see also Crissman 1976. In terms of practical applications, Skinner 1964, 1965 offered ways in which $K = 19$, $K = 4$, and $K = 3$ models, operating at different levels, might make sense of a given marketing network, and C. A. Smith 1976b argued that western Guatemala was sectored into a number of different levels each of which could be represented by a different central-place model.

[28] Jones 1974: 37; Duncan-Jones 1974: 367–9. See the *Edict on Prices* 17, Graser 1940: 368; Lauffer 1971: 148–149.

[29] See Bagnall 1993: 39.

[30] I have assumed that in general tenants had relative autonomy in how they spent their time, provided they produced a sufficient return to cover rents. Cf., however, the "cultivators of the land" (*cultores agrorum*), who might be sent to bring items to market,

freedom in terms of time, and possibly less to spend (although perhaps with a larger proportion of wealth in coin) than independent farmers. All of this suggests further that what central-place theory represents as a neat geometrical abstraction (a circle or hexagon) corresponds to an aggregation of socially conditioned choices or judgments that leveling generalizations may in fact obscure.

The working assumption, both above and in what follows, is that central places correspond roughly to settlement hierarchy, which, in turn ranged from farmsteads[31] and non-market-bearing villages to sizable cities. The case for this is easiest to make in terms of cities, and some of the material discussed below in Section C further suggests that ancient Palestinian texts also might assume that market hierarchy coordinates with size or complexity of settlement. By contrast, the geometry of the central-place landscapes discussed above assumes an even distribution of population. In fact, market locations need not coordinate with "settlements" at all, since, at least in the "market" and "transportation" settings, the criterion of location is proximity to other market sites and for $K = 4$, proximity to roads. Theoretically, it matters not at all if B-level sites do not serve as settlements, but rather are simply places between three or two A-level sites where marketers set up shop.

Once we assume that hierarchy of settlement does correlate with market hierarchy (as Christaller himself did) the landscape becomes much more complex.[32] Cities, for instance, with their higher concentration of demand, might have a smaller minimum threshold, but in practice might be able to extend their effective range beyond that predicted by the theory by appropriating some of the market functions of the nearest lower-level sites. In practice we might expect to see differential levels of intensity in the production or marketing of the same goods. To return to the examples of bakers above, in cities, where there is higher concentrated demand, we might expect to find not only bakers, as in lower-level markets, but more bakers, or bakers baking more bread (as *t. Pesaḥim* 2 [1]:1–2, to be discussed in Section C below, implies in schematized fashion), or bakers specializing in kinds of bread, as might be suggested on the basis of documents relating to the nome capital Oxyrhynchus and the rather sizable village Karanis, both from second century Egypt.[33] Karanis appears to have

---

referred to in *Dig.* 50.11.2 (Callistratus). For the possibility that these are tenants see de Ligt 1993: 221. See further Kehoe 1997.

[31] For farmsteads in the northern regions see e.g., Safrai 1994: 82–99; Hirschfeld 1996, 1997; Frankel, Getzov 1997: 34–35, 34*, English section.

[32] See, e.g., Crissman 1976.

[33] Oxyrhynchus: Rea 1982: 195, lines 9–10, with p. 201 (commentary); Karanis: Geremek 1969: 92 (no. 10) (following Geremek who translates *mouliōn* "meunier-boulanger"). For the size of Karanis: Geremek 1969: 37–39, cf. Rathbone 1990: 130, 132.

supported less – and less diversified – marketing than Oxyrhynchus: tax documents from Karanis include references to some five to eight categories of something like retail trade (involving some seven to twelve people), depending on what one includes; a list of market taxes from a market at Oxyrhynchus may have as many as eighteen categories.[34]

In this case, thinking about the lack of fit between pure theoretical types and what one might in practice expect to find on the ground may be productive. Consider the question discussed above of a "transportation" landscape and the way that cities may have shaped the economic landscape of the region. In a late-antique Palestinian setting, assuming that market levels coordinated roughly with site size, not only was demand more concentrated as one moved up the settlement scale (cities were more populous than farmsteads), but wealth – in absolute terms and in terms of availability of coin – also was distributed unevenly in favor of cities, and a larger proportion of the urban population may have relied on markets for basic goods than in rural villages.

As a result, at the highest-level sites ("cities") prices may have been set in relation to internal demand in the cities or – at least for higher-order goods – through interurban competition, perhaps mediated by potential customers or traders in "towns" (i.e., B-level sites), but, as before, not necessarily in order to attract rural purchasers. At the same time, high levels of demand in cities might require cities to draw on wider or more intensively worked hinterlands than "naturally" assumed by the central-place model. In theory such demand might trickle down in the form of greater commercialization overall, as rural producers meet the demands of competing traders working to stock "city" and "town" markets. In practice, however, certain sites are strategically better placed than others – sites in close proximity to the cities themselves, for instance, or to some strategic resource, or, particularly in a $K = 4$ landscape, to roads (and thus prime candidates, one might imagine, for the siting of estates[35]) – and might specialize in production for urban markets. The result of such a hypothetical process might well be a system in which much of the production and trade that is carried on is designed to feed urban elites, and in which there are "core" zones of specialized and commercialized production and peripheral zones of greater or lesser degrees of village or local autarky.

Considering the discontinuities between theoretical assumptions and what one might expect to find in practice, as well as the kind of evidence one actually does find, is thus helpful for raising analytical questions about

---

34 Geremek 1969: 92–93; Rea 1982: 195, lines 7–20. The documents are not entirely comparable to one another: a list of property owners and their property for Karanis, and a record of tax dues for one market in Oxyrhynchus.

35 Cf. de Neeve 1984: 23–25; see also Morley 1996: 68.

how "real" historical landscapes and economies may have been organized. One line of investigation raised by the preceding discussion and typically ignored both by those who see trade in northern Palestine as "natural" and self-evident, and by those who see cities as parasitic on an autonomous "traditional" peasant economy, is the economic landscape of the region as itself a historical artifact, and the place of cities within that landscape not only as islands separated from a vast rural ocean surrounding them, but in fact as playing a role in constituting that landscape. Attention to a regional context and to analytical and interpretive frameworks, may help also to place other aspects of the social history of northern Palestine (e.g., the distribution of ethnically or religiously marked remains) within a larger context, not governed solely by generalization from artifact to anecdote.

C. Markets and Hierarchy in Later Roman Palestine: Some Examples

The preceding discussion of central-place theory has specified a set of concepts and models that can be used to suggest possible distributions of markets and marketing in later Roman Palestine. Chapter 3 and Chapter 4 will turn to this issue in some detail and will address literary evidence for the distribution of marketing. This section addresses the question of the "fit" between the model and the "real" world of later Roman Palestine. To object that northern Palestine is not early-twentieth-century central Germany (the basis of Christaller's work), or China (Skinner), or Guatemala (C. A. Smith), or to object that Galilee is not a flat featureless plain, and that hence analyses of one region are inapplicable to another, is to miss the point of working with models in ancient historiography at all. Models constrain historians to bring to the analysis of the local and the particular, questions about how historiographical concepts that tend to be invoked as "givens," such as class, cities, peasants, demography, or trade, work as historically contingent processes that vary from period to period, from region to region, and from culture to culture. It is, however, a matter of concern that the model mobilized not, in and of itself, misconstrue the specific historical setting of later Roman Palestine. This is particularly true in the present instance, where the fit alleged between model and "world" is conceptual (i.e., how might central-place theory provide a vocabulary for analyzing economic and social history?) rather than statistical (i.e., how does the measured distribution of markets compare with predicted model distributions?[36]). I have, for instance, already pointed out problems with how

---

[36] Data suitable for such applications of models are rare in any ancient Mediterranean contexts. For examples see Bagnall, Frier 1994; Duncan-Jones 1994.

we might conceptualize range and threshold in the context of the later Roman economy. It is somewhat reassuring, therefore, that key concepts presupposed by the central-place models discussed above – notably the development of market hierarchy across a landscape – also appear to be fairly close to the surface in ancient Palestinian texts. A few examples follow.

1. t. Baba᾿ Meṣiʿa᾿ 3:20; Sipra, Bĕ-har, Parāšâ 3:8 (107d).

The Mishnah allows consumers who have been given bad coin in a transaction to return the coin within a limited time period. The time limit is set as follows: "In the cities (*kĕrakkîm*), long enough to show it to a moneychanger; and in the villages (*kĕpārîm*), until Sabbath eves [i.e., Fridays]."[37] In what is clearly a gloss to this rule in the Tosepta and the Sipra, the following is added: "Because it is in the manner of the market in the villages (*ʿayārôt*) to be suspended from Sabbath eve to Sabbath eve." It is not clear whether *ʿayārôt* should be read as corresponding to *kĕpārîm* in the Mishnah, or whether a hierarchical relationship exists between them (e.g., someone in a *kĕpar* given bad coin needs to be given sufficient time to visit a market in an *ʿîr*; cf. the discussion of *m. Megilla* 1:1–3 below). In either case, however often markets may meet in cities, in villages they meet only once weekly, and, as a result, the complainant may be forced to wait until the market convenes again the following week in order to have the coin examined.

The preceding discussion focused on the hierarchical organization of markets as expressed in goods offered. This example illustrates another aspect of hierarchical ordering of markets, one related to some of the expected "deviations" from central-place theory also discussed above: whether markets have sufficient volume of trade to meet daily, or whether demand is concentrated into less frequent periodic meetings.[38] The assumption in the Mishnah, and more explicitly in the gloss in the Tosepta and Sipra is that the rural markets are so ranked.[39] A similar assumption seems to underlie the following text as well.

2. m. Megilla 1:1–3; y. Megilla 1:1 (70b).[40]

The beginning of tractate *Megilla* in the Mishnah sets out the possible dates on which the book (scroll, *mĕgillâ*) of Esther is read in three types of settlements:

---

[37] *m. B. Meṣ.* 4:6.

[38] Skinner 1965; C. A. Smith 1976b 15–8; Plattner 1976; cf. R. H. T. Smith, ed. 1978: Introduction.

[39] Safrai 1994: 292 cites these passages to argue that there was no moneychanger in rural markets. Whatever the historicity of rabbinic texts, such a reading might make sense of *m. B. Meṣ.* 4:6 (although it is too strong even for that passage), but does not seem to do justice to the gloss in the Tosepta and Sipra.

[40] The following discussion is based on Lapin forthcoming.

cities (*kĕrakkîm*) "that were surrounded by walls in the days of Joshua the son of Nun," villages (*kĕpārîm*), and "large *ʿayārôt.*" Differences arise for three reasons: (1) as a matter of general practice walled cities read a day later than smaller sites; (2) the scroll is not read on the Sabbath, but is either postponed or pushed back one day; (3) villages (and, in one case in *m. Megillah* 1:2, large *ʿayārôt* as well) read on "gathering day," *yôm ha-kĕnîsâ*. It is this last factor that is of particular interest here. From the discussion in *m. Megilla* 1:2 it is clear that "gathering day" falls on Monday or Thursday. This passage is thus one in a series that attributes special functional importance (meeting of local courts, reading of the Torah, public fasts for rain) to Mondays and Thursdays.[41] That the meeting days are also at least connected with marketing activity is suggested by *m. Taʿanit* 1:6 and 2:9, which rule on the opening of shops on public fasts for rain held on Mondays and Thursdays. However, the identification of these periodic meeting days with market days remains an inference.

An additional ambiguity relates to the specification of "large" *ʿayārôt* (singular: *ʿîr*), defined as a settlement with ten "idlers" (*baṭlānîm*).[42] This qualification typically is taken to imply some sort of village council, but it may mean no more than that "large" *ʿayārôt* can always rely on a gathering of ten people. In repeatedly specifying "large" the Mishnah may merely be emphasizing the distinction between *kĕpārîm* and *ʿayārôt*. Alternatively, "large" may implicitly distinguish between kinds of *ʿayārôt*. A number of interpretations are possible, but the present discussion assumes that the Mishnah distinguishes between large and small *ʿayārôt*, understanding the schedule of reading to work as follows. The smallest sites (*kĕpārîm*) do not read on their own but gather on the nearest preceding "gathering day" in their local *ʿîr*, elsewhere in the Mishnah specified as the locus of court and synagogue meetings as well.[43] Large settlements – that is, walled cities or large *ʿayārôt*, by contrast – read on their respective statutory days, the fifteenth or fourteenth of Adar. The homology between central-place models of marketing, and the relationship between villages and *ʿayārôt* in this pattern of reading is fairly close, particularly if the "gathering day" is assumed in the Mishnah to have performed market functions for rural settlements. It is closer still if large settlements can be assumed to have double readings, once for their own inhabitants, and once, as much as three or four days earlier, for the villages in their hinterland.[44] In that case, in the same

---

41 See Safrai 1994: 239–40, which effectively reproduces Safrai 1983a: 182–3; see also Lapin 1996a: 111.

42 *m. Meg.* 1:3.

43 E.g., *m. Taʿan.* 2:1; 3:3–4; *m. Meg.* 3:1; *m. Ket.* 1:1 (arguably interpolated, but see also *t. Taʿan.* 2:4); *m. Ned.* 5:5.

44 A possibility that, for example, Tosafot, *b. Yeb.* 14a, rejected for exegetical reasons. The assumption of double reading may be presupposed in the Yerushalmi tradition

way that in the central-place landscapes discussed above, an A-level site also serves as a C-level site for non-market sites in its immediate area, large *ʿayārôt* and walled cities also serve as local "gathering day" centers for surrounding villages.

Unfortunately, even if this reading of *m. Megilla* 1:1–3 is correct, it is impossible to move from this passage to straightforward historical conclusions. I leave aside for the present the entire complex of problems relating to the "historicity" of rabbinic texts, and focus merely on textual problems. For one thing, the previous passage (the gloss to *m. Babaʾ Meṣiʿaʾ* 4:6), assumed that markets in *ʿayarôt* met once weekly on Fridays, but the present passages understand these as meeting on two days weekly, neither of which is Friday. Moreover there is some uncertainty because the passages may mean different things by the term *ʿayārôt*. One factor that both agree on, however, is the *coincidence* of periodic markets at the rural level. In the case of neither *m. Megilla* 1:1–3 nor the gloss in the Tosepta and Sipra to *m. Babaʾ Meṣiʿaʾ* 4:6 are we given much context for evaluating how a system of periodic markets might be articulated. If the periodic markets presupposed by the rabbinic texts were organized so as to be exclusive of one another, rather than, for instance, to coordinate the markets at one level with markets at higher central places, this might accentuate the divide between levels, and work against "commercialized" production at the lowest levels.[45]

---

attributed to Philippa b. Prota to be discussed presently, *y. Meg.* 1:1 (70b). *t. Meg.* 1:1 refers to "those [settlements?] adjacent to the city and seen with it" as reading with the city itself, but this may refer to the built up area outside the walls of a city rather than rather than presupposing that the villages in the immediate territory of cities gather for reading on the reading day of the cities. At any rate that Tosepta passage does not presuppose a separate gathering day for villagers gathering in the city.

[45] Skinner described systems in China in which the timing of lowest-level ("standard") markets was prevented from coinciding with "intermediate"-level markets. This facilitated the movement of itinerant buyers and sellers between the higher-level central place and the lower-level market places surrounding it, and, by extending the range of "central" services and commercial functions (e.g., the buying up of produce) closer to the village level, fostered the fuller economic integration of lower- and higher-level centers (Skinner 1964: 24–7, see also 15). An analogous coordination organized the timing of "intermediate" markets with their "central" marketing town (Skinner 1964: 29–30). By contrast, Smith suggests that the coincidence of periodic market days (Sundays) across market levels (including "major urban centers with populations in the hundreds of thousands") in highland Guatemala was the result of Spanish colonial policy to restrict trade so that it remain with in the administrative and economic control of a colonial elites (C. A. Smith 1976b: 17–8). These suggestions will not necessarily work for Roman-period Palestine (Smith's suggestion, for instance, presupposes a mercantile basis for imperial that does not fit the Roman context particularly well), but are offered here as examples of the kinds of possibilities that are raised when we address the historiographical questions raised by texts about economy from a broader theoretical framework.

A post-mishnaic tradition suggests a further connection with marketing: "Samuel taught: 'Why do they push [the reading of the *mĕgillâ*] back to the gathering day? So that they may supply their brethren in the cities (*kĕrakkîm*) with food.'"[46] A reasonable reading of this passage is that the dating of the reading in villages facilitates the functioning of those markets that supply the cities with food.[47] It is imprudent to insist on this interpretation, since it rests on a choice between textual variants, and since, in any case, even in this amplification of the Mishnah the "market" explanation is not the only one possible. Nevertheless, it is worth considering for a moment how such a system might work.

One possibility is that *ʿîr*, the smallest locus for both religious functions and markets, corresponds to a lowest-level central place. As a result of the way in which the Mishnah organizes the dates for reading, the regular market day in these places (and, if we assume a practice of double reading in large *ʿayārôt* and cities, there too) would never be disturbed.[48] In contrast, the reading date for "large *ʿayārôt*" and for walled cities is adjusted only once for each, when the statutory day for reading falls on the Sabbath.[49] From lower-level rural markets (as from higher-level central places), produce might be bulked by wholesalers and make its way to cities (see further, Chapter 4).[50] In this way, by meeting regularly on the "gathering day," and by altering the day for reading the scroll of Esther accordingly, villagers might indeed "supply their brethren in the cities with food."

An alternative reading of the tradition attributed to Samuel in connection with the Mishnah is based on the passage that follows it in the Yerushalmi:

> R. Philippa b. Prota said before R. Yonah: "This [i.e., the tradition attributed to Samuel] means [lit. "says"] that [Purim] is prohibited with respect to performing labor."
>
> Said [Yonah] to him: "From this you cannot learn anything. Lo, the intermediate days of the festival are prohibited with respect to performing labor, but they supply their brethren in the cities with food."[51]

---

[46] *y. Meg.* 1:1 (70b). The reading follows the Leiden manuscript. The Venice *editio princeps*, following a marginal correction in the manuscript, reads "with water and food," as in *b. Meg.* 4a, with parallels at 2a and 19a, but I suspect that this is a correction influenced by the Babli; the reading "food" alone is supported by the sequel in the Yerushalmi, on which see below.

[47] As already argued by Safrai 1994: 242.

[48] *m. Meg.* 1:2.

[49] *m. Meg.* 1:2; see also *t. Meg.* 1:2.

[50] For the combination of periodic markets with wholesale purchase in rural China see Skinner 1964: 20–1, 29–31. For eighteenth- and-nineteenth century Egypt see Cuno 1994: 49–51.

[51] *y. Meg.* 1:1 (70b).

Based on the rejoinder, the initial suggestion attributed to Philippa b. Prota appears to assume that by bringing produce to the city on "gathering day" villagers avoid doing so on the Purim itself. According to this reading, the tradition attributed to Samuel does not specifically presuppose hierarchically organized *networks* of markets. Instead, it understands the Mishnah to rule as it does in order to make sure that (*kĕdê še-*) villagers supply cities by coming to town directly on the "gathering day." Possibly, by extension, we might understand Samuel's tradition as concerned with the provisioning of food for *ʿayārôt* as well, although it may well be that that tradition, on this reading, is concerned with cities and with their particular reliance on periodic markets to draw on surrounding villages in order to provide food for the urban residents.[52] Even on this alternative interpretation of the tradition attributed to Samuel, market-bearing sites (at least cities) are in a hierarchical relationship with non-market-bearing sites of the kind discussed earlier in the chapter, although now framed from the point of view of the upper-level site as consumer of market goods rather than producer or distributor.

3. t. Pesaḥim 2 [1]:1–2.

Samaritans, as the betwixt-and-between ethnic category in rabbinic legal texts, were held (at least in early rabbinic texts) to be liable to the same restrictions as Jews on owning or possessing leaven on Passover, although differences in calendar might mean that Passover was celebrated by rabbinic Jews at a different date than it was by Samaritans. As a result, leaven that had been in the possession of Samaritans during Passover was, as in the passage that follows, deemed prohibited to Jews[53] until it might be conceived of as a new product.

> The leaven of Samaritans (*kûtîm*), from what time after Passover is it permitted [to Jews]?
> [The leaven] of householders, after three weeks of baking.

---

[52] This reading of the tradition of Samuel is somewhat closer to that of Safrai 1983: 182; 1994: 240 than my suggestion above of a hierarchy of markets implied in the statement. However, this second reading of the tradition of Samuel implies a rather less developed marketing system than Safrai appears to assume for the Roman period (see Safrai 1983: 182–5; 1994: 240–43). Since this reading is based on comments attributed to rabbis of the fourth amoraic generation (i.e., ca late third or early fourth century) it might go some distance toward undermining Safrai's confidence that by the Roman period "every town" (the Hebrew version uses *ʿayārâ*) had stores and courts that met daily (Safrai 1983: 183; 1994: 241) and that periodic markets had lapsed. In addition, particularly if the tradition attributed to Samuel refers specifically to cities, it is precisely such developed market towns that might cut into the flow of villagers making their way to cities and providing them with food (cf. de Ligt 1993: 202–17).

[53] I.e., as opposed to the leaven of gentiles, from which one was permitted to derive benefit after Passover, *m. Pes.* 2:2. See Lieberman 1955–88: 4, 484.

> Of bakers:
> In the villages (*kĕpārîm*) [it is prohibited] until three days.
> In the cities (*kĕrakkîm*) [it is prohibited] until three ovens.[54]

One of the glosses that follows in the Tosepta claims that despite the rule stated above, if a householder or a village shopkeeper, due to some exceptional need baked "three ovens one after the other," that the resulting leaven at the end of this process is permitted,[55] implying that "three ovens" is in fact the criterion in all three cases. The distinction apparently has to do with volume of baking: households are deemed to bake once a week, village bakers once a day, and urban bakers multiple times daily. In each case, once the process of setting aside leaven from fresh dough for the next time has been repeated three times, the leaven is deemed permissible. Here, again, we have an example of market hierarchy: the volume of demand in a *kĕpar* is such that baking and selling is carried out more intensively in towns.[56]

4. y. Baba᾽ Meṣiᶜa᾽ 5:8 (10c).

This final passage is cited as an example of the kind of intensive marketing that can at least be imagined to be taking place in cities. The Mishnah's prohibition of interest extends not only to outright interest-bearing loans, but to other transactions that could be considered usurious. Of special concern are those transactions involving repayment in produce, because of the potential shift in the market price of the produce.[57] In particular, *m. Baba᾽ Meṣiᶜa᾽* 5:7 prohibits sales of produce in which payment is made in advance but in which delivery is delayed, unless the "market price has come out," that is, unless the harvest for the seasonal produce is well underway and therefore there is ample produce

---

54 *t. Pes.* 2:1.

55 *t. Pes.* 2:1. Apparently, the assumption in this gloss is that new leaven is made by using all of the previous leaven in a batch of dough and separating out a lump of dough as starter for the next "oven." However, the objection in *t. Pes.* 2:2 to the rule pertaining to city bakers implies the possibility of a different strategy of leavening: using the same lump of leaven to leaven more than one batch of dough, although even this objection assumes that within three days the entire lump of leaven will have been used up three times.

56 The version of this tradition and its continuation in the Yerushalmi is somewhat different (*y. ᶜOrla* 2:7 [62b]; *y. ᶜAb. Zara* 5:11 [45a], corresponding to the latter part of *t. Pes.* 2:1 and 2:2; following the text in *y. ᶜAb. Zara*):

> In the cities (*kĕrakkîm*) [it is prohibited] until three days.
> In the villages (*kĕpārîm*) [it is prohibited] until three ovens.

Following the suggestion of Lieberman 1955–88: 4, 484–5, this version can be taken to mean that in cities, where bakers certainly might be assumed to bake daily, it was possible to set a fixed limit; but in villages there was no fixed limit set because the volume of baking might depend on the village. The basic import for market hierarchy is the same, although this version might be more conducive to a reading that involves market periodicity as well.

57 Lapin 1995: 193–5.

available at stable prices in the market. The Mishnah apparently presupposes a pricing cycle in which produce comes on the market in season, is readily available for standardized prices, and then, as time goes on, becomes increasingly unavailable, and accordingly, is priced erratically (and, presumably, high). Before the harvest, prices for the purchase of the produce may come down for wholesalers if farmers producing for market attempt to secure buyers by selling in advance below what they think the price will be. This may be the kind of contract envisioned here, but others are possible as well, such as a loan masked as a sale in which the expected produce is effectively the collateral for the loan, and the adjustment of the "price" of the produce may be the "interest" paid to the "buyer."[58] At any rate, the kind of transaction envisaged in *m. Baba᾿ Meṣiʿa᾿* 5:7 seems to suggest something of a higher financial order than buying of consumer goods in the market place in small amounts.

In the Amoraic discussion of this passage in the Yerushalmi, the following debate is offered:

> What is the rule with respect to making a bargain [for delayed delivery] on the basis of the market price of the *syrqy/sydqy* [market]? R. Yohanan says, "One may make a bargain"; Resh Laqish says, "One may not make a bargain."[59]

Just what is at issue here is not entirely clear, since precisely what *syrqy/sydqy* means is obscure, but given the suggestion that the Mishnah here deals with larger-scale transactions, *syrqy/sydqy* should refer to large scale merchants.[60] This passage is followed by the following:

> R. Bun b. Hiyya asked before R. Zera: "Does it not follow reasonably that Resh Laqish would concede to R. Yohanan in [the case of] the market price of Sepphoris [Escorial ms.: Caesarea], which never ceases, [that one may make a bargain]?"

This passage serves as an example of the intensity of commercialization that might conceivably be available in a regional city: wholesale bulking and warehousing, as well as, perhaps, imports through connections with other centers mean that Sepphoris (or Caesarea) might have wheat in the marketplace all year round. At lesser central places producers who want to guarantee a supply of grain therefore might be constrained to store their own grain, or in case of need to rely on the potentially expensive and distant market in the city.

---

58 See Bagnall 1977.

59 *y. B. Meṣ.* 5:8 (10c).

60 Lieberman 1983: 160 (to l. 122) suggests [*plateia*] *Syriaqē*, the Syrian street (or, perhaps, "plaza"), where imported, i.e., "Syrian" goods were sold. Perhaps *sitikē* [*plateia*] is an alternative: the street of wheat (i.e. where wheat sellers are found); cf. *šôqā᾿ dĕdagônā᾿* in Tiberias (*Gen. Rab.* 79:6, ed. Theodor-Albeck 1912–1936: 943–4). Cf. Kohut 1878–92: 6, 26; Levi 1876–89: 3, 598. At any rate, there seems to be little justification for the conclusion of Safrai 1994: 112 (see Safrai 1985: 118) that: "This would seem to imply that in Sepphoris the *farmers* did not grow grain but bought it in the market" (emphasis added).

In summary, in this capsule formulation of the theoretical claims of central-place theory, markets are expected to be distributed in hierarchical fashion across a landscape. Although no "real" distribution of markets will match the theoretical distributions with which central-place theory work, the considerations involved in constructing model landscapes, the kinds of hierarchical and spatial relationships between markets (and with them, plausibly, between sites as well) proposed by the model landscapes themselves, and the examination of areas where the expectations of the theory fall short of describing the historical landscape of a region, all offer opportunities to reexamine key features of the economic and social history of later Roman Palestine. This chapter attempted to further such a reexamination in two ways, first by discussing briefly, and on a fairly theoretical level, how basic problems of late Roman economic and social history (rural commercialization and the economic role of cities) could be articulated in spatial terms suggested by central-place theory as well as some of the most obvious gaps between theory and evidence, and second by examining a few ancient Palestinian texts that appear to be readily readable in terms of central-place theory assumptions about market hierarchy. With this in mind, the next chapter turns to the archaeological evidence for historical landscapes.

Chapter 2

Landscape, Archaeology, and Settlement Pattern

The preceding chapter introduced central-place theory and some of its implications for the social and economic history of later Roman Palestine. Chapter 3 examines northern Palestine in this period in greater detail, with a view to constructing a number of hypothetical central-place models for that region. That discussion is based on material from published archaeological survey and excavation reports, as well as from other publications (including brief notices in journals or encyclopedia articles, frequently the only formats in which some archaeological material is reported). The present chapter surveys the archaeological data collected, with particular focus on five areas published as part of the *Archaeological Survey of Israel*, ostensibly reporting all sites with surface ancient remains and therefore the most susceptible to close analysis. The chapter concludes with a consideration of the data taken as a whole, including a discussion of the possibility that the data collected on the size of sites (the "rank-size" relationship) might reflect a degree of regional integration.

A. Describing the Data

The primary archaeological data for this project comprise a database of some 728 records on the Galilee and environs in the western part of ancient Palestine, and an additional 215 records for the Golan. Primary data on location, size, and significant findings for the Golan were culled primarily from the 1972 survey published under the editorship of M. Kochavi, the 1985 study by Urman, and the more recent work by the same author on Jewish "public buildings" in the Golan.[1] For the Galilee as a whole there are no comprehensive surveys. For five regions I was able to utilize publications of the *Survey of Israel* project (see below). For the rest, data has been compiled from a variety of sources: primarily from surveys,[2] supplemented by the *Tabula Imperii*

[1] *JSG* Golan; Urman 1985; 1995; see also Ma'oz 1986; H. Ben David 1998.

[2] In particular, Saarisalo 1927; Zori 1962, 1977; Frankel 1986; Gal 1990; and Avi'am 1994.

Romani – Palaestina (hereafter *TIR*), and by the catalog of Byzantine sites in Israel prepared by Claudine Dauphin.[3]

Inasmuch as this study is dependent upon the methods, biases, and reporting standards of a variety of different authors writing over an extended period of time, it is important to note the significant limitations of the collected data. First, there are gaps in the evidence. While, for instance, sites may have been included in *TIR*, implying that the editors determined that the individual sites were occupied during the Roman and Byzantine period, it is not always possible to tell from the bibliography supplied when within that seven hundred year period (63 B.C.E.–637 C.E.) those sites was occupied.[4] Second, surveys are frequently selective in their sites. Saarisalo explored *The Boundary Between Issachar and Naphthali*.[5] Although Z. Gal's study of lower Galilee supplies much important data on Hellenistic, Roman, and Byzantine occupations, his research design is specifically focused on sites that contribute to Galilee in the Iron Age.[6] M. Avi'am's important study of Christianization in late-antique western Galilee does not survey small sites at which explicitly Christian remains were not found.[7]

Third, archaeologists differ in their periodization, sometimes significantly. The survey by Raban of the Nahalal area, to which we will turn shortly, divides the period from the Hellenistic to the Byzantine into the Hellenistic I and II, the Roman I, II, and III, and the Byzantine I and II.[8] Most surveyors are content to use a coarser dating system, referring merely to the Hellenistic, Roman, and Byzantine periods. The index to a survey of the Golan has, in addition to the usual Hellenistic, Roman, and Byzantine subdivision, two entries for the Roman Period III.[9] More frustrating, for the kinds of purposes to which the data are put here, are the substantial number of sites in the index to *JSG* Golan (forty-nine) dated to the vaguer "Roman-Byzantine."[10] In addition, archaeologists are far from unanimous in what they mean by the terms Roman and, especially, Byzantine. The most

---

[3] Dauphin 1998.

[4] See for example *TIR* 124, *s.v.* Ḥ. ʿEved; 136, *s.v.*, Ginneigar; 177, *s.v.* Ḥ. Zarʿit; 201, *s.v.* Parod.

[5] Saarisalo 1927.

[6] Gal 1990.

[7] Avi'am 1994: 126.

[8] Raban 1982. Confidence in the ability to separate out finer chronological subdivisions underlies Dauphin 1998.

[9] *JSG* Golan: 294. An insert included with the maps dates this period from 180 to 324.

[10] Messier still, the survey of the Golan was carried out by two units, and each has an introduction. That by S. Gutman refers to the period of the Mishnah and the Talmud (*JSG* Golan 245–247); and that by C. Epstein (p. 250) refers to the Hellenistic, Roman, and Byzantine periods.

common referent for "Byzantine" still appears to be the period after Constantine's conquest of the eastern Roman empire (324 C.E.), especially in older literature. I have retained this definition of "Byzantine" and the tripartite chronological division more generally because of their ubiquity in the secondary literature, and in the absence of any clear criteria in published accounts for re-dating particular subdivisions within the gross chronological framework. However, some Palestinian archaeologists begin the "Byzantine" period somewhat later, in the 360s,[11] and archaeologists working within the framework of classical archaeology use still a different set of periodizations.[12] Since surveys frequently do not make explicit the dates to which their chronological markers are pegged, there is the risk of mis-classifying sites or events (e.g., by assigning sites labeled "late Roman" to the Roman period – the practice followed below – although they may fit more properly the "Byzantine."

More serious, however, are the problems that result from discrepancies in reports of the same site, which result from differences as well as refinements over time (one can only hope) in dating pottery or in field or survey methodology.[13] At the most general level, for instance, Tsafrir has drawn attention to the problems of identifying the continuities or transitions between the Byzantine and Early Arab periods in the Negev.[14] Three sites referred to in particular by Y. Portugali in a study of population and settlement patterns in the western Jezreel valley, based on a field methodology that attempts to discern the sizes of settlements at particular sites during different periods, exemplify the problem.[15] Based on a table provided by Portugali, the size of the settlement at Tel Shimron could not be estimated for the Hellenistic and Roman periods, but in the Byzantine it had reached 78 dunams.[16] By contrast in Raban's survey of the Nahalal area, the size of "the fortified area" of Tel Shimron is given as 150 dunams, with no indication of the periods during which the site attained that size.[17] For Tel Qashish, Raban gives the size of the hill as 25 dunams and reports pottery from the Hellenistic, Roman, and Byzantine periods.[18] According to Portugali's table the site was not occupied at all during these periods. Tel

---

[11] E.g., Meyers 1982; Groh 1988.

[12] See e.g., Magness 1993, 11–2.

[13] See also Morley 1996: 129–30 on Roman Italy; Alcock 1993: 33–37 on Greece.

[14] Tsafrir 1994: 272; see also his comments, p. 273 on Gal 1991.

[15] Portugali 1986; see also Portugali 1982 with specific reference to Tel Shimron and Tel Qashish.

[16] Portugali 1986:14; in figure 9, Portugali offers hypothetical sizes for the Hellenistic and Roman periods.

[17] Raban 1982: no. 83.

[18] Raban 1982: no. 11.

Yoqneᶜam, in Raban's survey publication, has an area of 40 dunams at its top.[19] According to Portugali's table the site's size during the Hellenistic period is indeterminate (it is marked with a question mark), but the site was deemed unoccupied in the Roman (marked with a dash); in the Byzantine period it reached 35 dunams.[20]

To a great degree, the different conclusions in this case derive from Portugali's method for determining site size during specific occupation periods. Thus, although he acknowledges the presence of Hellenistic pottery at Tel Qashish, Portugali's methods lead him to the conclusion that "although the surface of the mound may have been exploited (probably for agriculture), there was no sedentary settlement there during this period."[21] However, these differing conclusions are in turn dependent upon the identifiable sherds that happen to be noticed and collected in survey, as well as simple disagreements over what dates to assign to the surface pottery. At Tel Qashish, where Raban found pottery for every occupation sub-phase except for the Byzantine II, the 1981 report on Tel Qashish, of which Portugali was a joint author, states that preliminary survey showed evidence of the Hellenistic but not the Roman or Byzantine periods, while Portugali himself reports none for the Byzantine.[22]

Differences such as those highlighted by the specific results of Portugali's project are in fact quite common. Z. Yeivin estimated the size of Kh. Shemaᶜ at 10 dunams, and of Meiron at 105 dunams. The Meiron excavation project estimated the sizes at approximately 40 and the massive 300 respectively, and explained the difference as resulting from the greater accuracy of excavation over survey.[23] In the survey by N. Zori published in 1977, Ḥ. Gobel (map ref. 18632370) is listed as covering an area of 250 m. by 300 m. (thus on the order of 75 dunams), and Byzantine pottery is

---

[19] Raban 1982: 16.

[20] For occupation history see also Ben-Tor, Avissar, Portugali 1996: 2, and the various subsections; note, however, the discussion of Roman remains on pp. 32–4. Cf. Ben-Tor, R. Rosenthal 1978: 73.

[21] Portugali 1982: 184; see also 177 (Table 1), 183.

[22] Raban 1982: no. 11; see his key to sites; Ben-Tor, Portugali, Avissar 1981: 138; Portugali, 1981: 177 (Table 1); in this case perhaps reflecting refinements in survey method described in that article.

[23] Yeivin 1971: 11; cf. Meyers, Meyers, Strange 1978: 97; Meyers, Strange, Groh 1978: 22 n. 3. It should be noted that neither the Khirbet Shemaᶜ report (Meyers, Kraabel, Strange, 1976) nor the Meiron final report (Meyers, Strange, Meyers 1981) offer plans complete or detailed enough to allow estimation of the size of the site by the reader. The entire area covered by the plan in Meyers, Kraabel, Strange, 1976: 4 (Figure 1.1) is not much more than 27 dunams, including areas left blank. The plan for Meiron in Meyers, Strange, Meyers, 1981: 4 (Figure 1.3) covers an area no more than 62 dunams. Moreover, the Meiron final report pointedly avoids precision on this matter (Meyers, Strange, Meyers 1981): "several dunams or more."

said to predominate. Z. Gal's entry for the same site estimates its size at 10 dunams, mentions no Byzantine pottery, and reports that Roman pottery accounts for 95 percent of that recovered at the site.[24] In a different survey, Zori reported that the ancient site at ʿEn ha-Yadid (map ref. 19962218) was some 100 by 250 meters (on the order of 25 dunams), and had pottery from the Byzantine periods. According to Gal's publication of the Gazit section for the *Survey of Israel* the size of the site was 5 dunams and the pottery dated to the Hellenistic, Roman, and Byzantine periods.[25]

Even under the best of circumstance, the data collected for this study yield only the coarsest kinds of historical conclusions. The estimation of the size of a site is a difficult business, particularly when the site has not been extensively excavated.[26] Only rarely do archaeologists attempt based on surveys to assess changes in the sizes of particular sites over time, and the methods for this tend, as surveys go, to be labor intensive and time consuming.[27] Hence, there is almost never a way of determining from published survey reports (or, for that matter, excavation reports in many cases) how much of a 40 dunam site occupied in the Hellenistic, Roman, and Byzantine periods was actually occupied during the respective periods. In fact, it is usually unclear when the site attained that size at all (might Byzantine remains reflect a small nucleated farm settlement on the remains of a substantially larger Bronze age settlement?). However, the implications of this uncertainty must be faced squarely. Not only are the dynamic processes of settlement growth or decline of any given site over a given period usually impossible to determine. Even if, as I shall argue below, there is a correlation between the very largest sites and major thoroughfares, it remains impossible, on present evidence, to show conclusively that such a correlation is particularly the product of late-antique social or economic history. This is because it is unclear to what extent the correlation reflects the persistence of travel routes ("roads") and sites from earlier (or, for that matter, later) periods that at some point in time were "large."

The moral of this cautionary tale is that the data that can be collected from published archaeological sources is, at bottom, profoundly problematic. This bears stressing, given the claims to "materiality" and hence to a privileged kind of facticity that is still sometimes made for archaeological evidence. No doubt, further research could have cleaned up a number of incomplete entries, but the examples cited above are sufficient to indicate the extent to which work on the historical geography of what is now northern Israel, with its particularly heavy dependence on surveys, is constrained by

---

[24] Zori 1977: no. 155; Gal 1990: no. 1.18.
[25] Zori 1962: no. 33a; Gal 1991: no. 61; see also Zori 1977: no. 147.
[26] A point brought home to me by James F. Strange, personal communication.
[27] Cf. Portugali 1982; Alcock 1991; 1993: 96–98.

the incomplete, indeterminate, and frequently contradictory quality of the available data on particular sites.

B. Five *Archaeological Survey of Israel* Regions

Having said this much about the problems involved with the information about individual sites, I wish to turn now to a discussion of five regions surveyed as part of the *Archaeological Survey of Israel* project.[28] These publications claim to record all sites with visible antiquities and, problems notwithstanding, offer the best snapshots of the regional distribution ancient sites. Four survey areas are regular 10 kilometer by 10 kilometer regions on the Survey of Israel grid; the fifth is distorted by boundaries both geographical (the Mediterranean coast) and political (the Israel-Lebanon border). The first of these surveyed regions, the Gazit area, is located in the southeastern portion of Galilee (see Map 1). This area is instructive, first, because it immediately makes clear the problem with one of the fundamental assumptions of central-place theory: that of a featureless plane with equal distribution of resources. An examination of the 1:20,000 map that accompanies the survey shows that the settlements all are oriented along the wadis that cut through the survey area. Moreover, according to Gal, nearly all were built along natural springs that formed along the wadis; only three of the settlements were on the plateau, and these were built on limestone outcroppings suitable for cisterns.[29] Of the three sites, Kafra has no pottery before the Roman period, and el Ṭira and Ḥ. Riv have none before the Byzantine.[30]

This, together with the sizes of the sites (see below), suggests that in antiquity the area was agriculturally marginal and only brought under consistent cultivation during the expansion of sites and population in the Roman and Byzantine periods. At any rate, it was apparently during the Byzantine period that the terracing along Naḥal Tabor was constructed.[31] Even in the Byzantine period a number of sites remained widely spaced from one another and perhaps, to all intents and purposes, isolated from one another. However, at least in the eastern section of the survey area, between Sirin and Wadi el Bira (Naḥal Tabor) nearly all the sites are accessible to one another by tracks noted on the British Survey of Palestine

[28] Gal 1991; 1998 (ʿEn Dor and Tabor areas published together); Raban 1982; Frankel, Getzov 1991.

[29] Gal 1991:10; 11* in English section.

[30] Kafra: Zori 1977: no. 145; Gal 1991: no. 59; el Ṭira: Zori 1977: no. 174; Gal 1991: no. 10; Ḥ. Riv: Zori 1977: no. 176; Gal 1991: no. 28.

[31] See Gal 1991: 10, and, for terracing, no. 44.

Map,[32] despite a rise from approximately 150 meters below sea level at the site labeled below as "Nahal Tabor [c]" to 75 meters above sea level at Naḥal Shaḥal, and higher still to approximately 250 meters at Sirin. This suggests that even in the absence of modern technologies (paving, mechanized transportation), these sites could have been in contact with one another. The survey and maps also draw attention to another problem: the 100-square-kilometer grid is too abstracted from its wider geographical context to place it within a regional framework. Thus, although Gal (not implausibly) understands the new Roman and Byzantine settlements as agricultural dependencies of Beth Shean[33], the data of the survey in and of themselves cannot support this.

Table 2.1: NUMBERS OF SITES BY PERIOD

		Hellenistic	Roman		Byzantine	
Region	*Median*	*Number*	*Number*	*Percent Increase*	*Number*	*Percent Increase*
I. Gazit	3.6					
Gal		9	12	*33*	37	*208*
Alternative		11	12	*9*	30	*150*
II. En Dor	5					
Gal		4	13	*225*	25	*92*
Alternative		5	10	*100*	18	*80*
III. Mt. Tabor	10					
Gal		10	30	*200*	49	*63*
Alternative		11	14	*27*	27	*93*
IV. Nahalal	5.5?					
Raban		22	54	*145*	51	*-6*
Alternative		15	54	*127*	41	*21*
V. Akhziv/Ḥanita	15					
Frankel, Getzov, sites		28	41	*46*	45	*10*
Frankel, Getzov, settlements		26	35	*35*	41	*17*
Alternative		22	31	*41*	35	*13*
VI. Regions as a whole						
Galilee, Bet Shean valley, etc.	11	179	323	*80*	568	*75*
Golan	18	16	132	*725*	180	*36*
Galilee, Golan Combined	15	195	455	*133*	748	*64*

This survey by Gal can be compared to surveys by Zori and to Gal's own survey of the Galilee, all of which have some overlap with the Gazit area. Although there are examples of differential reporting,[34] overall the surveys

---

32 1:20,000, Sheet 19–23; 1932, with 1942 overprint.

33 Gal 1991: 13, 13* in English section

34 En ha-Yadid (Gal 1991: no. 61) was given above as an example of differential reporting. See also Gal 1991: no. 4 (Zori 1977: no. 209), 5 (Zori 1977: no. 210), 12 (Saarisalo 1927: no. 27; Zori 1977: no. 175; Gal 1990: no. 3.4); 33 (Zori 1977: 178, 180, cited

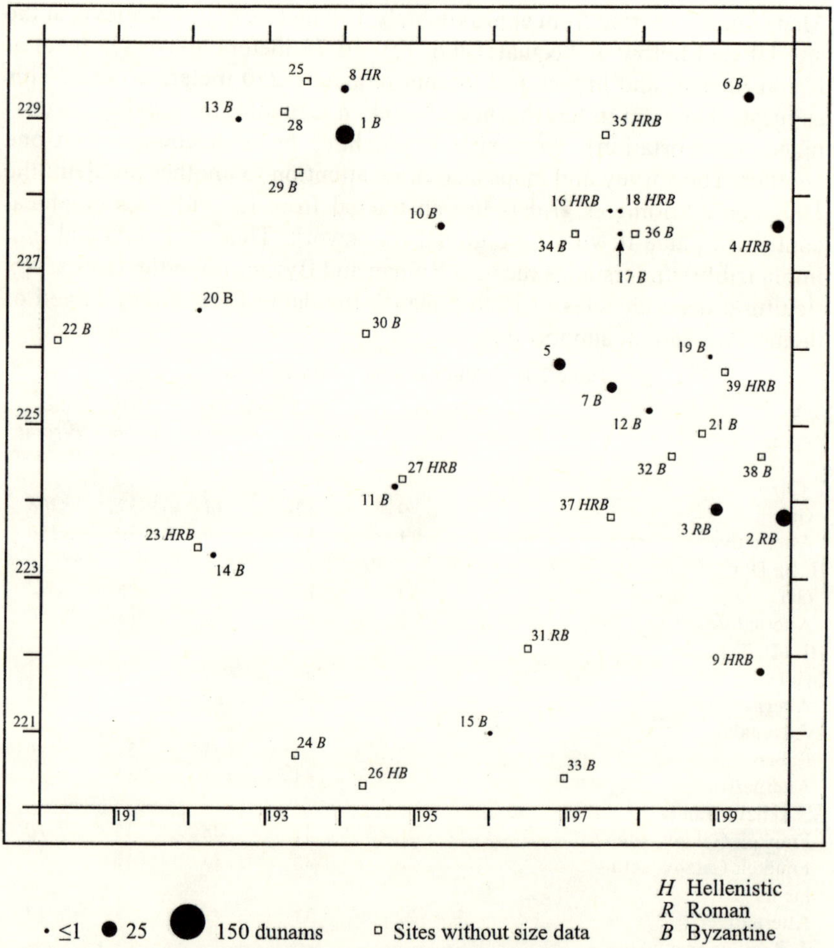

Map 1: GAZIT AREA (after Gal 1991)

tend to support each other. One site that possibly might be added to Gal's list is what Zori calls "Northern Kokhab ha-Yarden" (map ref. 19902239), which reportedly had some Roman and Byzantine pottery (the majority from the Early Arab), and building stones.[35] Also, in at least one site where

by Gal), 34 (Gal 1990: 3.2), 40 (Zori 1977: no. 185; Gal 1990: no. 3.3; 42 (Zori 1977: no. 143, cited by Gal), 43 (Zori 1977: no. 142), 57 (Zori 1977: no. 144; Gal 1990: no. 3.1; no two map references are identical).

[35] Zori: 1977: no. 148; cf. Gal 1991 no. 51, map. ref. 19902240, which, although quite close, does not match Zori's description.

Map 1: LIST OF SITES

1 T. Rekhesh	14 Ḥ. Ḥadad	27 Danna
2 Naḥal Tabor [d]	15 Byz. structure	28 Ḥ. Maᶜog
3 Kokhav ha-Yarden	16 Ḥ. Ukkal [c]	29 Ṭirat Gazit
4 Ḥ. Ḥagal	17 Kh. ᶜUkkal [a]	30 Ḥ. Riv
5 Ḥ. Šaḥal Taḥtit [a]	18 Kh. ᶜUkkal [b]	31 Kafra
6 Ḥ. Ḥardon	19 Naḥal ᶜAkhin	32 ᶜEin et Tina
7 Ḥ. Šaḥal Taḥtit [b]	20 Gazit	33 Naḥal Ziqqa
8 Kh. Qamal	21 Naḥal Tabor [b]	34 Ḥ. Salsilla
9 ᶜEn ha-Yadid	22 Dabu	35 Sirin
10 Ḥ. Zeev	23 el Tayyibe	36 Naḥal Šaḥal
11 Sheikh Daniel	24 Naḥal Issachar	37 el Bireh
12 Naḥal Tabor [a]	25 Saᶜideh (?)	38 Naḥal Tabor [c]
13 Ḥ. Ṭeḥavit	26 Yubla	39 Ḥ. ᶜAkin

Gal found no remains of the Hellenistic through Byzantine periods, Zori refers to Roman, Byzantine and Early Arab remains.[36]

The distribution of sites that are dated to the Hellenistic, Roman, and Byzantine periods for the Gazit area is summarized in part I of Table 2.1. In that summary, the first line is based on the key in Gal's publication and could have been adjusted somewhat by inclusion of sites 43 and 45 in Gal's numeration also as "Roman" (they are listed under the heading "Roman-Byzantine"; in the text Gal does not refer to Roman pottery at these sites). The second line presents my retabulation. The difference between the tabulations depends partly on the comparison of descriptions of the sites in Gal's publication with other published descriptions, partly on a decision to combine under one heading sites treated as two in the survey, and partly as a result of my effort to distinguish settlements from areas with remains of agricultural and other activity.[37] Despite the increase in the number of settlements, it seems likely that over the course of the Hellenistic and Roman periods, there was not simply absolute growth in the number of settlements (however we count them), but also a certain amount of turnover. According to Gal's listing Danna may have become deserted, to be reoccupied in the

---

[36] Kawkhab el Hawa, Kokab ha-Yarden, Belvoir; Gal 1991: no. 60; *TIR* 168–9, *s.v.* Kokhav ha-Yarden; cf. however, Gal 1991: 13; 13* in the English section; Zori 1962: no. 33.

[37] Gal 1991 does not refer to Hellenistic remains for nos. 57 and 65, although Zori 1977: nos. 144, 132 does. For the Roman and Byzantine periods I have counted Gal 1991: nos. 61–62 together (as Gal suggests), but added, for the Roman, Gal 1991: nos. 43 and, with some hesitation, 60 (see Zori 1977: nos. 142, 148; Zori 1962: 33; for the second of these sites see also *TIR* 168–169, s.v. Kokhav ha-Yarden; Dauphin 1998: no. 4.211). Ḥ. Shaḥal Taḥtit [a] (Gal 1991 no. 33; Zori 1977 nos. 177, 180) is included under the Byzantine heading based on the description of Zori; but Gal 1991: no. 16 (marked as questionable in the table of sites by date) is not included. On the other hand, in attempting to

Table 2.2: Gazit area, Sites with Reported Size Data

Name	*Size*	*H*	*R*	*B*	*Name*	*Size*	*H*	*R*	*B*
Gazit	0.11			•	Ḥ. Zeev	4.2			•
N. ᶜAkin	0.15			•	Kh. Qamal	5	•	•	
Ḥ. Ukkal [c]	1	•	•	•	ᶜEn ha-Yadid	5	•	•	•
Kh. ᶜUkkal [a]	1			•	Ḥ. Shaḥal Taḥtit [b], ᶜEn Shaḥal	10			•
Kh. ᶜUkkal [b]	1	•	•	•					
Byz. structure (Zori 1977: no. 146. Identical with Gal 1991: no. 66?)	1.2			•	Ḥ. Ḥardon, Kh. Ḥureidna	10			•
					Ḥ. Shaḥal Taḥtit [a], ᶜEn Shaḥal	14			•
Ḥ. Ṭeḥavit	2			•	Ḥ. Ḥagal	15	•	•	•
Sheikh Daniel, ᶜEn Daniel	3			•	Naḥal Tabor [d]	30?		•	•
Naḥal Tabor [a]	3			•	T. Rekhesh	40?			•

Byzantine period; and according to the alternative listing, el Bireh and Kh. Yebla did so as well (see Map 1).

Table 2.2 summarizes the data from this survey area for settlements for which I was able to find size estimates. The median size, based on this sample, is quite low: between 3 and 4.2 dunams. Moreover, granting for the moment that sizes as recorded are indicators of actual size in the Hellenistic through Byzantine periods, it is instructive that no site is larger than 40 dunams. In fact, based on the description of the remains in Gal, the actual Byzantine settlement at Tel Rekhesh and Naḥal Tabor [d][38] appear to have been smaller than the sizes given. Interestingly enough, the majority of new settlements in the Byzantine period according to this listing appear to be below this median. Although the "representativeness" of this sample is in doubt, the increase at the level of small settlements is interesting particularly because it is minute sites that are likely to disappear due to agricultural work or stone removal, and will become important when we examine the data as a whole.

The ᶜEn Dor area comprises the 10 km by 10 km square immediately to the West of the Gazit area (see Map 2). The number of sites is summarized in Part II of Table 2.1. As before, a tabulation different from that of Gal's is included. Here the primary reason for differences between the figures is the large number of sites where the description implies agricultural activity (winepresses, often found outside of settlements; oilpresses; cisterns or reservoirs; but also quarrying) but not necessarily a settlement.[39] Even at

include primarily settlements, I have not counted Gal 1991: nos. 10 (Zori 1977: no. 174), 25, 44, and 67, for which Gal lists Byzantine remains; and no. 52 for which he lists Roman remains as well.

[38] Gal 1991: nos. 12 and 52.

[39] Gal 1998: ᶜEn Dor nos. 2 (Byzantine); 6 (Roman); 13 (Byzantine); 16 (Byzantine); 20 (Byzantine); 30 (Byzantine), 32 (Byzantine), 39 (Roman, Byzantine; cf., however, Zori

Table 2.3: ᶜEN DOR AREA, SITES WITH REPORTED SIZE DATA

Name	*Size*	*H*	*R*	*B*	*Name*	*Size*	*H*	*R*	*B*
Ḥ. Sahar, Kh. Maluf (west) (Zori); Mughr el Saghira	0.5?		•	•	Ḥ. Ṣafṣafot, Kh. el Ṣafṣafa (TIR: Endor)	5?		•	•
Kh. Maluf (east), Ḥ. Elef	2		•	•	Tell el Ḥarfeh	10	•		•
Ḥ. Tomer, Kh. Dabu	4.8			•	Sulem, Shunem	10		•	•
Ḥ. Ṣur, Kh. el Ṣireh	5			•	Ḥ. Qara	20?	•	•	•
					Tel Qishyon, Tell Kasyun, el Khirbeh	50?	•	•	•

Gal's higher figures, however, the apparent settlement density is rather low, for which Gal accounts by pointing out that a substantial portion of the area covered by the survey (by Gal's estimate about two thirds) is either rocky, or covered by heavy alluvial soil.[40] Based on the 1:20,000 map accompanying the survey, the sites with preserved remains, whether serving as "settlements" or not, tend to appear along the slopes of the hills that dominate the central portion of the area, and consequently appear in Map 2 as a band across the middle portion of the map. The map may suggest a pattern of intensification of settlement over time: the attested remains at Nebi Daḥi, Naᶜurah, and Tel el Ḥarfeh appear in areas where there already had been substantial numbers of sites in the Byzantine period. This is true to a lesser degree for Tel Qishyon (see also the southeastern section of the Tabor area, discussed below) and Ḥ. Qara.

The rather skimpy data relating to site size are summarized in Table 2.3. The median size is small, about 5 dunams, although even more than with the Gazit area, it is difficult to know how representative reported sizes are. Tell Kasyun (Tel Qishyon), for instance, has a reported size of some 50 dunams, but both Zori's and Gal's descriptions suggest that it was occupied more heavily in periods substantially earlier than the Hellenistic through Byzantine.[41] By contrast, the minute size for Ḥ. Sahar is based on Gal, whose accompanying figure implies a substantially larger area for the settlement.[42]

Immediately to the north of the ᶜEn Dor area, and published by Gal together with it, is the Mt. Tabor survey area (see Map 3). The differences

---

1977: 59, which assumes a settlement; dating to the Roman follows Zori). Excluding also nos. 28 (Roman) and 29 (Hellenistic, Roman, Byzantine) reduces the numbers to: 4 Hellenistic sites, 8 Roman, and 17 Byzantine.

[40] Gal 1998: 59, 45* English section. Note also Isaac, Roll 1982: 87 on the disappearance of sites in the Jezreel valley.

[41] Zori 1977: no. 164; Gal 1998: ᶜEn Dor no. 1. Neither Dauphin 1998 nor *TIR* appear to list the site.

[42] Gal 1998: ᶜEn Dor no. 34, with figure 34.6 (the enclosure labeled 1 should be on the order of 15 dunams); Zori 1977: no. 92 (93) gave the area as 18 dunams.

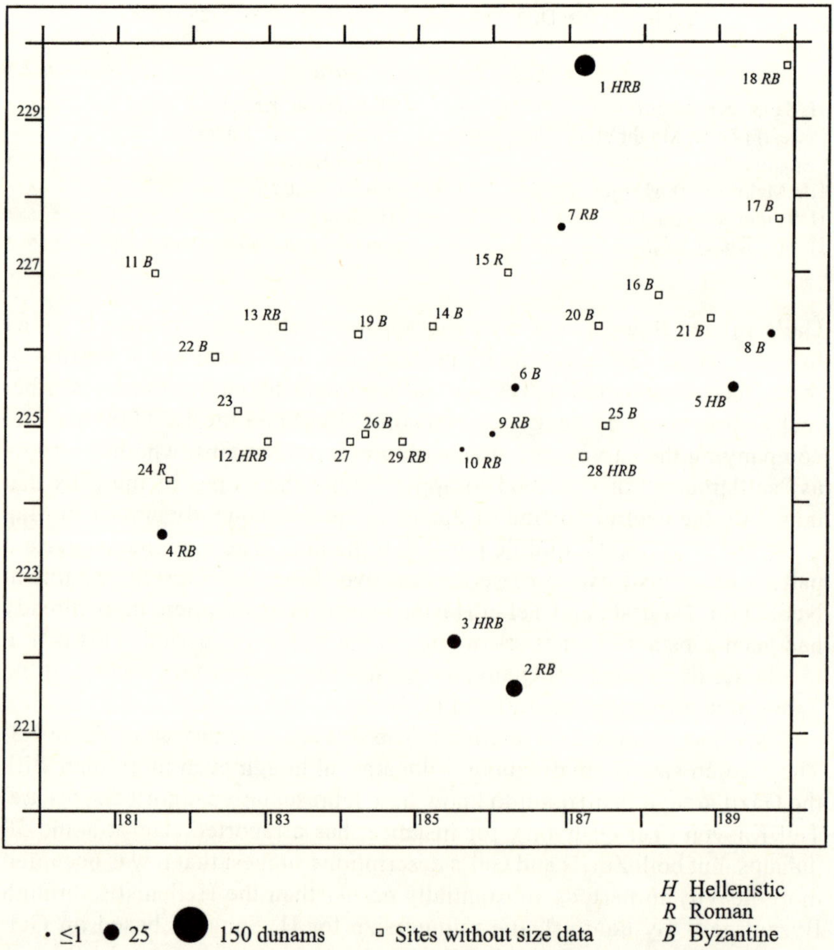

Map 2: ʿEn Dor Area (after Gal 1998)

between raw tabulations as provided by Gal and the alternative figures (see Part III of Table 2.1) are suggestive of the impact late-antique settlement had on the landscape itself. Although some of the differences are accounted for by comparing the survey report with other accounts of finds at the site,[43] the single largest factor is the large number of sites where Gal reports pottery, frequently in association with wells or springs, agricultural

43 E.g., I have included Shibli as a site with Hellenistic occupation (Gal 1998: Tabor no. 66, listed under sites with no datable remains; Gal identifies the site with Bir el Luza, Zori 1977: no. 156, where Zori noted Hellenistic remains). Jebel el Ṭur (Mt. Tabor) is listed in Gal 1990: no. 1.3 as having Hellenistic, Roman, and Byzantine remains; for his own

Map 2: LIST OF SITES

1 Tel Qishyon	11 Ḥ. Tevet	21 Shunet Ṭumrah
2 Kh. Buleiq	12 Nebi Daḥi	22 ᶜEn ha-More
3 Ḥ. Qara	13 Nain	23 el Daḥi (West)
4 Sulem	14 Tel ᶜAgol	24 Gibeᶜat ha-More [a]
5 Tell el Ḥarfeh	15 Ḥ. Endor	25 Bir el Naᶜura
6 Ḥ. Ṣur	16 Ṭamra [a]	26 Gibeᶜat ha-More [b]
7 Ḥ. Ṣafṣafot	17 Kafr Miṣr	27 Gibeᶜat ha-More [c]
8 Ḥ. Tomer	18 el Qaṣr	28 Naᶜurah
9 Kh. Maluf (east)	19 Tel ᶜAgol (Southwest)	29 Bir el Siyyaḥ
10 Ḥ. Sahar	20 Naḥal Neᶜurah	

installations or burials built or hewn into the bedrock itself, or quarrying, but without explicit description of a settlement.[44] Given the limited evidence available, it seems possible that despite the general trend toward greater density of settlement from the Hellenistic to the Byzantine period, there was a certain amount of turnover in the use of sites. Shibli may have had Hellenistic but not later remains; Karm el Ras may have had remains from the Hellenistic and Roman but not Byzantine; while Kh. Beiyin (Binit), Kh. ᶜArbita (ᶜArpad), and Mugheiyir (Ḥ. Zelef) appear to have Hellenistic and Byzantine but no Roman remains.[45]

Compared to the Akhziv/Ḥanita and Nahalal regions (to be discussed presently), and even to the Gazit area discussed above, the number of settlements seems somewhat low. Ecological factors, both of ancient settlement and of preservation, are presumably at play here: a substantial proportion of the sites clusters in the northwestern portion of the map; the southwestern portion of the map, marking the outer reaches of the Jezreel valley, has the fewest sites; while the eastern portion marks the transition to basalt plateaus, which, according to Gal, "impeded large scale agricultural activity" in antiquity.[46] In any case, it seems fairly clear that the hill

---

survey report, Gal 1998: Tabor no. 68, Gal listed only Byzantine remains E. M. Meyers, Strange, Groh 1978: 7 (Fig. 9), Byzantine, and possible late Roman pottery; cf. the text on the same page. I have included Kh. el Ṭira (Ḥ. Ṭirya, Gal 1998: Tabor no. 56; see also 1990: no. 1.9) among the Hellenistic sites, following Zori 1977: no. 149.

[44] These include Gal 1998: Tabor nos. 2 (Roman); 6 (Roman, Byzantine); 8 (Byzantine); 14 (Byzantine); 20 (Byzantine); 22 (Byzantine); 24 (Byzantine); 27 (Byzantine); 28–30 (two Byzantine, one Roman); 31 (Byzantine; see also no. 34, Roman, Byzantine); 32 (Roman, Byzantine); 33 (Roman, Byzantine); 35 (Byzantine); 40 (Byzantine); 43 (Roman, Byzantine); 49 (Roman, Byzantine); 50 (Byzantine); 51 (Hellenistic, Roman); 52 (Byzantine); 60 and 61 (Roman); 73 (Zori 1977: 163: Byzantine pottery but no remains of a settlement); 75 (Roman); 76 (Roman). Given the descriptions in the survey publication, I have, however, found it difficult to be exhaustive.

[45] Gal 1998: Tabor nos. 66; 3; and 11, 38, and 72 respectively.

[46] Gal 1998: 11–12, English section 12*–13*, the quotation is from the English section.

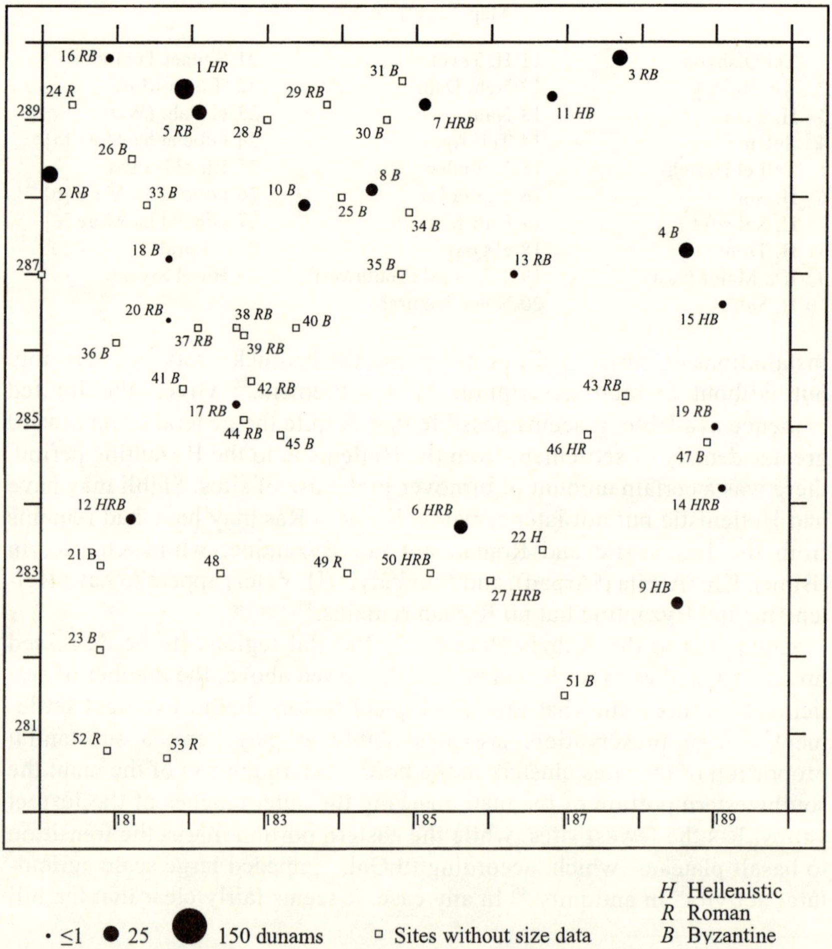

Map 3: MT. TABOR AREA (after Gal 1998)

country that served as the immediate hinterland to Sepphoris (at map reference 176239, just four or five kilometers to the East of Kh. Kenna or Mashhad [Tel Gat Ḥeper]) was fairly extensively settled in the Roman and Byzantine periods.

The evidence for site sizes for the Mt. Tabor area is summarized in Table 2.4. The median size for sites occupied in the Byzantine period is 10 dunams, somewhat lower than the median for the same period in the area surveyed by Frankel and Getzov (see below). Compared to the *Survey of Israel* areas as a group, this figure appears a bit high. At the same time, on comparison with the Akhziv/Ḥanita or Nahalal areas, the maximum site size is fairly small. It is possible that the particular configuration of eco-

Map 3: LIST OF SITES

1 Karm el-Ras
2 Tel Gat Ḥefer
3 Sejera
4 Kh. Qasṭa (?)
5 Kafr Kanna
6 Ḥ. Deborah [A?]
7 Ḥ. ᶜEn Kibšan
8 Kh. Banna
9 Kh. Mugheiyir
10 ᶜEn Lapidot
11 Ḥ. Binit
12 Ḥ. Ṭirya
13 Ḥ. Gobel
14 Kh. Sheikh Muhamad
15 Ḥ. Arpad
16 Kh. Kenna
17 ᶜEn Šiᶜin
18 En Amitai
19 Kh. ᶜEin el Saudeh
20 Har Yona area [?]
21 Meᶜarat Kesulot
22 Shibli
23 ᵓIksal
24 Mashad (North)
25 ᶜEin el Joz
26 Mashad (East)
27 Mt. Tabor
28 Jebel Khuwweikha [a]
29 Jebel Khuwweikha [b]
30 Jebel Khuwweikha [c]
31 ᶜEn Kibšan (Northwest)
32 el Reina
33 Mashad (Southeast)
34 Naḥal ha-Shibeᶜa [a]
35 Naḥal ᵓAzenot
36 ᶜEn Rani
37 ᶜEn Avinoᶜam
38 Nahal Baraq [a]
39 Nahal Baraq [b]
40 ᶜEin Mahil
41 Naṣerat ᶜIlit road
42 Nahal Baraq [c]
43 Bet Qeshet
44 Nahal Baraq [d]
45 Har Deborah [c?]
46 Naḥal ha-Šibᶜa [b]
47 Naḥal Qeshet
48 Naḥal Baraq [e]
49 Har Deborah [d?]
50 Dabburiye
51 Ḥ. Ṣonim
52 Biqeᶜat Kesulot [a]
53 Biqeᶜat Kesulot [b]

Table 2.4: MT. TABOR AREA, SITES WITH REPORTED SIZE DATA

Name	*Size*	*H*	*R*	*B*	*Name*	*Size*	*H*	*R*	*B*
En Amitai	4			•	Kh. Banna,	15			•
Kh. ᶜEin el Saudeh, Qa-saṭil (?); Gal: ᶜEn Sheḥor	4?		•	•	Kh. Mugheiyir, Ḥ. Zelef	15	•		•
Ḥ. Arpad, Kh. ᶜArbita	5	•		•	Ḥ. ᶜEn Kibšan, Kh. Kabs-hani	15	•	•	•
Ḥ. Gobel, Kh. Umm el Jubeil	5		•	•	Ḥ. Deborah [A?], Kh. Dabbura	20?	•	•	•
Kh. Kenna,	5		•	•	Kafr Kanna, Cana?	23?		•	•
ᶜÊn Šiᶜin, ᶜEnôt Šôᶜîm	5?	?	•	•	Kh. Qasṭa (?),	25?			•
Kh. Sheikh Muhamad,	5	•	•	•	Tel Gat Ḥefer, Meshed, Geth Hefer	30		•	•
Ḥ. Binit, Kh. Beiyin	10	•		•	Karm el-Ras	45	•	•	
Ḥ. Ṭirya, Kh. el Ṭira	10?	•	•	•					

logical or historical factors in this region lent itself to a somewhat more homogeneous distribution of settlements (modest sizes, with fewer very large sites).[47] Nevertheless, there is a signicant margin of error (i.e, a substantial proportion of sites without size data, and, as usual, a fair degree of uncertainty about individual site sizes), and a safer assessment may be merely that the data on size collected for this survey area is truncated.

---

[47] From the point of view of some of the theoretical adjustments to central-place theory discussed in the previous chapter, one might think in terms of Sepphoris inhibiting the growth of larger villages in its immediate hinterland.

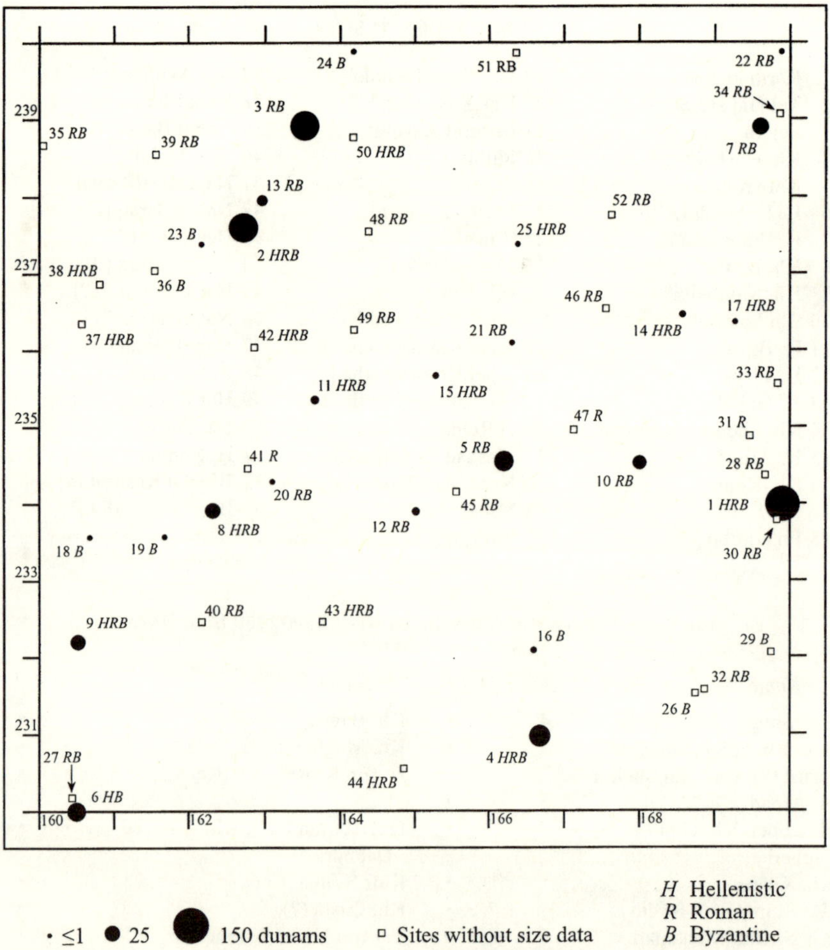

Map 4: NAHALAL AREA (after Raban 1982)

Raban's publication of the survey of the Nahalal area yields rather different results (see Map 4). I noted above that Portugali differed in detail about a number of sites in this area. Here, however, the focus is not on the histories of individual sites, but rather on this collection of data as a whole. Notable, first, is the rather higher settlement density, particulary based on Raban's summary table (see Part IV of Table 2.1). Again, there seems to be a lower density of settlement in the southern section of the area, where the western hills of lower Galilee end in the Jezreel valley. In retabulating these figures, a number of factors had to be taken into account. First, Raban's tabulations in the key to sites by period are not always consistent with his descriptions of the site. Thus, for example, in connection with Tel

Map 4: List of Sites

1 Tel Shimron
2 Ḥ. Buṣim
3 Kh. Umm Rashid
4 [unnamed Tel]
5 Ramat Yishai
6 Tel Yoqneʿam
7 Miṣpeh Zebulun
8 Bet Šeʿarim
9 Tel Qashish
10 Zebed
11 Beʾer Tibʿon
12 Tel Risim
13 Ḥ. Buṣin
14 Kh. el Khudeireh
15 Ḥ. Ḥazin
16 Tel el Ghalṭa
17 Tel Ḥaṣir
18 [Byzantine farm]
19 Pinnat ha-Šomerim
20 ʿEn ʿAmiel
21 Beʾer Abba
22 [Roman farm]
23 ʿUzbeidat (East)
24 [unnamed farm]
25 Umm el ʿAmad
26 Ḥ. Seifan
27 Tel Yoqneʿam (No.)
28 ʿEin el Resmeq
29 [agricultural buildings]
30 ʿEin el ʿAleiq
31 [prehistoric site]
32 Ramat David
33 [tombs/presses]
34 Sur el Musheirifa
35 Kh. ʿAjajleh
36 ʿUzbeidat
37 Kh. el Ḥarithiyeh
38 Kh. el Ḥaritiye [North]
39 [Khirbeh]
40 Tel Iṣḥaqi
41 [tombs?]
42 Tibʿon
43 Kh. Ṣeror
44 Tel Shem
45 Ramat Yishai (W)
46 Ḥebraya
47 Newe Yaʿar
48 Ḥ. Zeroʿa
49 ʿArdasqos
50 Ḥ. Qoshet
51 Kh. Shabaneh
52 Bet Leḥem (Gal.)

Shimron, the Hebrew text discusses pottery from the Hellenistic, Roman, and Byzantine periods.[48] In the Persian period, according to Raban, settlement was "mostly on the acropolis," implying that Hellenistic through Byzantine remains are spread more widely at the site. However, in the English summary Raban gives a rather more detailed picture: "At the beginning of the Roman period, settlement resumed [implying desertion during the Hellenistic?] and grew toward the west and on the slope of the tell, and remains of buildings and pottery from this period were found." On his Map 4 Raban lists this site as occupied only during the Roman period; but in the key to sites he lists the site for every sub-period from Hellenistic I to Byzantine II. Similarly, for Umm el ʿAmad Raban gives references to the Hellenistic, Roman, and Byzantine periods, in both the key and the description but does not mark Hellenistic occupation on the corresponding map.[49] In general, in the interests of consistency I have in most cases followed Raban's Hebrew text.

Second, there are a number of "sites" that Raban lists separately but describes as part of an extended single site, and I have treated these as single sites.[50] Third, Raban's key to sites frequently attempts greater

48 Raban 1982: no. 83.

49 Raban 1982: no. 45.

50 E.g., Raban 1982: nos. 15 and 16, 26 and 20, and 24 and 30. Note also sites in which Raban associates tombs or other installations with a particular settlement, e.g. 63 and 64; by name, at least, Raban appears to associate nos. 52 and 53 with the settlement at no. 54, and he explicitly notes the proximity of the installations at no. 64 with the site at 63. In

Table 2.5 (a): NAHALAL AREA, SITES WITH REPORTED SIZE DATA

Name	*Size*	*H*	*R*	*B*
Tel Ḥaṣir, Tell el Ḥudeira	2		•	•
Ḥ. Ḥazin, Kh. Bir el Baidar	3	•	•	•
Tel el Ghalṭa [after Dauphin 1998: no. 3.213]	3			•
Kh. el Khudeireh,	3.5	•	•	•
Ḥ. Buṣin	5		•	•
Tel Risim, Tell el Rish	5.5		•	•
Beʾer Tibʿon, Tell Tabʿun	6	•	•	•
Zebed, Zebdah el Alaly, Zebod de-Galilaʾ?	20?		•	•
Tel Qashish, Tell el Qassis	25	•	•	•
Bet Shearim, Sheikh Abreik	25	•	•	•
Miṣpeh Zebulun, Kh. el-Musheirifa	30		•	•
Tel Yoqneʿam, Tell Qamun	40	•	•	•
Ramat Yishai, Jeida, Bibl. Yideʾelah (?)	45		•	•
[unnamed Tel] (16682311)	52	•	•	•
Kh. Umm Rashid	100		•	•
Ḥ. Buṣim, Kh. Buseima	100	•	•	•
Tel Shimron, Kh. Semmuniye	150	•	•	•

Table 2.5 (b): NAHALAL AREA, ESTIMATED SIZES FOR ADDITIONAL SITES

Name	*Size*	*H*	*R*	*B*
[Byz. Farm] (16072336)	2			•
Pinnat ha-Shomerim	2			•
ʿUzbeidat (East)	2			•
[unnamed farm]	2			•
[Roman farm]	2		•	•
ʿEn ʿAmiel, ʿEin el Khashaba	2		•	•
Umm el ʿAmad, Allonei Abba	2	•	•	•
Beʾer Abba, Bir es Samandura	2		?	•
Kh. el Ḥaritiye, Gaba Hippeon?	large	•	•	•
ʿAjajleh	large		•	•

precision than the description in the body of the text. According to his tabulation, the breakdown by period is as follows: Hellenistic I: 19; II: 18; Roman I: 20; II, 27, III, 50; Byzantine I: 45, II, 38; Arab 35, in other words a steep increase in the later Roman period with a gradual decline over the course of the Byzantine period. The presentation in Table 2.1 collapses his tabulation into the coarser periodization used by the other surveys to facilitate comparison. Finally I have, even more tentatively than in the case of the preceding survey areas, attempted to distinguish between settlements and non-settlements.[51] Given the relatively large number of explicitly labelled "farms" reported for the Nahalal area (see below), at least in comparison with the areas just discussed, it is not clear whether the Nahalal

some cases Raban describes a site as a "suburb" of another site, e.g., nos. 4 and 5; 41 and 48, although in these cases the sites seem widely spaced enough to consider them independently of one another.

[51] Raban 1982: nos. 17, 18 (?), 58, 76, 78, 79, and 82 appear to be good candidates for non-settlements. See also no. 74, a prehistoric site with some Byzantine pottery.

area preserves the archaeological traces of a different kind of agricultural regime than that of the eastern end of the Jezreel valley, or whether, conversely, clusters of agricultural installations routinely were interpreted by Raban as farms.[52]

The primary difference between Raban's reported results and the retabulated figures relates to whether there is a net increase between the Roman period and the Byzantine period or a net decline, and this question cannot be answered conclusively on the basis of present evidence. It is worth noting that a net increase in the number of settlements fits with the data as a whole, as well as various regional surveys, although the data for other regions presumably implicitly collapse more complex processes of change (much as the Table 2.1 does for Raban's survey area). It is notable, too, that however we count the data for the Nahalal region, the rate of growth in the number of settlements is weighted differently here than for the other regions discussed thus far, with a lower rate of increase in the Byzantine period for the Nahalal region than the other areas (compare the Akhziv/Ḥanita area discussed below).

Turning now to the sizes of sites, the data from Raban's survey are summarized in Table 2.5 (a). Based on these numbers, the median site size is 25 dunams (rather large compared to the other survey areas discussed so far, and, as we shall see, compared to the data as a whole as well). Here, based on this limited sample, half the new sites that emerged in the Roman period were below the median. If we assign nominal sizes to other sites where size was characterized but not quantified by Raban (i.e. two dunams for sites described as "farms," on comparison with similarly characterized sites for which he does give sizes, and something in the 100 or 150 range for Kh. el Ḥaritiye and ᶜAjajleh, described as "large," again in comparison with the other "large" sites), we can add the items listed in Table 2.5 (b). This brings the median size down to 5.5, still larger than for Gazit, but comparable to that of ᶜEn Dor, and smaller than for the data set as a whole. These additional data also accentuate the growth at the lowest stratum of settlements. Of the five large sites, at least three are on or close to Roman roads:[53] ᶜAjajleh, el Ḥaritiye, and Tel Shimron (although, as we have seen, Portugali calls the size and occupation history of Shimron into question).

The last *Archaeological Survey of Israel* area directly relevant here is the Akhziv/Ḥanita area, published by Frankel and Getzov, comprising the northernmost coastal plain of the State of Israel (it ends at the border with Lebanon), and in its eastern portion including the western plateaus of upper

---

[52] See Raban 1982: no. 72 (Ras el ᶜArqub), where a cluster of installations is presumed to be associated with the Roman or Byzantine farm at Tel Ḥaṣir (no. 73, where the remains appear to be quite scanty, and not sufficient to date them).

[53] *TIR* map, Northern Sheet; the road is attested by milestones; see further Chapter 3.

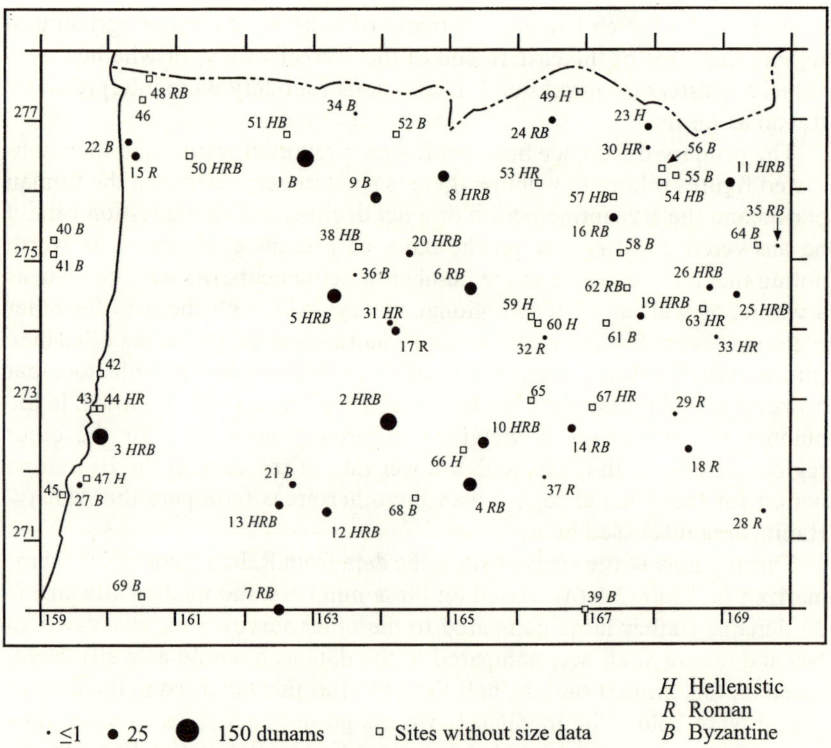

Map 5: AKHZIV/ḤANITA (after Frankel, Getzov 1997)

Galilee (see Map 5). The distribution of sites by period for the area as a whole is summarized in part V of Table 2.1. As before, the authors' tabulation of the sites by period[54] is accompanied by an alternative retabulation. In this case, I have also supplied numbers that Frankel and Getzov give in their introduction for sites that they there identify as "settlements," as opposed to sites that merely have remains dated to these chronological periods. Although Table 2.1 counts two sites not indexed under a particular chronological period by the authors,[55] the main reason for the differences in tabulation is that, like the authors,[56] I have made an attempt to include only those sites that appear from the authors' descriptions to be settlements.[57] The numbers are roughly comparable to Avi'am's reported figures

[54] Based on the index in Frankel, Getzov 1997: 53, 53*–54*, English section.

[55] Frankel, Getzov 1997: nos. 2.43, 2.74.

[56] Frankel, Getzov 1997: 33–36, 33*, 34*, 36*, English section.

[57] Thus, I have not included milestones: Frankel, Getzov 1997: nos. 2.4, 2.130, listed as "Roman"; or burial places, e.g., nos. 1.5, Hellenistic and Roman; 1.8 Hellenistic. In ad-

Map 5: LIST OF SITES

1 Baṭ el Jebel	24 Ḥanotha	47 el Buqbaq
2 Kh. Ḥumṣin	25 Ḥ. Remaḥ	48 [unnamed site]
3 el Zib	26 Ḥ. Seraf	49 Miṣpeh Ḥanita
4 Ḥ. Sugar	27 Ḥ. Nemal Ahkziv (N)	50 Kefar Rosh Haniqra
5 Ḥ. Kenesiyya	28 Ḥ. Bet Uriyya	51 [unnamed site]
6 Kh. el Ghureiyib	29 Kh. Shaumariya	52 [unnamed site]
7 el Ṭuweiri	30 Kh. el Mizrath	53 Ḥ. ʿEn Kovshim
8 Kh. el Maʿṣub	31 [unnamed site]	54 Meʿarat Kukhim
9 Bezeth	32 Ḥ. Zibdi	55 (Mugharat Abu Sabʿa)
10 Tel ʿAbdon (?)	33 Kh. Juʿarran	56 Mugharat el Baiyaḍa
11 Kh. Idmith	34 (unnamed)	57 Meʿarot Eder
12 Ḥ. ʿEmed	35 Kh. Daqdaq	58 [unnamed site]
13 Ḥ. Shaquf	36 Shelomi (West)	59 Har Poreaḥ
14 Kh. Dureijat	37 Kh. Jazirat el Sidrah	60 [unnamed site]
15 Kh. Masref (South)	38 Kh. Judeideh	61 [unnamed site]
16 Ḥ. Bannay	39 edh Dhur	62 Ḥ. Ẓurit
17 [unnamed site]	40 ʾI Shaḥaf	63 [unnamed site]
18 Ḥ. Ṭabburit	41 ʾI Naḥlieli	64 [aqueduct]
19 Ḥ. Gez	42 [unnamed site]	65 Giveʿat Ezov
20 Ḥ. ʿOvesh	43 [unnamed site]	66 [unnamed site]
21 Kh. Umm el ʿAmad	44 [unnamed site]	67 [cistern]
22 Kh. Masref	45 Minat el Zib	68 Ḥ. Manot
23 Tel el Ṣarijah	46 [unnamed site]	69 Saʿar

for upper Galilee as a whole: 93 sites in the Hellenistic period, 138 in the Roman (an increase of 58%), and 168 in the Byzantine (an increase of 21%).[58]

As in the case of surveys by Gal and (after my retabulation) by Raban, the "Byzantine" period shows the largest number of sites. The rates of change between one period and the next are different from these other regions (as might perhaps be expected), but it is difficult to know how much of this is the result of different techniques of data collection and pottery dating. Frankel and Getzov argue for a fairly sharp decline in the "Late Byzantine" (17 sites), with almost no settlements in the "Early Arab," although in both cases they acknowledge doubts as to the reliability in detail of these conclusions.[59]

---

dition, and unlike Frankel and Getzov, I have excluded such sites as 2.141, where the authors describe a scatter of pottery (including Hellenistic), but not remains of a settlement; 2.151, Hellenistic and Roman pottery near a cistern (perhaps for irrigation purposes?); or 2.67, an underground reservoir (with pottery from the Byzantine period in the first layer of plaster) and a nearby winepress (typically, although not exclusively, found outside of settlements, as noted by Frankel, Getzov 1997: 43, 42*, English section).

[58] Aviʿam 1993: 453, 455

[59] Frankel, Getzov 1997: 36–37, 36*–37*, English section.

In any case, within this area there is no one, single, chronological development. Out of 28 sites with "Hellenistic" remains, for instance, some 13 do not have remains from the Byzantine period (of these, 7 have Roman period remains); an additional 4 Hellenistic sites have Byzantine remains, but not Roman. This may imply a comparatively high turnover in the use of sites. An examination of Map 5 suggests subregional variations. Focusing now on sites that appear to have some sort of settlement on them, in the northeastern section of the region (the 4 km by 4 km square between map coordinates 16602740 and 17002780), it appears that although roughly the same number of sites are said to have been occupied in both the Hellenistic and the Byzantine periods, a different set of sites was occupied in the Hellenistic period (Ḥ. Gez, Ḥ. ᶜEn Kovshim, Tel el Sarijah, Kh. el Mizrath, Kh. Idmith, Meᶜarot Eder, Ḥ. Seraf; possibly Har Poreaḥ and the unnamed site at map reference 16632741 [site no. 2.91]) than in the Byzantine (overlap at H. Gez, Kh. Idmith, Meᶜarot Eder; and Ḥ. Seraf; additional sites at Ḥanotha, Kh. Remah; and Ḥ. Bannay; possibly Kh. Daqdaq; and no. 2.95), with the Roman period serving as a kind of transition.

By contrast, the southeastern section of the area (the 4 km by 6 km area between coordinates 16402700 and 17002740) shows a different pattern. Two settlements occupied in the Hellenistic period (Kh. Ḥumsin and Tel ᶜAbdon; cf. Kh. Juᶜarran, not occupied in the Byzantine) were occupied also in the Roman and Byzantine, although in that last period more sites were occupied. What is striking, however, is that on the evidence provided by Frankel and Getzov this sector includes a number of settlements that were only occupied in the Roman period: Kh. Zubdiyye, Kh. Bit Iriya, Kh. Shaumariya, Ḥ. Tabburit, Kh. Jazirat el Sidra. In fact, Frankel and Getzov connect at least one of these sites (Kh. Zubdiyye) with the complex of land subdivisions identifiable on the plateaus, suggest that it and other sites like it were rural farms rather than villages, and relate the land subdivisions to the political status of Akko-Ptolemais.[60] If their chronological data are correct, the evidence suggests that the Roman period saw a different *kind* of settlement and agricultural regime than either before or after.

Data about size are summarized in Table 2.6. The median is 15 dunams for Byzantine sites alone, somewhat lower if we include all the sites with size data. As in the previous examples, there remains some uncertainty as to size. The size of Kh. Judeideh is given only as "a few."[61] In the case of Kh. Ḥumsin about half of the area given for the site is said to be in the

---

[60] Frankel, Getzov 1997: 34–35, 34–35*, English section; they also discuss Kh. Juᶜarran in this context.

[61] Frankel, Getzov 1997: 2.52, English section: "several."

Table 2.6: AKHZIV/ḤANITA AREAS, SITES WITH REPORTED SIZE DATA

Name	*Size*	*H*	*R*	*B*
Kh. Jazirat el Sidrah	0.5		•	
Shelomi (West)	0.5?			•
Kh. Daqdaq	1		?	?
[unnamed] (16362771)	1			•
Kh. Juʿarran	1.7	•	•	
[unnamed] (16412741)	2	•	•	
Kh. el Mizrath	2	•	•	
Ḥ. Zibdi, Kh. Zubdiyyeh	2?		•	
Kh. Shawmariya, Ḥ. Shomeriya	2.5		•	
Ḥ. Bet Uriyya, Kh. Beit Iriya (vel sim.)	3		•	
Ḥ. Nemal Ahkziv (N)	5			•
Ḥ. Seraf, Kh. Samaḥ, Kh. Samakh	8	•	•	•
Ḥ. Remaḥ, Kh. Ramaḥ	9	•	•	•
Tel el Ṣarijah	10	•		
Kh. Masref, Minat el Musheirifa	10			•
Kh. Umm el ʿAmad	10			•
Ḥ. ʿOvesh, Kh. el Abbasiyeh	10	•	•	•
Ḥ. Gez, Kh. el Jauzazia	10	•	•	•
Ḥanotha, Ḥanita	10?		•	•
Ḥ. Ṭabburit, Kh. Ṭibiriya, Kh. Thableh, Kh. el Suyyuḥ	11		•	
Kh. Masref (South)	15		•	
[unnamed] (16422740)	15		•	
Kh. Dureijat, Kh. el Wawiya	15		•	•
Ḥ. Bannay, Kh. Banna	15		•	•
Ḥ. Shaquf, Kh. Shuquf (?); Kh. Umm el Shuquf	15	•	•	•
Ḥ. ʿEmed, Kh. el Amud	20			•
Kh. Idmith, Kh. Edmeth (?); Ḥ. Idmit	20	•	•	•
el Ṭuweiri, Kh. Thuwaireh	30		•	•
Bezeth, el Bassa	30?			•
Kh. el Maʿṣub, Maẓuva	30?	•	•	•
Tel ʿAbdon (?), Kh. ʿAbdeh	30?	•	•	•
Kh. el Ghureiyib, Ḥ. Ghureib (?) + Tel Bad, Tell el Baiyad	40?		•	•
Ḥ. Sugar, Bibra (Bēt Karia/Badia of Rehov ?); Kh. Suweiyireh, Kh. Suweijireh	50		•	•
Ḥ. Kenesiyya, Kh. el ʿAmariyye; Kanisat el ʿAmariyye	50	•	•	•
el Zib, Ecdippa, Achziv, Akhziv	70	•	•	•
Baṭ el Jebel	80			•
Kh. Ḥumṣin, Gibʿat Ḥamudot; Ḥ. Hamudot (Aviʿam)	80?	•	•	•
Kh. Judeideh	several	•		•

valley, where the remains consist of pottery alone; it seems reasonable to suppose that at least part of 80 dunams is the result of erosion from the slopes.[62] Other sites have been given different estimates by Aviʿam.[63]

The Akhziv/Ḥanita survey pays particular attention to aspects of the economy and material culture of the region, with a discussion in the introduction of the distribution of quarries, oil and wine presses, and the traces of large scale agricultural intensification.[64] Based on the evidence given for their distribution, oil and wine presses do not appear to reflect subre-

---

[62] Frankel, Getzov 1997: 2.134 following the Hebrew section; cf. p. 12–13, English section 11*.

[63] E.g., for Frankel, Getzov 1997: 2.8, 2.77, and 2.87 cf. Aviʿam 1994: 124–6.

[64] Frankel, Getzov 1997: 38–46, 38*–45*, English section.

gional specialization; indeed, a number of sites are associated with remains of both.[65] Of particular interest are the remains of walls subdividing the highland plateaus[66] and terracing on the slopes. The editors date these phenomena to the Roman and Byzantine periods respectively, and link them with increased settlement in the area.[67]

The absence of any clear traces of regional specialization in the Akhziv/Ḥanita area, even in a cycle of agricultural intensification, is worth noting given H. Ben David's argument about olive oil specialization in the Lower Golan, or, more generally, Tchalenko's classic reconstruction of the economy of northern Syria.[68] At least with respect to wine or oil presses or parts thereof, such as crushing stones for olives (given the nature of the survey reports, these are among the most explictly attested aspects of agricultural production) none of the survey areas discussed above appeared to be marked by exclusive production.[69] As a rule, the evidence as reported in the surveys does not allow for quantified assessments (the precise number or size of installations), and therefore may mask specialization.

At any rate, the absence of specialization (if such it was) does not exclude intensive, possibly market-oriented production. The complex of presses at site no. 82 in the Nahalal survey (no. 33 in Map 4) implies some sort of organized production (whether through estate management, cooperative activity, or some other mechanism). The proximity both to Tel Shimron (even by Portugali's estimation a relatively large local site in the Byzantine period, see Section A) and to a Roman road linking Sepphoris, Legio, and, rather farther away, Scythopolis, supports speculation (but not more than that) that the production is for consumption at Tel Shimron or at some higher-level consumption center, rather than exclusively for local use by peasant producers. Evidence for crafts arises in connection with el Reineh (in the Mt. Tabor survey area) and Tel Masref (in the Ḥanita area), which had remains of the production of stone vessels and pottery production respectively.[70]

---

[65] See, e.g., Frankel, Getzov 1997: 2.8, 2.102, 2.104, 2.125, 2.134, 2. 142, 2.156, 2.166.

[66] See, e.g., Frankel, Getzov 1997: 174, ill. 2.154.2.

[67] Frankel, Getzov 1997: 42, 40*–41*, English section.

[68] H. Ben David 1998; Tchalenko 1953–58.

[69] Examples (not comprehensive) are as follows. Gazit: winepresses, e.g., Gal 1991: 5, 15 (see Zori 1977: no. 211), 16, 62; olive presses, Gal 1991: no. 13 (see Zori 1977: no. 201), 31, 43, 53, 59 (see Zori 1977: no. 145). En Dor: winepresses, e.g., Gal 1998: En Dor nos. 7, 34, 39; oilpresses, Gal 1998: En Dor nos. 20, 30, 34, 39. Tabor: winepresses, e.g., Gal 1998: Tabor nos. 5, 6, 7, 10, 23, 24, 32, 65; oil presses, Gal 1998: Tabor nos. 23, 32, 45, 65. Nahalal: Raban 1982: nos. 42, 43, 54, 79, 63; wine presses, Raban 1982: nos. 37, 57, 58, 64, 82.

[70] Gal 1998: Tabor: no. 18; Frankel, Getzov 1997: no. 2.14.

Gal mentions terracing in connection with a number of sites, particularly in the Mt. Tabor areas, although it is rarely clear from the report whether they date to the period under review here.[71] In addition there are numerous notices for the ʿEn Dor and Mt. Tabor areas of pools, cisterns, or other water storage installations apparently outside of settlements (suggesting, if these can be dated to the late-antique period, intensive farming of irrigated crops).[72] Kh Sireh (Ḥ. Sahar), in the ʿEn Dor area had as many as eight such installations on the slopes to the West of the settlement, some at a distance of 100 meters or more from the site.[73] These, together with the notices regarding watch towers (associated by Dar with wine production in Samaria),[74] point to the transformation of the late-antique landscape through increased settlement and agricultural production.

C. The Data as a Whole

The preliminary review of the data from the five extensively surveyed areas of the *Archaeological Survey of Israel* suggests that the late-antique period is one of multiplication of settlements, although apparently at different rates in different subregions. A cursory examination of data for the region as a whole shows that the Roman and Byzantine periods were periods for which we can trace the growth in the number of settlements. These results are summarized in part VI of Table 2.1. The upward trend is unmistakable. However, as that table, and the preceding discussion, also make clear, the data from the *Archaeological Survey of Israel* areas suggest that different, if in aggregate, perhaps, complementary, processes were taking place in different sub-regions. Similarly, some portions of Samaria may in fact have seen a fall off in the number of settlements during the Byzantine period.[75] Individual sites may have gone out of occupation in the Byzantine period in upper Galilee, but on the basis of numbers reported by Aviʿam the Byzantine period saw a growth in the number of sites occupied overall, but again, with different rates of change than that of the area covered by this study as a whole.[76] Indeed the differential rates for the

---

71 See, e.g., Gal 1998: Tabor nos. 8, 20, 35, 40, 43.

72 E.g., Gal 1998: Tabor no. 14 (a pool, in association with ancient (?) terracing); ʿEn Dor no. 32 (a covered reservoir with a capacity of some 400 m^3).

73 Gal 1998: ʿEn Dor: no. 34, with Fig. 34.6. The descriptions mention winepresses and an oil press, neither marked on the drawing.

74 E.g., Gal 1998: ʿEn Dor nos. 13, 30; Tabor nos. 7, 27, 50. See Dar 1986a: 110–113.

75 Dar, Safrai, Tepper 1986: 137–138; despite overall increase in settlement in Samaria in the Byzantine period, see *JSG* Samaria, 237–238; Zertal 1992–: 1, 581–582; 2, 808, with extensive discussion in the introductions to the respective volumes.

76 Meyers, Strange, Groh 1978: 8–10; Aviʿam 1993.

Galilee and Golan, and, for that matter, contiguous areas in the present-day Kingdom of Jordan,[77] suggest that different rates of settlement growth or decline characterized more extensive areas as well. Portugali has argued that in the western Jezreel valley the period of demographic growth peaked in the Roman period, and had reversed itself by the Byzantine period, despite the rise in the absolute number of settlements in the Byzantine period. However, subject as the present study is to published data, it is impossible to evaluate changes in site size over time, and therefore to attempt similar modeling of demographic change.[78]

For the area covered by the study as a whole, the median size of sites from the Byzantine period (the period with the largest number of sites and sizes) is 15 dunams, similar to the median of Byzantine sites in the the Akhziv/Ḥanita area, but higher than any of the other *Archaeological Survey* areas. My calculation of the median for the Golan is higher still, 18 dunams. By contrast, the median size for the western territories covered by this study (Galilee and adjacent areas) is 10 dunams. It is not clear whether the higher median in the Golan is the result of different demographic conditions or settlement patterns, or whether it results from the methods of, or the political and military constraints upon, the surveys executed immediately after the 1967 war, which serve as the source for much of this data. At any rate, attention to the area around Beth Shean, another well-surveyed area, again yields a small median size: between 3.75 and 4 dunams.[79] As a result of the evidence from this area and from the *Archaeological Survey* areas, it seems likely that in aggregate the data collected here tend to fail

[77] See the data for what is called Sector 1 in the recent publication of *JADIS: The Jordan Antiquities Database and Information System*, the sector that includes the site of ancient Gadara and Pella and much of the southeastern section of what would have been, from the fifth century onward, Palaestina Secunda (Palumbo, ed. 1994: 1.14, and the corresponding maps in the map section). That publication lists the following settlement numbers: Persian and Hellenistic: 86; Nabataean: 3; Roman: 321; Byzantine: 424. A similar trend occurs in the adjacent Sector 2. See also the data summarized in Kennedy 1999: 93.

[78] Portugali 1986; see also Portugali 1982; cf. Safrai 1986b. Were Portugali's conclusions generalizable to the rest of the region covered by the present study (the growth in the number of sites on the order of 2 dunams, but the decline in the size of sites in the range of more than 80 dunams), and combined with the manifest spread of certain urban centers (for instance, Caesarea, see Holum, *et al.* 1988: figs. 50, 86, 112; or Scythopolis, Tsafrir, Foerster 1994: 106; see further, Table 3.1), this would shed important light on the resulting divide between urban centers and small rural settlements.

[79] For the Bet Shean area it was easiest to tabulate data based on map reference; because I have collected no data on the Jordanian side of the Jordan river, the sites are effectively limited to the 280 km^2 rectangle between 19002000 and 20402200), rather than on any geographical boundaries or on administrative subdivisions. Effectively, this area incorporates data from Zori 1962, and to a lesser degree from Zori 1977, as well as other sources.

to represent the very smallest sites, and therefore to inflate the median size of the sites. A small median size is also consistent with the tendency noted by Portugali in the western Jezreel Valley for expansion in the number of settlements during the Byzantine period precisely at the bottom of the scale, and the observation by M. Avi'am that larger villages in the north-western Galilee of the late Roman and Byzantine periods tended to have a substantial number of satellite settlements (eight and eleven in his two examples) of a few dunams or less within a two-kilometer radius.[80] If a small median settlement size was the general norm, at least in western Palestine, the Akhziv/Ḥanita material should remind us that within broader tendencies there were also different localized settlement patterns (in this case, possibly to be connected to the survey area's position on and near the coastal plain; see also Chapter 3, Section D).

The figures collected in Table 2.1 give some sense of the range of possible real settlement densities. The higher figures reported by the archaeologists are themselves samples of presumably larger, but uncontrolled for, numbers of sites where remains have either not been preserved at all, or are not visible on the surface. The generally lower figures representing my retabulation of the number of settlements provide something like a lower limit, within the constraints of the published data: it is certainly possible (even likely in some cases) that places where installations or scatters of pottery were found also served as settlements. Leaving aside the clearly low number of settlements for the ʿEn Dor area, and taking the retabulated figures as a base, the Mt. Tabor area had 3.7 km^2 per settlement in the Byzantine period, the Gazit area had 3.3, the Nahalal area 2.4, and the Akhziv/Ḥanita[81] area 2.5. The Gazit area, again, may have been fairly marginal and have had a somewhat low settlement density. In connection with the Mt. Tabor area, it is worth recalling that it is particularly the southwestern section of the map (representing lowlands) that is rather sparely represented; at any rate the northwestern section (corresponding to the hill country of central lower Galilee) had a comparable settlement density to that of the Nahalal and Akhziv/Ḥanita areas.[82]

---

[80] Portugali 1986; cf. Frankel, Getzov 1997: 34–35, 34*–35*, English section for section western upper Galilee, where they argue for the development and then the desertion of small farmsteads in the Roman period. Avi'am 1994: 125–6, exemplified with reference to Fassuta and Ḥ. Bata.

[81] Taking that area to be roughly 82 km^2, and leaving off two islands: Frankel, Getzov 1997: nos. 1.1, 1.2, 1.7 (nos. 40, 41, and 45 on Map 5).

[82] Within the triangle marked by the western and northern boundaries of the map area between 180239 and 189240 (i.e., 40.5 km^2) there at least some 17 settlements, or 2.4 km^2 per settlement.

Again, these figures may represent a minimum settlement density (assuming, not unproblematically, that all the sites counted under a given period were occupied at the same time). The raw figures offered by the surveyors suggest the possibility of even higher settlement densities (for the Nahalal area, less than 2 km^2 per site). Still, it is not clear how representative these figures are. The figures generated from Frankel and Getzov's survey of the Akhziv/Ḥanita area (contiguous with upper Galilee) seem low (i.e., and the settlement density high) for upper Galilee as a whole, which, if we may take the figures reported by Avi'am as representative (see above), may have had a ratio of area to settlements on the order of 6.5 km^2 per site.

A report of a survey by Frankel immediately to the South of the Akhziv/Ḥanita area gave a settlement distribution of 3.51 km^2 per settlement in the Byzantine period.[83] Here the median size for settlements in the same period was fifteen dunams, comparable to the median for the Akhziv/Ḥanita area. However, the median for Akhziv/Ḥanita is higher than the median for any of the other *Archaoelogical Survey of Israel* areas discussed above or, for that matter, than that calculated for the Galilee and adjacent areas in western Palestine. Frankel's western Galilee survey is titled a "preliminary report" so it is not clear whether the relatively high median size together with low settlement density reflects a general under-reporting of (small) sites or whether the correspondence in median size with the area immediately to the north implies a fairly representative assessment of settlement density to the West of Galilee. (Note again, the proximity of both areas to the coast, which may have supported somewhat larger settlements; see Chapter 3, Section D.)

To the South of lower Galilee, in the area in western Palestine around Scythopolis, settlement distribution was 3.29 km^2 per settlement in the Byzantine period, based on data collected from surveys by Zori. However, an examination of the northern section of this area (immediately to the South of Gal's survey area) shows very few settlements until the Byzantine period, suggesting a settlement history similar to that of the Gazit area (economic marginality until the Byzantine period).[84] Discounting that area of the map yields a density of 2.88 km^2 in the Byzantine period, approaching

---

[83] Frankel 1986, supplemented in part by Avi'am 1994.

[84] For instance, by my count, the 60 km^2 immediately to the South of the Gazit area had one site in the Hellenistic period (Bet ha-Shiṭṭah, Zori 1977: nos. 119, 120; see also Ovadiah 1970: no. 21; *TIR* 82, *s.v.*), two in the Roman (Bet ha-Shiṭṭah and Gibeʿat Ṣebaʾim, 19312173, Zori 1977: no. 124), and eleven in the Byzantine (in addition to the preceding: Kh. Yaḥmi, 19862178, Zori 1977: no. 140; agricultural installations at 19192179, Zori 1977: no. 122; a site identified as a monastic farm, 19212172, Zori 1977: no. 121; Sede Naḥum, 19562146, Zori 1962: no. 126 [162]; Ovadiah 1970: no. 160; *TIR*

that of the Akhziv/Ḥanita and Nahalal areas, as well as portions at least of the Mt Tabor area. The median size of sites with settlements reported for the Scythopolis area is low enough (about 4 dunams in the Byzantine period; see above) that it is harder to presume that a large number of small sites have been missed. Nevertheless, given uncertainties about methods used, it remains possible that the number of sites has been underreported, or that for other reasons we should assume a higher density.[85]

So far, I have discussed settlement density in sections of the western portion of late-antique northern Palestine. Based on the surveys published in *JSG* and by Urman,[86] the Golan as a whole was more sparsely settled: if we estimate an area of some 1,200 square kilometers, with 180 settlements in the period of maximum settlement, the distribution of settlements is 6.67 square kilometers per settlement, comparable to upper Galilee. However, the distribution of settlements in the Golan was quite uneven. For example: the 100 square kilometers between map references 22002700 and 23002800 had some 6 sites datable to the Byzantine period; the square between 21002700 and 22002800 had 10 sites, and the square between 21002400 and 22002500 had 25 sites. The numbers of each of these could have been swelled somewhat by sites for which the surveys did not specifically report Byzantine remains, but in the case of the third of the above squares, abutting the Sea of Galilee and including a "city," Susita-Hippos, this would bring the distribution ratio up to 3.22 square kilometers per settlement, a figure only slightly higher than for the "marginal" Gazit area.

Given the heterogeneous nature of the evidence, it is impossible to come to any hard and fast conclusions regarding settlement distribution other than the rather obvious one that it must have varied by region. Based on the data collected for this study, upper Galilee and the Golan appear to have had rather low settlement densities overall (lower even than the density in the ʿEn Dor area of 5.5 km^2 per site – possibly artificially low). In contrast, the hill country of lower Galilee may have had substantially higher density

225, *s.v.*; Kh. Sahad, 19622193, Zori 1977: nos. 134, 135; Daba Sudi, 19732178, Zori 1977: no. 139; Kh. Shaḥuḥ, 19642197, Zori 1977: no. 137; Khuneizar, 19992143, Zori 1962: 174 [316]; Kh. el Sauda, 20002141, Zori 1962: no. 20).

[85] An examination of the 1958 Israeli reprint of the British map (1:100,000 Palestine, Sheet 5, Nazareth, 1924; rev. 1944, with roads corrected in 1956–7) shows that a substantial number of sites are close to the routes of existing roads. At the same time, the modern routes are approximately those of the major thoroughfares of late-antique Palestine. Thus it is uncertain whether the concentration of settlements results from modern accessibility or from ancient patterns of settlement. Higher density of settlement would also result if we deduct much of the extreme western portion of the map below Bet Shean where there are steep rises into the northern Samaritan hills. Again, note the comment of Isaac, Roll 1982: 87 on under representation of low lying sites in Zori's survey.

[86] Urman 1985; see also Dauphin 1998.

of settlement. This is suggested not only by the generally higher settlement densities for the western surveys discussed above, but also by consideration of portions of the Mt. Tabor area.[87]

D. Regional Integration?

The suggestion that, despite more or less localized variations, the number of settlements across the region as a whole increased between the Hellenistic and Byzantine periods raises the further question of regional integration. Of particular interest is the extent to which all of the areas under discussion here may have taken part in common long-term processes (tied, it will be argued below, to Roman imperial control and urbanization, and with them certain kinds of orientation to markets, and so on) that would have linked sites to one another. On that very general level, it might be possible to suggest a wide area of rough "integration," including, for instance, northern Syria, and perhaps even Greece, assuming that one could substantiate that the demographic or settlement patterns were more or less parallel.[88] However, precisely because such a framing of the question of "integration" links it with an exceedingly wide area (potentially, the entire eastern Mediterranean), it is not particularly helpful for addressing local and regional integration, understood as the extent to which the social and economic lives of the residents of a region were tied together through, among other things, political and administrative control, communication, trade, or redistribution.

One of the kinds of information that surveys typically provide (although as noted above, not necessarily as fully or as consistently as one might like) is some measure of site size. Data on size lends itself to rank-size analysis, and this, in turn, may be used provisionally to frame the question of more narrowly construed local or regional integration. Rank-size analysis compares the size (i.e., population) of each of a series of sites, arranged in descending order, with the position of the site in the series. The claim, based on a fair amount of empirical observation, is that "integrated" systems appear to have a regular relationship between site sizes that, when plotted on a double logarithmic scale produces a straight-line, descending curve. Although other relationships are possible, the standard "ideal" curve

---

[87] Compare Dauphin 1998: 1, 91. The apparent anomaly (i.e., her finding an unexpectedly low settlement density in lower Galilee) may be due to, or at least sharply accentuated by, the relative absence of surveys; the boundaries of survey areas to the west of lower Galilee are clearly visible on her map 23; the denser area of settlement to the South and East of lower Galilee corresponds to areas surveyed by Zori.

[88] See, e.g., Tate 1992: 297–301; 303–14; Alcock 1993: 48, summarizing 33–48.

is one in which the second largest site is roughly half the largest site, the third largest is one third of the largest site, the fourth one quarter, and so on.[89]

Understandably, much of the data for the discussion of the rule and of deviation from it comes from the modern world-economy, where there is ample statistical data. According to a widely cited study by Berry, the existence of a regular rank-size relationship in a given country did not, in 1961, correlate with size, with degree of urbanization (percentage of population resident in cities larger than 20,000), or with level of "development" (e.g., industrialization) of a region as such. However, where a regular rank-size relationship did occur (especially in the absence of "development") it was in regions (e.g. China and India) that had long histories of urbanization (and one presumes, long histories of stratification as well as of inter-urban trade, and so on).[90]

Deviation from the rank-size rule, at least in the form of "primacy" (where the first site is disproportionately larger than succeeding sites; see the plot of the Scythopolis region in Figure 2.2), did, according to Berry, seem to correlate with the integration of a particular territory into a wider system: primate cities tended to occur in former imperial capitals (e.g., Vienna, Madrid, or Lisbon), or in the main cities in former colonies.[91] In either case, primacy may be associated with the orientation of the largest site in a given geographical area to a system larger than its immediate territory. The other type of variation is "convexity," where sites at the top of the scale are larger than predicted by the rank-size rule. Johnson has argued that the "convexity" of the rank-size relationship is connected with one of two phenomena: either "pooling," in which case the data set combines more than one autonomous or semi-autonomous region, so that there is a

---

[89] The most basic form of the relationship is: $P_r = P_1/r$, where P_r is the size (the model is based on population hence P) of the r-th site, P_1 the size of the first site (the largest), and r the rank of the site in the rank order. In other words, size should vary inversely with rank order. Taking the logarithm of both sides of the equation yields the following, which when plotted on double-log scale produces a straight line: $\log P_r = \log P_1 - \log r$. The first equation above can also be generalized to the form $P_r = P_1/r^q$. Taking the logarithm of both sides of this equation yields: $\log P_r = \log P_1 - q\log r$. Effectively, this allows the slope of the line to vary while maintaining a straight-line function on a double-log scale, and the first equation becomes a special case (when $q = 1$). A convenient discussion of the rank-size rule in geography (on the level of an introductory textbook) can be found in Bradford, Kent 1977: 58–68. Harris 1970: 129–47 is a good example of the potential significance of the investigation of rank-size relationships. Credit for the development of the concept usually is given to G. K. Zipf (see Zipf 1949: 374 n., who in turn cites earlier formulations). See also Pumain 1997.

[90] Berry 1961: 575, 579, 585–7.

[91] Berry 1961: 582; for primacy in London see also Johnson 1980: 243–4 and Figure 6; for former colonies see also C. A. Smith 1976b: 31–32.

disproportionate clustering of larger, essentially mutually independent, sites at the top of the scale; or "partitioning," in which the data set only incorporates a segment of what is actually a larger system.[92]

The data collected for this study lend themselves to the plotting of rank-size curves and the measurement of their variation from a "normal" rank-size relationship. It is important to stress at the outset just how impressionistic the results are. The relationship of site size to population, for which it serves here as a proxy, is complicated, since even within the same general region different sites may have different densities of settlement. Moreover, the vagaries of estimating settlement size (even assuming that sites were typically at their largest in the late Roman or Byzantine periods) are such that it hardly seems necessary to measure the statistical significance of apparent conformity or deviation from the rule.[93] The point here is, rather, to examine whether in aggregate the collected data allow certain kinds of rough assessments of integration that might reward further investigation. Again, as with the comparison of settlement patterns with ideal central-place landscapes, such assessments can be posed in terms that can be compared across time and space.

Despite the fact that, as noted above, much of the data on which the rank-size rule was worked out came from modern contexts, the correlation between regularity of the rank-size curve and "integration" has profitably been used in historical and archaeological contexts. The argument about rank-size convexity by Johnson, himself a near eastern archaeologist, drew comparative evidence from eighteenth- through twentieth-century North America, China, India, and England, for archaeological cases drawn from fourth-millennium B.C.E. Iran.[94] Others have used rank-size relationships to measure changes in regional integration in the Bronze Age Levant or elsewhere in the Near East.[95] The implication of all these cases is that while system integration does appear to manifest itself in greater rank-size regularity, the scale at which this integration takes place – whether measured in terms of geographical area, the populations involved, economic or technological complexity, or the chronological rate of change in relationships of rank to size – is historically specific, the product of entirely different and complex histories. The payoff for rank-size analysis in late antique Palestine, in the "impressionistic" sense in which it is used here, is particularly its utility for framing study of the degree or the geographical scale of regional integration.

---

[92] Johnson 1980: 240–1; see also Skinner 1977a, Harris 1970: 129–32.

[93] See Savage 1996.

[94] Johnson 1980.

[95] Levant: Bunimovitz 1989, 1995; Savage 1997; Mesopotamia, Adams 1981.

The graphs in Figure 2.1, based on the *Archaeological Survey of Israel* publications discussed above, serve as likely examples of "partitioning." In each case, the survey area is based on a regular grid that inevitably and arbitrarily (from the point of view of either geography or ancient history) subdivides sections of larger systems, and in the case of the Akhziv/Ḥanita survey the area is also partly bounded by both geographical and contemporary political boundaries. The curves representing four of the five survey

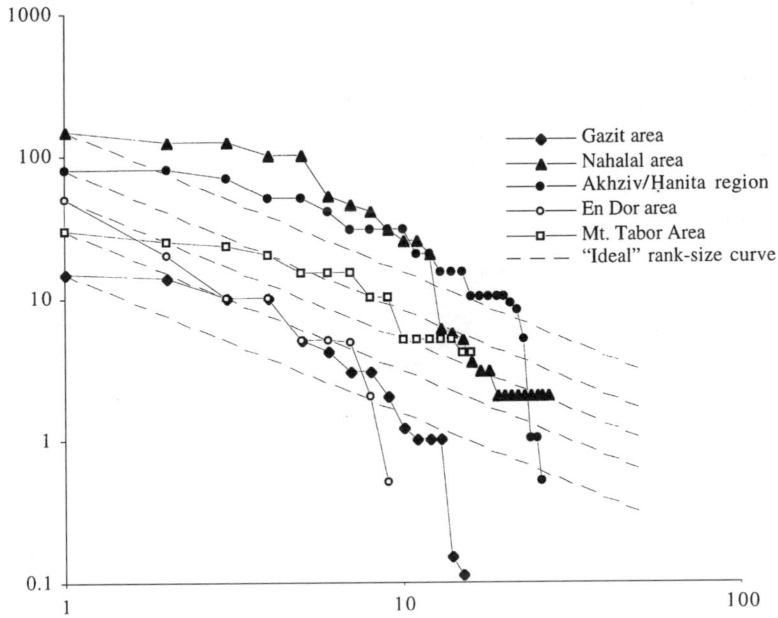

Figure 2.1: RANK-SIZE CURVES, *SURVEY OF ISRAEL* AREAS

areas are convex, as expected. The fifth, for the ʿEn Dor area, is based on a very small sample, and I have suggested above that Tell Kasyun (Tel Qishyon) probably had a smaller settlement than the reported fifty dunams in the Byzantine period. (The graph for Gazit leaves off the questionably sized Tel Rekhesh and Naḥal Tabor [d]; the curve would have been convex, although substantially less so, had those sites been included.) It should be noted that each of these graphs also represents an incomplete data set: for the Gazit area 15 sites with size data are plotted out of some 30 Byzantine period settlements, or as many as 37 according to Gal's calculation; for ʿEn Dor 9 of 18 (or 25); for Mt. Tabor 16 of 27 (or 49); for Nahalal 27 of 41 (or 51); for Akhziv/Ḥanita 26 of 35 (or 45). Nevertheless, if we assume that unsized sites are likely to have been smaller rather than larger, these gaps in the data are also unlikely to substantially alter the shape of the left-hand side of the curve.

Johnson's "pooling" phenomenon also may be seen in the two upper plots in Figure 2.2.[96] In the absence of better evidence, these two graphs attempt to represent cities in Palestine in two different but overlapping groupings. The first utilizes Broshi's study of population in western

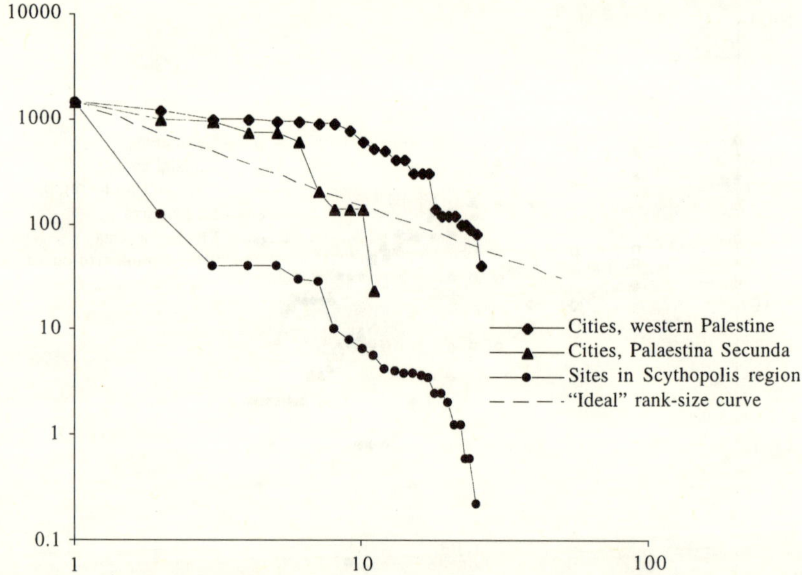

Figure 2.2: RANK-SIZE CURVES, WESTERN PALESTINE, *PALAESTINA SECUNDA*, SCYTHOPOLIS

Palestine as a convenient corpus of urban size estimates, but consequently one that does not take into account connections (administrative, economic, or other) between portions of eastern and western Palestine throughout the

---

[96] The graph of sites in western Palestine is based heavily on Broshi 1979, 1982 (with some corrections for sites that fell within the area covered by this study; see further Table 3.1). The graph of Palaestina Secunda plots approximate sizes for the cities listed in Georgius Cyprius, *Descriptio* 1028–42 (ed. Honigmann 1939: 67–8; Gelzer 1890: 52–53): Scythopolis, Pella, Gadara, Capitolias, Abila, Legio, Sepphoris, Tiberias, Gaba, Helenoupolis, and Hippos (cf. Hierocles, *Synecdemus* 720, ed. Honigmann 1939: 42–43). Where the sites overlapped I have used the same sizes in both graphs. Gadara may have been on the order of 720 dunams (Wagner-Lux, Krueger, Vriezen, Vriezen-van der Flier 1978: 135, following Schumacher; see also Dauphin 1998: 4: 151: 750 dunams); Abila

Roman and Byzantine period. As a result, it may reflect a degree of "partitioning" as well. The second uses estimated sizes for the cities in Palaestina Secunda, established by the beginning of the fifth century.[97] Underlying my choice to use these sites in particular is the assumption that the contours of the provincial subdivision that made up Palaestina Secunda bore at least some relationship to the economic and other forms of integration within the province. Both graphs suffer from uncertainties about site sizes. In addition, both make use of urban sites, which, although they are the largest sites in their immediate hinterlands, may be outsized by non-urban sites in other subregions of the area covered. Thus both plots risk conflating the degree of integration of a site within a large economic framework with juridical classification of a site.

The rank-size plot of cities in western Palestine and of cities in Palaestina Secunda are both visibly convex. It is tempting to see in both of these rank-size curves the result of the pooling together of more or less autonomous "solar" urban economies, each reproducing more or less the same economy based ultimately on surplus production from their hinterlands, and each showing a fair degree of primacy within their immediate regions (compare the plot of the Bet Shean area in Figure 2.2).[98] Alternatively (or complementarily), we might see both curves as partitioning off a region that is better seen in still a wider context, one that places these mostly modestly sized Palestinian cities in connection with the major centers of Antioch, Alexandria, Rome, and, increasingly from the fourth century, Constantinople. Based on a formula provided by Johnson, the index of convexity for the plot of cities in Palaestina Secunda is actually quite low (0.057).[99] However, this figure is due partly to the disproportionately small size of Capitolias (the last site on the curve). Leaving off Capitolias, and counting only the first ten sites yields, the more substantial, but still

---

may perhaps have been a city on the same scale in this period (Mare 1996: 259 and n. 3 describing the archaeological site as a whole as roughly 1.5 km by 0.5 km; see also Mare 1993); Pella, some 210 dunams (Walmsley 1992: 250; 1996: 150; cf. R. H. Smith 1987: 57 n. 33, estimating a population of 25–30,000); Capitolias, some 23 dunams (based on Lenzen, Knauf 1987: 29, fig. 3, after Schumacher). For Helenoupolis, I have assumed a (perhaps inflated) size on the order of what are, with the exception of Capitolias, the two smallest sites (Gaba and Hippos, both 140 dunams).

97 See the discussion of Tsafrir 1982: 371–372 and *TIR* 16; see also Mayerson 1984: 228–230; 1988: 294–295.

98 Despite the fact that Bet Shean is substantially larger than the other urban sites, I illustrate urban primacy here because the region is so well surveyed (see Zori 1968, 1977). Moreover, had Bet Shean been a half or a third the size (something on the order of Tiberias or Sepphoris, see further Chapter 3), the curve would still be primate.

99 Johnson 1980: 239; the formula yields an index figure where 1.0 is a straight horizontal line, 0.0 is perfect rank-size regularity, and primacy yields a negative figure.

relatively modest, index of 0.184. By contrast, the plot of the first ten cities in Western Palestine has an index 0.696.

It is worth considering whether the decreased convexity in the curve representing the cities of Palaestina Secunda is not the result of a closer approximation of a unit of economic integration of a region centered on Scythopolis. That is to say, it is possible to suggest on the basis of the rank-size plots (it can be no more than this, given the limits of the evidence) that inland portions of northern Palestine in the Byzantine period saw a certain degree of regional economic integration around a large regional city that eventually served as a provincial metropolis. This connection between provincial "capital" and territory is not inevitable: the rank-size distribution of towns in Roman Britain appears far more convex than that of Palaestina Secunda; while Egypt, skewed by the massive size of Alexandria, almost certainly had a primate curve.[100] If, in fact, the rank-size curve representing Palaestina Secunda does reflect a greater degree of integration than that of the cities of western Palestine (i.e., and does not represent merely a different, but no more "representative" sample), it suggests that in the later Roman period, at least in Palestine, individual cities and their hinterlands may have been integrated into larger regions.

With this in mind, I wish to take a brief look at three more rank-size plots: the western portion of the data set assembled for this study; the eastern portion (i.e., the Golan), and the data set as a whole (Figure 2.3). Once again, it is important to remember the limits of the data on which these charts have been based. The sites for which there is size data account for 259 items in a data base with a total of 728 sites in the western portion (36%); for 128 of 215 for the eastern portion (60%); and for 387 of 943 (41%) over all; and the number of items in the data base is itself an uneven sample of the settlement distribution. Given these gaps, it is certain that there is at least some distortion to the overall shape of the curves in Figure 2.3. Nevertheless, to the extent that it is precisely the smallest sites that are likely to be unrepresented, the left-hand side of the curves, corresponding to the very largest sites, may be usefully compared with Figure 2.2, again, for the purposes of forming general impressions that might reward further research.

Visually, the curve of sites in the Galilee and environs in western Palestine shows close conformity to the rank-size rule, and indeed the index of convexity for the ten largest sites is 0.014 (0.007 for the first 11

---

[100] Britain: Woolf 1997: 6, Fig. 3, after Millett. The scale is too rough to calculate an index of convexity, but by rough inspection of the graph, the tenth site is on the order of three times the "expected" size, and the twentieth roughly twice. Egypt: Woolf 1997; see also Rathbone 1990: 120–121. The histogram of cities in Achaia in Alcock 1993: 162, Fig. 56, suggests primacy for Corinth, but it is also an extremely incomplete list; cf. 130–131.

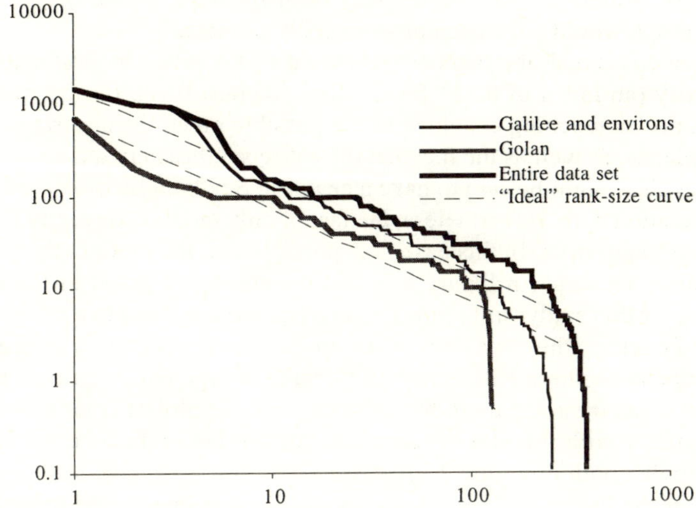

Figure 2.3: RANK-SIZE CURVES, GALILEE AND ENVIRONS, GOLAN, ENTIRE DATA SET

sites). Here, however, it is necessary to conclude that the close conformity with rank-size regularity is accidental. The alternative is to argue that Galilee and the Bet Shean valley were integrated into a regional economy centered on Scythopolis, but only those territories, to the exclusion of other territories to which Scythopolis was adjacent and had ready access. The graph for the Golan poses a number of problems.[101] It is primate for the largest sites (for the 10 largest sites it has an index of –0.079; –0.055 for the 11 largest sites), but for the middle range of sites it is actually convex. However, the large site that creates the impression of primacy is Caesarea Philippi (Paneas) at the extreme northern border of the region, and which, by the "Byzantine" period was included in Phoenicia.[102] Without that site, the curve is actually quite convex with an index almost as high as for the cities of western Palestine (0.66 for the ten largest sites after Caesarea

---

[101] In addition, I am not entirely confident about sizes for sites in the Golan. Thus, for instance, for a number of large sites Ben David 1998 has given rather different sizes than Urman: Dabura, Urman 1985 no. 61: 100 dunams, Ben David: 21, 50 dunams; Rafid, Urman 1985: no. 97: 100 dunams, Ben David: 24, no. 16, 15 dunams; el Dura, Urman 1995: 463: 75 dunams, Ben David: 23, no. 12, 35 dunams; Qaṣrin, Urman 1985: no. 83, 50 dunams; Ben David 1998: 23–24, no. 12, 20 dunams.

[102] Georgius Cyprius, *Descriptio* 980, ed. Honigmann 1939: 66; Gelzer 1890: 50; Hierocles, *Synecdemus* 716.9, ed. Honigmann 1939: 41. For an earlier assignment to Phoenicia (hence to Syria) see Avi-Yonah 1962: 71, 150.

Philippi). Moreover, had Scythopolis been included within the plot, the entire graph would have been pronouncedly primate.

When combined, the two data sets yield a plot with a modest degree of convexity (an index of 0.151 for the first 10 sites; 0.132 for the first 11). Again, no far-reaching conclusions are possible given the uncertainties of the evidence, as well as the fact that the entire southeastern quadrant of the territory that might be said to have a center in Scythopolis is omitted from consideration here. Nevertheless, the fact of only modest convexity for this region is suggestive. In this case, it is possible that the plot of city sizes in Palaestina Secunda (in Figure 2.2) and the combined graph of the entire data set for this study (in Figure 2.3) in a limited way tend to confirm each other. Together they may allow us to at least hypothesize a regional landscape in northern Palestine with a degree of regional integration (more marked when we compare it, for instance, with the plot of cities in western Palestine, or with the plot of just those sites in the immediate vicinity of Scythopolis, both in Figure 2.2).

Given the limits of the evidence available, it is impossible to push the question of rank-size distributions much further. Indeed, some will no doubt object that I have pushed it too far. As I noted above, the value of this kind of analysis is its ability to promote further study. Thus, the discussion of rank-size curves suggested a number of different hypotheses that point in different (but, in practice, not necessarily in mutually exclusive) directions. First, the convexity of the Palaestina Secunda and western Palestine curves suggests that regions were divided into more or less independent "modules," each centered on cities (the largest regional sites) that were economically dependent on their respective hinterlands. Alternatively, convexity might suggest a larger module of integration than individual cities and their hinterlands: perhaps the eastern Mediterranean. Third and finally, the relatively modest levels of convexity for Palaestina Secunda and the data set as a whole may mean that groups of cities and their immediate regions coalesced into moderately integrated regions.

It is this last possibility that I have spent the most space on here, primarily because it lends itself to an alternative model of "regionalism" in northern Palestine in late antiquity, one that does not begin with ethnicity, or religion, or "natural" geomorphological boundaries.[103] Instead, the model of integration discussed above, centered on the late Roman and Byzantine Scythopolis and organized first and foremost around cities, will have been facilitated by Roman administrative structures (roads to be sure, and eventually the selection of Scythopolis as a *mētropolis*), but more so by long-term ties (notably, but not exclusively, of commerce) between the

---

[103] See, e.g., Meyers 1979; 1985; 1995; 1997.

inhabitants, and especially the elites, of the cities.[104] In the case of northern Palestine, such a module of integration – if it could be substantiated – would have cut across putative ethnic lines, incorporating territories with populations of Jews, Samaritans, "pagans," and, increasingly, Christians (both "Arian" and "Orthodox"), and across ecological and geomorphological zones. And this, in turn, opens wide the question of the extent to which the contours (geographical and cultural) of the social and economic history of late-antique Palestine were in fact the product of negotiations across territories constructed and reconstructed in a later Roman political economy. It is to this question that I return in Chapter 5.

---

[104] My formulation is influenced by Woolf 1997: 8–12, although I am interested here in somewhat smaller units of integration than that essay is.

Chapter 3

Reconstructions of an Economic Landscape in Northern Palestine

Having introduced central-place theory (Chapter 1) and having discussed the archaeological data upon which the present discussion is based (Chapter 2), I now turn to hypothetical reconstructions of central-place hierarchies in northern Palestine. It is worth stressing both "hypothetical" and the use of plurals in the preceding formulation. Underlying this and the following chapters is the general recognition that in aggregate there may well have been a fair amount of rural marketing and of commercialized agriculture and other production. Nevertheless, the reconstructions offered below treat city and rural marketing as organized into two distinct but nonetheless closely interrelated tiers, with rural markets relatively few and widely spaced, and with the majority of rural production going to fill the immediate subsistence needs of producers. The fact (if such it was) that much village production was not commercialized directly does not mean that peasant households did not interact with marketing networks centered on cities in economically and socially meaningful ways, if only because it may have been in part through such small-scale and localized interactions (together with the local ties of sociability or of patronage that they fostered) that cities gathered the supplies they required to feed their inhabitants.

Given the indefiniteness of the periodization of sites discussed in the previous chapter, the historical "present" of the following discussion, although nominally the fourth century (see the Introduction), is in more than one sense fictive. This chapter deals with the distribution of sites at the time of its apparently greatest density in most areas, the Byzantine period. However density of settlement varied by sub-region (see Chapter 2), and although the Byzantine period does appear to be the most densely settled period in general, it is by no means clear that this was specifically true of the fourth century. Moreover, the mapping of hypothetical central-place landscape against administrative urban boundaries based, with some changes, on the work of Avi-Yonah[1] (see Map 6), necessarily brings together in a static relationship subdivisions of the territory that may have

[1] Avi-Yonah 1966: 131–53; see also Avi-Yonah 1940: Map.

shifted over time. It is possible in the case of Gaba, for instance, that a city founded in the first century B.C.E. had lost its civic status by the early fourth century, only to regain it by the date of the Council of Ephesus, which a bishop of Gabae attended.[2]

The fit between the distribution of cities in northern, late-antique Palestine and central-place paradigms is a fairly comfortable one, especially if we focus on sites that had attained or retained civic status by the beginning of the fourth century (Caesarea Paneas, Ptolemais, Sepphoris, Tiberias, Hippos, Legio, Scythopolis; excluding Helenoupolis, wherever it might have been located, as a foundation by Constantine, and Gaba). These cities (presumably the largest consumers of market goods and the loci of markets) are widely spaced, and are set on nodal points of a road system. Moreover, I will argue below that not only cities, but the largest sites more generally, at least in the lower Galilee and Bet Shean valley, also can be correlated with Roman roads (see Map 6). On that basis, Section B proposes a hypothetical central-place landscape that resembles a "transportation" ($K = 4$) system, where, in the language used in Chapter 1, B-level sites are expected at the midpoints between A-level sites on the roads that connect them (see Figure 1.1 (b) and Map 6).

If the spatial relationship between highest-level sites (cities) is fairly straightforward, the lower levels of any proposed hierarchy are far more difficult to analyze. Limited and problematic data, again, pose one problem. The sizes offered for sites are frequently rough at best and not always directly assignable to a particular period, the periodization available for estimating growth and decline is very long-term and therefore extremely coarse, and overall the collected data tend to under-represent the very smallest sites. Together, these factors obscure whatever hierarchical organization may have existed in northern Palestine. The manifest irregularity of Palestinian geography, over against the idealizing assumptions

---

[2] Loss of status: Safrai, Linn 1988a: 127; later episcopal see: Abel 1938: 201. See further Chapter 5. If this is correct (and it need not be), Gaba is not the only example. A similar case might be made for Dor, described in the revision by Jerome of the *Onomastikon* by Eusebius as abandoned (ed. Klostermann: 1904: 79. 9–10; the state of the site in Eusebius' Greek text appears in an editorial correction, presumably on the basis of Jerome; again at 137.20 the deserted state of the site appears only in Jerome, but not in the corresponding Greek text). It had been argued that the city as a whole was abandoned in the Byzantine period despite a fourth-century church near the site (E. Stern 1992: 172–4; 1995: 180–2; Dauphin 1993b); it now appears that settlement may have continued or have been re-instated below the mound itself running to some 68 dunams (Dauphin, Gibson 1994–5: 31). Dor appears as an episcopal see as early as the fifth century and is on the lists of Hierocles (*Synecdemus* 718.2, Honigman 1939: 41); and Georgius Cyprius (*Descriptio* 1000, ed. Honigman 1939: 66; ed. Gelzer 1890: 51); see also Jones 1971: 546; Dauphin, Gibson 1994–5: 32.

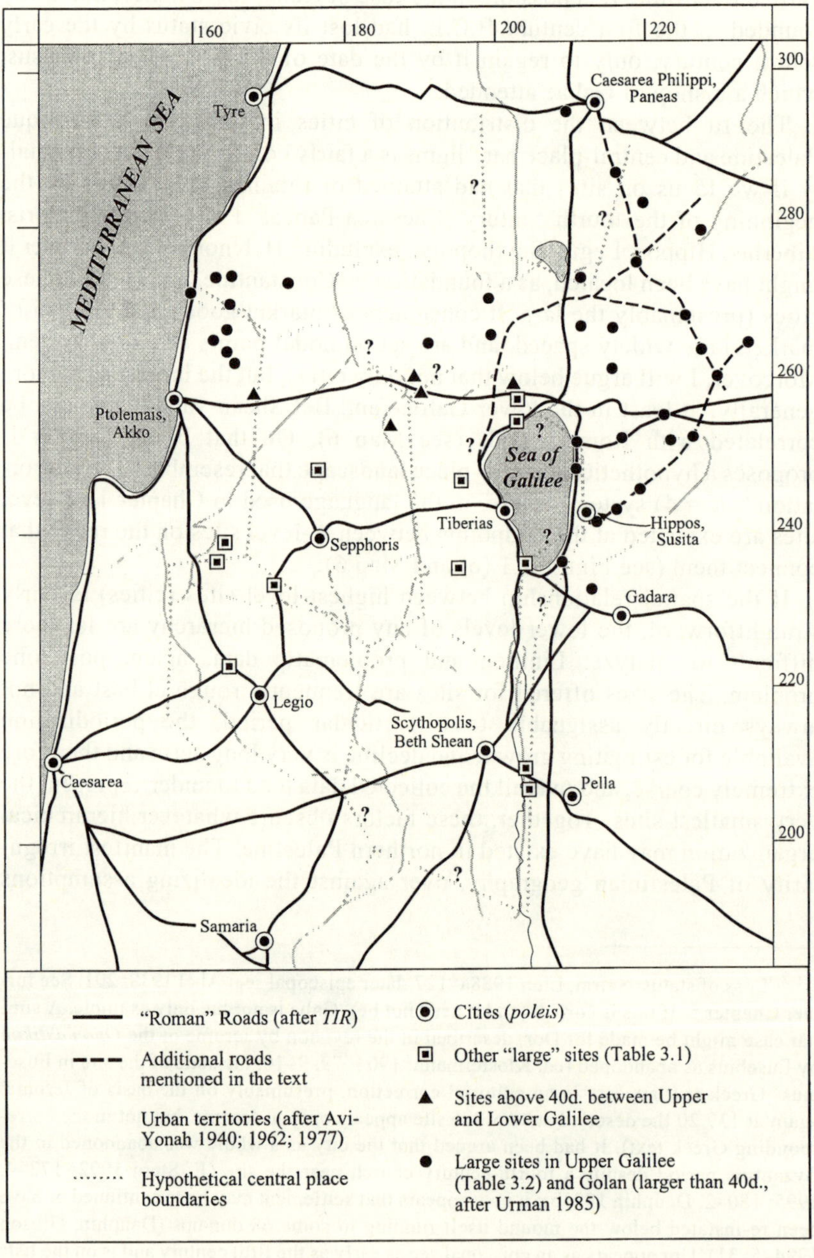

Map 6: NORTHERN PALESTINE: CITIES, SITES, AND ROADS

made by central-place theorists, should further caution against a simple "reading" of the hierarchical distribution of economic or social institutions. Moreover, size (i.e., area), or even population, is not necessarily an indicator of economic centrality, reasonable though that may be as a working assumption.

The second problem is one of assessment. There does not appear to be any straightforward and unproblematic way of refining the picture from geographical distribution for assessing the role of trade and markets in integrating the rural economy of late antique Palestine. Beyond the roughest allusions in literary texts, it is not possible to compile a hierarchical index of markets based on the kinds of goods available for sale or on the intensity of the presence of marketers, and to correlate that index with spatial or temporal relationships between markets.[3] For the production side of the relationship, there is little evidence, with the exception of pottery, on the basis of which to assess what kinds of rural production made their way into a marketing system, much less to attempt to assess the specific markets with which various kinds of production were coordinated.[4] As for pottery, sophisticated study of pottery distribution from point of production to point of deposit in the archaeological record is only in its infancy for this region.[5] Even if a broader base of such studies were available, however, it remains difficult to estimate, for instance, what a reasonable repertoire of domestic pottery might consist of, and therefore how great the day-to-day demand for pottery might be, because of the rarity of fully published, well-preserved destruction layers, the lack of published domestic (especially village) sites, and, more generally, the lengthy time before excavated material is published fully. For much the same reasons, but also because pottery is preserved in great quantities while other goods leave little or no trace, it is not clear how well pottery serves as an index of the integration of the local or multi-regional economy beyond some rough guidelines (e.g., that amphorae imply transportation of liquids; finewares in Palestine are imports; "common wares" are locally made).[6] The final section of the chapter returns to some of these questions.

Partly in response to these problems, the present chapter offers not one (and certainly not "the") central-place landscape of northern Palestine in

---

[3] Cf. Appleby 1976: 164–70; Crissman 1976: 190–91; Bromley 1976, 1978. See also Stobart 1996, arguing against a Christaller-like model.

[4] Cf. Biddick 1985.

[5] See Adan-Bayewitz 1993; Adan-Bayewitz 1995; Adan-Bayewitz, Perlman 1990; and the contribution of Adan-Bayewitz, Asaro, Perlman, and Michel in Strange, Groh, Longstaff 1995: 180–87; Porat, Killebrew forthcoming.

[6] See Peacock 1982; see Arnold 1985; Price 1987: 168–205 for general a discussion of "pottery economics."

late antiquity, but instead three different kinds of reconstructions, representing three potential types of hierarchical organization of the rural landscape. Hence the insistence on plurals ("reconstructions," "hierarchies") above. While the limitations of theory and evidence for central-place models yield results that are fictive, hypothetical, and plural, these conclusions are not without historiographical significance. Thinking through how roads are laid out across the landscape and whether large sites are coordinated to them may help to distinguish between core and peripheral areas in northern Palestine, and to better understand the role of cities in organizing the economy. Thinking seriously about minimum population or settlement size thresholds for marketing in villages, and about the distribution of settlements of such sizes across the region, may allow us get some sense of the structural limits of rural marketing. And, finally, thinking about how settlements across a landscape may have been organized in a hierarchically ordered network with cities forming the apices may help to refine the view of the multiple relationships between cities and countryside.

A. Large Settlements and the Roman Road System

As noted above, cities in late-antique Palestine tended to be linked by roads and to be among the very largest sites in the region. Ancient cities were also the location of at least some marketing activity, a matter to be returned to in different ways in Chapters 4 and 5. What we have, by and large, in northern Palestine (the closely spaced Samaria and Neapolis are an exception), is a geographical distribution that at the coarsest level matches the expectations of central-place theory: a series of widely spaced very large sites with the intervening territories occupied by a large number of smaller sites. What is less clear is the extent to which those intervening territories were hierarchically organized and how that hierarchy might be traced. In the absence of better criteria for determining market orientation and level in the hierarchy, the examination of the relationship between site size and orientation to a road network serves as a limited tool for identifying possible central-places and drawing the boundaries between them. The limitations are not only due to the problems of collecting or interpreting the data (see below), but also based on theoretical expectations. The primary difference between a "transportation" ($K = 4$) network and both of the other "standard" types of central-place landscapes is that, although the other landscapes also may assume that major roads link the highest level market sites (particularly for a "market" [$K = 3$] model, which is presumed to reflect a fair degree of commercialization), in a "transportation" landscape roads offering communications between those sites are thought to constrain the location of lower-level sites as well (see Figure

1.1 (b)). However, the absence of such a correlation would not mean the absence of some regular hierarchical relationship between sites of various sizes, or even the absence of marketing as a significant factor in the organization of the landscape.

As it turns out, a correlation can be made between site size and roads, at least for lower Galilee and the Bet Shean valley, and this lends itself most neatly to a $K = 4$ landscape. However, it should be noted that in an ideal "transportation" landscape only the B-level sites are coordinated with major roads. For lower-level sites, only half of C-level sites, one-quarter of D-level sites, and one-eighth of E-level sites are expected on those major roads. Thus, even assuming close correspondence of the actual distribution of sites with a theoretical landscape, a correlation between large sites and roads should only help to identify the contours of the upper levels of the system.

Beyond the issues of variations in site distribution (mentioned above), regional variations in site size, and ecological factors that might shape a regional economy, the question of the actual placement of roads in the face of incomplete evidence poses its own problems (see Map 6). A review of maps of the Galilee and its Roman period roads even in fairly recent scholarship shows very different basic judgments about where to place the course of roads.[7] Differences include such features as the direct connection between Sepphoris and Tiberias, the route of roads at the northern end of the Sea of Galilee, the presence or absence of a road through upper Galilee from Ptolemais, and the connections between Banias (Caesarea Paneas) and points to the South. A somewhat more subtle problem is that of the use of "Roman" to describe these roads[8] (assuming – and even this is problematic – that the dating is more or less secure): is this a chronological marker – routes built, maintained, or renovated during a particular period – or a judgment about the impetus and administrative function of particular roads. In coming to terms with these problems I have been guided largely by the work of B. Isaac and I. Roll on both the road pattern itself, and the significance of state sponsored and directed road building in antiquity. In Isaac's view, road building should be seen, at least in its initial phases, as a military activity and, in the case of provinces such as Judaea, as part of the pacification and policing of the province. Thus, roads connected military sites (such as bases) as well as urban sites, which needed oversight and which might in fact be garrisoned themselves.[9] Of particular interest in the present context is the observation by Isaac that at the very end of the

---

[7] See, e.g., Safrai 1986a: 215; Ilan 1989–90: 15, fig. 13; Isaac 1992: Map IV; *TIR*, Northern Sheet, 1:250,000 and p. 21 (by I. Roll).

[8] See Urman 1985: 109.

[9] Isaac 1978; Isaac, 1992: 107–13; cf. Roll 1978 = Roll 1983.

second or the beginning of the third century, the responsibility for maintaining the roads shifted to the cities, hence, among other things, the system for counting miles shifts to cities as fixed points, and errors arise in milestone inscriptions suggesting local rather than central stone cutters.[10] Although Isaac argues vigorously for the military and administrative function of the roads (e.g., for the collection of taxes) even after responsibility had shifted to the cities (as a system "maintained by rather than for civilians"[11]), it is worth wondering whether a system of comparatively well paved, regularly maintained roads, organized to connect cities to one another, would have influenced the kinds of relationships urban populations or their elites were able to cultivate with their hinterlands and with other cities, or have favored the growth of settlements or clusters of settlements along their course.[12]

It is beyond the scope of the present study to present a history of the study of roads in Palestine. It is worth noting, however, that compared to the map accompanying the collection of milestones by P. Thompsen,[13] where the only Roman road deemed "*sicher*" in the north skirts the Galilee entirely, connecting Sycaminum (more or less at present day Haifa) on the coast with Legio and northern Samaria, and to the studies of Avi-Yonah,[14] the system of roads in the map of the *TIR* (based on I. Roll; the basic routes are represented in Map 6) shows both an increase in data (reflected in the marking of milestones), and a correlative change in the shape of the road system and its interpretation. Most markedly, the map has been redrawn, so that cities appear as the nodal points. For example, the route mentioned above from the coast drawn by Thompsen (and Avi-Yonah's "Map of Roman Palestine") from Sycaminum is now traced from Ptolemais,[15] and Sepphoris and Caesarea Paneas are now intersections rather than points that roads pass through.

Still, uncertainties and gaps remain. Although partial roads are apparently well attested, the actual connections between Ptolemais on the coast and any of the inland sites is marked as "inferred" in the *TIR* map including the route crossing to the site identified as Beth Saida-Iulias.[16] A milestone is noted south of the Jisr Banat Yaʿqub (a bridge crossing the Jordan north

---

[10] Isaac 1978: 55–59.

[11] Isaac 1978: 58; see pp. 57–59.

[12] Isaac, Roll 1982: 89–90; Fischer, Isaac, Roll 1996: 328–334.

[13] Thompsen 1917, with map.

[14] Avi-Yonah 1940: 178–83, 1940: 41–46, 1977: 180–7; see also Abel, 1938: 225–31 and *carte* X.

[15] See Avi-Yonah 1940; and cf. Avi-Yonah 1966: 84; 1977: 187 where it is traced from a point south of Ptolemais.

[16] The map in Isaac, 1978: 48; Isaac, 1992, maps III and IV; and Roll 1976: 39 omit.

of the Sea of Galilee), strengthening the supposition that a road followed the course of the Jordan on the eastern side down to the Sea of Galilee, as drawn, but traces of built roads have been discovered consistent with a route from the northwestern shore of the sea of Galilee, north through upper Galilee and across that bridge, as drawn in older maps.[17]

The eastern section of the area of this study is no less problematic (see Map 6). On the *TIR* map, only three roads in the vicinity of the Golan are marked as attested by milestones (and therefore as having clear connections to the kind of provincial administrative policies described by Isaac).[18] The first is a route along the length of the eastern shore of the Sea of Galilee (with a segment connecting the southeastern end of the Sea of Galilee with southern points) that Roll has connected from Beth Saida-Iulias northwards towards Banias (partially inferred). The second is a route from the East or North East, that meets the sea of Galilee below Kafr ʿAqab (Map Ref. 21172521).[19] A third road approaches the Golan from the North (from Damascus?) and meets an "attested" road running southeast from Paneas. Another road, drawn as "attested," but not marked as having milestones, links the northern Sea of Galilee with the Jisr el Ruqqad, and from there perhaps to Nawa.[20]

However, there were presumably other roads in the Golan. Dauphin reported finding an anepigraphic milestone at Naʿaran "in a courtyard beside a road which runs North–South along the wadi," which she and Gibson associated later with what they took to be a *mansio* (a road station) on the Roman road system crossing the Jisr Banat Yaʿqub – in fact, on "the junction of the *Via Maris* ... and of a branch running southeast towards Khushniye."[21] Dauphin and Gibson further report paved sections at Kafr Nafakh along the same route from the upper Galilee, and Ma'oz apparently traces it through Quneitra.[22] Another road drawn by Roll in an essay published in 1976, but not drawn on the *TIR* map, would have run from Caesarea Paneas, southward and eastward through Kafr Nafakh (Map ref. 21942742) and Tell el Jukhadar (23022594).[23] At issue here is the extent

[17] Ilan 1989–90; see also Stepanski 1992: 15; it is also so drawn in Safrai 1986a: 215.

[18] Cf. Ma'oz 1986: Map 3; 1993: 536, Map, who does not include this road.

[19] Labeled C in Urman 1985: 111, fig. 45, based on a map by Roll; cf. Ma'oz 1986: Map 3; 1993: 536, Map, where the course is somewhat differently drawn.

[20] As drawn in Isaac 1992: Map IV.

[21] Dauphin 1984: 268; Dauphin, Gibson 1992: 11; cf. the maps in Thompsen 1917, Ilan 1989–90: 15.

[22] Dauphin, Gibson 1992: 11, citing Ilan 1989–90: 14; Ma'oz 1986: Map 3; 1993: 536, Map.

[23] Roll 1976: 39; labeled B in Urman 1985: 111, fig. 45, who suggests, p. 116, that that road should be deemed probable, not certain; see also p. 108; not drawn in Ma'oz 1986: Map 3; 1993: 536, Map.

to which the Roman-built roads served to integrate the rural economy of eastern Palestine by itself or with other regions. As drawn in the map in *TIR*, the two East–West roads crossing the southern Golan manage to bypass just about every large site in the region. By contrast, if I have traced it correctly, the road from Caesarea Paneas to Tell el Jukhadar, but omitted on the *TIR* map, would have connected Caesarea Paneas with Bostra (as noted on the map by Roll), while passing through or near Sukeik (21872865, 120 dunams), Ramsaniyye (225626560, 60 dunams), and Tell el Jukhadar (23022594, 200 dunams) in the Golan.[24]

A similar problem involves a road already noted by Schumacher as the winter route for communication with Damascus in the late-nineteenth century, and along which he reported seeing stretches of "Roman" road. Following Schumacher, other older studies of the Roman road system drew this road as turning South at Kafr Ḥarib and meeting the Jordan River valley near the southern end of the Sea of Galilee.[25] A road with a similar route was drawn in earlier maps by Roll, where it was connected instead with Susita-Hippos, but was omitted in other maps by Roll and others including the *TIR* map.[26] If, in fact, the existence of a Roman-built road that connected Susita-Hippos to Syria could be confirmed, Hippos would be one more Roman city in northern Palestine at a junction of a Roman road system. What is particularly striking about this stretch of road in the southern and eastern Golan, if such it was, is that it connected two of the four sites assigned the size range of 120–200 dunams by Urman,[27] four of the seven sites to which he assigned the range of 80–120, and passed within a kilometer or two of a fifth.[28]

---

[24] Roll 1976: 39; size follows Urman 1985: Appendix A, nos. 35, 71, 108 respectively; cf., however, Yeivin 1971: 11: Jukhadar is assigned the size of 40 dunams (see also Ma'oz 1986: Map 3; 1993: 536, map). Given the discussion below of whether villages of about 30 dunams might have supported markets and about their distribution, it is worth noting that five sites along this one route are between 30 and 40 dunams (more than one-sixth of all the sites to which Urman 1985: 87 assigns the range 20–40 dunams): Sumaqa (21282848, 35 dunams), Baidarus (21842764, 35 dunams), Kafr Nafakh (21942742, 40 dunams), Khushniyye (22612669, 30 dunams), and Farj (22842627, 40 dunams) (Urman 1985: Appendix A, nos. 42, 5, 58, 84, 96 respectively).

[25] Schumacher, 1886: 72, Schumacher 1888: 63–64; on the map in the English edition, this road is explicitly marked "Roman Road"; see also Thompsen 1917: 33–34 and Map; Abel 1938: *Carte* X; Avi-Yonah 1977: 187.

[26] Included: Roll 1983: 139; Isaac, Roll, 1982: 118, 120; see also Isaac 1992: Map IV; omitted: in addition to *TIR*, Roll 1976: 39; Ma'oz 1986: Map 3; 1993: 536, Map and 537.

[27] Urman 1985: 87. Tell el Jukhadar, 23022594, 200 dunams; Susita-Hippos (Qalʿat el Ḥusn), 21202420, 140 dunams; size follows Urman 1985: Appendix A, nos. 108, 186 respectively.

[28] el Rafid, 23402620, 100 dunams, Urman 1985: Appendix A, no. 97.

Here the question of the relationship between "Roman" roads and site development becomes crucial: a disproportionate number of large Golan sites from the Roman and Byzantine periods fall along the course of what Schumacher recognized as old roads.[29] It seems a reasonable guess, given the way that apparently large ancient sites between Hippos and Rafid are arranged, that this "old" road runs along the course of a road that existed in antiquity. In that case, to take a position at one end of the spectrum of possibilities, if the route from Hippos-Susita to Tell el Jukhadar and toward Damascus (?) was a "Roman" road built and maintained under military or provincial auspices for the purposes of facilitating troop movement or the collection of taxes, the implication is that those same military or provincial authorities linked together major sites or, that alternatively, sites managed to grow due to their proximity to roads. If, on the other hand, this was a road built entirely on the initiative of local cities and villages, and of local significance, rural sites – at least in the Golan – it would have appeared to have developed entirely separately from the flow of government and military officials and other travelers, information, and goods along the main roads that linked the cities of western Palestine to those of southern Syria. (Note that Tell el Jukhadar, a site of some 200 dunams according to Urman, would have been located at the intersection of two roads previously drawn by Roll but omitted in the *TIR* map, perhaps relegated to the status of secondary routes.) On the present state of published evidence there does not seem to be any way of deciding the issue, or even of refining it by staking out some middle ground between two extreme positions.

In sum then, the question of the road system in Roman and late-antique northern Palestine is by no means a settled one. As drawn by Roll in *TIR* (and in many respects paralleled by Isaac, with whom he has collaborated), the network of Roman roads, at least in western Palestine, is fairly dense and connects major local centers (cities). The same reconstruction shows the roads of the Golan as effectively passageways to points further north or east but do not serve to integrate the Golan as a region.

It remains to ask to what extent a correlation between site size and roads can be drawn, and, in the following section, what implications this may have for a central-place analysis (for the following see Map 6). Much of

---

[29] Khisfin, 22662506; el ʿAl, 22002457; Fiq, 21602420; Kafr Ḥarib, 21212405; according to Urman 1985: Appendix A, nos. 148, 178, 187, 191 all were 100 dunams. These sites are more or less along a major road marked on the 1972 map of the Golan supplied with *JSG*. This raises the possibility that road access (and perhaps security constraints) have artificially created the impression of disproportionate concentration of large sites. However, Urman insists that the survey coverage is sufficiently extensive that "it is doubtful whether future surveys and excavations will substantially alter" maps of settlement distribution (Urman 1985: 80).

Table 3.1: LARGE SITES IN NORTHWESTERN PALESTINE

Site name	*Map Ref.*	*Size*	*Bibliographical references (for size)*
Scythopolis, Beth Shean	19702110	1500	Tsafrir, Foerster 1994: 106; cf. Foerster, 1991: 223, ca. 1300 dunams; Broshi 1979: 5: 1100 dunams.
Lejjun, Legio, Caparcotani, Kefar 'Otnai, Maximianopolis	16702200	1000	Broshi 1979: 5; cf. Dauphin 1998: no. 3.354
Tiberias	20102420	920	Hirschfeld 1993a: 11; the figure is for the combined area of Tiberias and Hammat Tiberias (given as 230 acres); cf. Hirschfeld 1993b: 1470: area enclosed by the Byzantine walls (of Tiberias proper?) is ca. 740 dunams (185 acres). Vitto 1993: 1470 gives area of the "Roman city" as something on the order of 300 dunams (1200 m. x 250 m.). Broshi 1979: 5 put the size (of the city itself?) at 400 dunams. Dothan 1983: 5 gave the size of Hammat Tiberias as 140 dunams. See also Meyers 1997: 59 "an area of 80 hectares" (the context is a discussion of the first century!); Reed 2000: 81. Dauphin 1998: no. 4.108 (Tiberias): 300 dunams; 4.104 (Hammat Tiberias): 71 dunams.
Sepphoris, Diocaesarea, Saffuriye	17602390	600	Broshi 1979: 5; cf. Safrai 1994: 374: 800 dunams; Weiss, Netzer 1996b: 86: above 40 ha (400 dunams) in Byzantine; Meyers 1997: 59: "at least 60 hectares" (date? see under Tiberias); J. A. Strange, personal communication, ca. 375 dunams. Cf. Reed 2000: 79–80
Philoteria, Kh. Kerak; Bet Yeraḥ	20302350	200	Maisler (Mazar), Stekelis, Avi Yonah 1952: 165; cf. Joffe 1996: 312, 250 d. for the size of the tel.

the relevant data for the Golan has just been discussed. Although the major Roman roads accepted by Roll (and hence published in the *TIR* map) do not connect sites within the Golan, other possible roads, if such they were (they were deemed "attested" by both Roll and Isaac in some of their publications, but are not represented in the *TIR* maps), do indeed serve to connect sites that in local terms were relatively large. In addition, Dan, a fairly large site in the Hellenistic and earlier Roman periods but apparently eclipsed by Caesarea Paneas in the later periods,[30] Caesarea Paneas itself, and Susita-Hippos are all along major roads, and Caesarea Paneas (and possibly Hippos as well, see above) was at a junction of roads. Dabura, another site of some size,[31] is located close to (but not along) a major North–South route

---

[30] Biran 1994: 271–2; according to Biran 1993: 331–2, Dan was abandoned in the fourth century.

[31] Urman 1985: no. 61: 100 dunams.

Table 3.1: LARGE SITES IN NORTHWESTERN PALESTINE (Continued)

Capernaum, el Ḥum	20402540	170?	Reed 2000: 149–51. See also Tsaferis 1989: 2, 216, with the possibility of even greater extent. Dauphin 1998: no. 4.37: 320 dunams. Loffreda 1987: 18: 40 dunams at largest; 1997: 418: some 6 ha (60 dunams) in the Byzantine.
Ḥ. Sarona	19402350	150?	Saarisalo 1927: no. 10 (estimated on the basis of the spread of the "ruin area").
Tel Shimron, Kh. Semmuniye	16992340	150?	Raban 1982: no. 83 (cf. Portugali 1986:14; see discussion above, Chapter 2).
Tell abu Shusha (Tel Shosh) = Gaba in Palaestina Secunda, Gaba Philippi?	16302240	140	Siegelman 1984: 92 (14 hectares); cf. Broshi 1979: 5: 90 dunams (a guess based on mean sizes).
Tel Peḥah, Tell el Basha	20272097	125?	Zori 1962: no. 78.
Halashon (?), el Qad	20372073	125	Based on Zori 1962: no. 60 (250 m. x 500 m.).
Chorazin, Kh. Kerraze	20302570	100	Yeivin 1971: 11. cf. Yeivin 1973: 144, 70 dunams; Dauphin 1998: no. 4.17, 350 dunams.
Arbel , Arbela; Kh. 'Irbid	19502460	100	Ilan 1988: 35; cf. Yeivin 1971: 11, 90 dunams.
Iotapata, Kh. Shifat, Yodfat	17642485	100	Gal 1990: no. 2.2
Kh. Umm Rashid	16372391	100	Raban 1982: no. 29.
Ḥ. Buṣim, Kh. Buseima	16292378	100?	Raban 1982: no. 23 (more than 100 dunams). Cf. Gal 1990 no. 1.19 (map reference 16302380): 5 dunams. The two authors report similar pottery for the sites by this name. Raban shows no ancient settlements in square 163-238.

Turning now to the lower Galilee and Bet Shean valley, where the road network is delineated most securely, and where it is possible to proceed more systematically, I have examined below the placement along the road network of the sixteen largest sites.[32] The sites are listed in Table 3.1. On the basis of this list of sites there is a clear association between site size

[32] For convenience I have taken the East-West line of 260 on the Survey of Israel grid as the border between upper and lower Galilee. This means that the road between upper and lower Galilee, linking Ptolemais with Bethsaida, as well the southern reaches of upper Galilee are treated as "lower Galilee." My choice of number is determined in part by the conviction that a $K = 4$ roughly describes the relationship of large sites, and that lower Galilee and the Bet Shean valley together make up no more than about 4 complete central-

and roads. Eleven of sixteen sites are sited on or near major Roman roads (as drawn by Roll). Moreover, if we leave off the four largest sites (administratively defined as cities by the early fourth century and arguably linked for military and administrative reasons out of the control of the cities themselves), still, of the remaining twelve sites, seven are associated with roads. Of the exceptions, Arbel is just over three kilometers to a major road (as both the site and roads are drawn on the *TIR* map), a substantial, but still manageable walk, and placed on the route of an uncertain ancient road on the map of Avi-Yonah.[33] Ḥ. Sarona is on the route of what Avi-Yonah marked as an uncertain Roman road.[34] Iotapata and Umm Rashid (possibly inflated in Raban's survey) do appear to be exceptions to the rule. while Ḥ Buṣim is problematic (as noted in Table 3.1) and should perhaps be left out of consideration here.

Again, the limitations of the available evidence restrict the ability to draw far-reaching conclusions. It is impossible to tell with any certainty how many sites on the same order of magnitude (say, approximately 100 dunams) for which no sizes are reported might have been located along roads, or, for that matter, entirely off roads.[35] At the same time, it is precisely these largest sites that are least likely to be overlooked in surveys.

---

place systems (see further below Section D). However, these are also large sites (around 100 dunams or larger), and I hope that the sample is sufficiently large to indicate at least that there is a correlation between site size and roads. In addition, if we take the next series of sites, those larger than 45 dunams (about half of the smallest sites listed in Table 3.1), some 15 addtional sites, then, on the spotty evidence available, the correlation is not much lower than we might expect based on a $K = 4$ distribution of C-level sites (of which only half should appear along major roads). Five of the sites are near or on major Roman roads (Kh. Ẓavon, 20112214; Kh. et Twal, el Hammam, 19902130; Kh. Jedora, Gedora?, 17522130; Kh. Waziya, 16822597; T. Zabadon, Kh. Zabid, 17422145). Kh. Anu el Shiba, Galilean Beer Sheba, 18952595, is probably under two kilometers from a major road. Tell Kasyun, Tel Qishyon 18722297 is not on a major road, but it is not clear that it was a major site in the Byzantine period (see Zori 1977:, no. 164; Gal 1998: ʿEn Dor no. 1). I have not included Tel Ḥanaton (Asokhis? Shiḥin?, 17432434), although it, too, falls on a major road, following Dauphin 1998: 3.81, who gave its size as approximately 30 dunams; but cf. Safrai 1985: 45, 52, who gave the size of the tel as 60 dunams. Safrai 1986a: 94 placed Umm el ʿAmad (Ḥ. ʿAmmudim, 18872647) on a "natural" road from the lower Galilee to the Sea of Galilee basin; and at least Yafa (Yafiaʿ, Iaphia, 17612325) is on a road that Avi-Yonah labeled "other ancient roads, certain," Avi-Yonah 1940: Map); if Meshhed (Tel Gat Ḥefer, 18012383) fits in this size category (Gal 1998: no. 13 gave the size as 30 dunams; cf. Gal 1990: 1.23, 50 dunams), it fell along a similarly designated road. Nevertheless, once again, this is merely evidence of a correlation (and one that fuller evidence might alter) and not sufficient to allow the construction of a central-place system.

[33] Avi-Yonah 1940; see also the map by Safrai 1985: 215.

[34] Avi-Yonah 1940.

[35] See, e.g., the discussion of the Nahalal region, above Chapter 2. To the list one might have added, for instance, el Ḥaritiye, possibly the site of Gaba Hippeon if it was not

Moreover, it is clear that what constitutes a relatively large site locally varies by subregion. Thus, Hippos-Susita, the only *polis* in southern Golan – and it is on its western edge – is estimated to have been 140 dunams according to Urman,[36] less than half the smallest estimates of the sizes of cities in the western portion. As we shall see, the northern portions of the Galilee may also show a tendency toward smaller-sized sites. By contrast, the Bet Shean and Jordan valleys (perhaps because of more intense survey work here, primarily by Zori) appear to have supported a number of large sites, two within close proximity to both Scythopolis and Pella.

On the basis of the preceding discussion I would propose as a working hypothesis that in the lower Galilee and Bet Shean valley, large sites – and not merely cities – frequently were coordinated with built Roman roads. In the case of the very top tier of sites (i.e., cities) this may be understood as the linking of existing sites, and possibly along more or less well traveled existing courses. Whether roads were designed to link existing second tier sites (i.e., those falling between 90 and 200 dunams), is as yet an open question, but the possibility should be considered that proximity to roads might favor the development of strategically placed sites (e.g., Legio in its transition from military base to city).

Finally, I consider northern Galilee. Unlike fairly large parts of the southern portion of the region, surveys of the northern areas are less well published and much of the published evidence relates to the distribution of synagogues and churches.[37] Table 3.2 lists the largest sites for which I have found both size and occupation data in northern Galilee. The list includes Firʿin although I have not located specific information on periods of occupation. Given the increasing tendency of scholars to date synagogues later (i.e., not before the fourth century), if Ilan is correct in seeing the remains of a synagogue here, the site is likely to have been occupied in the Byzantine period.[38] Other problematic items, not included on the list, are: Meiron (Map ref. 19102650), because the excavators argued that the site

---

identical with "Gaba in Palaestina Secunda"; cf. Raban 1982: nos. 4, 5, with no size given; see also *TIR* 125, *s.v.* Gaba Hippeon. It is located on the road connecting Ptolemais and Legio. Similarly Jezreel, on the road between Legio and Scythopolis, is referred to by Jerome (in the revision of Eusebius's *Onomastikon*) as large (ed. Klostermann 1904: 109.11), and by the Bordeaux pilgrim as a *civitas*, "city," *It. Burd.* 585, ed. Geyer, Cuntz 1965: 13.

[36] Urman 1985: nos. 185–86.

[37] E.g., Ilan 1991 and earlier studies; Avi'am 1994; for more systematic survey compare Frankel 1986; Frankel, Getzov 1997; and Meyers, Strange, Groh 1978, the last a comparatively limited exercise; the results of a survey of upper Galilee are also reported in Avi'am 1993.

[38] See, e.g., Magness forthcoming; Netzer 1996; cf., e.g., Foerster 1992; Tsafrir 1989; Tsafrir 1995; Ma'oz 1996.

was largely vacant from the middle fourth century on; Tel Dan (Tel el Qadi, Map ref. 21102940), because the site may have been unoccupied from some time in the fourth century; Tel Qedesh (Map ref. 20022798), because it is not clear to me whether and to what extent the site continued to be occupied during the Byzantine period; "Tell Kabri" (Map ref. 16342680), because later work suggests that there was no Roman or Byzantine settlement on the site, which was replaced during those periods by el Kabri (Kabritha, 16452690).[39]

Table 3.2: LARGE SITES IN NORTHERN GALILEE

Site name	*Map Ref.*	*Size*	*Bibliographical references (for size)*
Firᶜin	20002650	90	Yeivin 1971: 11, 29.
Kh. Ḥumsin	16412727	80?	Frankel, Getzov 1997: 2.134
Baṭ el Jebel	16312767	80?	Frankel, Getzov 1997: 2.24, 2.22
Kh. el Zib	15992725	70	Frankel, Getzov 1997: no. 1.6; see also nos. 1.5, 1.8; 2.107, 2.131, 2.155.
Ḥ. Kenesiyya, Kh. el ᶜAmariyye; Kanisat el ᶜAmariyye	16332745	50	Frankel, Getzov 1997: 2.77; cf. Avi'am 1994: 95–96.
Kh. Maṣlaḥ	16212656	60	Frankel 1986: no. 26
Ḥ. Sugar	16532718	50	Avi'am 1994: PP
Tel ᶜEmeq	16462634	50	Frankel 1986: no. 39
Merot, Kh. Marrus	19902700	45	Ilan 1987a: 19 (between 40 and 50 dunams).
Kh. Buda	16432661	45	Frankel 1986: no. 31
Kh. Shemaᶜ, Teqoa (II)?	19102640	40	Meyers, Strange, Groh 1978: 22 n. 3; cf. Yeivin 1971 11: 10 dunams.
Kh. Jelil, Gelil?	17322733	40	Avi'am 1994: 88; cf. Ilan 1986: 516: 150 dunams.
Dar el ᶜArabiyeh	16492621	40?	Frankel 1986: no. 60. Avi'am 1994: 108 describes a site by the same name and that is less than a dunam and might have been a monastery.
Kh. el Ghureiyib, Ḥ. Ghureib (?)	16532746	40?	Frankel, Getzov 1997: 2.87; cf. Avi'am 1994: 79–83, 125–26.

Strikingly, all of the sites listed appear to have been 90 dunams or below. Most tend to be located in western portions of upper Galilee, but this may in part be due to the fact that the western portions are more intensively surveyed, but may also reflect regional shifts in sizes along an East-

[39] Meiron: 300 dunams, E. M. Meyers, C. L. Meyers, Strange 1978: 97; cf. Yeivin 1971: 11: 105 dunams; see Chapter 2 above; for fourth century occupation: E. M. Meyers, Strange, C. L. Meyers 1981: 156–61. Tel Dan, Tel el Qadi, for size see Biran 1993: 323: ca. 200 dunams for the mound itself; but according to Biran 1994: 321 the site was "considerably reduced" in the Roman period; fourth century occupation: Biran 1993: 331–32). Tel Qedesh, Aharoni 1993: 855: between 22 and 25 acres, hence approximately 94 dunams; the chart in Aharoni 1993: 856 shows Hellenistic and Arab levels but not Roman;

West gradient moving away from the plain (see secition D below).[40] Clearly, there is no question of correlation with Roman roads, since the major roads did not pass through the region. Firʿin, the largest site on the list, is several kilometers from either the North-South route from Caesarea Paneas to Bethsaida or the East-West route linking Bethsaida to Ptolemais, drawn on the *TIR* map. El Zib is on the North-South coastal road, but since it is on the coastal plain it should hardly be taken as typical of upper Galilee. From the point of view of the Roman administration, it may well be that upper Galilee, like the Golan but unlike lower Galilee, was a territory to pass through in connecting with other places.

The question of local roads is an open one at present. If the route in antiquity from the western Sea of Galilee to the Jisr Banat Yaʿqub was along the roads marked on the British Survey of Palestine Map,[41] Firʿin (at least the location of the present village) is within some two kilometers of a major route; it is somewhat closer to the Safed–Rosh Pinah road passing to the south. One can make a similar case for some of the excluded examples as well. The excavators at Meiron attempted to place Meiron on the "ancient road system" on the basis of thirteenth-century Jewish pilgrims' routes.[42] Although this is an extremely problematic approach, it turns out that at least part of the reconstructed route was the basis for a "first-class road" by 1942.[43] Similarly, the site of Kabri is near the route of a road running east from the coast, and Tel Qedesh is connected by a road to the North-South route connecting Tiberias and Metullah.[44] In both cases, the road had been upgraded by 1942 from a "second-class road" to a "first-class road." The evidence of the road system in the British Mandatory period is hardly probative for the placement of sites in antiquity. It does, however, suggest that some of the larger ancient sites were along or near routes that by topography (as well as the administrative needs of later periods) were suitable for modern road construction.

---

the temple, built in the second to third centuries, may have been destroyed in the earthquake of 363 but the excavators do not discuss the occupation of the rest of the site; Ovadiah, Fischer, Roll 1993: 859. "Tell Kabri," Frankel 1986: no. 4: 300 dunams; absence of Roman or Byzantine settlement: see Kempinski 1993: 893–91; for a summary of the stratigraphy of excavated areas see Kempinski, Niemeier 1994: 5–7 (Hebrew section), 6*–7* (English section).

[40] Frankel 1986; Frankel, Getzov 1997; Aviʿam 1994.

[41] Survey of Palestine 1:20,000 Series, 1932, with 1942 overprint; see Sheet 20–26 and Avi-Yonah 1926: Map; cf. the course drawn in the sketch map accompanying Ilan 1989–90: 15, which passes even further to the East.

[42] E. M. Meyers, Strange, C. L. Meyers 1981: 6–7 and Fig. 1.4.

[43] Survey of Palestine 1:20,000 Series, 1932, with 1942 overprint, Sheet 19–26.

[44] Survey of Palestine 1:20,000 Series, 1932, with 1942 overprint, Sheet 15–26, 16–26 Composite (Kabri); Sheet 20–27, 21–27 Composite (Tel Qedesh).

The situation, therefore, may have been analogous to the Golan: Roman roads proper passed through or around the territory, but to the extent that the sub-region was integrated through roads, these were secondary, local roads.[45] However, if, as I am inclined to think, the above list suggests that in the upper Galilee sizes of the largest sites were likely to have been smaller than they were in the lower Galilee and in the Bet Shean valley – although this is certainly far from proven – it is worth examining the placement of sites larger than 40 dunams in the border area between upper and lower Galilee (for present purposes, those between the East-West lines of 250 and 260 on the Survey of Israel grid). Of the five sites for which size data were located, only one (Kh. es Sallama, Ṣalmon, 18592543[46]) does not fall on the road (admittedly deemed "inferred" on the *TIR* map) connecting the north of the Sea of Galilee and Ptolemais. The remaining four are along or near that road (Map 6): Kh. Waziya (16822597, 60 dunams); Kh. Anu el Shiba (Beer Sheba, 18952595, 50 dunams); Kafr ʿInan (Kefar Hananiah, 18902580, 45 dunams); and Kh. Kerraze (Chorazin, 20302570, 100 dunams).[47] If this correlation is not accidental it suggests, again, that the course of (inferred) Roman roads might be correlated positively with sites that were, in local terms, large, and in this case might also reflect the development of sites along these routes.

B. Proposed Reconstruction of an Upper Tier

The preceding discussion has yielded some tentative results. First, at least with respect to the lower Galilee and Bet Shean valley large sites do tend to be located along major roads. Second, if the course of Roman-built roads as drawn by Roll is correct, the absence of such roads in the Golan and upper Galilee (and, in upper Galilee, absence of sites larger than 100 dunams or so) means that the same correlations cannot be made for these regions. Third, even here, however, it may well be that relatively large sites coordinated with secondary or regional roads. The rough correlation between site-sizes and roads suggests, at least provisionally, a central-place landscape resembling (at its upper tier) a "transportation" ($K = 4$) model to describe lower Galilee and the Bet Shean valley. This fits with Skinner's suggestion that such a system is expected in places where road building is difficult, such as mountainous areas. However, such a model does not fit the territories to the North and to the East

[45] Cf. Villeneuve 1985: 80 on the Hauran.

[46] Gal 1990: no. 2.10.

[47] Kh. Waziya: Aviʿam 1994: 69; Kh. Anu el Shiba: Gal 1990: 2.15; Kafr ʿInan (Kefar Hananiah): Yeivin 1971: 11; Kh. Kerraze (Chorazin) Yeivin 1971: 11.

of the lower Galilee. Nor does this appear to be entirely due to the preservation, publication, and collection of data. It may well be that as a result of the relative ruggedness of these areas, the distance from the "core" areas of the coast, the Bet Shean valley, and lower Galilee, these regions developed as "peripheries." At least for the southern Golan an alternative "dendritic" mode of organization, may be in evidence, which may further fit the "peripheral" development of the Golan.

My proposed reconstruction of a "transportation" ($K = 4$) landscape for lower Galilee and the Bet Shean valley was produced more or less mechanically (see Map 6). Starting with the very largest sites (*poleis*) as the highest-level central places, where there was evidence for a fairly large site roughly midway between two cities (e.g., Simonias, Ḥ. Zavon[48]) I drew a line marking the hypothetical boundary between those two large sites through the smaller site. In other cases, I have attempted to make educated guesses about likely "large" sites.[49] Since the study did not focus on Samaria the southern portion of the territory of Legio is left open; that of Scythopolis too is quite tentatively drawn. Similarly, the way in which the northern portions of Galilee connect with lower Galilee is not clear on the basis of this study. Consequently, the map does not show the northern portions of the polygons approximating the areas of Sepphoris or Tiberias as closed. Furthermore, it was not clear whether the southeastern border of the area of Tiberias should be drawn through Philoteria or with a straight line down to a point close to Scythopolis. Further work on the region around Gadara (Umm Qays) might help clarify the question of the relationship of northern Jordan to the area of Scythopolis.

One of the interesting aspects of the resulting pattern is the general overlap of territorial boundaries with central-place boundaries as drawn here. In fact the analogy is closest if we omit those cities that did not have civic status by the very beginning of the fourth century (see the introduction to this chapter). The northern end of the territories of Sepphoris and Tiberias is somewhere above of the line between Kh. Kerraze (Chorazin) and Ptolemais. The proximity of Pella and Gadara to the Jordan valley

---

[48] Simonias (Shimron): Raban 1985: no. 83; cf. Portugali 1986:14 (see above Chapter 2); Zavon: Zori 1962: no. 38.

[49] For el Ḥaritiye (16092369), see Raban 1982: nos. 4, 5, possibly the site of Gaba Hippeon; for Lavi (18952415) see Safrai 1986a: 172, who claims that Lavi served as a local center on the basis of remnants of its road system; for Jezreel (18122181) see Zori 1977: no. 34; Isaac, Roll 1982: 33; Ussishkin, Woodhead 1994: 47 (summarizing discussions earlier in the report); Ussishkin 1997: 247; I have found no suitable candidate on the Ptolemais-Sepphoris road. ʿAbelim (16802470) is well placed but I have found no size data for it; the line I have drawn passes through Sheparʿam (16602450), which Safrai claims, again on the basis of the road pattern, had local centrality, Safrai 1983b: 282, 284; Safrai 1986a: 35.

suggests that a hypothetical central-place boundary of Bet Shean should run along the Jordan, and the same may well be true for the southern part of the area of Tiberias. The mapping of territorial boundaries is based on Avi-Yonah's reconstruction, and this depends, in part, on notices in the *Onomastikon* of Eusebius of distances between villages and cities, and on milestones marking distance from a city. In both cases, the named city was taken by Avi-Yonah to be the city in whose territory the village or location on a road was found.[50] If Isaac and Roll are correct that both conclusions are false, the boundaries of city territories will have to be reassessed. The question of the analogy between central-place and political-administrative boundaries is therefore a bit premature, and is offered here only very tentatively.[51] It may well be, however, that a reconsideration of the administrative boundaries between cities will yield results more closely analogous to that of central-place boundaries.[52]

In terms of their outlines, the most obvious difference between the two systems of boundaries (and one that in general terms is not likely to be altered by a reconsideration of territorial boundaries of the cities) is the place of Hippos in the overall scheme. In the administrative system of *poleis* and their hinterlands, Hippos serves as an independent city and as an episcopal see in the later Roman and Byzantine periods (it is referred to as a city by Eusebius, *Onomastikon*[53]). By contrast, spatial analysis of the kind I have attempted suggests that economically Hippos should be thought of as within the orbit of Tiberias.

This is an important point, because it signals that if there is any historicity to the proposed models, the administrative and economic landscapes – although they may well have overlapped in many respects – were not identical. First, the logic of an administrative system is to include or to separate: for a system of obligations (such as for payment of taxes administered through cities) to function efficiently it makes sense to group villages and their residents unambiguously under one heading, and not another. In other words, the borderlines, however inaccessible they may be to us at this late date, may have been of enormous importance. Hence both documents and literary texts specify the location of villages within city

---

[50] See Avi-Yonah 1940: Map and, e.g., Avi-Yonah 1977: 127–8; Safrai 1980: 218–9, who agrees with reservations.

[51] See Isaac 1979: 57–9; Issac, Roll 1982: 11–2; see also Isaac 1992: 309 n. 244.

[52] E.g., on the Tephen area, Avi'am 1990: 372–3; Di Segni 1991, 1993; see also Safrai 1980: 232 n. 1, which may yield a border between Legio and Sepphoris that more closely approximates the central-place boundary drawn in Map 6.

[53] Ed. Klostermann 1904: 22. 21; for further literature and references see *TIR* 147, *s.v.* Hippos.

boundaries.[54] With the top levels of the kind of central-place landscape proposed here, the logic of organization is quite different.[55] Although the very largest sites typically are also administrative centers, the sites at the second level are strategic points of contact *between* two higher-order sites, and their own economic hinterlands are *split between* those two higher-order sites. Two of the proposed reconstructions below assume at least one additional tier of sites functioning in much the same way (see Table 3.4 and Figure 3.1). Moreover, the example of Hippos suggests that administratively "autonomous" cities might have served as subordinate market or economic centers.

Second, administrative decisions to elevate a site to urban status may not be entirely in keeping with its economic role or spatial placement. Byzantine Gaba, if it is to be placed at Tel Abu Shusha, seems too close to Legio to be an obvious candidate for a developing central place based on the expectations of central-place theory. If it is correctly located, just what might account for the (re-)elevation of Gaba is far from clear, and may include both economic and administrative concerns, as well as the fact that the place had a history as an urban site. The proximity of Samaria to Neapolis is an old example of two very closely placed cities. If Helenoupolis was in the general vicinity of the Mt. Tabor area, this administrative adjustment may have been associated in part with Christian religious significance attributed to sites in the general area (see the area south of Sepphoris marked on Map 6).[56] At least here, however, we are dealing with an area not too distant from where three civic territories and three possible central-place regions meet; much the same can be said of the apparently independent village territory of Nain.[57]

Third, a dichotomy between economic hierarchy and administrative organization conceivably might be reproduced at higher levels as well. If we could reconstruct a still higher order central-place system organized on more or less the same principles, with nodal points at, say, Caesarea, Scythopolis, Tyre, and Bostra (*mētropoleis* and the seats of governors in late antiquity) the lines of that system would split the territories of smaller cities and cut across boundary lines between provinces as they were

---

[54] E.g., *P. Yadin* 16.13–14; 37.2–4; Rehov inscription, Naveh 1978: no. 49, ll. 9–13, 26–29; cf. *t. Šebi.* 4:8–10; *y. Dem.* 2:1 (22c–d); Eusebius, *Onomastikon*, ed. Klostermann 1904: 14.18–19, 16.13, 30.24–25, 70.9–10, 78.6–7, the examples from Eusebius are from northern Palestine.

[55] See Smith 1978: 178–79; Skinner 1977b; see especially the introductory comments, pp. 275–76.

[56] See Abel 1938: 205; Avi-Yonah 1966: 137; Safrai 1980: 125–6, 127, 129–30.

[57] See Georgius Cyprius, *Descriptio* 1042, ed. Honigmann 1939: 68; ed. Gelzer 1890: 53.

constituted in late antiquity.[58] Just what such a landscape centered on Scythopolis would have looked like is not clear, but this higher-level central-place region would have incorporated territories in Palaestina Prima (e.g., with a border possibly at Neapolis, modern Nablus) and Palaestina Secunda (e.g., with a border possibly at Sepphoris, Tiberias, and Legio), Arabia (e.g., with a border possibly at Gerasa), and possibly Phoenecia.[59] Precisely the question of large-scale regional integration is difficult to substantiate. The discussion of rank-size relationships in Chapter 2 raised the possibility that a fairly large region centered on Scythopolis may have been the unit of economic integration in the general area under consideration here. However, that discussion focused on a region that more closely approximated the administrative boundaries of Palaestina Secunda. Just how (and how well) large regions may have been integrated through the provincial *mētropoleis* raises the question of the extent to which the social, political, and economic horizons of metropolitans were shaped by the overlapping networks of relationships (some "vertical," others "horizontal") in which their cities were embedded.

The discussion thus far has dealt with areas more or less within the territories of Sepphoris, Tiberias, Scythopolis, and, to a lesser degree, Legio. Northern Galilee and the Golan are more difficult to assess. In the former case this is in part because data fall off at the modern border of Lebanon and Israel, and in part because the data, based on published surveys and reports, are certainly incomplete. Thus for the area in western upper Galilee surveyed by Avi'am the settlement distribution index based on the data collected for the present study is perhaps as low as 4.8 km^2 per settlement;[60] but for the area around Meiron it is 8.3 km^2 per settlement. Assuming a very rough total of some 900 km^2 in upper Galilee (the boundaries of the survey area are unclear), Avi'am's reported figure of 138 settlements in the Byzantine period suggests an average settlement distribution of 6.5 km^2 per settlement. Still, it makes sense to view much of upper Galilee not as outside the orbit of the urbanized "core" areas, but rather as the outer reaches of the urban networks centered on Ptolemais, Sepphoris, Tiberias, Caesarea Paneas, and presumably Tyre. Certainly, the work by Adan-Bayewitz, showing that the production of Kfar Ḥananiah was distributed as far north as Tel Anafa and Cadasa (Tel Qedesh) as well as the heart of lower Galilee, suggests that production in upper Galilee was integrated into the consumption patterns of the Galilee as a whole.[61] On the

---

58 For *mētropoleis* see Di Segni 1996.

59 For administrative divisions see Tsafrir 1982 359–80; and briefly in *TIR* pp. 14–9.

60 Avi'am 1994.

61 Adan-Bayewitz 1993: 211–9; see especially 215–9 for the problem of the northern extent of the distribution of Kfar Ḥananiah ware.

basis of the distribution of coins found at Nabratein, compared to that of other upper Galilean sites a few kilometers to the West, it has been argued that Nabratein fell into a somewhat different economic orbit than those other sites.[62] This, in turn, makes it possible to hypothesize that within upper Galilee itself sites may have been differently integrated into a wider system of economic interaction based on their position (geographically as well as hierarchically) in the system.

Based on the maps of the Golan prepared by Urman, as part of his study of the region, settlement was quite dense in the western Golan (abutting the Jordan valley and the Sea of Galilee) below the level of Dabura (Map Ref. 21252724).[63] It therefore may be possible to make much the same argument for southern and western Golan as one can for Upper Galilee: the more densely settled areas are the outer extensions of a Galilean central-place system. By way of concluding this section, it may be useful to return to the question of local roads in the Golan. It was noted above that two roads in particular that appeared in earlier studies by Roll but were omitted from the *TIR* map linked large sites. One route linked Hippos with areas to the North and East.[64] In fact, based on Urman's map, sites seem to be arranged in lines, with smaller sites aligned on either side of the row of large sites connected by this road, and relatively few sites placed between those large sites.[65] No doubt in part this has been shaped by geography, but this linear arrangement is striking, and deserves comment.[66] This linear arrangement (and the road, if such it was, that connected it) is a kind of a "dendritic" organization. Like an "administrative" ($K = 7$) landscape, a "dendritic" organization classically links lower-level sites series to one upper-level site, but in a spatial arrangement (e.g., along transportation routes) organized to move raw materials from a production zone to a core consumption or processing zone, or to the local (e.g., coastal) link in a wider (colonial) network.[67] Based on the sizes provided by Urman this is

---

[62] Raynor 1981; see also Raynor, Meshorer 1988; Hanson 1980; Meyers 1982; and Raynor in E. Meyers, C. L. Meyers, J. F. Strange 1990: 232–3.

[63] Urman 1985: 85–6; see also Chapter 2 above for settlement density in sample areas within his survey area.

[64] Ma'oz 1986: Map 3, 1993: 536, traces the road but, based on the legend, assumes different figures for site sizes than Urman.

[65] Urman 1985: 86.

[66] Given the argument of Dauphin, Gibson 1992: 11, the presence of sites along regular intervals perhaps might be interpreted as implying organization for the Roman *cursus publicus*. This seems, however, to read far too much into the evidence.

[67] See C. A. Smith 1976b: 34–6; 1976b: 345–53; 1978: 581–2; see also Hodges 1988: 42–52. Smith, viewing dendritic systems in the context of a capitalist world economy organizing the production and interaction of nation-states as well as colonies (see, in addition to the above, C. A. Smith 1976c: 345–53), explores the implications of such a system

not a "classical" dendritic system, nor is it organized in clearly identifiable "branches"; but if this proposal is correct, the implication is that to the extent that the southeastern Golan highlands were integrated with the lower Galilee and Bet Shean valleys it was to funnel surplus production.[68] The road stretching to the South East from Caesarea Paneas may perhaps have played a similar role.

C. Settlement Distribution and Rural Marketing

The preceding sections explored the possibility of reconstructing the upper levels of a central-place system organized around the cities of northwestern Palestine. Turning now to the question of the lower levels of such a system, this section considers the capacity of small sites to support regular, local marketing. Although the discussion is of necessity hypothetical, this issue forms part of the undergirding of any "real" geographically structured agrarian economy in which marketing plays a significant role.

I begin with a set of simple calculations of the implied minimum threshold of a single household whose sole income comes from marketing. Athough in practice marketing may be carried out by a variety of people for whom it is only a partial source of income, such a procedure is a useful way of getting at least a rough measure of the potential limits of commercialization. The calculations make rough assumptions about the average size of households and basic subsistence requirements.[69] In addition, they assume that all of the purchasers of market goods supporting a marketing household live in the settlement in question, and that subsistence requirements effectively make up the entirety of a household budget. Given these crude assumptions, the minimum size for a settlement to support a marketing household depends on three factors: the density of population

---

for ethnic differentiation and the structuring of national economies. The phenomenon I am describing operates at a far more localized level and without the massive machinery of production and trade of the twentieth century. Nevertheless, it is worth exploring further how a regional landscape as described here might be integrated into the imperial landscape of the later Roman world.

[68] Based on the map of agricultural installations in Urman 1985: 146, perhaps wheat; but perhaps also animals, meat, or other animal by-products, Urman 1985: 150–5; cf. H. Ben David 1998.

[69] See Foxhall, Forbes 1982: 49, n. 26, based on UN (Food and Agriculture Organization) estimates. The caloric minimum for their sample household (an elderly adult female, a male and a female each 20–39, and three children) is roughly 4.6 times that of an adult male (for purposes of calculation this has been rounded to 5). For a discussion of the Roman period family structures of Roman-period Egypt see Bagnall, Frier 1994: 67–68; Martin 1996; see also Peskowitz 1993.

(which I take to be between 20 and 30 people per dunam in rural settlements),[70] the percentage of the amount paid by purchasers that accrues to sellers as profit, over and above business expenses, from which marketing households must maintain themselves, and the degree to which potential customers rely on a market to provide basic subsistence goods.[71] Table 3.3 presents eighteen hypothetical cases.

Table 3.3: AREAS (DUNAMS) REQUIRED TO SUPPORT A MARKETING HOUSEHOLD

		Percent of Subsistence from Markets (Degree of Dependence)					
		10%		25%		100%	
Population density:		20/d	30/d	20/d	30/d	20/d	30/d
	1.5%	200	133.3	80	53.3	20	13.3
Profit:	5%	60	40	24	16	6	4
	15%	20	13.3	8	5.3	2	1.3

---

[70] Broshi 1978 and 1982 proposed that for cities settlement density was about 40 people per dunam, but assumed that one-quarter of urban area was uninhabited public space, giving an estimate of 30 people per dunam (1978: 5) (cf. Broshi, Gophna 1984: 42; Broshi 1993, which gave a lower density coefficient in general for the Early Bronze (II–III)). Tsafrir 1996: 270 suggests that the index for villages should be lower since residences are spaced more widely. At the same time, relatively little space is set aside for public functions in villages (see the plan of Umm Riḥan in Dar, Tepper, Safrai, 1986; the authors suggest the existence of an open marketplace, pp. 37–38; Dauphin, Gibson 1992: 13 and Figure 2, a paved square; Yeivin 1993: 302–303 discusses a "civic center" in Chorazin, but there is no clear suggestion of marketing here; see also Hirschfeld 1997: 63, n. 118). Compare Ma'oz 1986: 72–73, who estimated population density at 16–20 per dunam for villages and 30 to 40 for cities; and Reed 2000: 73–89 for still lower estimates. On the other hand, some archaeologists have suggested rather higher densities of settlement in villages, on the basis of the counting of rooms and the assumption that each corresponds to one "nuclear family" (see, e.g., Dar 1986a: 55, 85–6; Safrai 1995: 41–44; for Syria see Foss 1995: 222; 1997: 201). See also Hirschfeld 1995: 134–135; and the general discussion by Biger, Grossman 1993; Zorn 1994; cf. Bagnall, Frier 1994: 54–56.

[71] The figures are based on the following calculations. A household requires a minimum of S (a unit of household subsistence, here assumed to have a specific monetary value). A marketing household gains that basic subsistence by retaining as profit a percentage of the proceeds of purchases made by customers. So for our purposes, a marketing household can survive if $S = mMsP$, where m is the margin of profit, M the degree of market dependence (i.e., the percent of basic goods attained by means of the market purchases), s the value of basic subsistence requirements for one person, and P the population of the site. For any population size (P), the area of the site (A) is: $A = P/D$, where D is the density of population. Combining the two equations gives: $A = S/mMsD$. On the basis of n. 67, I have assigned the notional value of 5 to S and set household size as 6, so that s (subsistence needs for one person) is 5/6. Since D = 20 or 30 people/dunam, $A = 0.3/mM$ or $0.2/mM$, and the result is in terms of dunams. In Table 3.3 the horizontal rows correspond to

On one extreme, given low profit margins and low levels of dependence upon markets, markets are expected only at sizes well above 100 dunams, or at the largest tier of sizes in northwestern Palestine (see Section A above). Particularly with a threshold on the order of 200 dunams, it is reasonable to modify some of the assumptions given above. Thus, for instance, doing away with the assumption that all purchasers live in the same settlement as the marketer (but maintaining, for simplicity alone, the assumption of even density of population per site, as well as even distribution of market dependence across sites), we could instead imagine a single market center of, say, 50 dunams, serving an additional six sites of 25 dunams, or, keeping the likely median size of sites in view, perhaps serving six sites averaging 15 dunams each, and an additional twelve averaging 5 dunams each. With the latter arrangement, we should expect markets more frequently than only at very large sites. However, if we assume some 40 settlements per 100 km^2 (2.5 km^2 per settlement) as in the (perhaps uncharacteristically dense) Nahalal and Akhziv/Ḥanita areas (see Chapter 2, Section C above), this is still only about two markets for every 100 km^2. A more refined model of market distribution would also have to take into account possible gradients of market dependency both in terms of size (are small hamlets likely to be more or less market dependent?), and in terms of distance from markets.

At the other extreme, based on the hypothetical examples represented in Table 3.3, markets could exist in just about every place with a population of 40 or more only if marketers were assured high profit levels (15%) so that they could rely on fewer sales, and if all of the residents' subsistence needs were met through marketing. This is an exceedingly unlikely scenario for late-antique Palestine, if only because it implies (given the rough assumptions used to generate the figures in Table 3.3) that every five to six households supported the services of an additional, local household that sustained itself based on marketing. Moreover, at that level of marketing nearly every site would be expected to support some marketing, and, given the working assumptions about settlement density, each would be within competing distance of one another (from any given site there are an additional eighteen within a radius of under 3.5 km). Even assuming exceedingly high levels of market dependency, such a framework might reasonably give way in favor of larger sites, where marketers were positioned

---

sample values of M, the vertical columns to sample values of m at each of two coefficients of population density. (Note that for simplicity, these calculations effectively assume that marketers purchase their subsistence goods at the same prices as other consumers, an assumption that presumably inflates the areas that result. A model that assumed that overall areas were, say, 20% smaller would not substantially alter the following argument.)

to be able to rely on lower margins of profit (hence lower prices), serving a wider rural hinterland.

Although real distributions of sites are not regular distributions on a hexagonal lattice, it is worth considering the area around and between Bet Shearim[72] and Tel Shimron (about 7 km apart) in the Byzantine period, where the number of settlements seems to have increased through intensification rather than along a progressive "front" (see Map 4, the sites labeled 8 and 1 respectively). Assuming for the sake of argument that these two sites were capable of supporting markets from the Hellenistic period onward, the location of potential marketers at developing sites within their environs would be undermined by conditions that distinctly favored the existing markets at larger sites (and possibly by social ties of patronage or kinship that might continue to draw residents of smaller settlements into the larger ones). Over time, settlements that became villages of some size (e.g., Ramat Yishai [Jeideh] [site 5 on Map 4][73]), might develop sufficient concentrated demand that potential marketers could operate there on terms comparable to those of the existing sites, and they, too, might do so "earlier" if they drew upon non-market-bearing rural settlements.

Moreover, the basic assumption that rural producers would rely on markets to supply them with subsistence goods, and therefore could produce exclusively for market, is unrealistic in comparison with other agrarian economies.[74] Nor does it fit with such evidence as there is for rural production in Roman and Byzantine Palestine, to the extent that this can be examined. By and large, agricultural plots in later Roman Palestine tended to be small. By itself this gives only limited insight into the structures of landholding (it is impossible to tell, for example, whether these plots were owned or rented from others), but the distribution of land plots plausibly has been associated with a pattern where the unit of production was something like the household farm (whatever the structure of that household).[75] Overall, large landholders may have held only a fraction of the agricultural land under cultivation (although if Egypt is any indication, the

---

72 Vitto 1996 has argued persuasively for a continued and thriving village at Bet Shearim long after the middle fourth century.

73 Raban 1982: , no. 48 (cf. no. 41); see also *TIR*, 212, *s.v.* Ramat Yishay.

74 Cf. Scott 1976; Wolf 1966; Garnsey, Saller 1987: 75–77. Tate 1992: 243–253 has argued that the region characterized by Tchalenko as organized in late antiquity around monoculture (specifically production of olives; summarized, Tchalenko 1953–58: 401–402, 413–416), had, instead, a rather more varied production and a greater degree of peasant self sufficiency (see also Foss 1997: 199–200; Gatier 1994). The same is likely to be true of regions in Palestine said to "specialize" in production of certain goods (see e.g., Ben David 1997).

75 Dar 1986a: 61–73; 245–49; 1986b; Safrai 1985: 127–29; 1994: 357–63, Safrai, Linn 1988a 125–126; 1988b: 199–200; Dauphin, Gibson 1992.

fraction was large).[76] However, such landowners could, on the one hand, afford to produce for market at lower prices than might a smallholder, taking advantage of economies of scale, and on the other hand, could afford also to wait for optimal market conditions. Even among the wealthy, however, traditions of self-sufficiency, as well as strategies of economic security, may have resulted in the production of at least some day to day consumption goods for "home" use.[77] Within such a setting – where small households worked with a narrow margin of error, and where larger landowners could determine or evade market conditions, if not corner markets entirely – we should expect that Palestinian peasant households pursued strategies that filled subsistence needs first, and that kept market dependency to a minimum.

D. Models of a Lower Tier

Based on the preceding discussion, we should expect markets at only some relatively large places. How many and how large is unclear given the present evidence. In light of this basic uncertainty this section does not attempt to construct a single central-place model for the region, but rather proposes three models representing three different types of organization of rural marketing (see Table 3.4 below). These are worked out with particular reference to the lower Galilee and Bet Shean valley.

Although the figure is chosen rather arbitrarily, it may be helpful to consider for the moment the possibility that the smallest market-bearing villages had populations of about 900; assuming a coefficient of density of between 20 and 30 persons per dunam, this corresponds to villages on the order of 30 to 45 dunams.[78] Based on Table 3.3, a minimum threshold of this size would presuppose modest levels of market dependency (between 10 and 25%) and fairly modest levels of profit over all for marketers (between 1.5 and 5%). A more sophisticated model might attempt to take into account the significance of non-market villages in supporting markets (allowing for smaller market-bearing settlements, but also requiring wider

[76] Bagnall 1992; 1993: 114–27; Rowlandson 1996: 118–24. For large landholding in Palestine, see, e.g., Safrai, Linn 1988b, 186–90, arguing for the transformation of public agricultural installations into an estate; Holum 1996: 625, with particular reference to Procopius, *Hist. Arc.* 29.17–25.

[77] On estate management in antiquity compare Kehoe 1992; 1997; Rathbone 1991.

[78] Cf., e.g., Safrai 1995: 41–46 for size categorizations of *ʿir*. The same reading of a rabbinic text that yielded Safrai the result of 100 dunams as a reasonable size for large "towns" should yield a size of 40 to 50 dunams for a small "town" (pp. 41–42), although Safrai also both assumes much higher population density per settlement (40 to 50 per dunam) and wants to see "towns" as small as 10 dunams.

hinterlands), as well as other modalities of marketing including, on the one hand, itinerant marketers (amply attested in rabbinic literature), and, on the other, the possibility that marketers will favor larger sites where other marketers and patterns of marketing already are established. These considerations point in different directions and underscore the provisional character of this discussion.[79]

Nevertheless, this range of sizes is not without interest. Based on the *Archaeological Survey of Israel* publications, discussed in Chapter 2 (see Tables 2.2–2.6), sites above 45 dunams are not found in the Gazit area. They account for at most one in nine in the ᶜEn Dor area (Tell Kasyun, Tel Qishyon is likely to be smaller than 50 dunams); at most one in seventeen in the Mt. Tabor area (including Karm el Ras, which apparently had no Byzantine occupation); fewer than one in five in the Akhziv/Ḥanita area; and close to one in four in the Nahalal area, without adjusting for sites for which I have not found size data. Assuming that these latter were typically smaller than 45 dunams, for the Akhziv/Ḥanita area (with an additional eight sites) the proportion drops to less than one in six, and for the Nahalal area (with an additional 14 sites) about one in six.

Even the lower figure of 30 dunams is a little less than three times the median size of the sites in northwestern Palestine for which data on size was collected, twice the rather high median of Byzantine sites in the Akhziv/Ḥanita area (15), and several times the medians for the remaining *Archaeological Survey of Israel* areas in the Byzantine period (see Table 2.1). Sites at or above 30 dunams also may have been fairly rare. The Gazit area surveyed by Gal yielded a ratio of two sites at or above 30 dunams out of 17 sites for which I found references to size and to occupation in the Byzantine period. As noted in Chapter 2, however, on the basis of Gal's description both sites probably should be considered smaller than their assigned sizes, so the actual ratio may well be smaller.[80] In addition, there

---

[79] For what it is worth, and it may not be much, Karanis in the 170s had between seven and twelve people engaged in something like retail trade listed among 647 taxpayers (i.e. males of taxpaying age), a number that appears to correspond to something like a total population of some 2,300. By those proportions our notional village of 900 should have between three and five males so engaged. At 2,300, however, the population of Karanis was something over 2.5 times as large as a village of 900, so that it might support greater commercialization. Karanis was, in addition, much reduced from its population of a generation earlier, so that the proportions of artisans or traders to the rest of the population may be skewed. (See Geremek 1969: 39, 92–93, with Rathbone 1990: 114–119, 130, 132.) In addition, once we allow that not all of the income to traders comes from trade (as Bagnall 1993: 128 points out for Karanis), and that, as I will suggest below, villages that served as market centers did so for a wider area population than the inhabitants to the village itself, it seems reasonable to begin to factor in additional traders.

[80] Gal 1991: no. 12, Tel Rekhesh; no. 52, Naḥal Tabor [d].

remain 18 Byzantine sites without size data. However, as noted by Gal, the region may have been agriculturally marginal, and the low proportion of sites above 30 dunams may not be representative.[81] Similarly, in the ᶜEn Dor area there was at most one site out of nine larger than 30 dunams. In the Mt. Tabor area the ratio was one out of sixteen, or, if Karm el Ras is included, two out of seventeen.

The Nahalal and Akhziv/Ḥanita areas again had somewhat higher ratios. The area surveyed by Raban yielded a ratio of one out of three (9 out of 27 sites). If the remaining seventeen sites without assigned sizes were assumed to be below 30 dunams, the ratio would drop to something above one out of five (9 out of 41 sites). In addition, some of the problems of site sizes and occupation for this area have been discussed in Chapter 2, and it is possible that site sizes are inflated for this area.

For the Byzantine period, the Ḥanita/Akhziv area yielded a ratio of sites of 30 dunams or larger to all sites with assigned sizes of over one in three (10 out of 27 sites), with eight sites without assigned sizes. Note the possible effects of rounding sizes here: had the cutoff been 28 dunams, the ratio would remain unchanged, but had it been set at 31 dunams four sites would have dropped out and the rather high ratio would have dropped to something over one in five. If this were combined with the assumption that all of the eight remaining sites with no assigned sizes were below 30 dunams the ratio would have approached one in six sites. In at least one case, moreover, the tendency to assign rounded sizes was compounded by my own practice in tabulating data: the figure of 30 dunams for Kh. el Maᶜṣub[82] results from my averaging the size assigned to the medieval occupation (10 dunams) and the size assigned to the spread of Byzantine pottery (50 dunams), but in fact no secure size for the Byzantine settlement is given. For Tel ᶜAbdon the size follows that reported by Frankel and Getzov for the size of the tel as a whole; the description and drawing by no means make it clear that the site held a 30-dunam built settlement.[83] It hardly seems a foregone conclusion, then, that apparent high ratio of sites 30 dunams or greater effectively represents the number of hypothetical markets for this survey area, much less for the region as a whole.

Perhaps more significantly, the survey area covered by Frankel and Getzov spans from the coast and coastal plain to the western portion of Upper Galilee, and this affects the distribution of large sites (see Map 5). Of the three sites with the largest assigned sizes (70 or 80 dunams) none is further east than Kh. Ḥumsin (Map ref. 16412727)[84]; and all seven sites

---

[81] Gal 1991: 10.

[82] Frankel, Getzov 1997: no. 2.30.

[83] Frankel, Getzov 1997: no. 2.142 and Fig. 2.142.2.

[84] Frankel, Getzov 1997: no. 2.134.

with assigned sizes between 30 and 50 fit within a central band of about three kilometers more or less corresponding to the westernmost reaches of the Galilean hills, between el Ṭuweiri (Map ref. 16252700) and Tel ʿAbdon (Map ref. 16552724).[85] The extent to which this correlation between geography and site size is related to the structure of the later Roman economy, and to which residence patterns inland may have been organized with respect to cities on the coast, remains to be studied. At any rate, if the sizes recorded for sites east of this band of settlements are more representative, at least of the upper-Galilean hill country, sites of 30 dunams or more would appear to be rare indeed. This fits with the observation above that sites of about 40 dunams may have been relatively "large" for upper Galilee.

If a size of 30 to 45 dunams is a reasonable, if hypothetical, working estimate of the minimum threshold for supporting markets in northern Palestine the preceding discussion has some bearing on the way we reconstruct theoretical marketing landscapes in the region. It suggests that at the very bottom of the hierarchy we should not expect to find patterns of the "market" ($K = 3$, with one in three sites serving as a market) or "transportation" ($K = 4$, with one in four serving as a market) variety, but instead a framework in which each market serves rather more non-market sites. Nor should this be surprising. Based on the discussion of the distribution of settlements in northern Palestine in Chapter 2, moderately densely settled areas of western Palestine (excluding upper Galilee, for instance, or the ʿEn Dor or Gazit areas surveyed by Gal) may have had a distribution of settlements of something like 40 sites per 100 km^2 (or 2.5 km^2 per site) in the Byzantine period. Individual regions will, of course, have varied, but if this figure is taken as a rough working measure, settlements will have been about 1.7 km from one another on average (see Chapter 1). In a setting that had one market per three non-market sites ($K = 4$), the lowest-level markets would be within about 3.4 km of each other, requiring a round trip of 3.4 km from non-market sites. However, second-level markets would be merely 6.8 km apart, close enough that they could easily serve as lowest-level markets for more non-market sites than assumed by central-place theory for a "transportation" landscape, and might have strategic advantages over marketers in lowest-level market sites.[86] Consequently, particularly given the absence of industry and the fairly limited range of goods beyond

---

[85] Frankel, Getzov 1997: nos. 2.184 and 2.142, respectively.

[86] Simply because of the way such a landscape is constructed, with respect to markets one level higher, half of the non-market sites are between one lowest-level and one second-level market, see Figure 1.1 (b), putting lowest-level markets in competition with second-level markets for lowest-level marketing. But in the present example, because of the assumed settlement density even the remaining non-market sites are still within a modest

basic agricultural products produced and marketed rurally, a "transportation" ($K = 4$) landscape may place markets too close together for "predicted" lowest-level markets to function.[87]

With all of this in mind, I now turn to a hypothetical reconstruction of central-place landscapes in later Roman northern Palestine. The area of Galilee and immediate environs in western Palestine covered by this study is very roughly 2,800 km^2; for the southern portion of this area, lower Galilee and the Bet Shean valley, the area is some 1,950 km^2.[88] If, again, we take the figure of 2.5 square kilometers per site (40 sites per 100 km^2) as a rough index of settlement distribution, these two areas for argument's sake may be said to have 1,120 and 780 sites respectively (an indication of

---

distance from second-level markets (a round trip of under 6 km (5.89), as opposed to 3.4 km to the nearest lowest-level market).

[87] For Roman Britain see Finley 1985: 127; citing Hodder, Hassall 1971, who give a theoretical maximum average distance to "minor unwalled settlements" of four miles (ca 6.4 km) and who discuss the marketing implications, p. 404. For what it is worth, Skinner 1964: 33–34 estimated the distance between standard market towns in "agricultural China" to be between 5.84 and 11.1 km in sixty percent of cases, with a modal case of 7.79 km; for the vills in the medieval Bedfordshire tax rolls studied by Biddick 1985: 826, the average distance between a vill and the nearest market was 3.7 miles or about 6 kilometers, and average distance between markets is thus presumably correspondingly greater. Thorpe 1978: 90 reports the average distance between one marketplace and its nearest market neighbor to be 6.2 km in one region in Iran 1915, and 6.7 km in 1973. If by market towns Braudel means the lowest-level, regularly meeting places for markets (Braudel 1982: 42–47), these appear to have been more widely spaced in early-modern England and France than any of the models to be proposed below (in England, under 12 km apart where they were at their densest, based on the legend to Figure 2 assuming for the sake of consistency a hexagonal distribution), although, interestingly enough, there appear to have been fewer markets in sixteenth-century England than in in the thirteenth century (with towns supplanting village markets), and, even in the later period, market towns themselves on average may have had populations of about 1,000, tolerably close the hypothetical population of 900 suggested above. According to E. A. J. Johnson 1970: 193–195, over 42% of all villages in Uttar Pradesh were more than 5 miles (8 km) from any market, and 11,239 villages were served by some 30 market towns.

[88] These estimates (based on the 1:250,000 Map, Northern Sheet, published with *TIR*) are intended only roughly, and were derived as follows: for upper Galilee, by counting 50 times the roughly 17.5 km between the East-West line corresponding to 260 on the Survey of Israel grid (875 km^2) and the Lebanon border; and for the southern portion, by counting the 30-by-40 km rectangle between 16002300 and 20002600 (1200 km^2), the 300 km^2 between 17002200 and 20002300; the 200 km^2 between 18002100 and 20002200; and the 100 km^2 between 19002000 and 20002100; and, in addition, with the allowance of about an additional 100 km^2 for the western portion of the Jordan Valley below the Sea of Galilee and 50 km^2 for the remaining territory immediately to the North and West of the Sea of Galilee. Together, these yield a total of 2825 km^2. Omitting the northern 875 km^2 leaaves 1950 km^2.The Huleh Valley and the area to the West of it were left out of consideration (in the database, this area provided only about four sites, and is meaningless without information from present-day Lebanon).

the potential shortcomings of the data set assembled, which contains information on no more than 728 sites for the entire region). The entire region presumably comprehends no more than about five upper-level central-place systems centered on cities (three corresponding to Tiberias, Sepphoris, and Scythopolis, of which at least some part may have extended into present day Jordan; only part of the territory of Ptolemais and Legio are included (although the latter city itself was included in the data set); and at most a small portion of the territory of Tyre. Some portion of upper Galilee may have fallen outside the immediate sphere of Sepphoris, Tiberias, or Tyre. Dividing by five central-place systems gives a total of about 224; dividing by 4.5 (assuming slightly fewer than five upper-level central places) gives a total of about 253. For the southern portion alone, dividing 780 by 3 or 3.5 (primarily Sepphoris, Tiberias, and Scythopolis; and assuming that the areas of Sepphoris and Tiberias have been truncated, but compensated for by the territories of Ptolemais and Legio included) gives more or less the same range: approximately 260 or 223 sites.

Based on the preceding discussion, it seems highly unlikely that a "market" or "transportation" landscape ($K = 3$, $K = 4$) describes the bottom tier of the landscape. Instead we expect more non-market sites per market (i.e., a higher value of K). Because of the way hexagons are expected to superimpose upon one another, the next available values for K are: 7, 9, 12, 13, 16, and 19. What is common to all of these is that they all involve a ring of sites oriented entirely to one higher level site. In the case of $K = 13$ and $K = 19$ additional sites are brought into the exclusive orbit of one higher-level site; in the case of $K = 9$, 12, and 16, additional sites coincide with the outer boundary of the higher-level site's area (as in the case of $K = 3$ and $K = 4$, see Fig. 1.1 (a), and 1.1 (b), but here we may ask whether these sites are also peripheral to the higher-level site).

As for the upper tier, the discussion in Section B above has suggested that it may be reasonable to describe the relationship between the largest sites as based on the "transportation" landscape ($K = 4$). Within these constraints ($K = 4$ at the top; $K = 7$ or higher at the bottom), it is possible to elaborate a number of possible configurations, of which three, illustrating three different kinds of hierarchical organization, are presented below. These are summarized in Table 3.4 and illustrated schematically in Figure 3.1. For each of the columns labeled I through III in the Table, the rows labeled A–D refer to hierarchically ranked markets ("central places"). For each level I have put the expected distance between markets, and, for B–D, the value of K with which this level is organized with respect to the level above.

The configuration in column I assumes the highest degree of commercialization (i.e., the greatest number and spread of upper-level markets, and an additional hierarchical level as well). As before, however, such a

Table 3.4: HYPOTHETICAL CENTRAL PLACE MODELS

	I			II			III		
	No. of sites	*Distance (km)*	*K*	*No. of sites*	*Distance (km)*	*K*	*No. of sites*	*Distance (km)*	*K*
A ("City")	1	27		1	23.8		1	25.6	
B	3	13.5	4	3	11.9	4	3	12.8	4
C	8	7.8	3	24	4.5	7	8	7.4	3
D	24	4.5	3						
Non-market:	216		7	168		7	216		19
Total number of sites:	252			196			228		
Percent of market sites:	14%			14%			5%		

configuration may in fact place second-level (C) markets too close to one another and to lowest-level (D) markets for those lowest-level market sites to be functional.[89] Hypothetically, we might expect such a configuration to give way in one of two ways: toward still greater density of market distribution with greater commercialization and greater hierarchical delineation (an unlikely result), or toward the higher-level market places supplanting the functions of the level-D markets (and bringing us closer to the configurations of columns II and III).

Columns II and III illustrate two other possibilities. Both assume a less developed hierarchy of markets (only two levels of rural marketing below the city level). In column II, below a level of inter-urban markets, sites are coordinated with respect to one another according to a $K = 7$ plan.[90] In this configuration, because one level of intermediate markets has fallen out, second-level markets (here B) are now further apart and are spaced so that one can imagine lowest-level markets (C) actually functioning. As noted in Chapter 1, "administration" ($K = 7$) landscapes are associated in central-

[89] Given the geometry of a landscape that combines $K = 7$ with $K = 3$, and assuming a distribution of about 2.5 km^2 per settlement, for every cluster of six non-market sites and one low-level market, three of the six non-market sites are only 2.94 km from an upper-level site (C or higher), not very much further in absolute terms than they are from the nearest level-D market (1.7 km); and for the remaining three non-market sites, the distance to an upper-level site is about 3.4 km, twice the distance to the lowest-level market, but still, in absolute terms, quite close.

[90] A variant on this configuration involves $K = 9$ in the bottom level. This brings the total number of sites up to 252 and the total number of non-market sites up to 224 (11% of all sites); and the distance between markets is correspondingly higher as well, so that the distance between "cities" is 27 km (as in Column I). With $K = 9$ at the bottom, an additional six non-market sites occur at the outer boundary of the hexagon describing the market territory, and these are each shared with two additional neighboring market territories and so count together as two additional complete markets.

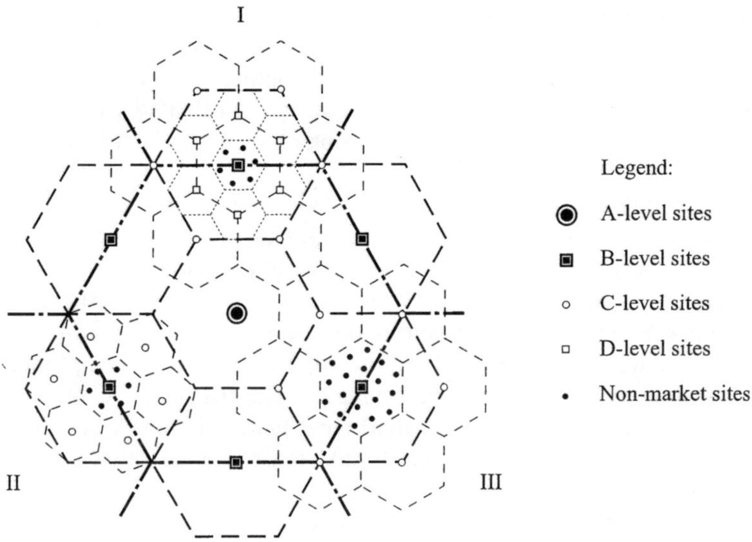

Figure 3.1: HYPOTHETICAL CENTRAL PLACE LANDSCAPES (see Table 3.4)

place theory with monopolistic control of markets from places that are both administrative and market centers. Such a picture may be attractive in light of rabbinic passages such as those discussed in Chapter 1 that appear to assume a Monday-Thursday or a Friday periodicity in rural markets, since market meetings on coinciding (and hence mutually exclusive) days limit the extent to which producers can gather and utilize information from competing markets, and further shore up monopolistic control.[91] Such a configuration also might serve as a kind of modified "solar central place" organization with cities and larger towns oriented to each other along commercial lines, but with markets and trade organized to draw surplus production into the larger sites, and rural production organized correspondingly to increase autarky.[92] If so, however, in the configuration as described in column II the unit of controlling centrality is not necessarily the city, but the B-level market. (The cities, since they are also B-level markets, would serve as "solar central places" for a more restricted area than their entire *territorium*.) In practice, such a system would be fairly difficult to police from the cities. However, there is very little evidence that might suggest

[91] Cf. in a very different social context, Shaw 1981: 64–65; the specific argument is critiqued in de Ligt 1993: 190–96.

[92] C. A. Smith 1976c: 318–19; cf. de Ligt 1993: 234–40; and the oversimplification in Hodges 1988: 126–32.

that the administration of village marketing was autonomous of cities,[93] but limited evidence of concern at the level of the cities or the provincial governors to regulate rural marketing (see below). The model represented in column II is also interesting from a developmental point of view in the context of provincialization, since it might be coordinated with the incorporation of Hasmonaean or Herodian toparchies into a Roman provincial structure centered on cities.[94]

Finally, column III presents a sort of hybrid between columns I and II. Like column I it assumes that all the rural markets are organized with respect to one another to maximize commercial connections ($K = 4$, $K = 3$). However, the bottom of the system assumes a fairly limited distribution of rural markets with respect to non-market bearing sites, which, again, are coordinated with only one rural market, and where, again, rural production may be oriented primarily toward autarky. The reason for choosing this particular variant of this kind of marketing pattern is not its low level of commercialization, but rather that it looks quite like the pattern described by Skinner for rural China and can be compared profitably to it (e.g., in terms of hierarchical organization of markets, credit, the social divisions manifested in market hierarchy, and Skinner's suggestion that it is the market town and its surrounding villages, and not the individual village, that ought to be seen as the locus of rural culture).[95] It is worth noting that the household with which Skinner lived for three months made (between the husband and wife of the family) 46 visits to the local market town – a fairly regular interaction with the marketplace – but at the same time Skinner comments on a fairly low level of demand and a widespread tendency towards self-sufficiency.[96]

It should be noted that the preceding discussion – for all its generality – is based primarily upon sites in north-western Palestine. Based on the surveys published in *JSG* and by Urman, the Golan as a whole was more sparsely settled, with settlements rather unevenly distributed. As with the relatively high figure for the median size of sites in the Golan, it is unclear how to interpret this low settlement density. It may be that relatively small sites (or perhaps the remains of a non- or partially-sedentary population) are under-reported or are no longer discernible.[97] Nevertheless, the apparently low settlement density in the Golan (and upper Galilee) also fits with the suggestion made above that the Golan (as also upper Galilee) were

[93] See Safrai 1995: 125–27 for the assumption that village markets had *agoranomoi*.

[94] Jones 1971: 272–78; Avi-Yonah 1962: 67–77. Safrai 1980: 119–31 (on Galilee), 1995: 286 dates the process to 300 C.E., far too late in my estimation.

[95] Skinner 1964; modal distance between markets: see pp. 33–35.

[96] Skinner 1964: 10–11, 27.

[97] Cf. Urman 1985: 80.

"peripheral" from the perspective of the "core" areas of lower Galilee and the Bet Shean valley.

E. From Theoretical Landscape to Historical Region

If the central-place landscapes described above offer some approximation of historical organization of the landscape, the upper tier consisted of a group of cities connected to each other by, among other things, ties of trade and markets. It requires no special documentation to note that cities in the eastern Roman empire were commercialized, at least to the limited extent that inhabitants might expect to be able to purchase day-to-day requirements in the city markets, that the city was the locus of exchange for money of a range of craft and other goods, and that part of the administrative roles of city, and sometimes provincial, government, was the overseeing of these markets.

What is more important but less easy to reconstruct is the organization of village economies, and their orientation toward a market network centered on cities, as suggested above. All three models represented in Figure 3.1 were based on the assumption that only a modest proportion of the basic needs of rural households were met through purchases in the marketplace. The corollary of such a proposal is that only a modest proportion (although in aggregate possibly a large volume) of rural production was sold in the marketplace. Although the distribution of settlements and settlement hierarchy across the landscape only can be roughly estimated, it is clear that the higher the proportion of non-market sites to market sites, the greater the proportion of the population that did not have marketing institutions in the villages they inhabited. All three models, if they may be taken for the moment to describe the organization of the countryside, presuppose that a substantial minority of the population as a whole, and quite possibly a majority of the rural population, lived in sites that did not bear any markets at all.[98] Nevertheless, rural markets, serving more or less

[98] Columns I and II assume that only one in seven sites (14%) is market-bearing. For the Gazit area, this means in theory that four out of thirty Byzantine sites were market-bearing. Even assuming that Naḥal Tabor [d] and Tel Rekhesh were 30 and 40 dunams each respectively (an inflated assumption), and assuming further that the 13 unsized sites were on average about 1.8 dunams each (half the calculated median), the 4 largest sites account for about 60 percent of the area occupied by all the sites (99 out of 164 dunams). If occupied area correlates roughly with population, a corresponding 40 percent of the population will have not lived in market-bearing villages. If the two largest sites were substantially smaller (say 20 dunams each) the percentage rises to close to 50 percent. The same procedure (as with Gazit, focusing only on the largest sites relative to the survey ares, and not based on any specific criteria for market-bearing capacity) suggests 41 to 46 percent of the population not inhabiting market-bearing sites for the ʿEn Dor area (assum-

self-sufficient peasants operating at a fairly low level of commercialization, may have tied rural production to a more highly commercialized urban and interurban economy in complex ways.[99] In addition, the models described above allow us to imagine some of the ways markets may have been tied to rural social relations, particularly if market days were arranged periodically so that they brought large numbers of people together at regular intervals. And if, as a guess, larger, market-bearing villages were more likely to have synagogues or churches, or religious functionaries such as Scripture readers, preachers, or teachers, the movement to and from market may have structured (divisively or integratively) aspects of the religious life of the rural population. Some of these issues are returned to in Chapter 5.

There is no "real world" test for these models. Subregional variation and the uncertainty of site size makes any calculation of "typical" market towns across the region less than secure, as the discussion of sites on the order of 30 dunams in the preceding section should make clear. Section A suggested a correlation between cities and roads that underlies all three models in Table 3.4, and this, at least is represented by the "real" distribution of cities and roads in late-antique Palestine. In addtion, judging by the map reference numbers (and in the case of Gadara the 1:250,000 Sheet on the *TIR* map) the straight-line distance between major cities in the area covered by this study is very approximately as follows: Sepphoris–Tiberias, 25 km; Legio–Sepphoris, 21 km; Legio–Scythopolis, 31 km; Gadara–Tiberias, 19 km; Sepphoris–Ptolemais, 29 km; Scythopolis–Gadara, 24 km. This yields an average of approximately 25 km, a distance that conforms fairly closely to the model in Table 3.4. This suggests that the model at least correctly approximated the number of central-place

---

ing the too-large size of 50 dunams for Tel Qishyon); 61 percent for the Mt. Tabor area; and 55 percent of the Akhziv/Ḥanita area. The rather low result for the Nahalal area (about 25 percent), suggests again that sizes for large sites in this region may be overestimated. Similar calculations, but assuming that only the largest 11 percent of sites bore markets (as in Column III) yields the following percentages of the rural population not living in market bearing sites: Gazit, between 57 percent and 76 percent (without adjusting the size of Naḥal Tabor [d] and Tel Rekhesh; higher if these are included); ʿEn Dor, at least 62 percent; Mt. Tabor, between 70 percent and 82 percent; Akhziv/Ḥanita, at least 78 percent; and even for Nahalal, at least 58 percent. For the data on which this discussion is based see Tables 2.1–2.6. If urban populations at maximum urbanization were as high as 30 percent of the population (see Broshi 1979; 1982; however, the urban population may have been rather smaller: cf. Bagnall, Frier 1993: 56, n. 15, assuming that a similar ratio in Egypt reflects unusually high urbanization), and between, say, 40 percent and 80 percent of the rural population lived outside of market-bearing villages (I am inclined to think the higher figure is more representative), then between 28 percent and 56 percent of the population as a whole did not live in market-bearing settlements.

[99] Wolf 1966: 41–48, on "network markets" in peasant economies.

regions centered on cities and their distribution over the area. However, the actual routes between cities are somewhat longer. (If we assume a factor of 20 to 30 percent the practical distance is on average 30 to 32.5 km.) To the extent that roads shaped the distribution of second- or third-level markets this may mean that in practice markets were rarer, and more unevenly distributed, than the models presuppose.

As for the lower levels of the system, M. Avi'am referred to Fassuta and Kh. Bata in western Galilee as examples of local centrality. Based on Avi'am's survey, Fassuta had eight surrounding sites and Kh. Bata eleven, in both cases within a 2-kilometer radius, and the latter, at least, was some 30 dunams in size.[100] The significance of these data depends upon a number of issues, especially how typical these two examples are, and, more complicated still, the role in the settlement distribution and the rural economy of monasteries and rural churches.[101] At the very least, Avi'am's examples suggest that the ratio of central villages on the order of 30 dunams to dependencies may in fact have been on the order of one to six or more. Similarly, Safrai and Linn's assessment of the region around Tel Abu Shusha (identified with Gaba) was that larger settlements had between six and fourteen dependencies.[102]

The proposed "upper tier" of the central-place system has markets not only at cities, but at sites roughly midway between these cities, and positioned so as not to fall entirely within the orbit of a city. All the models presented in Table 3.4 assume that there is at least one additional layer of rural marketing, and even the model in column III, with the lowest ratio of markets to non-market sites, has markets about 7.5 kilometers from one another. These reconstructions do not take into account the ability or interest of urban or imperial governments to regulate rural marketing – to foster or prevent the establishment of rural marketing. There is, in fact, a certain amount of scattershot evidence for such regulation, although I would hesitate before concluding that it derives from "an almost morbid fear of any unofficial assembly or association" on the part of Roman imperial authorities.[103]

An early second-century-episode mentioned in the younger Pliny's letters, in which a northern Italian city tried to prevent the establishment of a market on a nearby estate may offer comparative evidence from

---

100 Avi'am, 1994: 127–9; for the size of Kh. Bata see also p. 110.

101 For at least one example of a monastic farm see Dauphin 1977; 1979; 1993a; for other examples in Palestine see, e.g., *TIR* 82, *s.v.* Beth ha-Shiṭṭah; 212, *s.v.* el Rammun; 217, *s.v.* Ruḥama.

102 Safrai Linn 1988: 152 (Table 2). See also Roll, Ayalon 1989: 237 and Figure 142 on the southern Sharon.

103 Shaw 1981: 47–48.

elsewhere in the empire for a market center attempting to restrict marketing in its immediate environs.[104] A decree of "the city" (Aradus?) sent to Augustus, as reproduced in a third-century inscription from Baetocaece in Syria, regulates the activities of the *agorētai* (some sort of market officials? ll. 33–34 mention "the *agorētēs* of the city") in the periodic market that met at that rural holy site.[105]

A somewhat different problem is raised in an early-third-century inscription from near Magnesia in Asia Minor.[106] Here the right to hold a thrice-monthly market is requested from and granted by the provincial governor (and the request specifies that other settlements have received such a right "from you and from the governors before you," ll. 1–3). Moreover, the decree in favor of the village states that those making the request had specified that the new market day conflicts with no existing market days (ll. 29–32; see also 8–10), and the request itself specifies that the traders had to come through the village on their way to Magnesia (ll. 10–12). De Ligt places Mandragoreis some 10 kilometers away from Magnesia, and argues further that one might have expected a negative response on the part of the governor had the market been substantially closer to the city.[107] If this is correct and may be generalized to other places in the empire, it is possible that the models proposed above overestimate the number and degree of distribution of markets.

It should be noted, however, that what de Ligt has raised is distance from the city not the distance between markets (Attukleis appears to be only some 7 km from Mandragoreis, but on the far side of Mandragoreis from Magnesia).[108] Given the concentration of demand in cities even a theoretical model of market distribution should probably allow for larger catchment areas for cities, or, which may amount to the same thing, that cities usurp some of the marketplace functions in their immediate hinterland that might otherwise fall to lower-level sites.[109] If true, this would result in a larger than average distance between cities and their nearest markets.

At least in the case of Mandragoreis, moreover, what may be at issue is inter-urban trade. Traders are on their way from Attukleis to Magnesia.

---

[104] Pliny, *Ep.* 5.4, 5.13; de Ligt 1993: 202–24.

[105] *IGR* III 1020.30–37; the periodic meeting is called *hieromēnia*, "holy month," l. 32, but if it is identical with the meeting mentioned in the Hellenistic letter that appears earlier in the inscription, it is a twice monthly affair, ll. 24–25.

[106] Nollé 1982: no. 1; no. 2 also involves a grant by a provincial governor of a right to hold a once-monthly market in a rural village.

[107] De Ligt 1993: 125–26, 204–5.

[108] Nollé 1982: 24.

[109] Cf. e.g., Hodder, Hassall 1971: 394–95; C. A. Smith 1976b: 24–25; Crissman 1976: 206.

According to the identification of Mandragoreis and Attukleis by Nollé, both lie along a road connecting Magnesia with Tralleis on the East and Priene on the West.[110] It is possible that one of the functions of these traders was to bring higher-level "urban" goods to market, and if so, it may well be the potential disruption of a scheduled cycle linking urban sites together that underlies administrative concerns. If correct, it also fits the suggestion above that in later Roman Palestine upper-level markets may have correlated with roads. At any rate, de Ligt's assessment that "no rural market is known to have been situated within 10 kilometers of the nearest urban centre,"[111] assuming that this is representative, may only reflect the distribution of upper-level markets that might attract the attention of urban elites, and that larger or well-placed villages or their patrons, or the owners of large rural estates, might compete to establish.[112] Places of mere "rural exchange" (whatever role they may have played in bringing local agricultural production into the city) may have been outside the focus of direct urban concerns and consequently not well-attested in classical texts or inscriptions. It is worth noting in this context that in each of the three hypothetical cases represented in Table 3.4 the distance between B-level markets (and hence, between B-level sites and cities, even without adjusting for a wider catchment area for cities) is roughly twelve kilometers or more.

The kinds of hierarchical organization discussed in the preceding section – or the kind of bimorphism between more "commercialized" cities and more "autarkic" villages linked in part by networks of trade – are impossible to "prove" on the basis of preserved material culture. However, there does seem to be a sufficient amount of published data from village sites in northern late-antique Palestine to offer the impression that village inhabitants were touched by trade; this material is widespread enough and large enough in volume to assume networks of trading and not non-market "redistributive" mechanisms, or merely occasional, sporadic episodes of exchange. The work of Adan-Bayewitz on the distribution of cooking ware produced in Kafr ᶜInan (Kefar Ḥananiah) and of jars produced at Shiḥin argues for a certain degree of specialization at the village level and a wide regional distribution.[113] The "store jars" produced at Shiḥin are particularly interesting because they may well have been used for transporting

[110] Nollé 1982: 21, Map, and 24.

[111] De Ligt 1993: 128–29.

[112] Cf. Nollé 1982: nos. 2, 3, 4, 5, 6 cf. *Dig.* 50.11.1 (Modestinus), the right is given to a person; Shaw 1979, 1981; De Ligt 1993: 155–98.

[113] Kafr ᶜInan, Kefar Hananiah: Adan-Bayewitz, Perlman 1990; Shiḥin: Adan-Bayewitz, Perlman 1990; Adan-Bayewitz, Asaro, Perlman, and Michel in Strange, Groh, Longstaff 1995: 180–7.

goods.[114] A study of late-Roman mortaria (pottery bowls used for grinding, and made from very gritty ware) found at Caesarea has suggested that these originated in the northeastern Mediterranean; the authors propose a provenience of the "northeastern part of the Mediterranean" for their class 1 and cite examples (among Galilean village sites) from Capernaum and Chorazin (large sites), as well as Nazareth, Bet Shearim.[115] Examples of fine ware that almost certainly were imported also were discovered at village such sites as Capernaum, Jish (Gush Ḥalav), and Kh. Umm el ʿAmad (Ḥ. ʿAmmudim), of which the former two, at least, appear to have been villages of some size.[116]

Finally, coins have been found in significant numbers in rural sites, including in "marginal" upper Galilee. At el Jish (Gush Ḥalab) truly extensive numbers were found (although just how "typical" the site was depends upon its size); other sites include Capernaum (including coins from before the fourth century when the site became a pilgrimage site), as well as at Kafr Kanna, Kh. Shaṭṭah, and Kh. Maluf (west) found as part of

---

114 See, e.g., Adan-Bayewitz, Perlman 1993: 170–71. I thank D. Adan-Bayewitz and J. A. Blakely for discussing this material with me, both of whom suggested that the jars were used to transport goods. Blakely proposed that the thin, rounded bottoms of Shiḥin jars do not make them optimal for long-term use as storage vessels – although clearly round-bottomed jars of this kind were used for storage at Meiron, where they were found *in situ* with their contents preserved (E. M. Meyers, Strange, C. L. Meyers 1981: 60–69 and Photos 36–41) – and that this is not likely to be their primary function. A further point in connection with Shiḥin ware at Sepphoris involves the fact that in the most recent discussion, Adan-Bayewitz and his collaborators noted the wide distribution of jars, but refer to other forms of the same ware occurring at Sepphoris but "relatively uncommon outside the central hill area of lower Galilee" (Adan-Bayewitz, Asaro, Perlman, and Michel in Strange, Groh, Longstaff 1995: 184). Conclusions must await the final publication of this material, but this preliminary description makes it sound as if there is a two-level distribution: one, more restricted, for bowls and another, more extensive, for jars, which may have been used in transporting products, perhaps produced in or distributed from Sepphoris (cf. Peacock 1982: 108–12, on Alice Holt pottery).

115 Blakely, Brinkman, Vitaliano 1995: 202–3. For the size of Capernaum and Chorazin see Table 3.1; for Bet Shearim see Table 2.5. I have not been able to locate a reliable estimate of size in late antiquity for Nazareth, which Jerome's version of Eusebius, *Onomastikon*, refers to as a *viculus*, "small village" (ed. Klostermann 1904: 141.1), near the turn of the fifth century. On the basis of the distribution of early Roman tombs, Strange 1996: 113, estimated that the dimensions of the site were roughly 900 meters by 200 meters (i.e., approximately 180 dunams) and that "the total area comes to fewer than 24 ha [=240 dunams!] (60 acres) and reflects a population of about 500." Strange clearly presupposes a much smaller site, and, apparently, a lower settlement density. See too Strange 1992: 1050; and Reed 2000: 82–83 (4 or 5 ha, or 40–50 dunams).

116 For Capernaum see Table 3.1. Jish (Gush Ḥalav): Groh in E. M. Meyers, C. L. Meyers, Strange 1990: 139–48. Kh. Umm el ʿAmad (Ḥ. ʿAmmudim): Adan-Bayewitz 1982: 24–25; size: Yeivin 1971: 11: 70 dunams; Safrai 1986: 52: 60 dunams).

less intensive archaeological undertakings.[117] The connection between the distribution of coins and "markets" is far from simple, but the extent that coins circulated or were hoarded at the village level seems a rough index of the extent to which at least some members of the village population made use of money either for storing wealth or for exchange.

In short, the distribution of artifacts that may represent trade does not by itself allow for a sharp distinction in material culture between cities and villages, nor should it. The divisions between villagers and urbanites do not derive so much from what things they owned (especially not quotidian goods such as pottery), as from the lives they led (the availability of heated bathing facilities is perhaps a better marker[118]), and the respective places of villagers and urbanites in the network of social and economic relations that differentially brought trade goods into the hands of both. Village agriculturalists presumably did make use of a market system, and at least for village elites this is likely to have been quite important. Some scholars have attempted to identify marketing installations in villages, as at Umm Riḥan, Kh. Susiya, or Capernaum.[119] In addition, there was no absolute dichotomy between villages and cities in terms of the role of agriculture in the lives of residents. Substantial numbers of large town or city dwellers are likely to have engaged directly in agricultural production, although possibly as more highly commercialized "farmers," producing for the urban market, than most rural agrarian households.

Cities, as the centers of central-place systems, not only sat at the apex of a marketing hierarchy but also straddled lowlands capable, with drainage, of intensive agricultural production (Ptolemais, Sepphoris, Tiberias, Legio, and Scythopolis are all on or adjacent to such a lowland region), and hill country where small plots and possibly "vertical" diversification to take advantages of micro-ecological differences are expected.[120] As centers of consumption and as the seat of larger proportions of wealthy landowners, cities may have contributed to the development of a market system that engaged agricultural producers in different ways, while organized in the first instance to serve urban interests. Villages and villagers may have taken advantage of their relative position with respect

---

117 Jish: Raynor in E. M. Meyers, C. L. Meyers, Strange 1990: 230–45; Bijovsky 1998; also Hamburger 1954. Capernaum: Spijkerman 1975. Kafr Kanna: Bagatti 1964–5: 289–90. Kh. Shaṭṭah: Zori 1977: no. 119, a 40 dunam site. Kh. Maluf (west): Zori 1977: 92, an 18 dunam site. Note also the small collection of coins from the late sixth and early seventh century from Qasrin in the Golan: Ariel 1996.

118 Note the presence of a bath at Capernaum (second or third century), Laughlin 1993:56–59. Laughlin associates the bath with military presence; the bath is second or third century, a first-century bath is hypothesized but not attested.

119 Dar, Tepper, Safrai 1986: 37–38; Hirschfeld 1984. Tsaferis, Peleg 1988–89: 109.

120 See Marfoe 1979: 7–9, 20–23.

to marketing networks or to resources that allowed them to produce for markets, and indeed cities may have depended on such production from the countryside. However, in no way can villagers be seen as "driving" the economy, either as producers (in the sense that it is villagers' ability to produce specialized goods, or an ever-increasing variety of products, for market that stimulates a consumer economy) or, I suspect, as consumers (in that it is unlikely that either finewares or mortaria were imported for Capernaum, although both were found there).

That being said, there is some slight evidence for the hierarchical organization of goods. Based on recent studies by Fischer and others it appears that in the Roman period only one inland city, Scythopolis, made extensive use of marble for architecture and sculpture; almost all of the other examples on the distribution map of the use of marble, an import both expensive and costly to transport, coincided with cities.[121] If marble is a good imported largely for urban consumption and display, the making of mold-made lamps, or at least the sculpting of the molds themselves, may perhaps have been an urban craft, at least in northern Palestine. At the very least, based on a small number of examples, lamp molds in northern Palestine have tended to be found in cities (cf. the find of lamp molds at the village site of Beit Natif in Judaea).[122] Similarly, the design and laying of mosaics may have been a craft mediated by urban artisans.[123]

By contrast, "common pottery" was made in village sites, and was used more or less everywhere. The recent contributions of Adan-Bayewitz just discussed add additional dimensions to this picture by showing the likelihood that two villages in particular specializing in pottery production distributed this pottery throughout the region. A possible implication is that villages not only engaged in specialized production for market, but that highly commercialized specialization might have characterized village economies across the region.[124] Inasmuch as pottery is nearly the only trade item for which one can do provenience studies of this type, it is difficult to generalize on the basis of Adan-Bayewitz's evidence. It is possible, however, to take this evidence in a different way. (Since Adan-Bayewitz's work on Shiḥin pottery is not fully published, my comments are restricted to the work on Kefar Ḥananiah ware.) If Broshi's guess is correct that

---

[121] Fischer, Grossmark 1996; Fischer 1998: 30, 259–61; see also Friedland 1999: 7, 20–21. I owe the initial suggestion that marble be viewed as a central-place good to J. L. Reed.

[122] Adan-Bayewitz 1995.

[123] Gaza: Avi-Yonah 1975; contested by Hachlili 1987; Sepphoris: Weiss 1998: 239 n. 53.

[124] E.g., Safrai 1986a: 132–3: "industry" as one of the characteristics distinguishing an *ʿîr* from a *kĕpār*; see also Safrai 1986b: 36–38.

approximately two thirds of the population of western Palestine in the Byzantine period did not live in urban centers,[125] we can put the population of Galilee at not more than 300,000, or consuming households at no more than 50,000 to 60,000. (The sum of the areas of Sepphoris and Tiberias is perhaps 1,500 dunams, yielding a combined population of some 45,000 people, or 135,000 for the wider areas; doubling that figure for areas not within the urban territory of these cities yields 270,000.) According to ethnographic studies, the replacement rate of pots varies considerably by region and culture and is therefore far from secure, but if we estimate that each of these households replaces some 6 cooking pots per year[126] and, for ease of calculation, that all of those pots come from Kefar Ḥanania (i.e., that the percentage of pots from that village does not drop off with distance),[127] this presupposes a hypothetical annual demand of some 360,000 pots. This figure, which is clearly inflated, is itself well within a framework of production that involves no more than some households during the dry months of the year. Kefar Ḥananiah appears to have been approximately 45 dunams in the Roman and Byzantine period.[128] At 30 people per dunam and households of 6 people, this is nominally, 225 households. If half of those households were involved with pottery production, each would have had a quota of approximately 267 pots per week or approximately 3,200 over a three month season. Even at 20 people per dunam, half the households would have had a quota of no more than 4,800 for the season.[129]

These numbers are entirely hypothetical – and even as hypotheses are subject to dispute – but they serve to put the production level of Kefar Ḥananiah in perspective. First, the entire production can be seen as a

---

[125] Broshi 1979: 5.

[126] Price 1987: 296–7, Table 9.4 brings together data for a wide range of lifespans for cooking pots (0.8–1.5 to 9 years for small to medium pots; as long as 13–13.8 for larger pots); see also Wood 1990: 98, Table 4; Arnold 1985: 152–5 and Tables 6.2 and 6.3. For the purposes of calculation I have taken the figure of three years (something like the mean in a number ethnographic samples, but the figure is no more than a guess). The number of pots in a household also varies considerably: based on Price 1987: 304, Table 9.5, the number of cooking pots varies from some 3.9 to 48.7 cooking pots per household with a mean of 16.52, which I use for the sake of argument, although I suspect it may be high, (cf. Wood 1990: 97, Table 3, whose examples reflect somewhat lower numbers). The ratio of the number of pots to their average lifespan does not automatically yield the replacement rate because much may depend on other factors such as the reuse or repair rate of pots (Price 1987: 303). Nevertheless the resulting figure of 6 pots per year (16.52/3 = 5.5) may serve as an index of the turnover rate.

[127] Cf. Adan-Bayewitz 1993: 212, Figure 10.

[128] Yeivin 1971: 11.

[129] Cf. Wood 1990: 42, who cites the example of a pottery-producing town in Spain whose smallest workshop, employing four males, and making use of two wheels and one kiln as producing nearly 100,000 pots per season; see further Arnold 1985: 208–11.

supplement – although from the perspective of the villagers, no doubt a vital one – to an agrarian village economy.[130] Second, the persistence over generations of pottery production at Kefar Ḥananiah with no sizable competition (at least in northwestern Palestine) may suggest not so much the vigor of rural production and marketing as the limits of overall demand and absence of entrepreneurial competition. Third, the development of pottery production at Kefar Ḥananiah, which appears to have begun only in the middle of the first century B.C.E.,[131] may reflect the ability of village producers to tap into an existing marketing framework centered on newly developing urban centers. Overall, based on Adan-Bayewitz's quantified samples, the percentage of pottery appears to fall off as a direct function of distance, rather than being distorted by cities. However, the very small sample at Hammat Tiberias (32 items) did show a disproportionately high percentage of Kefar Hananiah ware, and Adan-Bayewitz suggests tentatively that sites on the coast of the Sea of Galilee may have had somewhat higher percentages and further considers it possible that Sepphoris and Tiberias served as marketing centers.[132] If that is the case, the spread of Kefar Ḥananiah pottery may also serve as an index of the degree to which urbanization could contribute to the integration of a substantial area in terms of the circulation of goods. It is striking, in fact, that on Adan-Bayewitz's evidence the Golan, although within the trading orbit of Kefar Ḥananiah pottery, shows considerably smaller percentages than expected merely by fall off due to distance. Although Adan-Bayewitz's suggestion that this can be accounted for at least in part by difficulty of transport is no doubt correct,[133] I would hazard the further guess that this, together with the absence of Golan ware in eastern Galilee, again suggests the relatively peripheral character of the Golan with respect to Galilee.

Thus far, I have attempted to base my argument on fairly restricted kinds of published archaeological material. Moving back and forth between the level of "evidence" and the level of "theory" in a deliberately heavy-handed fashion has allowed the construction of model landscapes for northern Palestine in late antiquity that between them may help to reframe questions about the social and economic history of the region. The fleshing out of those historiographical questions requires reexamining relevant, and, for elucidating how (some) people may have understood the world they inhabited, incomparably richer, literary material as well. It is to the way in which marketing is articulated in literary sources that we now turn.

---

[130] Adan-Bayewitz 1993: 235–36 who suggests that pottery supplemented olive production.

[131] Adan-Bayewitz 1993: 145–46.

[132] Adan-Bayewitz 1993: 213, 233–34.

[133] Adan-Bayewitz 1993: 213.

Chapter 4

Aspects of the Geography of Marketing in Palestinian Literature

The preceding chapter described the rough outlines of a central-place analysis of northern Palestine in late antiquity. The reconstructions in that chapter gave prominence to cities, but suggested that between the cities and small, non market-bearing villages there were intervening layers of markets that could serve both as the focal points of rural marketing and potentially facilitate moving produce upward to the cities. The point of the present chapter is to examine literary material on marketing in Palestine, particularly its northern regions. Ideally one would wish to map out a marketing system based on literary sources and compare that in detail with the hypothetical models proposed in the preceding chapter. In fact, however, no system can be teased out of the source material in any detail. In general, the literary sources give great priority to cities as location of marketing activity, and to this extent confirm the picture drawn above. In addition, a number of examples of non-urban marketing can be identified in the texts. However, the existence of a system of second-tier markets – much less third-tier – is impossible to substantiate, although one restricted series of non-urban markets was examined for how it might fit into such a systemic framework (see Section A.3 below).

It is useful to divide the literary material into two or three basic categories. The first category is Palestinian rabbinic literature, composed in Hebrew and Aramaic, and the product of a particular group of elite Jewish men who were – I have argued elsewhere – probably disproportionately concentrated in Palestinian cities.[1] Although all rabbinic works (or nearly so) are in part compiliations from a variety of sources whose datability, historicity, and historical significance are still debated, as edited collections the texts reviewed here span the third through the sixth or seventh centuries (perhaps later in some cases).[2] Literature in Greek and Latin can be divided into Christian and non- (or not specifically) Christian texts. "Christian" texts for present purposes are texts bound, not so much by the

[1] Lapin 1999; 2000.

[2] See Strack, Stemberger 1992 for discussion and literature.

religious affiliation of their authors, as by a particular set of ideological issues that the texts address. "Non-Christian" texts are the resulting, ill- and negatively-defined, assortment of texts that remain.

For questions relating to the economic integration of northern Palestine in late antiquity, these "non-Christian" Greek and Latin sources are not particularly forthcoming. Josephus, writing in the late first century, had first-hand knowledge of Galilee and but was uninterested, by and large, in questions of production or exchange, except to the extent of praising the great fertility of Galilee and the density of its population and cultivation.[3] Josephus does describe, rather critically, the large profit John of Gischala made by "exporting" oil to Jews, but this is better understood as a one-time undertaking on John's part than as evidence for an economy organized around export of a market crop.[4] At any rate, the direct significance of Josephus's first-century description for an understanding of Palestine in late antiquity is limited.

Beyond Josephus, Palestine – and certainly Galilee and its economic organization – does not figure prominently in preserved non-Christian writings in Greek and Latin. Certain products from Palestine apparently were known widely in the Roman empire, for instance to Pliny the Elder, also writing in the late first century, particularly balsam and dates.[5] The fourth-century *Expositio totius mundi et gentium* mentions Scythopolis, Laodicaea, Byblos, Tyre, and Berytus as prominent in linen production, in addition to the abundant agricultural produce of these cities, and Sarepta, Caesarea, and Neapolis in purple production, as well as the more famous varieties of fruit from Palestine.[6] One can, on the basis of such a notice, argue for cities specializing in the production of certain kinds of luxury goods for export (although based on this same description, not to the exclusion of basic production of staples), and it is worth noting that it is the city, presumably including its entire territory, but surely assumed to be organized through its urban center, that is the unit of specialization. Ultimately, however, the ill-defined body of material I have called "non-Christian" provides only limited material that can be interrogated along the lines set up in the preceding chapters.

---

[3] Josephus *BJ* 3.41–44.

[4] Josephus *Vita* 74–76 makes the scale of the transaction, its specific occasion, and circumscribed geographical scope – oil for the besieged Jews of Caesarea Philippi – explicit; cf. *BJ* 2.591–2. Compare Alon 1953–57: 99–100; Avi'am unpublished: 41; Meyers, Strange 1981: 45; Safrai 1994: 59; Safrai 1995: 135.

[5] See, e.g., Pliny the Elder, *NH* 12.11–124, 13.26–29, 43–49, M. Stern 1976–84: 1, 485–94; for other products see pp. 485–501 more generally.

[6] *Expositio* 30–31; M. Stern 1976–84: 2, 496–8; for linen production at Scythopolis see also Diocletian, Edict on Prices 26–28, ed. Graser 1940: 385–403; ed. Lauffer 1971: 169–79; *Cod. Theod.* 10.20.8 (374). See also *y. Ket.* 7:8, 9 (31c); *y. Qid.* 2:5 (62c).

"Christian" sources have a range of interests in Palestine. The Gospels place the early career of Jesus in the villages of Galilee, and for that reason are not without interest for an understanding of the cultural and geographical dimensions of the history of Palestine. The absence of any references to Sepphoris in the Gospels has been noted.[7] (Tiberias is mentioned only in John 6:23, but Jesus is not active in the city) Nevertheless, cities do play a role in structuring the space through which Jesus is said to move in Gospel texts, first and foremost Jerusalem, but also Tyre, Sidon, the Decapolis, Caesarea Philippi,[8] and possibly Gadara.[9] As with Josephus and with Pliny, however, on chronological grounds alone this material is of only limited utility in teasing out a history of fourth-century economic relationships and their spatial dimensions.

Late-antique Christian texts, by contrast, are more directly relevant to the questions at hand. In very rough terms, these relate to Palestine in two ways. First, discussions of Palestine arise in relation to the history of christological and other doctrinal controversies that may have involved the bishops of a number of cities of Palestine as participants in councils or synods as more or less prominent players. Second, Christian texts, particularly from the fourth century onward, describe a Christian "Holy Land" through the identification of biblical toponyms, and through the accounts of pilgrims of their own visits to those holy places.[10] Because of the prominence of Galilee in the New Testament as well in as the Hebrew Bible, the interest in a holy land generated a series of conceptual maps of northern Palestine, maps, moreover, that in placing sites in relation to roads, to other sacred places, and to the Biblical account, look nothing like the rabbinic conceptualizations of a Holy Land. This is true not only of pilgrim accounts, but particularly of Eusebius's *Onomastikon*, and of Jerome's translation and revision about a century later. These last texts are of great interest for the articulation of spatial relations between sites, and give us among the most explicit literary accounts of the way roads linked and therefore structured geographical space (organized primarily as a world of cities and villages).[11]

Ultimately, it is rabbinic texts that offer the richest source of material for investigation here, particularly in connection with the social geography of marketing. Questions of marketing and geographical space arise in

---

7 See, e.g., Meier 1991–: 1, 314–15 nn. 173–176; Sanders 1996; Reed 2000: 100–138.

8 "The villages [*kōmai*] of Caesaraea Philippi," Mk. 8:27; cf. Mt. 16.13, "the region [*merē*] of Caesarea Philippi."

9 See Mk. 5:1; Mt. 8:28; Lk. 8:26, and Metzger 1971: 23–24, following Baarda 1969.

10 Hunt 1982; Walker 1990; Wilken 1992; Leyerly 1996, 1999.

11 See also reconstructions of roads based on the Peutinger Table: Miller 1916: 803–804 (figs. 257, 258); 807–808 (fig. 260).

rabbinic discussions not only in the context of civil law (the structure of contracts, and so forth), but also (perhaps primarily) in terms of two other issues. The first has to do with the assumption that fairs held in the cities of Palestine (whose majority population is, with the exception of Sepphoris or Tiberias, presumed to be gentile), are "idolatrous" religious festivals and therefore (as far as the Mishnah was concerned[12]) prohibited, or at least (as in later sources) participation in these fairs needed to be regulated.[13] The second is the rabbinic articulation of a Land of Israel (*ʾereṣ yiśrāʾēl*) whose produce was, among other things, liable to biblical rules on gifts to levites, priests, and others, and whose territory was to lie fallow during the sabbatical year. The coincidence in Galilee and contiguous regions of a substantial number of Jews, including rabbis, a heterogeneous and unevenly distributed population ("gentile" cities or villages, for instance, or "Jewish" villages within "gentile" regions), and the northern reaches of a political territory governed once by Judaeans (i.e., "Jews") and then later by Romans, meant that rabbis have a fair amount to say about the cities and countryside of northern Palestine, as Sussman has already noted with regard to the far greater specificity of the northern areas in the contours of the so-called "*baraîtâ* of the boundaries of the Land of Israel."[14]

A full-fledged central-place "map" is not possible for late-Roman Palestine. Nevertheless, the literary material such as it is does allow for discussion of some aspects of regional economic integration that are relevant to a central-place analysis. In what follows, I first examine material that specifically locates marketing in specific places in northern Palestine, and then discuss some of the broader systemic issues raised by the textual material.

A. Aspects of a Geography of Marketing

This section examines some of the evidence for marketing in cities (Section A.1) and in villages (Section A.2), and then considers, very tentatively, the possibility that part of a second-tier central-place territory of Tiberias can be teased out (Section A.3). The preceding chapter has suggested that the sharp distinction between city and village, based on administrative and legal definitions, need not necessarily define the economic landscape. Indeed, the suggestion that Hippos-Susita, although a *polis*, may have played a subordinate market role to Tiberias makes a sharp distinction in roles problematic. The

---

12 *m. ʿAb. Zar.* 1:1–4.

13 Safrai 1984a, 1994: 253–54; Lieberman 1959: 78.

14 Sussman 1975–76: 245–47.

distinction remains useful for a number of reasons. The first is practical: references to at least some kind of marketing are readily found in connection with with nearly all the major urban sites in or around Galilee. By contrast, the evidence for village marketing was both sparse and scattered. This presumably reflects the urban biases of our sources, but I suspect that it also is the product of a general distinction between economic activity in cities and that in villages (taken for the moment as an undifferentiated group). Second, and related to the preceding, markets were part of the standard architectural repertoire of juridical cities of the Roman empire,[15] and the management of city markets through magistrates (*agoranomoi*)[16] or through other administrative means is one of the roles of functioning government.[17] That is to say, cities, unlike villages, almost by definition were organized to include commercial functions, at least for the urban residents.

Third, the distinction between cities and villages as such is reproduced in the literature at our disposal. It runs most strikingly through the text of Eusebius's *Onomastikon*, in which the description of a site as *kōmē* or *polis* is one of the standard pieces of information given. This does not mean that Eusebius necessarily gives the official status of individual places as they were at the time of his writing. It is sometimes argued that Eusebius made use of official maps or registries in Caesarea;[18] if so, it would be of interest to know precisely at what periods (if ever) Bethsaida had the status of an autonomous city.[19] As for villages in northern Palestine, Eusebius uses the noun *kōmē* almost exclusively to describe them throughout,[20] very occasionally placing them within the territories of one of the cities (such as Araba [in the territory of Sepphoris], Azanoth [cf. Josh. 19:34; Sepphoris], Arbela [Pella], Dabeira [Sepphoris], Gabatha [Sepphoris][21]), or mentioning the

---

[15] Jones 1940: 215–17; Shaw 1979: 92; 1981: 42–44; Sperber 1998: 9–25; Weiss 1998: 221–24.

[16] See, e.g., Nagy, E. M. Meyers, C. L. Meyers, Weiss, 1996: 201 (no. 67), a market weight; See Hirschfeld 1993c: 1467, on the sixth-century building taken to be a covered market.

[17] For Egypt, see, for example, Rea 1982, with Bowman 1984: 36–38; see also the price declarations from Oxyrhynchus, *P. Oxy.* LIV 3747–3753 (from 319), and the oath of egg sellers in the same city in 327 to sell eggs only publicly in the market place daily, *P. Oxy.* I 83. Aspects of control of markets elsewhere are discussed in Shaw 1979; 1981 (North Africa); Nollé 1982 (North Africa and Asia); and de Ligt 1993.

[18] Cf. Barnes 1981: 106–11; Roll, Isaac 1982: 11–13; Oppenheimer 1996: 223–24.

[19] Eusebius *Onomastikon*, ed. Klostermann 1904: 58.11: "city [*polis*] of Andrew and Peter and Philip," but echoing John 1:44; cf. Pliny *Hist. Nat.* 5.71; Ptolemy, *Geography* 5.15.3/5.5.16.4, in M. Stern 1976–84: 2, 167. See also Jones 1971: 274, 62 n. 64 and Schürer, ed. Vermes *et al.* 1973–87: 2, 172, both citing the same two passages in Josephus: *BJ* 2.252; *Ant.* 20.159.

[20] Cf. Klostermann, ed. 1904: 70.8–9: *polikhnē*, "town."

[21] Ed. Klostermann 1904: 16.13, 30.24–25, 14.18–19, 78.6–7, 70.9–10.

ethnic makeup of the population,[22] in addition to other notices that relate the toponyms to other geographical features (especially cities and roads) and to aspects of the biblical account.

Similarly, a number of the rabbinic texts already discussed in Chapter 1 assume some sort of hierarchically defined difference between cities and villages.[23] In *m. Qiddušin* 2:3, the Mishnah states that a man who makes betrothal conditional on the fact that he is from a from a village (*ʿîr*) but is in fact from a city (*kĕrak*), or from a city but is in fact a from a village has not made a valid betrothal. This example is part of a list of binary oppositions and should not be taken to comprehend all the possible definitions of where one might live. Compare, for example, the opposition between priest and levite in the same list: here the Mishnah chooses two terms from a standard tripartite division, priest, levite, Israelite, and one that could on occasion be expanded to include other divisions. Nevertheless, to the extent that the passage asserts that it is simply false to say that one is from a village when one is from a city (much as one is either a priest or is not, either has sons or not) suggests an underlying assumption that residence in a village and a city are substantively different from one another.

In later rabbinic texts this rough distinction is maintained as well.[24] For instance, *Pesiqta de-Rab Kahana* gives the following description of elite exploitation and benefaction: "Like those administrators (*ʾpwṭrwpyʾ*, from Greek *epitropos*) who go out to the villages (*qĕrayātâ*) and rob the tenant farmers, and go up to the city (*mĕdîntâ*) and say: 'Gather up the poor for we want to offer them charity.'"[25] A rabbinic story about the founding of Rome has an old man making his way to the Euphrates as a wine seller "entering a village (*qiryâ*) and leaving a village, entering a city (*mĕdînâ*) and leaving a city."[26]

Nevertheless, both rabbinic and non-rabbinic texts have a more graded hierarchy of settlement than might appear from the above discussion. In contrast to Eusebius, Jerome's revision of the *Onomastikon* regularly uses a variety of terms (*oppidum, vicus, viculus, villa, villula, castellum*) for Eusebius's *kōmē*. This usage suggests a scale of settlements that is more

---

22 E.g., Dabeira: ed. Klostermann 1904: 78.5–7.

23 *m. Meg.* 1:1–2; *m. B. Meṣ.* 4:6, with *t. B. Meṣ.* 3:10 and *Sipra, Bĕ-har, Par.* 3:8 (107d); *t. Pes.* 2 [1]:1–2; see Krauss 1914–23: 22–37; Safrai 1983a; 1995: 29–40.

24 Sokoloff 1992: 505–6, *s.v. qiryâ*, d.

25 *Pes. Rab Kah. ʿAśēr taʿăśēr*, ed. Mandelbaum 1987: 161; ed. Buber 1868: 95b–96a; cf. Lieberman 1946: 358–59.

26 *Cant. Rab.* to 1:6; see Rieger 1925–26; Feldman 1991. For this same image used elsewhere of a trader see *Lam. Rab.* 1 (to 1:16). That *mĕdînâ* here means "city" not "province" is suggested by the fact that the story is about the founding of the city of Rome, and that upon the standing of the first two huts, the Romans say of themselves (and their benefactor) "any *mĕdînâ* that does not have Abba Qolon is not a *mĕdînâ*."

finely graded. Since Jerome can use *oppidum* for Tiberias and Legio,[27] the "town" of Gaba (Eusebius: *polikhnē*),[28] and the "villages" of Cana, Capernaum, Chorazin, and Nain,[29] it does not seem likely that it is purely administrative distinctions between cities and villages that are at issue in the use of that term, at least. However, it is unclear just what the salience of the various terms was: how, for instance, might we distinguish between an *oppidum*, and a *pergrandis vicus*, "very large village," as Jerome describes Jezreel?[30] Finally, whatever the distinctions made by Jerome, his descriptions do not necessarily reflect full independent information on the contemporaneous situation: in addition to characterizing of Chorazin as an *oppidum*, Jerome appears to carry over from Eusebius (correctly or not) the notice that it was deserted.[31]

That in Palestinian rabbinic perceptions, settlement hierarchy was also more complex than the city-village divide is suggested by a variety of texts, particularly "tannaitic" texts (putatively predating the early third century). *m. Megilla* 1:1–3 (discussed above, Chapter 1), in which there are at least three grades of settlement (*kĕrak*, *ʿîr*, and *kĕpār*, with a possible further distinction between types of *ʿîr*) is an example. A similar grading is also found, for instance, in rabbinic comments on biblical uses of the term *ʿîr*, as in the following (commenting on a verse siege practices): "*ʿîr* and not city (*kĕrak*), *ʿîr* and not village (*kĕpār*)."[32] Interestingly for the place of marketing in a schematic rabbinic hierarchy of settlements, the siting of a biblically enjoined refuge city is placed in an *ʿîr* as opposed to either a *kĕrak* or a *kĕpār*, and in that same context explicitly connected with marketplaces: the city of refuge "may only be built at (?) a marketplace (*šûq*); and if there is no marketplace there, they build one there."[33] All of the above purport to be tannaitic traditions. Although occurring in a passage that is both dependent upon the Mishnah and exegetical in form, the hierarchy of settlements of *m. Megillah* 1:1–2 is reproduced in an explicitly amoraic context in the Yerushalmi (it is attributed to Simon in the name of Samuel b. Nahman).[34] The Yerushalmi glosses the terms of an earlier

---

[27] Ed. Klostermann 1904: 173.18–20, 99.12.

[28] Ed. Klostermann 1904: 71.8–9.

[29] Ed. Klostermann 1904: 117.7–8, 121.2, 175.24, 95.18.

[30] Ed. Klostermann 1904: 109.11; cf. Eusebius, ed. Klostermann 1904: 108.13: *episēmotatē Esdraēla kōme*, "most notable village." Notably, the Bordeaux Pilgrim in the 330s described Jezreel as a *civitas*, "city," *It. Burd.* 585, ed. Geyer, Cuntz 1965: 13.

[31] Ed. Klostermann 1904: 175.25.

[32] *Sipre Deut.* 199, 203, ed. Finkelstein 1939: 237, 238; also 180, ed. Finkelstein 1939: 232.

[33] *y. Mak.* 2:7 (31d); cf. *t. Mak.* 3:8; see also *Sipre Num.* 159, ed. Horovitz 1917: 221.

[34] *y. Meg.* 1:1 (70b). Both are of the third amoraic generation (late-third to early-fourth century?).

tradition about selling an *ʿîr*: "'Its remainder' – its outskirts; 'its daughters' – its villages," suggesting a hierarchical ordering of larger settlements and smaller, dependent villages.[35] That "small" villages may have different Sabbath practices than elsewhere seems to be presupposed by the way a comment in the Yerushalmi glosses one specification of the hour that the ritual obligation to read the *shemaʿ* (Deut. 6:4 and additional passages) begins as when people eat their Sabbath meals: "Said R. Yose [fourth amoraic generation]: 'It may be explained in connection with those small villages (*kôprānayâ dĕqîqayâ*), whose practice is to leave while it is still day because they are afraid because of wild animals'" (see further Chapter 5).[36] This is hardly a clear, graded hierarchy, but it still may imply an assumption of substantive distinctions between "town" and "village" life.[37]

1. Urban markets

a. *Tiberias*. The most explicit localized material connected with markets and marketing in Palestinian rabbinic literature is connected with Tiberias. A legend about the purification of Tiberias by Simeon b. Yohai mentions two possible identifications of a *šûq* that he had purified but in which an opponent had buried a dead body. In one version these are the *šûqâ dĕdagônâ* ("grain market") and the *šûqâ dĕ-saqāʾê* ("sack-makers' market"?).[38] *Šûq* frequently can mean nothing more than "street" so that we cannot insist here upon named markets in Tiberias, nor, even granting the identification of these toponyms as "markets," can we conclude that these streets continuously retained the market functions that gave them their names. Nevertheless, the names themselves are at least suggestive of the way that public space may have been allocated in late antiquity in Tiberias.

Another tradition, put in the mouth of Berechiah (fourth amoraic generation) in the name of Judah (a second century sage), offers a parable in which a man and his wife arrive at Tiberias and proceed from the "tannery," probably assumed to be at the outskirts of town, to the "upper *šûq*, and thence to the lower *šûq*."[39] Here landmarks are referred to and built

---

[35] *y. B. Bat.* 4:7 (14c), with Escorial ms., ed. E. S. Rosenthal 1984: 91, commenting on *t. B. Bat.* 3:5. Whatever the meaning of *ʿîr* in *m. B. Bat.* 4:7; *t. B. Bat.* 3:5, it is apparently taken as "village" rather than "farm" in the Yerushalmi (for this latter meaning of *ʿîr* see Applebaum 1976: 461–66).

[36] *y. Ber.* 1:1 (2a); cf. *t. Ber.* 1:1; *b. Ber.* 2b.

[37] *y. Šab.* 6 (8a); *ySanh.* 10:1 (28a).

[38] *Gen. Rab.* 79:6, ed. Theodor, Albeck 1912–36: 943–44; the version in *Qoh. Rab.* 10:8 gives two different identifications of which one, at least, *šûqâ dgrybh*, may be a textual corruption of *šûqâ ddgwnh*; for this whole legend see Levine 1978. According to the text of *Genesis Rabba* the enemy is from one of those places, so *šûq* may perhaps refer to residential "street," not "market."

[39] *Cant. Rab.* to 1:4; see Eliav 1995: 17–18 for discussion and bibliography.

public markets may perhaps be implied. Finally, the "shop of R. Hoshaya" is cited by "the Tiberians" as an identifiable landmark, and plausibly to be located in Tiberias.

b. *Sepphoris.* The *syrqy/sydqy* market of Sepphoris has already been mentioned in Chapter 1.[40] As a supplement to a story involving a butcher in Sepphoris who apparently sold improperly slaughtered meat, the Palestinian Talmud reads: "Said R. Yirmiya in the name of R. Hanina, the matter came before R. [Judah the Patriarch] and he said: 'It is not in our power to prohibit the *maqêllôn* of Sepphoris,'" where *maqêllôn* is a loan word ultimately from the Latin *macellum*, "provisions market."[41] In a story about a Sepphorean tailor who had become a *dux*, the locals hoped to determine whether the *dux* was indeed the former tailor by whether, when he passed in the *šûq*, he would glance at the bench where he used to ply his trade.[42] Here, taking *šûq* as "market," and the story as implying a former life as an artisan in the market of Sepphoris, seems reasonable.[43]

c. *Scythopolis (Bet Shean).* Traditions about markets or marketing in Bet Shean, as for other "gentile" cities, cluster around two issues: the status of the fairs during pagan religious festivals, and the status of produce in the marketplace with respect to tithes and related ritual requirements. The Mishnah mentions decorated shops during a festival at Bet Shean.[44] A story is told about Bibi who was sent by Zeira to buy a small amount (?) of thread (*ʿazîl qaṭîn*; perhaps, reading *qṭn* as "narrow," "fine thread"?) at the *Saturnalia* of Bet Shean.[45] Both the exemption of Bet Shean from the agricultural laws applicable to the juridical land of Israel (attributed to Judah the Patriarch), and the list of produce prohibited in Bet Shean (attributed in the Yerushalmi to Yose of Kefar Dan in the name of Rabbi ben Maadiya (?)) have to do with the produce that is available in the city markets of Scythopolis.[46] Hence, the details in the list of prohibited produce of how certain items are bundled or sold.

d. *Tyre.* In connection with Tyre, the Palestinian Talmud provides a version of an inscription commemorating the dedication of a fair ascribed

---

40 *y. B. Meṣ.* 5:8 (10c).

41 *y. Šeq.* 7:4 (50c), following the reading of fragment in Ginzberg 1909: 138; *LSJM*, *s.v. makellon*; *OLD*, *s.v. macellum*; Frayne 1993: 1–11; 101–17; cf. Sokoloff 1990: 326, *s.v. maqêllôn*, "kitchen."

42 *Cant. Rab.* to 6:12.

43 The designations "upper market" and "lower market" in Sepphoris occur in two passages in the Babylonian Talmud: *b. ʿErub.* 54b; *b. Yomaʾ* 11a.

44 *m. ʿAb. Zar.* 1:4. On the basis of *t. ʿAb. Zar.* 1:6, with *Ḥasdê dāwîd*, as well as on the general comment on this passage attributed to Resh Laqish in *y. ʿAb. Zar.* 1:4 (39c), a fair may be presupposed.

45 *y. ʿAb. Zar.* 1:2 (39c).

46 *y. Dem.* 2:1 (22c); see also Rehob inscription ll. 1–9; Sussman 1973–74: 109–21 (for the text of tradents' names see 109–110 n 113); Felix 1980–86: 2, 424 and n. 50.

to Diocletian himself and dedicated to the *genius* (*gād*) of *hrkwlys*. The latter was understood by Lieberman to refer to Maximianus who as co-emperor took the epithet Herculius.[47] In the same extended context, the Yerushalmi presents a story about Hiyya b. Ba, said to have sent someone to buy him shoes from the fair (*yārîd*) of Tyre, and the discussion that followed.[48] Hiyya and two other sages are said to have engaged in *pragmateia* ("trade") in silk at Tyre.[49]

e. *Ptolemais (Akko)*. The fair of Akko is mentioned as forming a set of three with the fairs of Gaza and Botna: "And it was taught thus [in a *bāraîtâ*]: There are three fairs [that are prohibited]: the fair of Gaza, the fair of Akko, and the fair of Botna, and the fair of Botna is the clearest (?) of all."[50] Although the tradition is marked as a tannaitic tradition (therefore arguably from the early-third century or before), it is impossible to locate a historical present in which precisely these three sites and no others are to be associated with fairs (or perhaps with unmistakably pagan fairs).[51] A story involving Mana who took his oil to Akko presumably presupposes some market function, although the discussion focuses rather on how to value produce set aside as second tithe.[52]

f. *Caesarea Paneas.* A tradition attributed to Yonah in the name of Simeon b. Zachariah, and supplemented by Gamaliel Zoga lists the "prohibited kinds" of produce at Paneas, despite the general exemption from agricultural laws.[53] As with Scythopolis, both the exemption and the restrictions on it appear to relate to produce in the city markets.

Casting the geographical net somewhat wider, the literary sources (in Hebrew and Aramaic or in Greek and Latin) easily allow the extension of this picture of urban based marketing or fairs to other cities in Palestine, especially Ashkelon, Gaza, and Caesarea.[54] Cyril of Scythopolis tells of a villager who went to Eleutheropolis to hire a magician to kill an opponent.[55] While not necessarily pointing to markets as such, this passage does

---

47 *y. ᶜAb. Zar.* 1:4 (39d); Lieberman 1959: 78–81; E. S. Rosenthal 1963: 23–8. For Maximianus as Herculius see Aurelius Victor *de Caesaribus* 39.18, in Dufraigne, ed. 1975: 50; Jones 1964: 38.

48 *y. ᶜAb. Zar.* 1:4 (39d).

49 *Gen. Rab.* 77:2, ed. Theodor, Albeck 1912–36: 910–1; cf. *Cant. Rab.* to 3:6; the named figures pose chronological problems.

50 *y. ᶜAb. Zar.* 1:4 (39d); *Gen. Rab.* 47:10, ed. Theodor, Albeck 1912–36: 477; see Jastrow 1886–1903: 438 *s.v. ḥwr*: "least doubtful of all."

51 A *yārîd* of Akko or of ᶜEn Beki is also mentioned at *b. ᶜAb. Zar.* 11b.

52 *y. Maᶜaś. Š.* 4:2 (54d).

53 *y. Dem.* 2:1 (22c–d); Rehob inscription ll. 18–20.

54 See Safrai 1984: 152–3; 1994: 256–9; de Ligt 1993: 256; Di Segni 1996: 575–77. See especially the elaborate description of the decked festival market in Choricius of Gaza *Laud. Marc.* 1.84–88, 2.59–61, ed. R. Foerster, E. Richsteig 1929: 23–24, 42–43.

55 *V. Euthy.* 57, ed. E. Schwartz 1939: 78.

at least suggest the hierarchical ordering of goods and services, with skilled, literate professionals concentrated in cities where villagers might have to travel to purchase their services.

2. Rural marketing

At least some village marketing is presupposed in rabbinic texts, particularly in "tannaitic" texts and texts that comment upon them. At times such presuppositions are made explicit, as in the passage about bakers and post-Passover leaven discussed above in Chapter 1.[56] However, even assuming that the texts accurately reproduce economic and social relations in Palestine, it remains impossible to reconstruct the extent and structure of village marketing. Thus, for instance, a reference to "village bunches [of vegetables] (*ʾagûdôt šel kĕpārîm*) that come from the market house (*mi-bêt ha-šĕwāqîm*),"[57] if this is how this text should be read, may refer to the marketing of village produce, but not necessarily at the level of the *kĕpār* itself, and the mechanisms through which it comes to market are far from clear.

A comment following a series of traditions dealing with "the whole village (*ʿîr*)" selling produce of one ritual status, and one person selling produce of a different status states: "With respect to what are the [above] said? When he bought, but he does not know from whom he bought; but if he bought from the marketplace (*šûq*) one follows the majority [i.e., the ritual status of produce sold by the majority]."[58] Clearly, the passage presupposes that a marketplace might exist in a village, but in specifying that marketplace purchases constitute a special category, this passage may well presuppose that an indeterminate (to us) proportion of transactions in villages are direct transactions with producers.

This issue becomes important in assessing one of the fairly few passages that directly addresses the sale of produce in upper Galilee, a story about an emissary from Laodicaea in Syria who comes to Gush Halab (Gischala) to acquire oil. The story does indeed assume that oil might be "exported" from upper Galilee, and it is cited occasionally in order to prove the participation of Galilee in an export economy, but it is worth noting how *Sipre Deuteronomy* frames the transaction.[59] The buyer is the representative of a city, not an individual consumer, an entrepreneur, or a professional marketer, and the transaction is set in motion due to the exceptional need of that city; the buyer makes his way to Gush Halab indirectly, by way of Tyre, suggesting the possible role of that city as mediator, at least of infor-

---

[56] *t. Pes.* 2:1.

[57] *t. Makš.* 3:8; cf. *m. Makš.* 6:2.

[58] *t. Dem.* 4:10, following examples in 4:6–10.

[59] *Sipre Deut.* 355, ed. Finkelstein 1939: 421. See Alon 1953–57: 99–100; Safrai 1994: 393–94.

mation about rural production; and while the point of the story is to illustrate the richness of upper Galilee in oil, the buyer is directed to a single producer, who despite his apparently humble status (the Laodicaean emissary finds him personally working his land) can personally fill Laodicaea's shortfall. In short, whether for rhetorical reasons or because of historical verisimilitude, the story gives no evidence that any regular patterns of marketing, trading partnerships, or standing routes of communication or delivery existed at all. The entire episode may just as easily illustrate the *ad hoc* character of the transactions through which individual landowners with large surpluses could sell those surpluses to distant buyers in exceptional cases of shortage as it does that upper Galilee "exported" produce.

Three sites, apparently to the West of the western edge of the hill country of Samaria and Judaea, are mentioned explicitly as places where one might buy produce.[60] I mention these here because these sites (only one of which is likely to have been a "city") are claimed to have drawn produce from fairly far afield (the Judaean hill country) and may suggest something of the possible range of village markets (see further Chapter 5). The account of the travels of the Piacenza pilgrim (in the late sixth century) gives a vivid description of rural trade in Samaria, with the contacts between Christians and Samaritan hedged in by purity rules driven, from the pilgrim's perceptive, by Samaritan animosity, and insisted upon by guards posted outside the village (*foris vico*).[61] This account is not specifically localized, but it can be read in terms of travelers visiting existing rural markets to get supplies. The account may also suggest some of the complex ways in which "subaltern" populations might at once orient themselves to an economic framework whose nodal points or centers of gravity are elsewhere (e.g., Jerusalem), and bracket that range of activity as "foreign."

---

[60] *t. Dem.* 1:11; for Patros and Hayyeshub (?) see *TIR* 151, 200 *s.vv.*Patros, Ieshub (for the latter see also Lieberman 1955–88: 1, 198–199. One of the sites, Antipatris, was a Herodian refoundation, issued coins under Elagabalus, and rather later was an episcopal see. Antipatris is likely to have been a fairly substantial site in the early third century, whatever its fortunes in the late fourth century (see Roll, Ayalon 1989: 147–48; 174–75; 233–37; Schürer, Vermes 1973–87: 2, 167–168; Isaac 1992: 361) and it is here that the Tosepta, if we may take it as the product of the early- to mid-third century, mentions a "market," (*šûq*). For the other two sites the text refers to a *kippâ/kuppâ*, which Lieberman 1955–88: 1, 198, understood as referring to a treasury. In that case the passage may involve something other than an unmediated marketplace, inolving, perhaps, the collection in treasuries of produce in payment of taxes, or estate rents on large estates, and their exchange for cash to buyers.

[61] *It. Plac.* 8, ed. Geyer 1965a: 133.

On balance, however, in contrast to the cities, for which there are clear attestations of marketing activity, for village marketing, there is very little specifically localized information for northern Palestine upon which to reconstruct patterns of marketing and trade with any confidence. The localized traditions that do exist relate in particular to fairs. Epiphanius describes how the young Patriarch once went to Hammat Gader for the bathing season, which was coordinated with an annual fair (*panēgyris de ekei kat' etos agetai*).[62] The reference in rabbinic literature to rabbis buying bread while at Hammat Gader also suggests a locus of marketing activity, at least in the context of a stay there, although not necessarily connected with a festival or fair.[63] In any case, the fair at Hammat Gader is perhaps better seen as an extension of urban marketing from Gadara itself or to have been driven by visitors to the hot springs in the famous suburb, whose fourth-century elite clientele is said to have included the Patriarch in Epiphanius's story, and Iamblichus, described by Eunapius as having come to visit the baths, and while there to have conjured deities.[64]

Perhaps the best example of a rural fair is the fair at Mambre (Terebinthos), particularly if it is to be identified with the archetypal rabbinic (prohibited) fair of Botna/Botnan in a passage cited above.[65] Mambre is mentioned in patristic texts as the site of a fair (*mercatus*, *panēgyris*) as well, which took place yearly in the summer and where people came to buy and to sell.[66] However, this site apparently long served as a local cultic center around which the annual festival may have been organized.[67] Moreover, nearby Hebron was a large site (Eusebius refers to it as a "very large [*megistē*] village"[68]) sitting at a crossroads of Roman built roads and, for a time, a military outpost.[69] The situation may therefore be roughly analogous to that of Hammat Gader, and not by itself a measure of rural marketing. At any rate, in northern Palestine fairs are associated with cities or their immediate suburbs.

---

[62] Epiph. *Panarion* 30.7.5, ed. Holl 1915–33: 1, 342.

[63] *y. Ter.* 3:1 (41b); see also *y. ʿAbod. Zar.* 5:15 (45b), a loan of money; and *y. ʿAbod. Zar.* 2:9 (42a), the permission of dumplings cooked by gentiles, possibly sold in the marketplace.

[64] Eunapius, *Vitae Sophistarum* 459.

[65] *y. ʿAb. Zar.* 1:4 (39d); *Gen. Rab.* 47:10, ed. Theodor, Albeck 1912–36: 477. See Krauss 1909; Mader 1957: 289–97; Avi-Yonah 1966: 170; Safrai 1984a: 150–52; 1994: 254–56.

[66] Sozomen *Hist. Eccl.* 2.4.2–3, ed. Bidez 1960: 54–55; Jerome *in Zachar.* 3 (to Zech. 11:4–5) ed. Adriaen 1970: 851; see also Jerome *in Hierem.* 4.18 (to Jer. 31.15), ed. Reiter 1913: 390; *Chron. Pasch.*, *PG* 92, 613.

[67] Cf. de Ligt 1993: 253–58 and the examples cited there of coordinated cult and marketing.

[68] Eusebius, *Onomastikon*, ed. Klostermann 1904: 6.8.

[69] See Isaac 1992: 430.

Otherwise, references to specifically localized marketing in villages or other rural communities are actually rather few. *Sipre Deuteronomy* uses the example of one who must travel to *Bêt ʾîlanîs*, and expects to expend ten to twenty thousand *dînārîm* (*denarii*), and lightens the burden by carrying golden *dînārîm* (i.e., *aurei*).[70] The location of this site is not known; it is typically, although not universally, taken to refer to the fair at Mambre.[71] It is worth pointing out that this transaction is not only large in its own right (particularly if it still coordinates one golden *dînār* with 25 *dînārîm*, rather than taking into account the debasement of Roman *denarii*), it is also one hundred times the size of the example that precedes it in the text, involving a person going to Caesarea (a major coastal city),[72] so that whatever the referent of the toponym, the text is, again, presumably not simply referring to rural marketing.

Turning now to traditions more explicitly related to northern Palestine, I have already noted in Chapter 1 a small number of passages that imply market hierarchy, including a tradition about the *sydqy/syrqy* of Sepphoris and its continuous market price (as opposed to other, less regular, markets). One possible reference to rural marketing is the exemption of Kefar [literally "village of"] Semah from agricultural laws such as those pertaining to tithes and the sabbatical year.[73] On analogy with the exemption of Bet Shean and other cities, this one village exemption may plausibly be taken to refer to marketing in the village. A *bārāîtâ* cited in the Palestinian Talmud refers to a gentile selling "books [i.e., Torah scrolls], phylacteries, and *mĕzûzôt*" in Saidan (Beth Saida-Julias), or possibly Sidon.[74]

A different kind of marketing is implied by traditions about *rôkĕlîm* (peddlers, associated by Adan-Bayewitz particularly with the selling of spinning goods and cosmetics).[75] In a gloss to a passage from the Mishnah that characterizes *rôkĕlîm* as "circulating (*mĕḥazzĕrîm*) in the villages," the Palestinian Talmud states "R. Simeon b. Laqish [said] in the name of R. Hoshaya: '[They are] like those of Kefar Hananiah who go out to four or five villages and sleep in their homes'";[76] the context implies that this is a single day's procedure. A story in *Leviticus Rabbbah* deals with a *rôkēl*

---

[70] *Sipre Deut.* 306, ed. Finkelstein 1939: 339, following a reading given in the apparatus; Finkelstein's text reads *ʾlyys*.

[71] After slight emendation, *ʾîlanîm*, or perhaps *ʾēlônîm* or *ʾalônîm*, understood as corresponding to "Terebinthos." Mader 1957: 292–93; Safrai 1994: 253, 254; 1984a: 150; cf. Krauss 1909: 300–302; Alon 1976: 2, 98–99; Sperber 1991: 89 and 232 n. 6.

[72] *Sipre Deut.* 306, ed. Finkelstein 1939: 338.

[73] *y. Dem.* 2:1 (22c); Rehob inscription, l. 10.

[74] *y. Giṭ.* 4:6 (46a); *y. ʿAb. Zar.* 2:2 (41a).

[75] Adan Bayewitz 1985; 1993: 232–33.

[76] *y. Maʿaś.* 2:3 (49d), commenting on *m. Maʿaś.* 2:3.

"who was circulating in the villages near Sepphoris and was proclaiming: 'Whoever would like the medicine of life let him come and receive [it].'"[77]

In glossing a *bāraîtâ*, the Palestinian Talmud presents a hypothetical example in which the rate for gold in terms of "silver" coinage is slightly different in Arbel than it is "here," perhaps Tiberias (and in which a "golden *dinār*" is worth no less than 2,000 of the lesser coinage, leading Sperber to propose a date for this tradition in the early fourth century).[78] That some sort of transaction based on the differential values of the gold coins is presupposed is clear. What is less clear – especially since the text itself is difficult to interpret – is the significance of the choice of Arbel as an example, that is, for our purposes, whether institutionalized money-changing is presupposed in Arbel.[79] Arbel may have been large in antiquity (see Chapter 3), and so could have supported money-changers.[80] However, it remains possible (following Sperber) to see this passage rather in connection with private large-scale transactions (it presupposes a sum of 250 units of gold coin) without the mediation of an institutionalized market at Arbel. The terms on which such transactions can be made may still involve the relative availability and consequently marginally cheaper price of gold coin in cities as opposed to villages.

As a final, dubious example, note the tradition attributed to Yohanan that "All the villages near Tiberias, once the market price of Tiberias has gone out, they [may] make a bargain."[81] This passage assumes the dependence of village transactions for agricultural produce upon prices in the local central place. However, this passage may not refer to village-based marketing at all. I have suggested above (Chapter 1) that *m. Baba*ʾ *Meṣiʿa*ʾ 5:7 may refer to large-scale transactions based on substantial amounts of produce, and the present passage (which depends upon that passage from the Mishnah) may in fact reflect the process of funneling produce into a local city (Tiberias) at terms set through market prices in that city. If there is an institutional framework in which such transactions may be carried out it may well be the city marketplace.

---

[77] *Lev. Rab.* 16:2, ed. Margaliot 1953–60: 349–51; for the problem of the connection of this story with a setting in Akbera in Upper Galilee as well see Adan-Bayewitz 1985: 79–80, n. 41.

[78] *y. Maʿaś. Š.* 4:1 (52d); Sperber 1991: 65, 91–92; cf. Lieberman 1955–88: 2, 732.

[79] Safrai 1986: 76 reads the passage in terms of regional agricultural specializations and systemic shortages in foodstuffs, for reasons that are unclear.

[80] Dolav 1988 discusses coins from Arbel, but these are not sufficient to ground a discussion of the degree of monetization at the site.

[81] *y. B. Meṣ.* 5:8 (10c).

3. Literary texts and a central-place landscape

Clearly, the material just discussed does not allow for a detailed map of rural marketing. However, such evidence as we have does match the proposal in the preceding chapter that we see in cities concentrated loci of marketing activity. Beyond this, the material that could be marshaled as evidence is very sparse. To see this as simply "fact" is to ignore the urban bias of all our sources. There are sufficient references to rural marketing to suggest that there is no immutable cultural divide between the commercialized cities and non-commercialized villagers whose surplus production made its way into cities only through rents or other means of extraction. Nevertheless, the scale of marketing outside cities and the degree of commercialized production is impossible to evaluate on the basis of these sources.

Still, and at the risk of collapsing sources that come from a large chronological range and of drawing far-reaching conclusions from accidents of preservation, it may be possible to amplify one segment of a central-place system on the basis of the literary material. In the discussion of rural marketing above, three sites in northern Palestine were noted in "amoraic" texts as the locus of some marketing activity: Kefar Hananiah, Bethsaida, and Kefar Semah. Kefar Hananiah is identified with Kafr ʿInan (map ref. 18902580). The precise location of Bethsaida-Julias is subject to scholarly discussion but it is unanimously placed close to the northern shore of the Sea of Galilee.[82] As for Kefar Semah, Klein identified the site with Ṣamakh (at the southern end of the Sea of Galilee); while Urman proposed an identification with Kh. Samra.[83]

To this brief list one may add two additional items. One tradition links Hippos-Susita to Tiberias. The tradition assumes that those kinds of produce of the sabbatical year that can be sold cannot be sold in the usual manner (by volume, number, or weight).[84] In commenting on this passage the Palestinian Talmud cites the following:

> [A *bārаîtâ*] teaches: Produce from outside the Land [i.e. the juridical land of Israel] that has come into the Land, let it not be sold either by measure, or by weight, or by number; but rather as the produce of the Land. But if it was recognizable [as imported], it is permissible.
> Said R. Yose b. R. Bun: "Like (Vatican ms. and the edition of Sirillo) that *qwrdq* [wheat (?)] that go out and are sold from Susita to Tiberias.

---

[82] Pixner 1985; Maʿoz 1986: 65–66; Urman 1995: 519–27; see also *TIR* 85–86; Arav, Freund, eds., 1995.

[83] See the map accompanying Klein 1939; followed by *TIR* p. 165; map ref. 20502340. Urman 1985: no. 203; 1995: 588–9; map ref. 20802360; see also Maʿoz 1986: 59.

[84] *m. Šebi.* 8:3.

Although it is possible to take this passage as referring to a kind of grain or other produce[85] literally sold in the territory between Tiberias and Hippos, such a reading does not make good geographical sense, since a lake accounts for nearly all of that area. A better reading may be that the sense is rather that this particular kind of produce is gathered into Hippos (outside "the Land," or at least exempt from the agricultural laws pertaining to it) and from there brought to Tiberias (inside "the Land"). The second item is an episode referred to in a "tannaitic" work (the Tosepta), set in the late first or early second century, and involves the marketplace of Meiron in upper Galilee.[86]

Plotting these sites against Map 6 yields an interesting result. Four occur along (or at least near) four separate sides of the hexagon representing the hypothetical central-place region of Tiberias.[87] The fifth, Meiron (usually located at map reference 19102650), falls a bit too far West to fit the hexagon as drawn (although on that map the northern portions of the region of Tiberias were drawn even more uncertainly than other portions). However, Meiron, too, falls near a boundary line.

As might be expected, there are problems associated with such a reconstruction. To begin with, if the passage about Arbel (well within the "hexagon" just described: map ref. 19502460[88]) discussed above is taken to refer to regularized market activity (in that example, banks), the whole schema is undermined. Moreover, the text that exempts Kefar Semah poses difficulties, over and above the dispute about where the site was located. First, while it is reasonable to read an explicit statement of exemption ("Rabbi [Judah the Patriarch] exempted Kefar Semah"[89]) as referring to markets, it is not entirely clear whether the list of "prohibited" villages from which Kefar Semah is excepted refers to their status as market-bearing villages or merely a kind of ethnico-historiographic statement put in legal terms (i.e., the population of those villages are presumed Jewish, and the ritual obligations on produce from there are presumed in force). I discuss the complex of texts dealing with "permitted" and "prohibited"

---

85 Sokoloff 1990: 484, *s.v. qwrdq*; cf. Felix 1980–86: 2, 176, n. 65.

86 *t. Dem.* 4:13.

87 Given the evidence of size alone, Chorazin might have been expected. Interestingly, however, Eusebius, *Onomastikon*, ed. Klostermann 174.23–5, writing at about the turn of the fourth century states that the site was deserted (so too the version of Jerome, 175.25–7). Assuming proper identification of the site, reoccupation does not appear before the late third century (Yeivin: 1973; Meshorer 1973), and may conceivably have been later.

88 Assuming it is not one of the other two northern villages called Arbela mentioned by Eusebius, *Onomastikon*, ed. Klostermann 1939: 14.18–21, one in the territory of Pella (present day Irbid) and the other located by *TIR* on the Legio–Scythopolis road (present day el Fuleh, Afula; see Zori 1977: 77 [Merhavia]; Roll, Isaac 1982:33).

89 *y. Dem.* 2:1 (22c); Rehob inscription, l. 10.

places in Chapter 5. For the present, note that of the other sites mentioned in the list of villages in the territory of Susita, all appear to be situated further East, and that even the other sites near the Sea of Galilee are some distance in from the lake and the coastal road, and are several hundred meters higher.[90] On that level, even if all the listed villages were market bearing, Kefar Semah is better situated as a "boundary" market than these other villages. A second problem relates to the status of Philoteria: if this Hellenistic city were still an active local center during the historical present of the text exempting Kefar Semah (theoretically about 200, since the exemption is attributed to Judah the Patriarch), it might have served as a better location for a "boundary" market.[91] (This problem is eased only slightly if we follow Urman in locating Kefar Semah at Kh. Samra, to the North and East.)

In short, it is just possible that a small number of sites discussed above might mark part of the boundary of the upper-level central-place region of Tiberias as described in Chapter 3. It is worth noting that even if correct, this suggested correlation between literary texts and theory allows at most an only very partial reconstruction of one subsection of the second highest tier of market sites. A full description of an integrated system of either marketing or extraction at the lowest levels of the system remains elusive. This is not to be explained entirely by the absence of marketing below these highest levels (although small village production may in fact have been less commercialized than production in the immediate region of cities or larger towns; see Chapter 3). At least in part, the apparent invisibility of village commercialization is to be explained by the fact that the producers of our texts were urbanites.

B. Aspects of a Marketing System

As noted above, the textual evidence cannot be made to support the reconstruction of a full-fledged network of interlocking markets and loci of production

---

[90] ʿAwanish (ʿAyyanosh), map ref. 21252471; Kafr Ḥarib (Kefar Ḥarub/Yaḥrib), map ref. 21212405; see the map of the Golan in *JSG*.

[91] Maisler (Mazar), Stekelis, Avi-Yonah 1952: 223 dated the bath at Kh. el Kerak (Bet Yerah, i.e., Philoteria) to the fourth or fifth century; Bar Adon 1953: 129 dated the synagogue to the fourth or fifth century; Ovadiah 1970: no. 26 dated the first construction of the church to the fifth century. Evidence for a full fledged occupation for the late second to early fourth centuries are lacking as far as I know. For the argument that the site was in decline during the Roman period see Safrai 1985: 68–73. The Palestinian Talmud refers to the servant of Levi of Sennabris (a settlement quite close, and possibly related, to Philoteria) as dealing in produce, *y. ʿAbod. Zar.* 2:10 (42a); but the locus of his activity is not mentioned.

or exchange. It is possible to supplement the material discussed in the preceding section with passages in which agricultural or other production is explicitly said to be geared toward sale, including one in the Tosepta that distinguishes between a place "where it was customary to sell in the market" as opposed to one in "where it was customary to sell in the field" (presumably to a single buyer who would dispose of the produce[92]); or a passage in the Yerushalmi where "a place where most people bring [produce from the fields] into the market" is opposed to a situation where most "bring into the houses."[93] Texts such as these suggest, at the very least, a countryside that might be differentially exploited with respect to markets or domestic consumption. Similarly, the hypothetical example given of a "great *agoranomos*" who puts pressure on sellers to sell cheaply[94] – where the rabbinic text imagines that a Jewish seller might be permitted to sell without tithing; and that consequently a buyer bound by tithing rules must assume that the produce is untithed – can be read in terms of market and non-market pressures that might be used to bring grain to market (presumably in cities, at least during shortages). Taken together, however, these texts only hint at how such differential organization or administrative pressures might have been played out in space and in time.

If literary texts cannot provide a detailed picture of rural marketing, they do at least offer a view of some aspects of economic activity, seen from the vantage point of urban-based groups. What follows is by no means a comprehensive treatment of ancient views of the Palestinian economy, much less a history of that economy itself – both areas that have only been incompletely studied to date.[95] Instead, I propose a sketch of some of the outlines of three issues that are directly related to a study of regional economic integration and the degree to which that integration is mediated or manifested in commercialized production and exchange: fairs, professional marketers, and the dependency of consumers on local markets.

1. Fairs.

The material discussed in the first part of this chapter already suggests that a good deal of the localized traditions about marketing refers to fairs, and much of that – at least in the North – would appear to be localized in or near cities.[96] The other recurrent feature is the connection of fairs with religious festivals. Less easily teased out, and perhaps ultimately unknowable, is the role such

---

92 See Lapin 1995: 143, n. 46; cf. and Kehoe 1992: 84, n. 69, see also 142–143; Morley 1996: 161–62; cf. Lieberman 1955–88: 9, 290.

93 *y. Maʿaś.* 2:1 (49c).

94 *y. Dem.* 2:1 (22c)

95 See for the present Heichelheim 1938, A. Ben David 1978, Sperber 1978, 1991; Safrai 1994.

96 See also *t. ʿAbod. Zar.* 1:5, 6.

fairs played in the local economy, from the point of view of both rural populations and urban populations. What I am referring to as a "fair" (Hebrew, Aramaic *yārîd*) is a short-term, possibly seasonal affair. This is implied by the "inscription" of Diocletian referred to in the Yerushalmi purportedly establishing a *yārîd* in Tyre for eight days,[97] and suggested also by the texts on the *panēgyris* at Mambre (where marketing is made explicit) and Hammat Gader (see above).[98] From the perspective of passages in the Tosepta, the *yārîd* might be understood as a framework for transactions involving expensive goods with limited circulation, notably medical treatments, and the purchase of houses, fields, vineyards, and male and female slaves; again one might use the opportunity to sell a slave; one might return from (illicit, from the rabbinic perspective) trading at a *yārîd* with livestock, textiles, *kēlîm*, money, or metal utensils.[99] In a fictional[100] life of Epiphanius, Epiphanius is said to have been sent to the *panēgyris* (presumably, but not explicitly, in Eleutheropolis) to sell the family ass to supply them with food.[101] It may be as a reflection of fairs as markets for fine goods that we hear of Hiyya b. Abba sending someone to buy him shoes at the *yārîd* of Tyre,[102] or the tradition involving Bibi, sent by Zeira to buy thread at the *Saturnalia* of Bet Shean (see above).[103]

The reference in the Tosepta to *tāgārîm* coming to a fair, that is, wholesaling merchants who, among other things, are said to buy up surplus rural produce,[104] opens up the possibility of seeing fairs as a vehicle (possibly the occasion for arranging contracts) for guaranteeing urban food supply on the level of individual householders, merchants, or administrators. This may perhaps fit with the suggestion of E. Kleiman that, among other things, seasonal fairs (coming at the end of a harvest season) would have helped to establish regional prices on agricultural produce.[105] The mention of *pragmateia* (see below) in connection with a *yārîd*[106] may imply that fairs offered the cities that housed them the opportunity to tap into a transit trade. The location in or near cities, in addition to utilizing an already existing concentration of population, also facilitated the registration of sale

---

[97] *y. ᶜAbod. Zar.* 1:4 (39c).

[98] Cf. de Ligt 1993: 57–105 and *passim*.

[99] *t. ᶜAbod. Zar.* 1:8 with Lieberman 1937–9: 2, 186; *t. ᶜAbod. Zar.* 3:9; since *kēlîm* is joined to "textiles," and one is required to let them rot rather than to smash them, the term presumably refers to clothing.

[100] See Williams 1987: xi.

[101] *V. Epiph.* 1, ed. Dindorf 1859–62: 1, 3.

[102] *y. ᶜAbod. Zar.* 1:4 (39d), perhaps a particular kind of shoe? His interlocutor admits to having bought loaves of bread.

[103] *y. ᶜAb. Zar.* 1:2 (39c).

[104] *t. ᶜAbod. Zar.* 1:9; Lapin 1995: 141–43, see also below.

[105] Kleiman 1986: 479.

[106] *y. ᶜAb. Zar.* 1:4 (39d).

or cession of land or slaves,[107] an issue that is made explicit in *t. ʿAboda Zara* 1:8. Finally, traditions in both the Tosepta (on the status of a fair given by the empire, by the city, or "a *yārîd* of idolatry") and the Yerushalmi (the tradition about Diocletian's dedication of a fair in Tyre) suggest that the institution and running of fairs was something that the local (i.e., civic) and imperial administration became involved in – a suggestion strengthened by evidence from other regions.[108] In particular, *y. ʿAboda Zara* 1:4 (39c) mentions benefits from (an exemption from) taxes as a characteristic of a *yārîd*.[109] Some sense of the annual rhythm of marketing, and the potential regional reach of marketing connected to a major religious event may perhaps be gained from Warren's observation in the mid-nineteenth century that, of 1,320 shops in Jerusalem, 278 (some 21%) were empty, "but these are quite filled up during the Easter festivities by merchants from Damascus and other cities."[110]

Fairs, on this view, will have operated on a number of levels – as religious festivals, as regional periodic markets for rare or expensive goods or services, as the occasion for contracting or registering transfers of real property, and as a structure for facilitating the funneling of surplus rural production into the cities – and fit reasonably well with a central-place analysis. It should be noted (although this is a matter for a different study) that different people (for example a peasant with surplus produce to sell, or a city-based grain merchant interested in laying in supplies) therefore will have experienced fairs differently, in ways at least partly structured by class, status, and geographical origin. At any rate, fairs centered on towns may both presuppose at least a partially integrated countryside, and have fostered further integration; they do not appear to be the artificial product of an imperial taxation policy.[111]

The institution referred to in rabbinic texts by the term *ʾiṭlîs* is of a different order than that of a *yārîd*, although, still more than with the *yārîd*, it is difficult to know precisely to what the term refers. Lieberman, following Benjamin Musafiah (in his seventeenth-century supplement to the *ʿAruk*) and Cohn, has given the most plausible etymology for *ʾiṭlîs*, arguing that the term originates as a borrowing from the Greek *atelēs* [s.c. *panēgyris*], "a tax-exempt fair."[112] It is in connection with *yārîd*, however,

---

[107] Brief bibliography in Lapin 1995: 138–39 n. 36.

[108] *t. ʿAbod. Zar.* 1:7; *y. ʿAb. Zar.* 1:4 (39d). Cf., e.g., *IG* V.1 18 B (Sparta); *IGR* III 1020 (Baetocaece); Nollé 1982; de Ligt 1993: esp. 199–240.

[109] See also *b. ʿAbod. Zar.* 13a.

[110] Warren 1876: 494.

[111] Cf. Safrai 1984: 158; 1995: 261–2; see the critique of Kleiman 1986.

[112] Kohut 1878–92: 1, 61; Cohn 1929: 33–34; Lieberman 1959: 77–81; see also E. S. Rosenthal 1963: 23–28. For *ateleia* and fairs in a wider Roman context see de Ligt 1993: 45–48, 229–34, 256–58.

and not with *ʾiṭlîs* that the Yerushalmi makes reference to special tax provisions (as noted above). Lieberman saw the two terms as more or less synonymous, using *ateleia*, for instance, as the corresponding term to the Aramaic *yārîd* in his rendering of the "inscription" of Diocletian.[113] Whatever the origins of the term, however, it does not appear to be used explicitly in Palestinian rabbinic literature with reference to a fair declared by the administration of a city (or by the emperor) combined with an exemption from duties for merchants.

In the "tannaitic" sources the term seems almost always to refer to a place where animals are bought, sold, slaughtered, and butchered.[114] The one exception would seem to be a passage in the *Mekiltaʾ*, which also connects *ʾiṭlîs* with idolatry and may therefore make the same association of cult and marketing that other rabbinic texts do for *yārîd.*[115] In "amoraic" literature the term may have the more generic meaning of "market" or "fair."[116] That, at least, is a plausible reading of a text that gives examples of a garment and of a woman slave being sold at an *ʾiṭlîs.*[117] Elsewhere in Palestinian "amoraic" literature, an individual coming from outside establishes an *ʾiṭlîs* and sells wares inexpensively.[118] It is possible that a market with a less official (and perhaps less regular) institutional character than a large regional fair is implied. It is worth noting that Jacob, the biblical patriarch, is used as a model. The immediate biblical context for this

---

[113] Lieberman 1959: 80; Safrai 1984: 143–44; 1994: 247–78, attempts to distinguish the two; Safrai 1995: 131 describes it as a kind of "Jewish" *yārîd*, citing *Gen. Rab.* 87:7, ed. Theodor, Albeck 1912–36: 762. See also Sperber 1998.

[114] *m. Bek.* 5:1; *m. ʿArak.* 6:5; *m. Tem.* 3:5; *m. Ker.* 3:7; *t. Bek.* 3:13; *Sipra*, *Ḥôbâ* 1:8, ed. Weiss 1862: 17b; ed Finkelstein 1983: 125; see also *b. Mak.* 14a; *b. Ḥul.* 91b; *b. Bek.* 31b; 32b.

[115] *Mek.*, *Wa-yĕhî bĕ-šallaḥ* 2, ed. Horovitz, p. 83; see the critical apparatus and notes. Cohn 1929: 83 and Lieberman 1959: 76 argued that the text of *Mek.* plays on *ḥîrôt* and *ḥērût*, "freedom," and that *ʾiṭlîs* is meant in a sense to gloss "freedom." This is problematic, since *ḥērût* generally refers to status as free or owned, whereas *ateleia* is the exemption from certain responsibilities (e.g., taxes, liturgies, or tithes, see *LSJM*, *s.v.*). It may be better to take *ḥērût*, with Jastrow (Jastrow 1886–1903, *s.vv. ḥîrâ*, *ḥêrût*; see also Lauterbach 1933–35: 188) as something like "libertinism"; in that case the *ʾiṭlîs* of the Egyptians (referred to in parallel with the place of their idolatry) may be a place of suspect sexual activity, as in *Gen. Rab.* 37:5, ed. Theodor, Albeck 1912–36: 348, but not necessarily a periodic regional fair granted a tax exemption.

[116] Lieberman 1959: 77 and de Ligt 1993:47 n. 49 offer evidence for the late-antique and medieval use of *ateleia* synonymously with other terms for markets (*mercatus*, *nundinae*, *panēgyris*).

[117] *Pesiq. Rab Kah. ʿAśśēr taʿaśśēr*, ed. Buber 1868: 98b; ed. Mandelbaum 1987: 168; note that, these items are also said to be sold in a *yārîd*: *t. ʿAbod. Zar.* 1:8; 3:19; Lapin 1995: 136–37, n. 27 omitted the woman slave.

[118] *Gen Rab.* 79:6, ed. Theodor, Albeck 1912–36: 940; cf. *y. Šebi.* 9:1 (38d) cf. *Pesiq. Rab Kah. Bĕ-šallaḥ*, ed. Buber 89b; ed Mandelbaum 1987: 192.

comment identifies Jacob as a shepherd just come from abroad, who has erected his tent near Shechem on land acquired from the inhabitants.[119] Given the connection between *ʾiṭlîs* and animals, at least in "tannaitic" sources, it is possible that we should connect *ʾiṭlîs* with seasonal patterns of transhumance (the existence of which remains an open question).[120] Elsewhere, *Genesis Rabba*, like the *Mekilta*, connects sexual license with the establishment of an *ʾiṭlîs*. This, of course, does not identify the kind of market presupposed in that passage, but the description in *Sipre Numbers* of Ammonite and Moabite women setting up tents near the Israelite encampment and selling goods and thereby seducing Israelites may offer an analogy: again "strangers" come and set up shop near the settlement.[121]

As an alternative to simply identifying *ʾiṭlîs* and *yārîd*, the follwing might also be considered. Despite the likely etymology of the term *ʾṭlys* from *atelēs*, it is the *yārîd*, with its assumed religious festival associations and connections to prominent cities, that is the more likely candidate for a successful appeal to the provincial governor or to the emperor for tax-free status, and indeed it is in connection with the term *yārîd* that the issue of tax is raised (see above). In the distinction between *ʾiṭlîs* and *yārîd* we may have something like the distinction between de Ligt's "local" and "regional" fairs: the former, on de Ligt's typology, might attract visitors from within fifty kilometers; the latter from up to several hundred kilometers.[122] Of the three paradigmatic *yĕrîdîm* mentioned in the above cited passage from *y. ʿAboda Zara*, two are set at major coastal cities (Gaza, Akko).[123] If the third (Botna/Botnan) is properly to be identified with Mambre, the shrine was significant enough to attract a visit from the mother-in-law of the emperor Constantine, and to have a church built on the site through imperial intervention.[124] As noted above, a third coastal city, Tyre, is explicitly said to have had an eight day *yārîd* (not said to be tax free) founded by imperial decree. Along these lines, traditions about *iṭlîs* may, by contrast, refer to fairly long-cycle periodic markets (say, monthly, or several times yearly?), that might draw on a wider hinterland, in terms of both traders and customers, than the daily or weekly lower-level periodic markets meeting in those same places, but not on the scale of the fairs

---

[119] Gen. 33:18–19.

[120] See Hodkinson 1988; Skydsgaard 1988; Marx 1992; de Ligt 1993: 79 n. 95, with reference to Epictectus, *Diatr.* 2.14.23–29. Villeneuve 1985: 118 links caravan trade with nomads as well.

[121] *Gen. Rab.* 37:5, ed. Theodor, Albeck 1912–36: 348; *Sipre Num.* 131, ed. Horovitz 1917: 170–171; cf. *y. Sanh.* 10:2 (28d).

[122] de Ligt 1993: 15, 77–78.

[123] *y. ʿAb. Zar.* 1:4 (39d); *Gen. Rab.* 47:10, ed. Theodor, Albeck 1912–36: 477.

[124] Eusebius *V. Const.* 3.50–53, ed. Heikel 1902: 99; Sozomen, *Hist. Eccl.* 2.4.6–8, ed. Bidez 1960: 55–56.

designated *yārîd*, either as places of trade or as religious festivals attracting a large number of visitors.

2. Professional marketers

A full discussion of professional marketers, artisans, and others who produce for, or trade in, regular marketplaces is beyond the scope of the present study. Instead, I have attempted to highlight aspects of the literary material that may help put texts about marketing in the context of the regional (and hierarchical) organization of trade. Shopkeepers are recurrent in rabbinic literature, and I have sketched elsewhere the Mishnah's descriptions of shopkeepers and large-scale merchants (*tāgārîm*), and the economic functions ascribed to them: shopkeepers as independent traders, or as agents or family members of a householder, and as engaged in the sale especially of foodstuffs and in credit transactions; *tāgārîm* as wholesalers in rural produce who can evaluate coins and who may be engaged in moving surplus rural production to the towns.[125] To shopkeepers in the general sense one can also add more specialized producers and sellers such as bakers, butchers, potters (who may be peripatetic), wine-makers (?), and grain merchants (who are larger-scale dealers).[126]

As for peripatetic traders, the most obvious example in rabbinic texts is covered by the term *rôkēl*, discussed above. Safrai has claimed that in the Roman period ass drivers (*ḥammārîm*) were the "major means of inter-village or inter-regional trade"; "by wandering from settlement to settlement, the donkey caravan served as the primary conduit of merchandise...."[127] There are indeed passages in which ass drivers apparently are engaged in trade with the merchandise they are carrying, such as the example given of ass drivers commenting on the ritual status of the grain that they and their fellows are carrying,[128] or a later text that makes use of a parable about a city (*mĕdînâ*) that was supplied by ass drivers.[129] More generally, however, a *ḥamār* may simply be a hired porter, as in the rule about one who hired ass drivers (i.e., to transport something) and they went to the pick-up place and found nothing to transport;[130] or as in an analogous story about Hiyya brought to gloss precisely such a case.[131]

Moreover, an assessment of the role of ass drivers in organizing rural exchange or commerce requires greater attention to the direction and

---

[125] Lapin 1995: 136–143; 154–155.

[126] Lapin 1995: 139–140, n. 38. For potters see especially Adan Bayewitz 1995: 228–35.

[127] Safrai 1994: 234, 237; reproducing Safrai 1983b: 271; cf. Lapin 1995: 139–40 n. 38.

[128] *m. Dem.* 4:7.

[129] *Gen. Rab.* 8:2, ed. Theodor, Albeck 1912–36: 57.

[130] *t. B. Meṣ.* 7:1.

[131] *y. B. Meṣ.* 6:1 (10d).

structure of trade when ass drivers are depicted as engaging in "marketing." What are typically depicted are two related aspects of the vertical organization of trade: ass drivers as a vehicle by which merchandise deriving from multiple producers with small surpluses is bulked in rural sites for movement to higher-level central places (and not a horizontal trading network running concurrently with that of central places), or agents through whom landowners with more sizable stocks might bring produce to market in cities.[132] A story about Simeon b. Yohai and his son may presuppose the first of these; the unfortunate ass drivers are apparently said to be buying, not selling, wheat (*Cant. Rab.*: "from the villages").[133] The second aspect may underlie a passage in the Tosepta that distinguishes between the ritual status of wheat in Tyre and Sidon in the treasuries from that sold by donkey caravans (since the latter might come from further afield, including territory governed for rabbinic purposes by biblical agricultural laws), or another about the price to be paid to the householder by the ass drivers "who receive from the householder and bring it up for sale ([?] *maᶜamîdîm*) in the place where it is expensive."[134] A story about Hiyya, from whom ass drivers wanted to buy flax (the location and destination of which are not specified) may be seen in the same light.[135] Lastly, even granting the organizing role of ass drivers as traders, it seems likely that these will have favored sites along well traveled routes rather than simply facilitating "horizontal" trade. Compare, for instance, the appeal on the part of the village of Attukleis in Asia Minor, which justified the foundation of a periodic market by stressing that the traders had to pass through the village in going from one existing market to another.[136]

In light of ongoing debates about the degree of commercialization of the Roman world in general and Palestine in particular, it is worth pointing out the "naturalness" of the fact of market sale, and especially market specialization – at least from the point of view of the literary texts. According to the Palestinian Talmud, "when Procla came to Sepphoris, R. Mana ruled that the bakers should bring [bread] out to the marketplace" on the Sabbath.[137] In other words, what appears to be a demand for provisions for a military presence is met through market professionals, not a levy on individuals (cf., however, another similar example on the same page where

---

132 Note the discussion of transportation in the management of a well documented estate in Egypt, Rathbone: 1991, 266–278.

133 *Pesiq. Rab Kah.*, *Wa-yĕhî bĕ-šallaḥ*, ed. Buber 1868: 89b; ed. Mandelbaum 1987: 194–5; cf. *Cant. Rab.* to 5:15.

134 *t. Dem.* 1:10; *t. B. Meṣ.* 4:8.

135 *y. B. Meṣ.* 5:8 (10c).

136 Nollé 1982: no. 1.

137 *y. Sanh.* 3:6 (21b).

baking by professionals is not specified).[138] In commenting on a rule having to do with the sale of produce collected during the sabbatical year, a tradition attributed to Yose b. Bun glosses the proviso "so long as they do not make him a marketer (*polêṭer*, from Greek *pōlētēs* or *pōlētēr*, "marketer"[139])," with "that he does not sell in that place every year (or: "every hour"),"[140] suggesting, at least, that taking on such a role (in this case: the authorized seller for the produce of five other people, brothers in the Tosepta) is possible. Isaac is said to have glossed Jeremiah 37:21 ("One loaf of bread daily from the street of the bakers"): "This is common (*qîbār*, cf. Latin *cibarium*) bread that is sold outside of the shops, which is darker than barley bran."[141] Yohanan is said to have had a conversation in the marketplace with a seller of honey cake, who made a regular (if precarious) livelihood doing so.[142] The Yerushalmi glosses one term in the Mishnah "the dumplings of the marketplace";[143] and [He]la is said to have given instructions to the dumpling makers on how to price their product during the sabbatical year.[144] In one tradition, brought to gloss a rule in the Mishnah about sellers of produce during the intermediate days of a festival, the Yerushalmi states that "the fishers of Tiberias, the grist makers of Sepphoris, and the groats makers of Akko took it upon themselves not to engage in labor during the intermediate days of the festival," and the sequel, which discusses the tradition in terms of "decreasing the joy of the festival" (i.e., because of lack of fresh food) seems to presuppose production for immediate sale in the market.[145] The specification of three urban communities may be accidental or may reflect the urban vantage point of our sources; however, it almost certainly also offers some indication of where market specialization may be expected to be localized.

One last aspect of specialization to be discussed here is that covered by the terms *prgmṭyy*ʾ and *prgmṭwṭs* (from Greek *pragmateia*, "affairs," but also "trade," and *pragmateutēs*, "merchant"). Unlike other forms of marketing activity, which rabbis occasionally disdain or disparage,[146] *pragmateia* is not typically stigmatized in rabbinic literature. Indeed, the traditional depiction of the relationship of Zebulon and Issachar was that

---

[138] Avi-Yonah 1976: 181 read this in terms of the "Gallus revolt."

[139] *LSJM*, 1560 *s.vv.*

[140] *y. Šebi.* 7:4 (37c); see Felix 1980–86: 2, 136; cf. *t. Šebi.* 6:22.

[141] *Cant. Rab.* to 1:6, following Jastrow 1886–1903, *s.v. palṭēr*.

[142] *y. Šab.* 8 (6c); see Sokoloff 1990: 309, *s.v. mlṭwm*.

[143] *y. Ḥal.* 1:5 (57d); glossing *m. Ḥal.* 1:4.

[144] *y. Šebi.* 7:4 (37c).

[145] *y. Pes.* 4:1 (30d); *y. Moʿed Qaṭ.* 2:5 (81b); cf. *m. Moʿed Qaṭ.* 2:5. For the question of marketing and food preparation cf. *y. Meg.* 1:1 (70b), discussed in Chapter 1.

[146] See, e.g., Lapin 1995: 141–42; Adan Bayewitz 1984: 82–83 for examples.

the former would engage in *pragmateia* and support the latter,[147] and at least one version of this tradition is preceded by a statement attributed to a rabbi supported by his own brother.[148] In addition, a number of rabbis are cast as having engaged in *pragmateia*,[149] or, in one case, as having pretended to be engaged in *pragmateia*.[150] That *pragmateia* presupposes travel over long distances is a regular feature of these traditions (Zebulon, for instance travels on the sea), and this recurs in midrashic traditions mentioning links of *pragmateia* with Syria and with Egypt.[151]

A number of traditions cited above mention cities as the context of *pragmateia*. More importantly, the material raises the possibility of examining attitudes to at least some kinds of commercial activity on the basis of a literature that has its origins and primary referents in the world of cities. Indeed, if the identification of Palestinian rabbis in late antiquity as wealthy urban-dwelling land-owners is correct, the focus on *pragmateia* serves at least to open the question of the degree of commercialized exploitation of that wealth open to such a class of people.[152] For instance, *pragmateia*, in one text, is simply what one does. A passage commenting on the process of life outlines five stages: gestation, birth, "when he is at his prime and goes out to his *pragmateia*," death, and the future age,[153] treats going off for business as what a man does, or perhaps as what a young man of a certain status does upon coming of age. This last possibility is echoed by the parable of a king who wishes to send his fearful son off for *pragmateia*.[154] *Deuteronomy Rabba*, a relatively late text and therefore not dealt with in detail here, has a number of references to *pragmateia*, some of which echo themes already encountered.[155] However, one passage in particular reminds us that we are still talking about an economy (and a class) that valued landed wealth for its great security, for it is a man's land that

---

147 *Gen. Rab.* 72:6, ed. Theodor, Albeck 1912–36: 843; cf. *Lev. Rab.* 25:2, ed. Margaliot 1953–60: 571–2; *Tanh.*, *Wa-yĕḥî* 11.

148 *Lev. Rab.* 25:2, ed. Margaliot 1953–60: 571.

149 *Gen. Rab.* 77:2, ed. Theodor, Albeck 1912–36: 910–1; 100:10, ed. Theodor, Albeck 1912–36: 1205; see also *y. Soṭ.* 9:14 (24b), with the emendation proposed by Lieberman 1929: 83, n. 131 and Sokoloff 1990: 458 *s.v.* *ṣbt*: "Let us engage in *pragmateia* together."

150 *Gen. Rab.* 76:8, ed. Theodor, Albeck 1912–36: 906.

151 *y. Sanh.* 10:9 (29d); *Gen. Rab.* 74:15, ed. Theodor, Albeck 1912–36: 872.

152 Cf., for instance, *Lev. Rab.* 37:2, ed. Margaliot 1953–60: 856–860, a story of how one might be driven into trade by poverty. For rabbis, cities, and wealth, see Lapin 1999, 2000.

153 *Lev. Rab.* 7:4, ed. Margaliot 1953–60: 94–5 and nn.

154 *Lev. Rab.* 25:1, ed. Margaliot 1953–60: 567.

155 E.g., *Deut. Rab.* 2 to 4:25 (a young man goes off for *pragmateia*); 7:5 to Deut. 28:6, ed. Lieberman 1974: 109 (one's "coming in" and "going out" is for *pragmateia*).

supports him if he goes off for *pragmateia* and all his *māmôn* goes down with the ship.[156]

3. Market dependency by consumers

In the same way that market specialization is presupposed in a number rabbinic texts, so is the dependence of consumers on a market. Thus, in a story about the reciprocal visits of Joshua b. Levi and Hiyya, Hiyya gives the disciples of Joshua b. Levi a sum of money and tells them to purchase the customary supplies.[157] The mother of Tanhum b. Hiyya, when she would buy a pound of meat or a bundle of vegetables, would buy an additional pound or bundle for the poor.[158] Zeira is said to have had to submit to a blow (in addition to a high price) when he wanted to buy a pound of meat.[159] A somewhat obscure passage in the Yerushalmi begins with a story about a Sepphorean who "wanted to buy meat and the butcher did not give it to him."[160] Moreover, it is twice said of Samuel b. Isaac that "all he eats is from the marketplace."[161] The notion that people buy food in the market is sufficiently unproblematic that it may be used to illustrate the relations of the Jews and Persians of the biblical book of Esther.[162] Although the discussion involves a sale of one hundred jars of wine, under certain circumstances a seller is able to claim legitimately "I sold it to you for drinking," that is, and not for long-term storage.[163] A string of stories in *Lamentations Rabbati*, set in pre-70 Jerusalem, involve an Athenian in Jerusalem and the wise Jerusalemite boy whom he gives money and asks to bring him something from the market (cheese and eggs, figs, "something that we may eat, and be sated, leave over, and take on the road").[164] The same motif of wisdom expressed through buying something from the market occurs elsewhere as well.[165]

Buying from the marketplace is implicated in distinctions of class and of status. The singling out of Samuel b. Isaac (above) suggests that not everyone in the orbit of rabbinic texts supplied all their day-to-day needs from the marketplace. Hence the distinctiveness of this rabbi's practice in terms of tithes, noted in the same two passages. An anonymous comment on Jacob's order to his sons to go down (*rĕdû*, from the root *yrd*) and buy

---

156 *Deut. Rab.* 2 to 4:41, ed. Lieberman 1974: 58.

157 *Lam. Rab.* 3:17, ed. Buber 1899: 131.

158 *Lev. Rab.* 34:5, ed. Margaliot 1953–60: 781.

159 *y. Ber.* 2 (5c).

160 *y. Šeq.* 7:4 (50c).

161 *y. Dem.* 2:2 (22c); *y. Šab.* 2 (5b).

162 *Est. Rab.* 7:12.

163 *y. B. Bat.* 6:1 (15b).

164 *Lam. Rab.* 1:1, ed. Buber 1899: 49; see also pp. 50–1.

165 E.g., *Lev. Rab.* 33:1, ed. Margaliot 1953–60: 756–8; *Ruth Rab.* 6:2, ed. Lerner 1971: 156.

grain from Egypt states: "From here you may learn that anyone who buys grain from the market is of low status (*yārûd*)."[166] Just why this so is not made explicit. Implicit, however, may be a distinction between those who rely on markets because they can, and those who do so because they must, that is, between people who maintain themselves – at least with basic commodities such as grain – on the rents or direct produce of land or from other sources, and those who cannot support themselves in that way, notably the urban working population.[167] In this context it is interesting to note a story about Hiyya and Simeon b. Halapta on the eve of a festival in Tiberias who heard the sound of people shopping and talking, and Hiyyạ explained that "one who has, buys; and one who does not goes to his employer (*mārê ʿabîdĕtêh*, "the master of his work"), and he gives [money]."[168] The story hardly suggests that only the poor shop in markets, but it does illustrate one way in which market dependency, employment for others, and patterns of indebtedness and patronage may come together for one sector of the population.

C. Conclusions

It is useful to compare the results of the present chapter with the proposed model that was the result of the previous chapter. As a "test" or a "check" on the model, the textual evidence discussed here clearly fails. Nevertheless, it is possible to point, at least in a general way, to texts presupposing hierarchically organized markets, and, more tentatively, to one possible network of markets. Despite this failure, moreover, the textual material is not without interest. First, it confirms – if confirmation were necessary – the role of cities as centers of commercialized activity. A portion of the textual material relating to market specialization and dependency on markets also centers on cities, and it is a reasonable guess that such specialization, and such dependency, would be more prevalent in cities (if only because of a greater degree of concentrated demand).

Second, the material reviewed here is indeed consistent with some degree of marketing in (or centered on, in the example of the *rôkĕlîm* of Kefar Hananiah) non-urban sites. Unfortunately, it is also precisely here that the limitations of the textual evidence become clear. Some sort of

---

166 *Gen. Rab.* 91:6, ed. Theodor, Albeck 1912–36: 1122.

167 Bagnall 1993: 70 discusses the possible size of this sector of the urban population in Egypt.

168 *Ruth Rab.* 3:4, ed. Lerner 1971: 88–90; see also the sequel involving Simeon b. Halapta himself.

marketing likely is based on these examples, but how it was organized and how thickly or thinly spread across the countryside remains unclear.

Third, the second part of this chapter discusses aspects of a marketing system that may shed light on the degree (or limits) of commercialization in northern Palestine in the late Roman period. Here it is important to recall that the texts that we have are all the products of urban populations (including rabbinic texts), and that they therefore have a peculiar vantage point that is not necessarily that of the majority of the region's population. For rabbis, at least, fairs seemed to have posed a question of religious significance. How much they are part of an annual cycle of commercial production is impossible to say. However, rabbis are said to have participated in fairs – at some distance from rabbinic centers in the Galilee. Similarly, some rabbis (although hardly all) are said to have engaged in *pragmateia*, and at least one passage specifies trade in silk at Tyre. As part of a wealthier urban population, rabbis may well have been able to take advantage of a trade in luxury items that involved substantial outlay and risk.

Beyond this, however, rabbis, at least, took for granted that people selling in marketplaces might be specialized. The world of their legal examples and their parables is populated by various kinds of market specialists. Similarly, they appear to assume the dependence of at least some consumers on markets as well as production specifically for market. Once again, it is hard to know how far down the (proposed) hierarchy of settlement and market institutionalization such specialization might go. Yet it seems reasonable to suppose that in the places where rabbis themselves appear to have lived, primarily the cities of Tiberias, Sepphoris, and Caesarea, a fairly highly specialized division of labor, or a high degree of market dependence was sufficiently prominent to be incorporated into rabbinic conceptions of the normal and the everyday. At the same time, some passages may be profitably read as implicating differences of class and status precisely in the level of market specialization or the degree of market dependence.

Chapter 5

Toward a Regional History of Northern Palestine in Late Antiquity

The foregoing discussion made use of a particular theoretical framework, central-place theory, as a tool for constructing a picture – of necessity artificial and static – of the late-Roman economy of Palestine. As noted above, the preceding discussion has as its "present" roughly the fourth century. By this period the road system linking cities was in place, the distribution of cities reached something close to its final form, and, according to the conventional dating of the "Byzantine" period by most Palestinian archaeologists, the number of settlements was approaching its highest level. This is also the period for which there is the greatest temporal overlap between Palestinian rabbinic literature (with its earliest surviving texts the product of perhaps the late-second or early-third century, and the latest Palestinian rabbis mentioned dating to the second half of the fourth century, but in texts whose redaction is in the fifth or sixth century, or even later) and a Christian literature relevant to Palestine (that we can trace back to Julius Africanus and especially Origen in the third century, but which begins in earnest with Eusebius at about the turn of the fourth century), both taken as wholes. The fourth-century focus is thus something of an analytical fiction, but one that defines a "moment" at which a variety of bodies of data can profitably be brought into relation with one another.

Working within the constraints of central-place theory has yielded a number of substantive suggestions that are susceptible to further archaeological, literary, and cross-cultural study. The apparent correlation between built roads and large sites (including, but not limited to, cities), suggested that these very largest sites could have been linked by commercial ties, whatever the original reason for the building of roads (plausibly linked initially to Roman military and administrative concerns[1]) or for the founding or subsequent development of sites, at least sometimes (as in the case of the military camp at Kepar ʿOtnai, later transformed into a city, Legio-Maximianopolis) the product of similar concerns. That city elites in

[1] Isaac 1978, 1992: 107–13; Isaac, Roll 1982: 7–9.

northern Palestine might be more or less commercialized (in the sense of depending upon markets for the provision of their basic subsistence, of engaging themselves in trade-based activities, or of using trade to dispose of surplus agricultural production) is suggested strongly by rabbinic literature, and in a more general way by some of the references in Greek and Latin literature (see Chapter 4). The correlation of large sites with roads also led to the suggestion, in Chapter 3, that we should see the development of lower Galilee on the one hand, and upper Galilee and the Golan on the other as reflecting different, but closely aligned processes, with the latter two regions perhaps developing as "peripheries" to the "core" territory of lower Galilee and the coastal region.

As for the substantially larger number of smaller sites, comprising the majority of the population, Chapter 3 suggested a number of ways in which these villages and other settlements (hamlets, farms, monastic settlements, and so forth) might have been organized with respect to larger, commercialized sites. The discussion there favored reconstructions that see rural producers as oriented to a market system that places them in a disadvantaged situation with respect both to buyers of their surplus or market products and to sellers of those goods that they do not or cannot produce or exchange within the immediate household or village (see Table 3.4 and discussion). Again, and in general, such a picture can be juxtaposed with the relatively few passages that deal explicitly with market periodicity, the presence of services (e.g., moneychangers) in villages and cities, or with the establishment of market prices. Such reconstructions suggest that we should not ask whether rural producers were oriented to markets (as if the market economy of the cities and the rural production of the countryside that fed those cities either were potentially disconnected or connected only by directly "exploitative" links,[2] or were somehow seamlessly and naturally connected[3]), but rather *how* they were oriented to a system built, ultimately, upon their surplus production.

This chapter examines the extent to which these general, static, and ultimately fictive suggestions toward a reconstruction of a later Roman Palestinian economy may help to frame an account of the history of later Roman Palestine. Although the discussion is broken down into section headings on political and administrative, economic, and cultural aspects, part of the argument of this chapter is that these fields are inseparable from one another. The chapter begins with a brief discussion of the political geography of northern Palestine as it became incorporated into a Roman provincial framework, focusing particularly on Galilee (Section A), and then examines select aspects of the economic (Section B) and cultural

---

[2] E.g., Horsley 1996.

[3] E. g., Strange 1997: 41.

(Section C) history of the region within the broader context of this process of provincialization.

A. Political and Administrative

Cities play a substantial role in the various reconstructions suggested above, and, as has been noted a number of times, those cities were also the centers of a Roman imperial administration in its provincial territories. It is worth asking, therefore, how the process of Romanization shaped the regional landscape of northern Palestine.[4] At the risk of vastly oversimplifying the place of ancient Galilee in the wider Roman world, between the first direct intervention by the Romans in the rule of Palestine in 63 B.C.E. and the end of the second century C.E., Galilee shifted from doubly peripheral territory – the periphery of a client kingdom – to core territory, organized as a Roman province around cities and their hinterlands.

At the beginning of this period Palestine itself was on the periphery of the Roman world system (to borrow a set of concepts from Wallerstein[5]), so that much of the territory was, for much of the next 130 years, governed through more or less autonomous and at least sometimes tribute-paying[6] client kingdoms (explicitly so under Herod and his successors). It was only after the death of Agrippa I (44 C.E.) that the entire territory of Herod's kingdom came under direct Roman rule, and even then, Agrippa II was granted the territories of Auranitis, Trachonitis, and Gaulanitis in 53 C.E.[7] Somewhat later, additional territory was assigned to Agrippa, including the toparchies of Tiberias and Tarichaeae on the eastern coast of the Sea of Galilee.[8] Moreover, despite the fact that Josephus stresses the authority of the new governor of Judaea, whom he labels, somewhat anachronistically, a procurator (*epitropos*),[9] the governor of Judaea appears, at least initially, to have been subordinated to the governor of Syria, if only because the latter had several legions under his command and the former only

---

[4] Alcock 1993; Woolf 1998.

[5] Wallerstein 1976; cf., e.g., the applications by Woolf 1988; Alcock 1993: 5; see also Woolf 1998: 27–28.

[6] For the payment of tribute by Herod and his successors see the much debated text of Appian, *Bell. Civ.* 5.75.319, in M. Stern, ed. 1976–84: 2, 186–189, with Stern's comments, Schürer, ed. Vermes *et al.* 1973–87: 1, 416 n. 85; Gabba 1999: 120–121.

[7] Josephus *BJ* 2.247; *Ant.* 20.138.

[8] In Josephus, *BJ* 2.252, Tiberias and Tarichaeae are called "cities with their toparchies"; in *Ant.* 20.159 Julias is called a city; Tiberias and Tarichaeae are not explicitly so called.

[9] Josephus, *BJ* 2.117; *Ant.* 18.2; on *epitropos* see Jones 1960; Schürer, ed. Vermes *et al.*, 1973–87: 1, 358–359.

auxiliaries.[10] Only after the suppression of the revolt against Rome in 70 C.E. was Palestine fully incorporated into the Roman provincial system, governed under a legate from the senatorial order and garrisoned with one, and later two, legions.

Within this political structure Galilee itself was peripheral. The short-lived subdivision attributed by Josephus to Gabinius in 57–55 B.C.E. of the "Jewish" territory (he divided the *ethnos*, "people," into five *synodoi/synedria*, "councils"), suggests that while Judaea proper required – or could support – in addition to Jerusalem at least one additional site (Jericho) within about 22 kilometers of Jerusalem, and possibly a second site within 30 to 40 kilometers (depending upon the identification of "Gadara" or "Gadora" in the relevant passages – Gezer? Adora?), all of Galilee was administered from Sepphoris.[11] Since this arrangement was explicitly understood by Josephus as replacing monarchy with aristocracy, it is reasonable to wonder whether this involved incorporating local elites, instead of a Jerusalem-based aristocracy, into the governance of the various regions. If so, the different treatment of Galilee and Judaea may reflect density of settlement or the size of a suitable ruling class in the two regions. Similarly, if we may take Josephus at least to have gotten the proportions right, when Cassius demanded 700 talents from the Jews/Judaeans

---

[10] Josephus, *Ant.* 17.355; 18.2; see also Tacitus *Ann.* 12.23.1; M. Stern 1976–84: 2, 75–76; Schürer, Vermes, *et al.* 1973–87: 1, 360, n. 35; 362, nn. 42, 43.

[11] Josephus, *BJ* 1.169–70; *Ant.* 14.90–91; Abel 1938: 148 n. 1; Marcus 1943: 494–95, n. d; Schürer, Vermes, *et al.* 1973–87: 1, 268 n. 5; *TIR* 58, *s.v.* Adora. It is worth noting also the descriptions of Palestine in Josephus *BJ* 3.35–58 and Pliny, *Hist. Nat.* 5.70. In both texts an elaborate – and overlapping if differing – administrative subdivision into toparchies is described for Judaea (which extends, in both, as far north as Acrabeta and, in Josephus, as far south as En Gedi), but not given for the other major subdivisions of Palestine (*BJ* 3.51–58 and Pliny, *Hist. Nat.* 5.70; M. Stern 1976–84: 1, 474–78; Schürer, Vermes, *et al.* 1973–87, 2, 190–96; for Galilee see especially 194–5, n. 43). Clearly this does not mean that other regions did not bear further administrative subdivision (particularly since if these lists of toparchies do reflect historical administrative subdivisions, precisely what period they reflect remains problematic; and since elsewhere Josephus does report two toparchies for Galilee: *BJ* 2.252; cf. Avi-Yonah 1962: 62–63; Safrai 1980: 119–21), but it is worth noting that "Idumaea" (excluding En Gedi) is treated by Josephus as a toparchy of Judaea as such. In what appears as a supplement to the description of Judaea proper, but which should perhaps be read as appendix to the description of Palestine as a whole, Josephus describes the territories held by Agrippa II as including Gamala (a region identified as centered on a single site), but also Gaulanitis, Trachonitis, and Auranitis (Josephus, *BJ* 3.59), again fairly large districts not identified by some central administrative site. Precisely because Judaea was the primary territory of both the Hasmonaean kings and of Herod, and, together with Samaria and Idumaea, came under direct Roman rule first, it may have loomed somewhat larger in the eyes of (and there may have been more information available for) first-century writers. But the elaborate description of Judaea proper also may reflect the greater density of governmental presence (and possibly of population) in core territories.

(Judaea in *Antiquities*) in about 43 B.C.E., the portion allocated to Galilee was 100 talents.[12]

Royal foundations also may indicate the peripheral status of Galilee within Judaea (in its larger sense). Herod build cities with Augustan names on the coast (Caesarea) and at Samaria (Sebaste); Jerusalem itself, where his kingdom was centered, saw major projects in the form of the rebuilding of the temple compound.[13] By contrast, Galilee did not see such major building projects. Under Herod Antipas, Herod's son, Sepphoris was fortified and possibly rebuilt, and Tiberias was founded, but at that point Galilee and western Transjordan were the sum total of the territory assigned to Antipas. Both projects, and especially the building of Tiberias, appear to have taken place well into Antipas's reign, postdating the deposition of Archelaus in 6 C.E. and the transfer of the core of Herod's kingdom to direct Roman rule. The fortification of Sepphoris, "the ornament of all Galilee," is placed by Josephus under Antipas after the deposition of Archelaus.[14] Somewhat earlier Josephus reports that after the death of Herod (in 4 B.C.E.) Sepphoris, which had been the site of a revolt, had been burnt and its inhabitants enslaved.[15] The foundation of Tiberias is placed in the *Antiquities* after the notice of the arrival of Pontius Pilate as governor (in 26 C.E.); in the *War* this is placed after the deposition of Archelaus.[16] On numismatic evidence the city's era began between 17 and 20 C.E.[17]

The one hundred and fifty years after the death of Herod (in 4 B.C.E.) saw the transformation of Palestine from client kingdom to fairly conventional province of the Roman empire. This involved the transformation of the area from a sphere of activity for a primarily military presence, centered in Syria, to a more or less self-regulating – although garrisoned – region subdivided into territories attached to nominally autonomous cities with Greek constitutional forms, most notably a council drawn from the local landowning elite.[18] One indication of how this transformation might have been set in motion is the abortive reorganization by Gabinius, the governor of Syria in the mid-first century B.C.E., as this is described by Josephus: the rebuilding and repeopling of cities that (apparently) had had a Greek constitution[19] and, in addition, the subdivision of the territory

---

[12] Josephus, *BJ* 1.220–21; cf. *Ant.* 14.272–74: with no specific amount given for Galilee.

[13] For Herod's foundations see Avi-Yonah 1962: 64–66; Jones 1971: 274–75.

[14] Josephus *Ant.* 18.27.

[15] Josephus *BJ* 2.68; *Ant.* 17.289.

[16] Josephus, *Ant.* 18.36; cf. *BJ* 2.168.

[17] Literature in Schürer, Vermes, *et al.* 1973–87: 2, 179, n. 514.

[18] For comparison see Mitchell 1993: 1, 80–99 for Anatolia; Bowman, Rathbone 1992 for Egypt; Sartre 1991: 335–39 for Syria.

[19] Cf. Isaac 1992: 336–40.

where there had not been such cities – it had been ruled directly from Jerusalem – into regions under the rule of aristocratic councils centered on the major town of the region.[20]

By the measure of urbanization, and the creation of a provincial ruling class, Judaea in general (much less Galilee) does not yet appear to have been well-incorporated into a system of Roman provinces by about 66 C.E. when the revolt against Rome broke out. Indeed, Goodman has argued that the failures of the ruling class in Judaea (particularly Jerusalem) as a Roman provincial elite were one of the primary causes for the outbreak of the revolt itself.[21] Formally autonomous cities of the type just discussed existed at the edges of Galilee, and quite possibly were detached from the administration of the province of Judaea: Ptolemais, Scythopolis, Hippos, and, presumably, the Gaba Philippi known from coins as early as the reign of Claudius and widely identified with Tell Abu Shusha.[22] Of these,

---

20 Josephus, *BJ* 1.166–70; *Ant.* 14.87–91. To the list of rebuilt cities cf. *BJ* 1.155–56; *Ant.* 14.75–76, where Pompey assigns the (Greek) cities (the list overlaps in part with that of Gabinius's refoundation) that had formerly been under Hasmonaean rule to the province of Syria.

21 Goodman 1987.

22 For coins: Rosenberger 1972–77: 2, 43–47; Meshorer 1984: 38, 114; Kindler 1988, which includes a coin from 37/6 B.C.E. with the legend *Gabēnōn*,"of the Gabans" among the coinage of Gaba Philippi. Tel Abu Shusha: *TIR* 126, *s.v.* Gaba Philippi; Siegelman 1984; cf. Dauphin 1998: no. 3.148: el Ḥaritiye. A Gaba is mentioned by Josephus as founded as a settlement for veterans of Herod's cavalry: see Josephus *BJ* 3.36 (adjacent to Carmel); *Ant.* 15.294 (on the "Great Plain"); also *Vita* 115–8; Schürer, Vermes, *et al.* 1973–87: 2, 164, n. 417. A number of problems relate to Gaba that are beyond the scope of the present discussion. (1) The identification of the Gaba founded by Herod (Gaba Hippeon) with the Gaba Philippi known from coins, apparently founded in ca 61–60 B.C.E. (2) The location of Herod's Gaba (a related problem). Gaba Philippi is presumably to be located at Tel Abu Shusha, only a few kilometers northwest of Legio. If Gaba Hippeon is not to be identified with its namesake (Linn 1988 identifies the two; so too Isaac 1992: 328–29; cf. Barag 1988: 8–9), it may perhaps be located at el Ḥaritiye (as did *TIR* 125, *s.v.* Gaba Hippeon, and Maps; the entry in the gazetteer, however, leaves the question open; see Raban 1982: nos. 4, 5). (3) The Gaba known from later sources (Hierocles, *Synecdemus* 720.11, ed. Honigmann 1939: 43; Georgius Cyprius, *Descriptio* 1037, ed. Honigmann 1939: 68; Gelzer 1890: 52; for references to Gaba as episcopal see in the fifth and sixth centuries see *TIR* 126, *s.v.* Gaba Philippi). If it was identical with Gaba Philippi (Barag 1988: 7; Linn 1988: 220), the latter may have lost its urban status, having been replaced by nearby Legio in the late-third or early-fourth century (as argued by Safrai, Linn 1988a: 127), and regained it again by some time in the fifth century. A church has indeed been found at Tel Abu Shusha (Ovadiah 1970: no. 140: dated to the fifth century). But an urban (re-)foundation at Tel Abu Shusha would have meant the existence of two cities and two episcopal sees within about 5 to 7 kilometers of each other. Might the later city have been located someplace else? (4) Pliny *Hist. Nat.* 5.74, 75, mentions two additional sites of similar name: a "tetrarchy" called Gaba in the general vicinity of the Decapolis; and Geba, sited on or near the coast (cf. *TIR* 126, *s.v.* Gaba on the Carmel).

Ptolemais was presumably in the province of Syria,[23] and Scythopolis and Hippos are mentioned by Josephus as cities that Pompey attached to the province of Syria.[24] In the case of Hippos, Josephus states that it had been assigned to Herod, but that after his death it was attached to Syria.[25]

By the end of the second century, lower Galilee had been tranformed into a characteristically Roman provincial territory. It now had at least two cities, Sepphoris and Tiberias, both minting coins under Trajan;[26] these cities were linked to the coast and to other regional cities by built Roman roads. The process of urbanization continued in northern Palestine with the elevation of the former military base at Legio (Kefar ʿOtnai, Caparcotna) into a city (Maximianoupolis) by about 301.[27] From a later period still, we hear of at least two more urban sites: Helenoupolis (named after the mother of Constantine, and probably founded under him) and Gabae. The latter is probably connected with the pre-revolt Gaba and located somewhere on the edge of Galilee (see above n. 22). The location of the former is unclear, but since it is listed on two sixth century lists as in Palaestina Secunda it is likely to be in the general vicinity of Galilee.[28]

Just how this process ultimately took place in Galilee is not entirely clear. Under Antipas, Tiberias minted coins under its own name, apparently the only one of the foundations of Herod's heirs to do so.[29] Josephus' description of his own interaction with the city assumes that it had standard Greek constitutional forms: a council, what appears to be a group of ten "first men" (*dekaprotoi*) and an archon.[30] Moreover, the city bore the name of the emperor Claudius as part of its title,[31] suggesting some sort of grant of status by Claudius (who died in 54), perhaps when Galilee had been transferred to Roman rule after the death of Agrippa I in 44 C.E.

---

23 Abel 1938: 236; Tsafrir 1982: 351; but cf., e.g., Josephus, *BJ* 2.188.

24 Josephus *BJ* 1.155–7; *Ant.* 14.75–4.

25 Josephus *BJ* 1.396; *Ant.* 15.217; *BJ* 2.97; *Ant.* 17.320.

26 Meshorer 1984: nos. 77–83, 87–90; Rosenberger 1972–77: 60–61, 64–65. Note also Josephus' reference to a hippodrome at Tarichaeae, Josephus, *BJ* 2.599; *Vita* 132, a characteristically "urban" structure.

27 For the date: Isaac, Roll 1982: 11. Ptolemy 5.15.3/5.16.4, in M. Stern 1976–84: 2, 167, mentions Kaparkotnei and Julias as *poleis* in Galilee, but it is unclear whether *polis* is used in the sense of juridical city. See above Chapter 4., n. 19.

28 Hierocles, *Synecdemus* 720, ed. Honigmann 1939: 43; Georgius Cyprius, *Descriptio* 1038, ed. Honigmann 1939: 67; ed. Gelzer 1890: 53; literature in Abel 1938: 205; *TIR* 142, *s.v.* Helenoupolis.

29 Meshorer 1997: 200–202; cf. 198–200 (Archelaus); 202–5 (Philip); Rosenberger 1972–77: 3, 64.

30 Council: Josephus *BJ* 2.641; *Vita* 169, and elsewhere; *dekaprotoi*: *Vita* 69, 296; archon: *Vita* 134, 278, 294. Jones 1971: 462 n. 67; Schürer, Vermes, *et al.* 179–80.

31 Meshorer 1984: nos. 77–85; *IGR* I 132 (restored).

If this means that Galilee had been reorganized as an urbanized territory, the process may have begun already in the first half of the first century C.E. However, there is no indication of a Greek civic constitution for Sepphoris in Josephus. Josephus puts into the mouth of Justus of Tiberias the claim that under Antipas himself, and until Tiberias was transferred to Agrippa II (under Nero, 52–68), Sepphoris was subordinate to Tiberias, and it was the latter that served as administrative center of Galilee.[32] The first surviving coins of Sepphoris to have been issued also date to the reign of Nero, but after the outbreak of the revolt.[33] Galilee thus conceivably may have been organized for some time under one city, Tiberias.[34] However, the process of urbanization may not have been fully underway until about the turn of the second century, after the suppression of the revolt against Rome, the upgrading (and garrisoning) of the province, and the reintegration of Agrippa II's western territories into the province of Judaea or possibly later still, after the suppression of the Bar Kokhba revolt.[35] The state of excavations at Tiberias and of their publication make it impossible to evaluate the history of that city.[36] At any rate, it is in this later period that not only Sepphoris but also such northern Palestinian cities as Scythopolis and Caesarea were undergoing major rebuilding and development projects, and these cities all continued to grow into the "Byzantine" period.[37]

One of the dimensions of the process of incorporation of northern Palestine into a provincial framework is the subdivision of the province into urban territories governed, at least in part, through the urban elites of the nominally autonomous cities, primarily a landowning class. By contrast, Herodian Judaea had been governed through toparchies, rather smaller subdivisions generally centered on a large village or town, and the mode of government may have given more space to royal appointment. Our evidence about toparchies in Galilee is far from full,[38] and how they were governed is still less well known. Jones claimed that the structure more or

---

[32] Josephus, *Vita* 37–38.

[33] Cf. Meshorer 1985: 36; 1997: 94–95, 208–209; Rosenberger 1972–77: 3, 61.

[34] Note that Tiberias, upon its transfer to Agrippa II, is described by Josephus as the center of a more restricted administrative district (toparchy) that does not include nearby Tarichaeae (Josephus, *BJ* 2.25; *Ant.* 20.159), not as a city with an extensive "natural" *territorium* attached.

[35] See Eck 1999: 87–88 on the possibility of unrest in Galilee in the Bar Kokhba revolt.

[36] See Hirschfeld 1993a, 1993c.

[37] E.g., Weiss, Netzer 1996a, 1996b; Raban, Holum, eds. 1996: Maps I–III; Foerster 1991; Tsafrir, Foerster 1994, 1997.

[38] Schürer, Vermes, *et al.* 1973–87, 2, 190–96, esp. 194–5, n. 43; cf. Avi-Yonah 1962: 62–63; Safrai 1980: 119–21.

less reproduced that of the Ptolemaic administration of Palestine, so that we could assume that *kōmogrammateis*, "village scribes," were royal appointees who were part of the administration of the villages.[39] Jones (and Avi-Yonah) cited an episode from Josephus, in which two sons of Herod, Aristoboulus and Antigonus, are alleged to want to make *kōmogrammateis* out of the other sons of Herod,[40] but the conclusion that all "village scribes" were therefore royal appointees is not absolutely required by these passages. At any rate, the description of the appointment by Herod Antipas of Agrippa I as market official (*agoranomos*) of Tiberias[41] suggests that a fair proportion of the prominent administrative functions within the territory may have been carried out by royal officials, possibly also related by ties of kinship to the king (whatever their local origins, and wherever they otherwise would have resided), rather than local elites with specifically local claims to authority; and there is at least one hint that the residents of Tiberias may have included royal officials.[42] In the transition from an administration organized around royal toparchies to one based on cities and their territories, a system of rule based, if not on a centralized government (as Jones saw it), then at least on patronage centered on royal (and supra local?) connections, gave way to one based on local elites with its nodal points in cities. The process of provincialization, and with it greater urbanization, thus also reconfigured the local structures of power and patronage by devolving a fair amount of the duties and privileges of office to local elites who might compete to get magistracies when the system worked, or to evade them when it did not.[43]

In accounting for the imperial role in all of this, it is almost certainly wrong to view urbanization as the product of "an imaginary 'State Ministry for Urban Development.'"[44] However, one does not need to argue for a state planning agency to notice the multiple, if rough, correlations between wealth (measured in monumental building), population (measured in size), degree of connectedness with other major sites (measured through roads built and maintained), and juridical status (as city). The apparent doubling in size of Scythopolis in the "Byzantine" period, and the involvement of provincial governors in construction in both Scythopolis and Caesarea (earlier the "capital" of Palestine, later of Palaestina Prima) reflect the

---

[39] Jones 1971: 272–73; Avi-Yonah 1962: 61; cf. Safrai 1995: 250. For the Ptolemaic period see Bagnall 1976: 19 (on komarchs).

[40] Josephus *BJ* 1.479; *Ant.* 16.203.

[41] Josephus *Ant.* 18.149.

[42] Josephus, *Vita* 35; see also Jones 1971: 276 and n. 67, citing Josephus, *Ant.* 18.37 in particular.

[43] See Duncan–Jones 1990: 159–73 (focusing primarily on the western Empire); Garnsey 1974; Jones 1964: 737–63; MacMullen 1988: 47–49.

[44] Isaac 1992: 370.

interconnectedness of political with social and economic processes.[45] To the extent that provincialization and urbanization relied upon, and also structured, a rural, agrarian society, it is reasonable to see cities as, in a sense, the stuff of empire.

B. Economic

The central-place models proposed in Chapter 3 all suggest that villages and the producers who lived in them will have been connected to a system of markets in complex and hierarchically organized ways (Table 3.4). What all of those models shared, despite their different hypothetical reconstructions of the density and distribution of markets, is the assumption that to the extent that peasant production is organized with respect to marketing networks, these hierarchically organized networks centered on *poleis*, cities. By itself, this hardly seems surprising. Sepphoris, apparently the smallest of the inland cities in the western portion of the region covered by this study, is still twice the size of the next largest site – even at the lower estimated size of 400 dunams.[46] At that estimated size, Tiberias (including Hammat Tiberias) and Legio at their largest may each have been twice or more the size of Sepphoris. The disproportionately large size alone will have served to concentrate demand and allow for the development of an internal division of labor and of markets to a higher degree than in a village of, say, 30 dunams.

Quantifiable data about the distribution of wealth both in absolute terms and in terms of its geographical dimensions are lacking for late-antique Palestine. There are, in fact, studies of surveyed land subdivisions, but given the uncertainties about the relationship of such subdivisions to landholdings at any given time, including the time of their construction (would the very smallest holdings – one dunam at Kh. Buraq, according to Dar; between one and three dunams in areas surveyed by Safrai in Galilee – ever have been the sole holding of one producing household?) it is impossible to draw any firm conclusions about land distribution.[47] Comparison with

---

45 Di Segni 1995, 1996; see also 1999; Tsafrir, Foerster 1994: esp. 103; Raban, Holum, eds., 1993: Maps I–III; see also Holum 1996.

46 Weiss, Netzer 1996b: 86; see above Table 3.1.

47 Dar 1986a: 68; Safrai 1985: 129; 1994: 360. Dar's study of western Samaria emphasizes reconstructed average holdings (see e.g., Dar 1986a: 58–76; see also Safrai 1994: 357; cf. Safrai 1985: 128–30). Such an approach flattens out the complexities of land ownership, and with it such questions as patterns of tenancy and the unequal distribution of wealth. If, for instance, at Kh. Buraq the subdivisions were to represent the actual distribution of landholding at one moment in time the owner of the largest plot of arable land (75 dunams; 2.3% of the plots) would have held some 16 percent of the land and the owners of the three largest plots (ranging from about 40 to 75 dunams; 7.1% of plots) would have held between 34 and

Roman Egypt, however, where documentation is more readily available, suggests that we should expect a disproportionate concentration of wealth in the hands of a fairly small number of urbanites, whose holdings may have included a fairly substantial proportion of the land in the villages.[48]

This group of landowners who did not farm their own land themselves (whether that land was exploited through direct management or tenancy is irrelevant at this point) might have had their day-to-day needs met by a number of means, but one of the strategies for meeting them may well have been markets. Moreover, to the extent that the monumental building projects (colonnaded streets, theaters, public baths, temples) needed human labor to carry them out and to maintain the buildings after they were in place, and to the extent that wealthy landowners may have drawn on the services of a more or less wide band of service providers in the form of porters and other laborers, as well as scribes and other professional artisans, cities also may have had a disproportionately large sector of people with little or no land to rely on. That some of these may have depended upon markets for at least some of their basic subsistence needs is suggested by the story of Hiyya and Simeon b. Halapta in Tiberias discussed in Chapter 4.[49] Indeed, markets, in Palestine as elsewhere, made up one of the standard features of both the material landscape of the city and its offices. The management of food supply mediated through markets appears to be one of the major, or at least recurrent, features of urban "commercial" policy.[50]

Of interest here is not whether cities had markets, however, but the extent to which cities, with their at least potentially more sharply

---

36 percent of the land, while nearly 60 percent of plots would have been smaller than the amount of cereal land in Dar's reconstructed "typical" private holding (Dar 1986a: 68–70, 74). Interestingly, the land Dar identifies as vine land ranges less widely in size (and there are more such plots): the smallest plot appears to be 1.5 dunams (no. 128?); the largest no more than about 12.5 (Dar 1986a: 62–63). At least 62 percent of plots (40 or more out of 65) were smaller than the average holding. The range in the size of plots for olive groves was also smaller than for cereal land, but given Dar's estimate of 230 dunams and 24 plots, even here the two largest plots (8.3%) account for between 18 and 25 percent of the land. In this case, all but three of the plots are actually larger than Dar's "typical" holding (Dar 1986a: 65–67). Moreover, Dar's reconstruction (assuming a rather high population density for Kh. Buraq: 40 to 60 people per dunam, with the population organized in 60 to 70 multi-generational kinship units, Dar 1986a: 55, 85–86; Dar 1986b: 140) means that there are fewer plots of arable land (42 plots) or olive land (24 plots, Dar 1986a: 65: the best agricultural land) per household. Given a 30 person per dunam density and a five or six person household, the 25 dunam site supports some 125 households, making the relationship of the distribution of land and village population even more complicated.

48 See Bowman 1985; Bagnall 1992; Rowlandson 1996: 102–18.

49 *Ruth Rab.* 3:4, ed. Lerner 1971: 88–90.

50 See, above, Chapter 3, Section E and de Ligt 1993: 217–24.

developed division of labor and denser concentrations of demand, not only for basic subsistence goods but for luxury or imported goods as well, may have contributed to the reshaping of the entire rural landscape.[51] Once again, it is impossible to separate the administrative aspects of the organization of the rural landscape of Palestine from economic or demographic ones. Roads are a case in point: if Isaac is correct, they were built primarily for administrative and military purposes, and the milestone inscriptions served ideological (and again administrative) purposes.[52] Yet, if roads did not make places accessible to one another in an absolute sense, they presumably did so in a relative way by making travel and transportation easier and by facilitating certain kinds of travel (e.g., with ox carts) – between cities. That roads channeled the way in which people may have moved across the landscape is suggested by the account of the Bordeaux Pilgrim, which regularly gives notice of *mansiones* (hostels) and *mutationes* (changing stations) along the course of travel,[53] and who, in going from the coast at Caesarea to Jerusalem followed along a major Roman road through Legio, Jezreel, and Scythopolis, and then South along the Jordan valley.[54] The route took the pilgrim substantially to the northeast, before turning toward Scythopolis (a point still to the north of Caesarea).[55] It is possible, too, that the route that Jerome describes in connection with the travels of Paula reflects the course of existing roads that made it practical to travel from Sebaste to Nazareth and then (via Sepphoris?) to Cana (whose precise location is unknown), but only upon return from the Sea of Galilee to stop at Mt. Tabor and Nain.[56] From a somewhat earlier period, the Mishnah appears to assume that travel "from Judaea to the Galilee" and "from the Galilee to Judaea" involved going West first (toward Antipatris and Kepar ʿOtnai, later Legio, respectively), again suggesting ways that existing routes shaped the movements of people.[57]

---

[51] Cf. de Neeve 1984; Biddick 1985; Morley 1996.

[52] Isaac 1992: 107–13, 304–9.

[53] Jones 1964: 831–32; Hunt 1982: 54–58.

[54] *It. Burd.* 584–587.1, in Geyer, Cuntz, eds., 1965: 12–13.

[55] See *TIR* 1:250,000 Map, North.

[56] Jerome, *Ep.* 108.13.4–6, ed. Hilberg 1910–18: 55, 322–323; cf. *Ep.* 46.13.2–3, ed. Hilberg 1910–18: 54, 343–344, where if an actual itinerary is intended it appears somewhat garbled. For literature on Cana see *TIR*, pp. 96–97, s.v., Cana. Cf. the course of the Piacenza Pilgrim in the sixth century: Ptolemais, Sepphoris, Cana, Nazareth, Tabor, Tiberias (the text places Neapolis before Tiberias, however), Scythopolis, *It. Plac.* 4–8, ed. Geyer 1965a: 130–33. Theodosius, *de Situ Terrae Sanctae* 4, ed. Geyer 1965b: 116–117 (sixth century?) gives distances to Sepphoris from Caesarea, to both Cana and Nazareth from Sepphoris; and from Nazareth to Tabor, although it is not clear that this reflects an expected route (i.e., with a return to Sepphoris from Cana).

[57] *m. Giṭ.* 7:7.

On the most general level, the relationship between rural landscape and urbanization is fairly clear. The data discussed in Chapter 2 – with all its problems – is sufficient to suggest that urbanization and urban growth coincided with substantial, long-term shifts in the way the population was distributed. This can be explored further in a number of ways. For instance, the results of the survey area of Gazit appeared to show that marginal land came to be occupied (and presumably brought under cultivation) in the Roman, and particularly in the Byzantine periods.[58] Notably, a large proportion of these sites are quite small (the median of sites with sizes reported and with occupation in the Byzantine period was between 3 and 4.2 dunams, Tables 2.1, 2.2; see also the results of the 'En Dor area, Table 2.3). Again in the Nahalal area there were a number of sites that were quite small, including a few sites identified as "farms" that appear to have been settled only in the Byzantine period (see Table 2.5).[59] These two observations fit in general terms with Portugali's claim for the western Jezreel valley that an increase in small sites matched a decline in middle sized sites,[60] although it does not necessarily follow that all of northern Palestine as a whole saw a decline in the Byzantine period as Portugali suggests for the western Jezreel valley.

It goes beyond the evidence collected here to argue that these changes can be correlated only with urbanization and Romanization.[61] Nevertheless, there are reasons to consider this connection further. The western Jezreel valley is potentially exploitable for intensive forms of agriculture not necessarily practicable in the hill country of Galilee. Indeed, it has been argued that precisely during this period the site on Tel Abu Shusha (a large local site and a Roman-period – and perhaps Byzantine-period – city) developed installations for processing flax.[62] So it is at least possible that the changing settlement patterns related to changing patterns of production,

---

58 Gal 1991.

59 Raban 1982.

60 Portugali 1986.

61 Cf., for the Hauran, Villeneuve 1985: 75, 126–7 who places the beginnings of some of the developments analogous to those mentioned here (e.g., the spread of villages, and apparent population growth; the bringing of more land under cultivation) in the first century B.C.E.; Sartre 1985: 193 on the impact of the rule of Herod and his successors on the distribution of settlements in some portions of the Hauran; Sartre 1991: 320, 330 n.3, and 344–47 for the process of urbanization in Syria more generally. See also MacAdam 1986: 47–90. In northern Palestine, too, it may well be that the processes described here under the rubric of Romanization saw their beginnings under Herodian rule. Note, however, the suggestion of Grainger 1995: 191 that direct Roman intervention in the area of the Hauran in the middle third century had "triggered off an economic boom, which manifests itself to us (in inscriptions) as a great expansion of building," and for Syria more generally Tate 1997: 58–59, 64.

62 Safrai, Linn 1988a: 130–135, 140 dating much of the evidence to the fifth century.

that are in turn related to (but not necessarily driven by, in a directed, top-down process[63]) connections with towns and production for marketing or processing in towns. Similarly, Raban reports a number of groups of winepresses close to Tel Shimron (a fairly large site, also near the road) just along the Roman built road connecting Sepphoris and Legio.[64] The presses are not, unfortunately, in explicit association with a village or farm. Here it is worth remembering Mattingly's observation that one does not need constructed presses to make oil or wine; they rather reflect an intensity of production.[65] The density of presses here (it is unclear from the diagrams just how many there were) suggests production on a large scale, perhaps to be connected with an estate. Elsewhere, in upper Galilee, Avi'am reported a cluster of eight wine presses on a hill near Ma'alot (map ref. 17592691), in a region where wine presses are apparently rare.[66] Similarly, the farmstead at Deir Samʿan (map reference 15501639) in western Samaria, which Dar connected with military oversight of the region, but which, in addition, could produce large amounts of wine, and possibly flax or wool as well, and which is not far from a Roman road, could afford another example of the presence of small sites with production capacities large enough and specialized enough to presuppose consumption of at least some of the product off the site itself.[67]

To the extent that it is possible to identify some regional specialization in produce, it seems reasonable to associate this with the development of a political economy dominated by an urbanized, commercialized sector of the population as well. It is worth recalling that none of the *Archaeological Survey of Israel* areas discussed in Chapter 2 show clear signs of such specialization. Other areas, however, may. Based on the catalog of sites compiled by Dauphin, one area, on the western hills of lower Galilee that meet the Plain of Akko (the 10 km by 10 km square just to the North of the Nahalal area surveyed by Raban) had more than twenty sites, typically with late Roman or Byzantine pottery, where remains of winepresses were found, in one case as many as thirteen presses associated with a single map reference.[68] Here, the general proximity to two Roman roads in the vicinity, as well as to Sepphoris and to the coastal plain South and East of

---

63 Cf. Sawicki 1997.

64 Raban 1982: no. 82 and p. 69 (diagrams); map reference 16992356; no. 33 in Map 4 (see Chapter 2). The road runs laong the eastern edge of that survey area; note the clustering of sites along that eastern edge.

65 Mattingly 1988b: 157; also Morley 1996: 117.

66 Avi'am forthcoming.

67 Dar 1986: 30–31; also Applebaum 1989: 97–110.

68 Dauphin 1998: nos. 3.18, 3.19, 3.23, 3.28, 3.31, 3.32, 3.38, 3.40, 3.41, 3.46, 3.47, 3.48, 3.51, 3.58, 3.59, 3.62, 3.65, 3.95, 3.108, 3.109, 3.111, 3.112 (the site with thirteen presses). See also Usha, Dauphin 1998: no. 3.68; Yeivin 1971: 207. In most cases, there is

Ptolemais make cities a likely destination for wine production. Avi'am correlated the large number and the density of oil presses in upper Galilee with the development of an agricultural regime producing oil for consumption elsewhere (he suggests Syria).[69] At least in those areas discussed by Avi'am in which the occurrence of oil presses is high, their density appears to be comparable to oil-exporting regions reviewed by Mattingly.[70] For the area of the "lower Golan" (that section of the western Golan opposite upper Galilee) Ben David has argued that olive production was particularly intense (with a production capacity four times that of local consumption), partly as a result of the scarcity of arable land, and that the population depended on trade in olive oil for its existence.[71] Given the limits of present evidence it is impossible to connect olive oil production in upper Galilee or the Golan direclty with urbanization in the region,[72] but the likelihood of sheer concentration of demand in cities and the utility of cities as nodal points for further redistribution should not be forgotten. What all of this suggests is the possibility of a certain amount of regional economic integration mediated through cities. In or near cities both landowners and local farmers could shed the production of at least some staples in favor of producing goods for an urban market or for external trade, because they could rely on a wider source of supply for those staples. In addition, relatively peripheral areas (e.g., the Golan) might develop as already tied to consumption or trade patterns centered on cities, whether their produce was sold by freeholding farmers, transported as rents to urban-based landowners, or produced, stored, and marketed by such landowners through directly managed estates.

The region studied by Frankel and Getzov suggests analogous processes, although in this case with different timing. As noted in Chapter 2, the archaeologists found that the southern and eastern section of their survey area, particularly on the highland plateau on the western reaches of upper Galilee, was settled with a number of Roman-period settlements that were not occupied in the Byzantine period, two of which, at least, they identify

---

no bibliography given for these sites, the data apparently coming from the Archaeological Survey archives; the northern and eastern boundaries of the survey responsible for the data are visible in Dauphin maps, Figures 7 and 23.

69 Avi'am forthcoming.

70 Mattingly 1988a.

71 H. Ben David 1998: 37 fig. 36; and 46–53.

72 H. Ben David 1998: 53 suggested the villages of the Hauran as the trading partners, but his discussion explicitly connects the development of the Hauran with a provincial political economy in the province of Arabia. For the Hauran itself see Villeneuve 1985: 126–127, who discusses the possibility of specialized wine production in the Jebel; with the absence of presses elsewhere in the Hauran, and the apparent absence of oil presses throughout the region.

as farm settlements of some kind.[73] In addition, "[o]ther hillcountry sites [presumably, without datable pottery retrieved in survey] in the surveyed area were also square in plan and should probably also be related to the Roman period."[74] Although they mention the possibility that the rise of these settlements is to be associated with the movement of Jews from Judaea in the wake of the revolt that began in 66 C.E., they appear to favor an explanation for these settlements that links this territory to Ptolemais (some 15 to 20 km away as the crow flies), and more specifically to the elevation of Ptolemais to the status of a *colonia*, apparently late in Claudius' reign[75] and to the settlement of military veterans in the territory of Ptolemais,[76] although specific evidence for either of these factors precisely in the area discussed by Frankel and Getzov is lacking.[77]

Frankel and Getzov connect these sites with the extensive area of land subdivisions on the plateaus, whose construction they also date, by association rather than on direct evidence, to the Roman period.[78] Thus if their explanation is correct, not only settlement but in fact the contours of agriculture and landscape in the countryside are linked with cities, and in this case also with Roman military and administrative concerns mediated, again, through a city.[79] The disappearance of these sites by the Byzantine period need not mean that the land was no longer worked (note that based on a preliminary report the area immediately to the South of this portion of the Akhziv/Ḥanita survey does not show the same pattern of disappearance[80]). The disappearance of these settlements might instead reflect a reorganization of settlement (with villages replacing farmsteads?). In any case the area just to the West appears to have more settlements dated to the Byzantine period than to the Roman.[81] If the area did go out of agricultural use, however, it is possible that these sites were producing for

---

[73] Frankel, Getzov 1997: nos. 2.125, Kh. Zabdi; 2.129, Kh. Juʿarran.

[74] Frankel, Getzov 1997: 34, 34* English section, quoted from English.

[75] See Pliny *Hist. Nat.* 5.76; and *Digest* 50.15.1.3 (Ulpian).

[76] See, e.g., Meshorer 1984: no. 2; Avi-Yonah 1946: 85–86; note the involvement of villages in the dedication.

[77] Frankel, Getzov 1997: 35, 35*, English section; cf. Applebaum 1989: 70–97; Schürer, Vermes *et al.* 1973–87: 125; Isaac 1992: 322–23; Millar 1993: 65–66.

[78] Frankel, Getzov 1997 34–35, 42; 34*–35*, 40*–41*, English section.

[79] Frankel, Getzov 1997: 35, 35* English section, imply that the subdivisions are connected with the settlements of veterans in the hill country. The implication is stronger in the Hebrew text. If Applebaum's reconstruction is correct, centuriation and assignment of territory will have taken place on the coastal plain, and the hill country would have been left in the hands of the original ("Jewish") inhabitants, Applebaum 1989: 81, 87–89.

[80] Frankel 1986. By my count, the area between map reference 16402660 and 17002700 there were something like two Hellenistic, five Roman and eight Byzantine sites, and four of the five Roman sites continued into the Byzantine.

[81] Cf. Frankel, Getzov 1997: 231–232 and Map 5.

markets on the coast that either contracted (the "crisis of the third century") or shifted their sources of supply, undermining the viability of the settlements. Like the Ager Cosanus and Campania in Italy in the first and second centuries as described by Morley, the areas further inland may have been insulated by their greater difficulty of access, and their correspondingly smaller reliance on market-based production.[82] The question of the settlements, the land subdivisions, and their connection to the coast also may be related to the apparent decrease in settlement size in this area over a West to East gradient (see above Chapter 3) as one moves toward western Galilee from the coastal plain. This phenomenon is matched roughly by the region immediately to the South, also surveyed by Frankel, but not as fully published,[83] and it is at least partly, but not necessarily entirely, to be explained by topography.

The purpose or function of the land subdivisions discussed by Frankel and Getzov cannot be resolved here. The dating that they favor for these subdivisions, if it is correct, makes impossible a specific association between the taxation reform associated with Diocletian – one that did involve attested land surveying in the region of Palestine.[84] Nevertheless, some system of taxation, perhaps organized through individual villages or village groups, may explain both the phenomenon itself and the local character of such subdivisions (as argued by Safrai), without requiring the assumption of autonomous Jewish local, regional, or national government carrying out land reforms.[85]

Turning now to another kind of evidence, the mosaic inscription from the floor of the synagogue from Rehob, near Bet Shean, is effectively the earliest preserved rabbinic text, and it offers some insight into the rabbinic construction of an economic and ritual landscape. Rabbinic legal texts considered laws relating to agricultural produce (such as the sabbatical year) fully applicable in the juridical "land of Israel," defined both through territorial boundaries and as land that was presumed to be (or to have been, depending on what one took to be the consequences of "gentile" acquisition of land in the "land of Israel") in the possession of Jews. Hence, a number of rabbinic texts, and in particular the ones in the Rehob inscription, are interested in territorial questions. At issue in the following selections is the assumption that the cities of Scythopolis (Bet Shean), Caesarea,

---

82 Morley 1996: 130–35.

83 See Frankel 1986.

84 See Millar 1993: 193–197 and App. A. See also the references to surveyors in the post-reform registration of property from Karanis in Egypt: *P. Cair. Isid.* 3, 4, 5.

85 Cf. Safrai 1995: 141–53, with additional examples of land subdivisions. Cf. Villeneuve 1985: 123, 126–128, and the figures cited there. Fig. 2 is significant for the different strategies of land subdivision (including both the results of regularized land survey – presumably attached to Bostra – and more *ad hoc* strategies).

and Caesarea Philippi (Paneas),[86] although ostensibly within the "land of Israel," had been deemed "permitted" (i.e., not subject in general to agricultural rules). However, some of the produce available in those cities was thought to come from areas where such restrictions continued to apply.[87]

i. Bet Shean (ll. 1–5):

> These [types of] produce are prohibited at Bet Shean in the sabbatical year, and during the rest of the sabbatical cycle (*šabuʿa*) they are tithed as produce deemed uncertainly tithed (*dĕmaî*): chate melons (?); melons; squash; carrots; mint that is bound by itself; Egyptian beans that are bound *bšyph* (?); leek heads – from *ʿaṣeret* [88] to Hanukkah [ca. December]; seeds [that are eaten as such[89]]; black cumin; sesame; mustard; rice; cumin; dry lupines; large peas that are sold by the measure; garlic; onion grown locally

---

[86] For "exemptions" for Scythopolis and Caesarea see *y. Dem.* 2:1 (22c).

[87] The citations are from the inscription rather than from the corresponding passages at *y. Dem.* 2:1 (22c). For the relationship with the Yerushalmi see Sussman 1973–74, 1975–76; Lieberman 1975–6; Feliks 1980–86: 2, 447–56. I have been aided in the translations below by those works and by Payne Smith 1903; Jastrow 1886–1903; Löw 1881; 1923–34; Sarason 1993; Wewers, Hüttenmeister 1995; and the unattributed translation (by Sussman?) in Levine, ed. 1981: 152–53. Lines 1–5 in particular have been treated by Feliks 1980–86: 2, 451–4. However, the translations are no more than approximate, and I make no claim to an independent contribution to botanical terminology.

A problem raised by the inscription from Rehob and the analogous texts from the Yerushalmi has to do with the description of the extent of the "permitted" area in Bet Shean and Caesarea (ll. 5–9, 25–26; both *y. Dem.* 2:1 [22c]). Since the passages from the inscription cited below appear to focus primarily on produce in Scythopolis, Caesarea, and Paneas themselves (as opposed to "within the boundaries of ..." in other sections of the inscription, ll. 9, 10, 11, 26–7; cf. *t. Šebi* 4:8–10; *y. Dem.* 2:1 [22c–d]), I am inclined to follow Sussman (Sussman 1973–74: 133) and to see the descriptions of the areas where the exemptions apply as referring more or less to the built up city area, although extending outside of the walls, both of whose "Byzantine" area extends beyond the Roman period walls. Thus the Bet Shean territory is organized by direction, and by city gate: "These are the permitted places in the vicinity of Bet Shean: from the South, which is the gate of the plain (*pîlî dĕ-qampôn*), until the 'white field'..." (l. 6). The end of the description, which describe gates leading out to two additional areas (ll. 8–9), seems to support this (cf. Safrai 1984b: 1113, 1116). The description of Caesarea is somewhat more difficult to read in this way, because it apparently refers to at least one site some distance away: Dor. However, even here we can, on analogy with the Yerushami's text ("the inn of Ammuda [or: "the pillar"], and the inn of Tibata/Tabita," *y. Dem.* 2:1 [22c], for variants see Schäfer, Becker 1991–: I/3–5 22–23), read in the inscription: "the inn of Tabita and [of] Ammuda and [of] Dor," and refer these to inns near the city itself on the road out towards these other places (but cf. Sussman 1973–74: 134–5 and n. 333). Alternatively, these passages describe the territory around the city that is presumed to supply the city with the permitted produce (whereas the prohibited produce comes from outside this restricted range and is deemed to have been produced on land possessed by Jews, see Safrai 1984b: 1110).

[88] I.e., Shabuʿot, early summer; cf. Sarason 1993: 70: end of Sukkot, autumn.

[89] According to Feliks 1980–7: 451 and n. 18 this serves as a topic heading for the following.

> (*bĕnê ha-mĕdînâ*) that are sold by the measure; bulbous onions (?); Ephes (?) dates; wine; and oil. [These are deemed as] of sabbatical status during the sabbatical year, and as uncertainly tithed produce [during the other years] of the sabbatical cycle. And bread is always subject to the priest's portion (*ḥallâ*).

ii. Paneas (ll. 18–22):

> These [types of] produce are prohibited at Paneas in the sabbatical year and in the other years of the sabbatical cycle are tithed fully (?) as uncertainly tithed produce: rice; nuts; sesame; Egyptian beans; some say even early ripening *ʾḥwnywt*[90]; lo, these are [deemed as] of sabbatical status during the sabbatical year, and [during the other years] of the sabbatical cycle are tithed as definitely untithed produce (*wādaî*), and even [if it comes?] from upper Tarnogala (?) and outward.

iii. Caesarea (ll. 22–25):

> These [types of] produce are tithed as uncertainly tithed produce in Caesarea: wheat (and bread is always [liable to the offering of] *ḥallâ*); wine; oil; dates; rice; cumin; lo, these are permitted on the sabbatical year at Caesarea, and during the other years of the sabbatical cycle are prepared as uncertainly tithed produce (*mittaqĕnîm dĕmaî*). And some prohibit white bulbous onions that come from *Har ʾha-melek*.

The legal issue of *dĕmaî* (i.e., produce whose status as tithed is doubtful),[91] is particularly connected with purchase of produce. Hence the concern in the present passages to identify how things are sold, or to specify how one might encounter certain varieties (e.g., by how they are bound). Marketing also underlies the way in which the analogous passages are handled in the Palestinian Talmud. For example, the statement at the end of the list pertaining to Caesarea (iii. above) that "some prohibit white bulbous onions" apparently derives from the following comments in the Yerushalmi: "R. Abbahu said in the name of R. Yose b. Hanina: 'Bulbous onions that are sold in the marketplace, lo, these are prohibited [during the sabbatical year as produce grown in the "land of Israel"], for most of them come from *Har ha-melek*.' R. Hiyya b. Ada said: '[This concerns] white [varieties]'; the sages of Caesarea said: '[This concerns] red [varieties].'"[92] Similarly, after quoting a version of the list of produce connected with Bet Shean (i.), the Yerushalmi explains a dispute by stating: "They do not disagree. What R. Yonah said – [that] they are doubtfully tithed – concerns one purchasing from the vegetable market; what R. Yose said – [that] they are certainly untithed – concerns one purchasing from the garden."[93]

---

[90] See Sussman 1973: 130, n. 296: a type of date or plum.

[91] The produce must be tithed, and a tithe of the tithe given to the priest; but the tithe itself is not given to the levite. For legal summary see Maimonides, *Laws of Tithing*, 9:1–2.

[92] *y. Dem.* 2:1 (22c).

[93] *y. Dem.* 2:1 (22c), with Lieberman 1975–76: 61–62: "vegetable market" corresponds to a term read as a transcription of the Greek *lakhanikē* (*plateia*).

This last passage distinguishes two strategies of acquiring produce: directly from the garden [i.e., presumably, directly from the producer], and in the city markets. A similar distinction between buying from a particular producer and buying in the marketplace underlies the talmudic discussion of the justification for exempting Scythopolis in the first place (and is presupposed by this inscription): "R. Zeira [said in the name of] R. Hiyya b. Abba in the name of R. Yohanan: 'Rabbi [Judah the Patriarch] permitted Bet Shean on the word of R. Joshua b. Ziruz son of the father-in-law of R. Meir, who said: "I saw R. Meir buying produce from the garden [i.e. directly from the producer] during the sabbatical year, and he [Judah] permitted the entire [city].""' The justification is, in context, thought to be at least partially specious since the same Zeira is said to comment immediately afterward: "This means [that] one may not do something (?) in public, for I say: that particular garden was set aside for him, but he [Judah the Patriarch] permitted the entire [city]."[94] That is, the earlier rabbi (Meir) would presumably buy only from a permitted field (permitted because it was deemed never – or at least not currently – to have been in Jewish possession), but his public practice was leveraged into general permission.

Whether buying for consumption directly from specific fields (mentioned also in connection with Joshua b. Levi[95]), presumably directly from the producer, is treated within this complex of texts as a general mode of acquiring produce or the specific practice of pious elites who take elaborate steps to acquire permitted produce for themselves is not clear from the present context in the Palestinian Talmud. In either case, but particularly if buying from specific producers is a generalized practice, these passages suggest strategies available to elites for supplying agricultural products through purchase but without resorting to a marketplace, a factor that ought to be kept in mind in assessing the extent of markets, and the dependence of urban markets on a rural market network (cf. Chapter 4). At any rate, what does seem clear, and underlies the lists of produce cited above, is that in general the lists of produce refer to produce available in the city markets.

If that is correct, these lists make claims to a fairly detailed knowledge about the produce available for sale in three cities in Palestine, and how these cities were supplied. That by itself ought not to be taken for granted, since it underscores just how well embedded in their cultural and political context – at least when it also suited their ritual or theoretical concerns – rabbis, as a provincial population, may have been. Moreover, and this is the primary reason for the rather lengthy excursus on this inscription here, it suggests that, at least from the perspective of these authors, the city

94 *y. Dem.* 2:1 (22c), reading Hiyya b. Abba and *wĕ-hittîr* with the Vatican ms., see also Sirillo mss.: Schäfer, Becker 1991–: I/3–5, 22–23.

95 *y. Dem.* 2:1 (22c); *y. Šebi.* 9:9 (39a).

markets themselves may have drawn on an area wider than the immediate hinterland of the cities themselves. If we start with two assumptions, (1) that the land immediately surrounding the cities will have been owned overwhelmingly by its inhabitants (and these will have been, for the texts we are considering, "gentile," hence exempt from tithing and sabbatical year restrictions), and (2) that the diet of most inhabitants will have included varying proportions of most of the same types of agricultural produce (cereals, wine, olive oil, and a variety of fruits and vegetables), it will be clear that for the authors of these lists all three cities drew at least some of these supplies from territory outside their immediate environs. Furthermore, they did so in three different ways: Caesarea "importing" wheat, wine, and oil; Scythopolis, oil and wine; and Paneas none of these three.

Rabbis register their interest here because of the presumption that the produce derives from areas where the agricultural restrictions do apply.[96] Some sense of the possible range may be given by the inclusion of bulbous onions among prohibited produce at Caesarea on the assumption that they derive from *Har ha-melek*, which Avi-Yonah identified as the hill country around Jerusalem.[97] Just how this produce was thought to make its way from the countryside into the marketplace is not specified in the lists of produce. Whether this is to be explained, for instance, through production for sale in cities by directly managed estates, through rent paid in kind by tenants, or through production and marketing of surpluses by peasant farmers mediated by marketplaces or market professionals, it seems reasonable to see in this complex of texts an attestation of the way in which rural production may have been structured by urban markets. A passage in

---

[96] See Safrai 1984b: 1116–17, whose reconstruction sees "Jewish" territory encroaching quite closely upon Bet Shean itself.

[97] Avi-Yonah 1962: 62; Schürer, Vermes, *et al.* 1973–87: 2, 191; see also Feliks 1980–86: 2, 246. The mention of *Har ha-melek* underscores the dangers of translating the various traditions brought together in the inscription into a demographic history of Palestine. Even assuming that claims about what was "once" Jewish territory correspond to areas predominantly owned or controlled by Jews, neither the inscription nor the rabbinic texts upon which it is based need be thought to be referring to a present day ownership or control. Thus, at least two traditions about *Har ha-melek* from the Yerushalmi mention the presumption that gentiles predominate: an abortive attempt to deem the territory "exempt" (i.e., "gentile") (*y. Dem.* 5:9 [24d]); and a question posed by a rabbinic landowner who owned fields in *Har ha-melek* about whether he was permitted to lease to gentile tenants is given in explication of the problem of "a place where Israelites are not to be found" (*y. Dem.* 6:1 [25a], cf. *y. ʿAb. Zar.* 1:9 [40b]) (see Alon 1953–57: 99, 246). Here it is plausible that the rural population was indeed now largely "gentile" (despite the possibility of some Jewish landowners) but the territory retained its status, at least for the authors of the texts. Both the definitions of the "land of Israel" as that which was "taken possession of by the returnees from Babylon" (e.g., *m. Šebi.* 1:1), and the "exemptions" from it are ideological constructs.

the Tosepta on a related legal issue rules that "all the villages (*ʿayārôt*) of the Samaritans along the road," are assumed to draw grains and legumes that are sold there from *Har ha-melek*, but other produce available there would appear to be either local or from other "gentile" territory.[98] The rule is presented as the revision of an earlier one on the status of produce sold in three places in the western hill country (Patros, Hayyeshub [?] if correctly read) or on the coastal plain (Antipatris), and follows on a rule about purchasing "from the ship" at Joppa or Caesarea. It therefore seems reasonable to ask whether, in the case of "all the villages of the Samaritans," it is proximity to "the road," and concentrated demand in coastal urban markets such as Caesarea that might structure the patterns of supply in rural market-bearing villages, whatever the means (market or non-market) through which the produce made its way into these markets.

Another complex of material that appears in the inscription may also refer to rural market centers: the lists of "forbidden" (or in one case, "doubtful") villages (i.e., deemed as having come into the possession of Jews) within "permitted" (i.e., gentile) territories,[99] or "permitted" villages in an apparently "prohibited" territory.[100] "Permitted" and "prohibited" here are shorthand for liability of produce to tithing before consumption and to the prohibition of working lands during the sabbatical year (cf. lines 12–13 in the inscription: "And (?) all [i.e., land?] that Israelites have acquired becomes prohibited"). These lists of villages, too, are organized by cities – a measure of the way in which the Roman administrative construction of space was appropriated by rabbis for their own purposes. Nine villages in the territory of Tyre, a similar number in the territory of Hippos, and eleven in the territory of Nawa in Batanaea (Bashan, within the former territory of Herod's kingdom[101]) are "prohibited." The "permitted" villages in the territory of Sebaste number nineteen.

Given the present connection, in both the Yerushalmi and the inscription, with the lists of produce liable to laws of tithing, it might be argued in the case of the enumerated villages too, that what is at stake is that produce for sale in "prohibited" or "permitted" villages was drawn from a supply area that included "Jewish" or "gentile" territory respectively. Indeed, Demsky has suggested that the list of villages of Sebaste is organized around routes that Jews might have traveled between Galilee and Judaea, where they might have bought produce (on analogy with the

---

98 *t. Dem.* 1:11; cf. 5:24; see Chapter 4, Section A.2, and n. 60.

99 Lines 9–13, cf. *t. Šebi.* 4:8–10; *y. Dem.* 2:1 (22c–d).

100 Lines 26–29 (villages in the area of Sebaste), no rabbinic parallel; "permitted" is based on a correction.

101 Note Eusebius, *Onomastikon* ed. Klostermann 1904: 136.2–3 on a "city of the Jews" called Nineveh in the corner (?) of Arabia.

tradition of "villages of Samaritans along the road" mentioned above).[102] In that case, the lists of villages in the Rehob inscription may offer a check on the scale of market distribution. The models presented in Chapter 3 (see Table 3.4) were worked out with an eye to the settlement density of lower Galilee and the Bet Shean valley, not the areas covered in these lists, but these suggested that we might expect no more than some eleven to thirty-five rural markets per city. The list of "permitted" and "prohibited" villages in the territory of Sebaste numbers as high as nineteen, and should imply a non-negligible number of additional villages that do not fall into the specified category (otherwise, why list these?). If the listed villages are market-bearing, the lists favor reconstructions that involve higher rather than lower distributions of rural markets.

Such a reading of these lists is far from certain, however. Versions of the lists of prohibited villages in lines 9–13 of the inscription appear in the Tosepta in a context that does not require taking them as concerned specifically with marketing, and it may be safer, on balance, to see these lists as merely specifying enclave villages deemed at some point to have been "Jewish" or "gentile," within a territory assumed to be populated by others (much as the *Onomastikon* of Eusebius occasionally and in a very different idiom specifies the "ethnic" makeup of the villages). Moreover, based on the suggested identifications of the villages (in some cases quite speculative) the sites seem to form a loose horseshoe, or perhaps a circle, of sites in close proximity to one another (and to that extent fit with a picture of a regional ethnic enclave),[103] but in some cases to be located closer to one another than one might expect for viable lower-level markets.

C. Cultural

The preceding sections have argued that the economic landscapes of northern Palestine – in terms of patterns of production, and in terms of possible marketing patterns – and the political and administrative landscapes were closely interconnected. The point bears repeating precisely because the

---

102 Demsky 1979: 184–185.

103 Lieberman 1975–76: 58–59, somewhat tentatively took the list of permitted villages in the territory of Sebaste (with no parallel in extant rabbinic texts) as referring to an unspecified group of "exempt" villages mentioned in *y. Šebi.* 6:1 (36c), perhaps located in a particular area. See also Sussman 1973–74: 136–137. For identifications see: Sussman 1973–74: 137–138; Safrai 1977: 1–12, 23; Demsky 1979: 188–92. See also: *TIR* p. 78, s.v. Belemoth; pp. 113–114, s.v. Dothaim; p. 152, s.v. Iezeth; p. 163, Kefar Kasdaya; p. 166, s.v. Kefar Yudith; p. 170, s.v. Leviya; p. 184, s.v. Merrus; p. 200, Pardesliya; p. 201, s.v. Pentakomia; p. 219, s.v. Salaba; p. 230, s.v. Shephirin; p. 231, sv. Shilta; pp. 262–263, s.v Ẓir.

distinction between town and country sometimes is essentialized and reified too easily. On one conventional analysis, the city "is," for instance, the locus of a pagan, graeco-roman, elite culture that sits at the edge of a gap on the other side of which resides "the" autonomous, rural, local, indigenous culture, a gap bridged only by practices and relationships that are ultimately exploitative. There are, of course, good analytical reasons to address the very real gap (a "non-relationship" as Brown described it) that may have existed between rural and urban cultures, particularly, as in the case of a now classic essay by Peter Brown on late antique Syria, where the goal is to assess how the terms in which the "village" and the "town" related to one another may have been transformed in late antiquity.[104] Such a view can be used to underwrite particular kinds of ethnic histories, especially in Palestine, such as Horsley's attempt to view the Jesus movement as an authentic northern Israelite revitalization movement marking cultural resistance to Roman imperialism and to its Judaean carriers and enforcers; or such as Safrai's attempt to describe the workings of an autonomous Jewish society organized through local, regional, and national structures, separate from a Roman imperial government and a pagan, urban society.[105] One of the very real dangers of such a view, however, is that it does not give sufficient attention to the ways in which both the "rural" and the "urban" have been shaped by the same complex history. The material on settlement patterns discussed in Chapter 2, and reviewed in the previous section, suggests that at least in northern Palestine rural peasantries did not, any more than did urban aristocracies, simply exist; they were made and remade in complex and historically contingent ways.[106] Without denying the reasonableness of historiographic attempts to trace the "trajectory" of a particular social or cultural formation (e.g., of "the Jews"), it seems equally necessary to remember that that formation is not simply "there" to "respond" to an "external" force (e.g., Roman imperialism; pagan cities; graeco-roman culture), but is rather in some very basic ways the product of the same historical processes that produced the local manifestations (e.g., these particular cities, within a given set of provincial boundaries, caught up in a specific web of economic and other relationships with rural settlements and groups of different kinds) of that "external" force.[107]

These considerations underlie the following discussion, which focuses more narrowly on examples in which aspects of Palestinian history may be further analyzed in terms of a provincial landscape that binds together

---

104 Brown 1982: 153–65; see also Mitchell 1993: 1, 195–7 for the relative separation rural and urban spheres in Roman period Anatolia.

105 Horsley 1996; cf. Reed 1999; 2000: 23–61. Safrai 1995; see also, e.g., Applebaum 1989: 92–94.

106 Sawicki 1997, with a rather different approach from that taken here.

107 See, e.g., Roseberry, O'Brien 1991.

villages and cities within a Roman provincial political economy. A fairly straightforward example has already been dealt with in the preceding section: the texts that appear in the inscription at Rehob. Here we have a group of texts that circulated in Hebrew for "local" consumption that addresses legal and ritual concerns of a group of local and apparently commercially aware provincials, engaged not only in regulating their own practices with respect to agricultural produce, but also in creating a "map" of sanctified territory in Palestine. Indeed, this text decorated a village synagogue built by provincials. The borders of the "Land of Israel" in this ritual sense do not appear to correspond directly to the political boundaries of Palestine in any specific period.[108] Yet the texts that the inscription brings together, in particular those sections listing villages permitted or prohibited within urban territories (lines 9–13, 26–29, see above), also make use of the Roman administrative division of space. There is room for teasing out a kind of "resistance" here: an appropriation for the use of the local population of the political geography of the imperial power, but toward the ends of articulating an "indigenous" (if geographically and temporally fragmented) territoriality. Whether or not this is the case, these sections suggest, at the very least, that imperial division of space gave rabbinic provincials a usable spatial vocabulary with which to pursue their own "theoretical" interests.

Inasmuch as the preceding example stems from the work of elite men (rabbis) with a primarily urban locus of activity, but is found as part of a group of inscriptions (of which only this one has been published[109]) in a village synagogue near Bet Shean in the sixth or seventh centuries, we should be careful in assuming a sharp distinction between village and urban cultures as mutually autonomous and hostile realms. Yet it equally misconstrues the ways in which villages may differ from urban settlements to assume that all inhabitants of northern Palestine (or, what is more commonly assumed, all Jews) shared a common and homogeneous culture. An apparently innocent illustration of such differences was referred to in Chapter 4, in connection with a passage that explained a problematic legal tradition by associating it with "those small villages, whose practice is to leave while it is still day because they are afraid because of wild animals.'"[110] As noted there, this statement appears to assume that small villages have different Sabbath meal practices than other, larger, places. Ginzberg suggested that the apparent problem that this statement aims at resolving (i.e., that "the time that people go in and eat their bread on

---

[108] Lines 13–18; cf. *Sipre Deut.* 51, ed Finkelstein 1939: 117; *t. Šebi.* 4:11; *y. Šebi.* 6:1 (36c); Sussman 1975–76: 252–53; Safrai 1984b.

[109] See, e.g., Vitto 1981: 91, photo.

[110] *y. Ber.* 1:1 (2a).

Sabbath eves" is rather later than nightfall, with which it is claimed to be synchronous) stems from the development of a practice of synagogue-attendance on Friday evenings, which thereby delays the Sabbath meal.[111] If this is correct (and it need not be), and assuming that the statement in question is also related directly to synagogues,[112] the passage might in fact be taken to refer to a differential structuring of public ritual and sociability. Particularly if we allow (for the sake of argument) that these "small villages" (*kôprānayâ dĕqîqayâ*) did not necessarily have their own synagogues, so that their inhabitants would have had to gather in local, central villages (and hence to return by walking through the countryside), the hierarchical ordering of settlements may have shaped the very rhythms of religious practice over the landscape, including distinctions in religious practice between "town" and "country," and within the "country" itself.

A differentially ordered culture structured in part by hierarchy of settlement presumably has implications for the organization of gender, and with it domestic structure and marriage patterns as well. In treating the question of the whether betrothal and marriage of a woman with disfigurements (*mûmîn*) about which the husband did not know constitutes an "erroneous purchase" (*meqaḥ ṭāᶜût*) one view in the Mishnah is said to state: "but if there was a bathhouse in that village (*ᶜîr*), he is not even able to make a claim [of erroneous purchase] about hidden disfigurements, since he may inspect her through his female relatives."[113] Here, a pattern of local marriage, cooperative relationships between kin, the relative position of men and women as agents, and the ability of a husband to inspect the object of what is explicitly treated as a commercial transaction, are linked to the practice of female bathing and especially the presence of public baths. These characteristically "Roman" (and typically urban) institutions are understood not to be everywhere, and presumably were located where population density or wealth, as well as the adoption of "Roman" bathing practices could support them.[114] Bathing patterns, marriage, and settlement

---

[111] Ginzberg 1941–61: 1, 8–9.

[112] This is no more than a supposition, but it is worth noting that the inhabitants of the small villages are described not as "entering" some place (as in the traditions that define the time of the reading of the *shemaᶜ*, nor as going home from their labors, but in terms of their habitual practice of "leaving" or at least "going" (*ʾorḥêhôn mistalĕqâ*), although just what they might be leaving is not specified. The immediate sequel in the Yerushalmi, which does refer to synagogue practice, may perhaps strengthen the supposition: "It is taught: 'One who reads [the *shemaᶜ*] earlier than this has not fulfilled his obligation.' If so why do they read it in the synagogues?..." However, neither the direct connection with the preceding passage, nor any connection with Sabbath practice are made explicit.

[113] *m. Ket.* 7:8.

[114] For a bath at Capernaum see Laughlin 1993: 56–59. For references to other non-urban baths see *TIR* 103, *s.v.* Chorazin; 148, *s.v.* Ḥurfeish; 203, *s.v.* Philoteria; 211, *s.v.* Rama; 216,

hierarchy are connected elsewhere as well. A tradition cited in the Yerushalmi (perhaps as a Babylonian tradition?) distinguishes the period of time a husband may restrict his wife from bathing in a bathhouse "in cities" (one week), from the period that applies "in villages" (two weeks).[115] It is, perhaps, possible to see here a reflex of the differential availability of public baths as well, but it seems that assumed differential standards of female personal comportment are the primary issue, inasmuch as the same passage continues with a similar rule about the application of a husband's vow to restrict a wife's wearing of shoes (three days "in villages"; a twenty-four hour period "in cities").

The concentration of third- and fourth-century rabbis in urban centers arguably would have allowed intensive relationships of discipleship without undermining domestic coresidence with spouses. That disciples from villages, by contrast, might have had extended stays with a master away from their home villages (assuming they returned to them), with some impact on the kinds of households, and the kinds of gendered division of labor or responsibilities in those households, such disciples established, is perhaps illustrated by a story told about second-century rabbis, but in a substantially later text, one of whom spent thirteen years away from a wife and daughter without contacting them and whose sudden appearance at home caused the death of his daughter.[116] At any rate, it is perhaps no accident that one widely cited text that invokes active attendance by a woman of rabbinic sermons (a context that sets the narrative stage for domestic tensions and "proper" gender roles) is a story set in second-century Hamat (presumably Hamat Tiberias), a site that by the time the Yerushalmi was edited had almost certainly been incorporated into the urban space of Tiberias itself.[117] Rather than explore in detail the possible correspondences or differentiations between village and urban culture, I focus here on examples that may indicate how these might be tied to the political economy. I begin with the apparent hostility of "village" inhabitants toward the "city."

> R. Yose taught: "Betar survived (?) fifty two years after the destruction of the Temple [in Jerusalem]. And why was it destroyed? Because it lit lamps [in celebration] after the destruction of the Temple." And why did they light lamps? Because the councilors of Jerusalem would sit in the center of the city, and when they would see a man going to Jerusalem, they would say to him: "For we have heard about you that you wish to

---

s.v. Rosh Pina; Urman 1985: no. 134, el Duga; 1995: 461–63, el Dura. See also Urman 1995: 528–530 citing Schumacher; Saarisalo 1927: no. 10.

115 *y. Ket.* 7:4 (31b). The tradition is attributed to Zeira (who has traditional Babylonian associations) and is introduced *tĕnî tammān*, "it was taught 'there.'"

116 *Gen. Rab.* 95, ed. Theodor, Albeck 1912–36: 1232; *Lev. Rab.* 21:8, ed. Margaliot 1953–60: 485–487; *b. Ket.* 62b; see Boyarin 1995: 156–58.

117 *y. Soṭ.* 1:4 (16d); cf. *Lev. Rab.* 9:9, ed. Margaliot 1953–60: 191–93.

> be a ruler or a councilor.'" And he said: "It is not my intention." [The Jerusalemites would say:] "For we have heard about you that you wish to sell a property." And he said: "It is not my intention." And his fellow would say to him [i.e., to one of the Jerusalemites?]: "What do you want from this one? Write and I will sign. And he would write and his fellow would sign. And they would send a bill of sale to a member of his household [in context, perhaps, a slave] and say to them: "If so and so [the owner] should come to enter his property do not let him for it is sold to us." And when he would hear this from them he would say: "Would that the leg of that man [i.e., myself] had been broken and that he had not gone to Jerusalem." And it is about this that it was written: "They hunted (*ṣādû*) our steps so that we could not walk in our open spaces" (Lam. 4:18)....[118]

Although the text purports to describe the relationship of Betar to Jerusalem in the first century C.E., it better reflects a later period[119] that more directly informed the tradents and editors of the Palestinian Talmud and the related texts. The passage blames two destructions at the hands of the Romans, one of Jerusalem (70 C.E.), and the other of Betar (in the Bar Kokhba revolt, 132–135 C.E.), on the overreaching of the Jerusalem leaders and on the inappropriate response of their victims. However, this text does not articulate class conflict in any simple, dichotomous way: the victim of the Jerusalemite councilors is certainly a property owner, probably an estate (*ousia*) owner. Nor does it utilize a distinction between the "gentile" urban elites and the "Jewish" rural residents. Indeed, the rhetorical force of the passage, linking as it does the destructions of Jerusalem and Betar, requires the Jewishness of the oppressors. Yet the story frames this "internal" Jewish narrative within a provincial political economy that is underscored by the use of Greek loanwords in text.[120] The text can be read against the background of attempts by cities to meet the pressure to fill the council or other magistracies left open by evasion of the wealthiest urban elites (certainly a recurring issue in the fourth century, if the *Codex Theodosianus* is any indication) by enlisting wealthy villagers who fell within the city's *territorium*, possibly – at least from the perspective of this passage – through extortion.[121] Other rabbinic texts suggest that rabbis, whose ranks included relatively wealthy landowners, might have fit into the category of those who might sometimes be called upon to serve in this capacity,[122] so

[118] *y. Taʿan.* 4:8 (69a); cf. *Lam. Rab.* 2 to 2:2; 4 to 4:18, ed. Buber 1899: 102.

[119] Cf. Safrai 1995: 248; see also Alon 1976: 1, 48 n. 50.

[120] "Councilor(s)": *bwlbwṭs/bwlwwṭy*, Greek *bouleutēs*, *bouleutai*; "ruler": *ʾrkwnts*, Greek *arkhōn*; "property" (perhaps better: "estate"): *ʾwsyyʾ*, Greek *ousia*; perhaps better: an estate; "bill of sale":*ʾwnytʾ*, an Aramaic form based on Greek *ōnē*, Sokoloff 1991: 40, *s.v. ʾwny*.

[121] The falsified sale in this passage may be related to the restrictions against decurions alienating property in order to evade service. See *Cod. Theod.* 12.9.49.1 (361); see also 12.3.1 (386), in this case apparently sale under constraint, 12.3.2 (423); see also Libanius, *Or.* 48.37; Jones 1964: 738 and n. 61.

[122] E.g., explicitly, *y. B. Bat.* 9:6 (17a); see also *y. Moʿed Qaṭ.* 2:3 (81b); cf. *y. Sanh.* 8:3 (26a–b); *Gen. Rab.* 76:6, ed. Theodor, Albeck 1912–36: 904.

that the description here (with its sympathy for the unfortunate landowner, and the none-too-disguised threat toward city elites) is not innocent of rabbis' own class interest. The significance of this passage for present purposes, however, is that social tension is given an explicitly geographical dimension that is more subtle than a simple hostility between "village" and "city." The coercive ability of the city to coopt the human and material resources of the countryside translates also, and more pointedly, into tension between wealthy villagers and urban elites who might, under other circumstances, have been the villagers' aspirational peers.[123] The passage is, thus, an example not so much of the natural antagonisms of town and country, as of the fact that both are caught up in the same larger political economy, one that could structure social tensions across the landscape.

The complement to the kinds of relationship described in the previous text, in which the councilors of Jerusalem are able to make use of their advantaged position with respect to other property owners (and also, it should not be overlooked, to the documentary mechanics of the ownership and registration of property) to extort property if not participation in urban magistracies, is the ability of urban elites to offer patronage. Despite the abiding utiltiy of the picture of the rural holy man drawn by Brown for rural northern Syria,[124] the lives of the Palestinian monks that Cyril of Scythopolis narrates frequently have their origins in urban and ecclesiastical society, including Cyril himself,[125] and some in those circles go on to become bishops or other holders of ecclesiatical offices.[126] Moreover, for all that the monks go off to monastic settlements in the desert, there remain carefully maintained connections to cities.[127] Christian holy men and rural patrons the leaders of these monastic movements may have been, but decidedly not because of a total disengagement from the city and its institutions.

For Galilee itself, we have a somewhat difficult account of the village rabbi who makes his way to town and suffers abuse for it (he is made to dance by children). The occasion for the visit is tied directly to the conventions of patronage: "A story happened involving one of the great ones (*gĕdôlê*) of Sepphoris, who had occasion to perform a circumcision, and the people of [ᶜEn (?)] Teenah came up to honor him, and R. Simeon b.

---

[123] Cf. MacMullen 1964: 47 and nn.

[124] Brown 1982: 103–65.

[125] *V. Sabae* 75, ed. E. Schwartz 1939: 179–181; and *V. Euth.* 49, 71.10–72.8; *V. Io. Hes.* 20, 216.8–24; see also: *V. Euth.* 16, 26.1–6, 11–14; *V. Sabae* 61, 163.5–13; 68, 170.1–5; 86, 193.16; 88, 196.7–11; *V. Kyr.* 14, 231.9–10.

[126] *V. Euth.* 16, ed. E. Schwartz 1939: 26.1–6; 37, 55.20–56.5; *V. Sabae* 37, 127.4–14; 56, 150.8–11; 68, 1701.1–5; 89, 197.19–23.

[127] E.g., hospices: *V. Kyr.* 7, ed. E. Schwartz 1939: 226.17–19; also Patrich 1995: 165.

Halapta went up with them."[128] In a public display of wealth and good will the father distributes good wine to his guests as a kind of downpayment for the hoped-for wedding feast. In practice, the story is a subversion of these conventions since we are told that the angel of death was authorized to take the life of the child as an infant, and it is (apparently) the rabbi's intervention that saves him. Nevertheless, this reversal of the flow of benefactions works against the patterns of movement (of the villagers to the city) and of generosity (from the "great one" to the guests) that place this story within the wider context of networks of patronage ties centered on city elites and extending outward into the village populations.

The final examples relate to issues of cultural change that are widely discussed by historians and archaeologists: the rise and extent of the rabbinic movement, the distribution of churches and synagogues in northern Palestine, and "Christianization." Here, again, I address possible connections between geography, political economy, and "culture." Rabbis are of particular interest here because, although it is impossible to determine the number of rabbis, or the extent of their influence, rabbis remain a rather densely documented movement. Catherine Hezser has argued that for all the institutional language that Palestinian rabbinic literature uses, the rabbinic movement should be seen primarily as arranged through loosely configured networks of personal relations.[129] While there may be room for more real institution-building than Hezser allows, her argument is, overall, illuminating. What I would hope to add to that analysis here is a particular focus on the geographical or spatial framework of those networks. Thus, for instance, on the basis of rabbinic texts rabbis of the third and fourth centuries appear to have been concentrated in cities in Galilee.[130] The archaeological evidence for rabbis appears to be scanty indeed, but the clearest attestations are from two villages: the inscription from Rehob (discussed above), and from Dabura in the Golan (a lintel inscription stating "This is the study house of R. Eliezer Ha-Qappar").[131] How we handle the disjuncture in evidence depends in part on how we date the inscriptions. The Rehob inscription is perhaps to be dated to the sixth or seventh centuries.[132] The Dabura inscription was dated by Urman to the late-second or early-third century on the basis of the identification of the named person.[133] This is far from conclusive, since even if the identification of the rabbi is correct there is nothing that requires the dating of the

[128] *Qoh. Rab.* 3:4, ed. Hirshman 1982: 223–9.
[129] Hezser 1995.
[130] Lapin 1999; cf. Hezser 1995: 157–84.
[131] Naveh 1978: no. 6; Gregg, Urman 1996: 129; see Cohen 1981–82.
[132] Sussman 1973–74: 153–55; Vitto 1981: 93–94.
[133] Urman 1970–71: 406–8 = 1972: 21–3.

inscription contemporaneous with him, or, consequently, that prevents the dating of this document of rabbinic "institutionalization" to the fifth or sixth century, to which the synagogues of this area in the Golan tend to be dated.[134] On balance, and although there are uncertainties connected with this position, I am inclined to think that to the extent that the rabbinic movement ever became prominent in the countryside of Galilee and its wider environs in late antiquity, this was the result of a spread outward from urban concentrations.

If this is the case, it is worth considering the geographical dimensions of such a spreading of influence. To begin with, the view suggested above implies that it is particularly cities – occupying peculiar positions in the regional political economy – that were the staging ground for this local, provincial, and indigenizing (i.e., "Jewish") movement of elite, literate, landowning men. As for the rabbinic reach into the countryside, "influence" presumably should be measured not by whether people at large believed in rabbinic claims to authority or power or followed rabbinic *halākâ*,[135] but whether they could convince those people who served as village judges, who ran synagogues, who wrote documents, or who taught the small percentage of children who ever learned to read at all, of the authenticity of the Torah of which rabbis claimed to be the guardians and transmitters. If we assume for the sake of argument that villages sufficiently large to serve as local marketing centers also provided other, non-market services such as scribes, local judges, or teachers (something like this may be the implication of such highly schematized traditions as *m. Megillah* 1:1–3 and other passages assuming Monday-Thursday periodicity), the discussion in Chapter 3 of hypothetical models for how market-bearing sites might be distributed (see Table 3.4), may offer some sense of the limited scale of such an enterprise.

In terms of the ratio of cities to market-bearing villages, that table suggests that we might want to think in terms of between 11 (column III) and 35 (column I) additional market-bearing sites for every city, not a very large number. Or, to go over the same ground another way, Chapter 3 estimated that the entire area in western Palestine covered by this study may have accounted for some 1,120 sites. That figure is almost certainly high, since it assumes that the density of sites in upper Galilee, or such marginal areas as the Gazit region, matched that in lower Galilee. For the Golan in the Byzantine period, the data collected for this study suggested

---

134 See Ma'oz 1981: 115, who dates the "heyday" of Dabura to the fifth and sixth centuries; see more generally Ma'oz 1981: 101–109; 1993: 538–45; but cf. Ma'oz 1986: 99; 1993: 545.

135 See, e.g., Oppenheimer 1977; Schiffman 1992; Safrai 1995: 24–26; cf. Goodman 1983: 93–118.

some 180 sites (see Table 2.1).[136] Allowing a generous 250 (for a substantial amount of under-reporting), gives a total number of settlements of 1,370. Based on the proportion of market-bearing to non-market-bearing sites in the models of Table 3.4, columns I and II assume a maximum of some 196 institution-bearing sites (1 in 7); the configuration in column III gives a maximum of 72 sites (1 in 19) for the entire area of northern Palestine covered by this study. If we restrict the area under consideration to those areas that are conventionally seen by contemporary scholars as predominantly "Jewish" (i.e., where synagogues appear in concentration, namely lower Galilee, eastern upper Galilee, and the "lower" Golan), the range of potential market-bearing sites presumably should be halved: between 36 and 98 sites.

The number of attested synagogues in the region – a very provisional indication of whether a village might serve as a local "institutional" center – might perhaps tend to justify the higher range of numbers (98 for the "Jewish" areas): Tsafrir estimated some 118 synagogues in western Palestine and the Golan;[137] by my rough count based on the synagogue map accompanying *TIR*, the narrower area under consideration here accounts for some 100 of these.[138] It is possible that upper Galilee and the Golan, with their relatively low settlement density (and, at least in the Golan, apparently a correspondingly high median size) may have supported a somewhat higher proportion of synagogue-bearing sites than more densely populated areas.

However, caution is advisable here, and it may well be that a more modest number of active synagogues at any one time should be assumed. On the one hand, archaeological evidence for synagogues leaves out undiscovered or unrecognized synagogues, so that the number of preserved synagogues is a sample of an unknown larger number. On the other hand, it is not clear that all buildings or remains claimed as synagogues by archaeologists served that purpose. Based on the map accompanying one recent assessment, the areas of northern Palestine covered by the present study are deemed to have had as many as some seventy-six synagogue sites, but only about fifty are based on more than "single finds," and of these seven are marked with question marks.[139] Of the evidence collected by Chiat (in a

---

[136] Based primarily on Urman 1985; 1995; *JSG* Golan. See Chapter 2.

[137] Tsafrir in *TIR* 19.

[138] Cf. Levine 1985: 100, Map.

[139] Bloedhorn, Hüttenmeister 1999: 284–285; by my rough count the numbers appear to be fairly close to the text of Hüttenmeister, Reeg 1977 for the regions under consideration here, although that collection, in both the body (volume I) and in the map of synagogues (attached to volume II) divides the sites somewhat differently, distinguishing between synagogues that are *archäologisch sicher* and those that are *unsicher* (see Hüttenmeister, Reeg 1977: 1, xv). Note also Dauphin 1998: Fig. 115 (which explicitly distinguishes archaeological and literary

1982 publication) for ninety-seven "synagogues" in roughly the area covered in this study, she deemed only some twenty four "validated" (18 in western Palestine; 4 in the Golan) and an additional thirty one "attested" (17 in western Palestine; 14 in the Golan), and rejected the attribution for thirty eight (18 western Palestine; 20 in the Golan).[140] By contrast Ilan and Urman appear to have a more expansive view of synagogues (in Urman's case: "Jewish public buildings") and their distribution.[141] Moreover, there is a fair degree of disagreement over the dating of synagogues, and, given the way they have been preserved in the first place, and subsequently dug or reported, it is rarely entirely clear whether any given synagogues were in use at precisely the same time. Nor is it clear, for instance, with what regularity any particular synagogue building was used, or whether it actually represents communal institutionalization (does the building represent a communal need to meet regularly in some capacity, or might it perhaps be the result of intercommunal competition and patterns of donation and benefaction?).

However the distribution of synagogues might have related to the distribution of local "central places," the numbers suggested for the latter, even at the expansive high of 196 across all of northern Palestine, are sufficiently small that a modest number of people (a total of several dozen to a few hundred), distributed in some or all of those institution-bearing villages, could reasonably have been cultivated by a small group of people centered in cities, through personal networks of affiliation, friendship, and patronage. To the extent that such "adherents" also served as religious or cultural functionaries, local arbitrators, or drafters of documents, this minuscule proportion of the population would potentially have been of enormous local influence. Nor must we assume a high degree of village institutionalization or a proliferation of offices in order to account for the playing out of this influence.[142] Even if local power in villages was the product of a combination of kinship and wealth, the preserve, at any given moment, of a few privileged families,[143] what is of interest here is the question of the cultural and ideological baggage (including what we might define as "ethnic" or "religious" identity) such privileged families might have

evidence), according to which the regions roughly corresponding to the area under discussion here had twenty-four sites with explicitly "Jewish" remains in the fifth century and an additional two possible sites (assuming that all of the "mixed" sites had Jewish remains, one can add an additional 5). For other periods see: Figs. 43–48; 116–117 (the latter with the corresponding maps); for the fourth century her assessment includes fewer than forty sites.

140 Chiat 1982: 263–94, 299–302, 305–13 for eastern portions; western portions summarized 332, Table 1, B.

141 Ilan 1991; Urman 1995.

142 Cf. Safrai 1995.

143 See Grainger 1995: 192–193.

shared, how the transmission and transformation of that baggage (through marital ties, for instance, and through more explicit forms of enculturation such as education) might have been mediated across a geographical landscape, and to what extent an elite group of men in cities might have been able to play a decisive role in that mediation.

Whether and when in antiquity rabbis ever managed to play such a role with any intensity is unclear, and I leave this question open. At any rate, a focus on the intersection of ties of personal influence or patronage with their possible spatial distribution may help make sense of some of the terms in which rabbinic influence is expressed in rabbinic literature. Thus, a story about Judah the Patriarch's assignment of a communal functionary to the village of Simonayans (an assignment with less than stellar results) casts that appointment as a response to a personal appeal.[144] Another example, involving Simeon b. Laqish and a community of Jews in Bostra (i.e., a city in this case), similarly involves a direct appeal to a rabbi who happened to be in town, and the choice of the candidate is also cast in personal (if perhaps dismissive) terms: "He [Simeon b. Laqish] saw a certain Babylonian and said to him: 'I've seen a good place for you.'"[145] The scripture teacher of Tarbenet who clashed with his community over his teaching practices "went [and] asked Hanina" (perhaps in Sepphoris?[146]); and upon being removed from his position turned up "here" (perhaps Tiberias?) where he discussed his situation with Simeon b. Yusina,[147] again giving play to the direct interactions between individual people, and possibly to the movement of the scripture teacher between his home and a city.

At the same time, rabbinic passages that describe great rabbinizing undertakings may also be put into a somewhat more circumscribed framework. For instance, a widely cited passage states that "R. Judah [III] the Patriarch sent R. Hiyya [b. Abba] and R. Asi and R. Ami to go through the villages of the land of Israel and to appoint for them scripture teachers and mishnah teachers."[148] As in the case of the story about Jerusalem and Betar, the point of the story presumably has less to do with its facticity than with its rhetorical claims: that the land of Israel is the purview of rabbis; that the patriarch directs such ventures; and that the teachers of Torah – the rabbinic bailiwick – are the true guardians of any village. Nevertheless, if the discussion above is useful for framing how we may think about

---

[144] *y. Yeb.* 12 (13a); cf. *Gen. Rab.* 81:2, ed. Theodor, Albeck 1912–36: 969.

[145] *y. Šebi.* 6:1 (36c); cf. *Deut. Rab.*, ed. Lieberman 1974: 60–61.

[146] See *y. Yoma*ʾ 3:7 (40d); cf. *Qoh. Rab.* to 3:11.

[147] *y. Meg.* 4:5 (75b).

[148] *y. Ḥag.* 1:7 (76c); cf. *Pes. Rab Kah.*, *ʾÊkâ*, ed. Buber, 120b, ed. Braude, 253; *Lam. Rab.*, proem, to 1:1; see also e.g. Alon 1953–57: 2, 140; Levine 1979: 671–72; 1987: 161–62; 1996: 11–12; Jacob 1995: 185–87; Hezser 1995: 96, 424; Safrai 1995: 242 and n. 191.

rabbinic influence, this passage can be viewed as giving narrative expression to one of the strategies available to rabbis for gaining influence in rural settlements: organizing a series of personal visits. Imagining such a project in these terms does not require thinking in terms of national "government" or "leadership" or even of a high degree of institutionalization. Nor would the raw number of "schools" need to be particularly high in order for the results of such an undertaking to mark the prominence of the rabbinic movement among those who claimed to read the texts of Israel's sacred tradition. Presumably, success required more inducement than simply the pious lesson about the true guardians of the village (with the implication that some villagers, those without teachers, do not know this) to gain adherents. Here the entire rabbinic repertoire (claims to an authentic tradition; to ritual expertise; to successful prayers for adherents; to work collecting charity; to reputation as judges) might be mobilized; but one should not rule out material support for the hiring of teachers based on the formulation in the Palestinian Talmud (cf. the parallels cited above, which have the rabbis going merely to inspect – a more circumscribed enterprise, and one that may fit better with the limits of rabbinic institutionalization).

There is an entire dimension, a depth, that is necessarily lacking in the preceding examples. Even granting the factual historicity of the stories cited (a dubious proposition), they may give us no more than a series of unconnected episodes involving individual rabbis and their interactions with some villagers, or one group of rabbis in a more or less systematic attempt to promote a religious agenda important to them. This lack of depth may be a function, at least in part, of the way that rabbinic literature uses stories: as anecdotes, giving the occasion for a particular legal, ethical, or other teaching, rather than designed to give detailed narrative histories. What I am suggesting, and where a focus on the geographical aspects of rabbinic relationships offers a point of entry, is that it is the forging or maintaining of such relationships in time, the cultivation of their intensity or their density – precisely those investments of cultural (and material) capital that are not always given play in rabbinic narratives about their own activities and practices – across a hierarchically marked landscape that may have at the same time structured divisions in agricultural and cultural practices, that may help us to frame the processes by which the rabbinic movement rose to prominence, to the extent that it did at all.[149]

As for "Christianization," the links between "culture," political economy, and its geography are perhaps more clearly seen in the more densely documented area of the Judaean Desert in the fifth and sixth centuries. I have already mentioned some of the links between cities (particularly Jerusalem) and developing monastic institutions in late antiquity as

---

[149] Cf. Bourdieu 1977.

described in Cyril of Scythopolis. The very spread across the Judaean desert of monastic settlements is some measure of the impact upon the rural landscape,[150] an impact played out, for instance, in mouths to be fed and land to be worked to provide food, and extending beyond the individual monasteries in terms of the social or economic connections that brought skilled artisanship (e.g., mosaicists) and its products (e.g. woven textiles), donated food, or benefactions to monasteries.[151] The ties to a wider imperial politics and economy are evident not only in ties to cities but also in the role that Sabas himself is said to have played in conflicts over the council of Chalcedon and, more specifically, in trips made to Constantinople. These trips, whatever their result in terms of ecclesiastical structure in Palestine, are described as bringing material benefits for the monasteries and remissions of taxation.[152] On a more mundane level, and set a generation earlier, the multiple connections between imperial conflicts, economic support for monasteries, the power of monastic figures as holy men, and cultural transformation on the part of the "indigenous" population (apparently partial sedentarization and Christianization) are all implicated in the stories about the healing by Euthymius of Terebon the son of Aspebetos (later Peter), the phylarch of treaty-bound Saracens in Arabia.[153]

In the northern areas covered by the present study at least some of these processes appear to be in evidence. Hirschfeld links the construction of the church on Mt Berenike at Tiberias, along with a sixth-century wall (attested by Procopius) with imperial involvement in establishing pilgrim sites.[154] There is evidence for the spread of monasteries in both western and eastern portions.[155] In addition, a number of sites have been identified as

---

[150] Maps: Hirschfeld 1992: 9; 1993b: 150; Patrich 1995: 52.

[151] See Hirschfeld 1992: 102–11; Binns 1994: 102–11; Patrich 1995: 194–95. Artisanship: e.g., *V. Sabae* 80, ed. E. Schwartz 1939: 186; *V. Kyr.* 6, ed. E. Schwartz 1939: 226.1–3; food: e.g., *V. Io. Hesych.* 12, ed. E. Schwartz 1939: 211.1–4; benefactions e.g., *V. Euth.* 48, ed. E. Schwartz 1939: 69.30.

[152] *V. Sabae* 50–55, 70–73, ed. Schwartz 1939: 139–48, 173–178.

[153] *V. Euth.* 10, 15, ed. Schwartz 1939: 18–21, 24–25.

[154] Hirschfeld 1999.

[155] For example, the following (without aiming to be complete) are among sites in the Galilee and Bet Shean valley with remains that have been identified as monastic: Tiberias (Ovadiah 1977: nos. 178a–b); near Beth Shean (monastery of the Lady Mary, see Fitzgerald 1939); Bet ha-shitta (Ovadia 1977: no. 21); Kh. ʿIribbin (*TIR*, 123, s.v. Ḥ. 'Erav); 'Ein Bala (see *TIR*, s.v. Beella); Tel Basul (Ovadiah 1977: 175; Ovadiah, de Silva 1982: 165, no. 53); Yehiʿam (see *TIR*, *s.v.* Yeḥiam); Nazareth (Ovadiah 1977: no. 147); near ʾIksal (see *TIR* 124, s.v. Exaloth); Mt. Tabor (Ovadiah 1977: no. 60; Ovadiah, de Silva 1982: 132, no. 17); Kh. el Deir (*TIR* 109, *s.v.*); Sede Nahum (Ovadiah 1977: no. 160); Magdala (Tarichaeae) (see *TIR* 173, *s.v.* Magdala); El Tabgha (Ovadiah 1977: 47). Possibly Mugharat el Rahab (Frankel, Getzov 1997: 2.42); Dar el ʿArbiyeh (?) (Avi'am 1994: 108 possibly a monastery); Kh. el Ghureiyib (Avi'am 1988–89: 93); and in the Golan: Kursi (Urman 1985: 154–55); Naʿaran (*TIR* 190, *s.v.* Na'aran;

monastic farms.[156] These sites, for the most part apparently to be associated with the fifth or sixth centuries, are an indication of possible intersections between the practice of agriculture, the rural inhabitants, and religious change that are worth pursuing further.

More striking, because it appears quite clearly on maps of later Roman northern Palestine, is the geographical distribution of churches and synagogues.[157] In lower Galilee churches appear primarily (but not exclusively) in connection with Christian holy places (among the same places that pilgrim texts mention), sporadically in the Golan, and, in upper Galilee particularly in the western portion, at the outer reaches of the territory of Ptolemais, and Tyre.[158] By contrast, the two areas in which there appears to be a dense concentration of synagogue building and little or no church building are in eastern upper Galilee and the region of the Golan immediately to the East of upper Galilee.

Given the attention to central-place theory throughout this study, it is worth noting that the areas of dense synagogue building (based on the synagogue map of *TIR*, more dense than lower Galilee, although this may be an artifact of surveying[159]), with fairly little overlap with church building, are precisely areas that in the list of Georgius Cyprius are labeled as areas separate from the urban territories of the cities of Palaestina Secunda[160] and that I have argued in Chapter 3 may have been peripheries in a central-place system organized around cities: upper Galilee at the northern reaches of the territory of Tiberias; and Gaulanitis in the region that falls between the territories of Caesarea Paneas and Hippos. The

---

Dauphin, Schonfield 1983: 199–200); Deir Qrukh (*TIR* 111, *s.v.*); Duer el Loz (Ovadiah, de Silva, 1981 no. 15). See also Dauphin 1998; Avi'am 1999. Note also Avi'am's use of the presence of oil presses (i.e., of some agricultural production) as among the criteria of rural monasteries, Avi'am 1999: 294–295.

[156] E.g., Dauphin 1977; 1979; 1993a; Bet ha-Shitta, *TIR* 82, *s.v.* Beth ha-Shittah; a site so identified in Zori 1977: no. 121; see also Avi'am 1994: 84–87; and the collocation of a church and agricultural installations at Qasr ʿAsheq (Ḥ. Hesheq), Avi'am 1993b: 55. Avi'am 1995: 57–59 suggests a pattern of "monasteries" in western Galilee (enclosures of some 2.5 dunams, some of which include the remains of churches) that also include agricultural installations (oil presses). Cf. Villeneuve 1985: 119–120, on the Hauran.

[157] See *TIR* Maps; see also Ilan 1987b; Avi'am 1995: 59 and 47 (map); Ma'oz 1985: 66, fig. 5; Gregg, Urman 1996: 297, 298; and cf. the maps in Dauphin 1998: Figs. 56, 73, 90, 107, 115–117.

[158] See Di Segni 1991; 1993, who favors placing Ḥ. Hesheq in the territory of Sepphoris, rather than Ptolemais.

[159] Again, some caution is advisable. Compare Chiat 1982: 21–65, 332: of the eighteen "synagogues" in Galilee whose attribution she rejects, twelve are in "Tetracomia," i.e., upper Galilee.

[160] *Descriptio* 1028–42, Honigmann, ed., 1939: 67–68; Gelzer, ed., 1890: 52–53 (if Tetrakomia is to be identified with upper Galilee).

differential distribution of synagogues and churches in northern Palestine is all the more striking if, as appears increasingly likely, Galilean synagogue building was more or less contemporaneous with that of the building of churches.[161] Nor, over the long term, should we dismiss the building of churches in the territories of Sepphoris and Tiberias as merely cosmetic. Tiberias was represented by a bishop at ecclesiastical councils by the mid-fifth century; a bishop of Sepphoris appears in councils by the early-sixth century (Jerusalem, 518);[162] and by some time in the fifth or sixth century a bishop of Sepphoris appears in an inscription commemorating what the excavators apparently understand as the rebuilding of a portion one of the main colonnades of the city.[163] The inscription from Sepphoris makes it at least possible that the bishop had emerged as a major benefactor with a local following, whatever its size.

The goal here is not to offer an explanation for the uneven distribution of synagogues and churches, much less to engage the question of whether there was a line that sharply divided Jews and gentiles in late antique Palestine.[164] Nevertheless, any explanation of that distribution will need to take into account not merely the putative regions of "Jewish" and "gentile" settlement throughout the territory of late-antique Palestine, but also the extent to which that settlement distribution was caught within, even constructed by, complex political, economic, and social frameworks. Thus, particularly if Ma'oz is correct that there was a gap in settlement in the "lower" Golan in the second and third centuries, with renewed settlement only in the fourth and fifth,[165] it is precisely in this later period that the region developed, and did so, I have suggested, as a periphery. In that case, we cannot attribute the "Jewishness" of this region solely to a long history of ancestral religion among an indigenous population, to a failure of Christianity to "reach" areas of greater difficulty of access, or, for that matter, to a resistance of "traditional" village communities to religious change. The "Jewish" Golan with its sizable number of synagogue-bearing villages developed as an area of expanding Jewish settlement precisely in the context of larger regional demographic changes, within an increasingly Christian empire.

As for churches, the story of Joseph of Tiberias, as told by Epiphanius, has Joseph, a former Jew and former member of the patriarch's retinue, build a number of churches in Galilee.[166] The story is understood by some

---

[161] See Magness 2000.

[162] References in Abel 1938: 201; Jones 1971: 547 and *TIR*.

[163] See Weiss, Netzer 1996b: 85.

[164] Dauphin 1982; Ma'oz 1985; Gregg, Urman 1996: 289–304; Isaac 1999: 186–88.

[165] Ma'oz 1986: 96–101; cf. Dauphin 1998: Figures 31–34.

[166] Epiphanius *Panarion* 30.4–12, ed. Holl 1915–33: 1, 338–348; see Rubin 1983; Thornton 1990; Goranson 1999.

as an example of the imperial policy of promoting Christianity through the building of churches ("we note the hostility of the Roman government under Constantine towards Judaism, for all its supposed impartiality"[167]). That may perhaps be, and given that the building of churches is presented as more or less an end in itself and that local resistance is explicitly addressed in the story, the story may imply that the presence of churches in Palestine, and elsewhere as well, do not transparently represent the Christianity of the local population so much as an emerging attempt on the part of Christian emperors to mark Christian and imperial space through the erection of monuments.[168] However, the aspects that place this story within a regional and imperial economy of patronage should not be overlooked. Joseph, a Jew from Tiberias in the circle of the Palestinian Jewish patriarch – a local aristocrat – through Christian connections cultivated while an advisor and "apostle" of the patriarch converts to Christianity and rises in the imperial administration, and in turn gets imperial support and funding to build churches in his home town and in nearby areas. But for the fact that this is a story about how the recalcitrant population resorted to any means including magic to prevent the completion of Joseph's unwanted churches (and, indeed, perhaps because of this), it reads like a paradigmatic story of fourth-century benefaction.

The story of Joseph of Tiberias thus suggests the ties that link local expressions of church building with an emerging imperial ideology that favored Christianity, and that favored urban elites who converted to Christianity. The choices for the location of Joseph's churches also are not accidental: Capernaum and Nazareth were significant places in the emerging notion of the Christian holy land;[169] but Tiberias and Sepphoris were cities – precisely the places where a local dignitary might be expected to make public displays of his allegiance to his imperial patron. It is not without irony that the site of Joseph's building in Tiberias is said to have been an unfinished Hadrianeion, presumably the site of cult for the emperor.[170]

D. Toward a Regional History

This chapter has attempted to shift the focus from the fairly static constructions developed in preceding chapters to a reconsideration of the history of northern Palestine in the later Roman period. The point of this reconsideration, exemplified by a discussion of several key issues in the administrative,

---

167 Avi-Yonah 1976: 168.

168 Epiphanius *Panarion* 30.11.9–12.9, ed. Holl 1915–33: 1, 347–348.

169 Walker 1990; Wilken 1992; Taylor 1993.

170 Epiphanius *Panarion* 30.12.2, ed. Holl 1915–33: 1, 348.

economic, and cultural history of the region, has been to draw attention to the geographical dimensions of that history. Thus, for instance, in reconstructing the second- and third-century province of Palaestina (and later), Roman administrators may have built on economic and administrative structures already in place under the Herodian rulers. However, the particular administrative choices made during this period reshaped social relations in the province, fostering a division of labor both within cities and across the landscape in terms of the development of "core" and "peripheral" areas. As noted in previous chapters, the extent to which the economy of Palestine was shaped by trade remains elusive, but a significant amount of material suggests both the role of cities in shaping both trade and the regional economy, and for the impact of the consumption needs of cities on production in the rural hinterlands. Nor can the cultural or social history of the region be separated from these phenomena. The impact of urbanization and provincialization may be seen in the way that rabbis understood the spatial dimensions of the ritual Holy Land, in the way such practices as public bathing were expected to be distributed in the countryside (with implications for patterns of marriage-making and the construction of gendered social expectations). Moreover, while the claim that "Christianization" in northern Palestine, at least as measured by the construction of churches, was tied to imperial politics should surprise very few, Epiphanius's story of Joseph of Tiberias suggests that the process of church building may have been more complicated, and more rooted in local patterns of elite status, than sometimes thought. Finally, by pointing to the connections between "Jewishness" and a regional landscape, I have attempted to underscore that much of what we now, from a distance of sixteen or seventeen centuries, tend to see as naturally Jewish, such as synagogues and the rise of rabbis, is in fact the product of a complex provincial history that itself has been at least partly shaped by regional administrative and economic structures.

The Introduction described the present project as an exploratory exercise toward a different kind of historiography of Palestine. Partly as a result of the constraints of working with central-place theory, but in part also of my own conviction that the material and day-to-day lives of people is central to our understanding of the period, much of the preceding discussion has focused on economy. The focus on trade and its limitations in the framework of a regional economy, the theoretical underpinnings of Chapters 1 and 3, and the nature of the data assembled in Chapter 2 paradoxically required a level of generality and abstraction that shifted focus away from those day-to-day lives. Yet they also helped to articulate the economic frameworks in which everyday lives were played out. Moreover, Chapter 4 attempted to bring the theoretical concerns of earlier chapters and the literary remains of ancient Palestinians to bear on one another, and

Chapter 5 pointed toward ways that we might bridge the gaps between trade and a lived, historical, regional economy.

By way of conclusion, it is worth stressing some of the implications of this exercise. The history of Palestine in this period, as it is conventionally written, is a history of "peoples" (e.g., Jews, Samaritans, Christians, "pagans"), institutions (e.g., the Church; the city of Scythopolis or Sepphoris; the Jewish patriarchate), or events (e.g., Jewish or Samaritan revolts). Such peoples, institutions, and events are, almost of necessity, treated as organic unities with life-histories all their own. The present study worked instead with a geographical or regional focus, asking, at least in a preliminary way, to what extent such features as the distributions of cities and villages and of trade or production might map onto religious, ethnic, or cultural history.

In suggesting the salience of such a focus, I am not proposing still another autonomous organic unity ("the Land"). On the contrary, part of the burden of the preceding chapter has been to stress the transformation of northern Palestine as a historical landscape. Yet the material, territorial landscape was the staging ground for the history of Palestine as we have come to understand it. Because it can only be studied in spatial, and hence relational, terms, a regional history is, furthermore, one that facilitates the juxtaposition of seemingly autonomous entities in productive ways that underscore their embeddedness in wider historical processes: long-term demographic or ecological shifts, patterns of consumption of agricultural products, craft goods, or cultural practices (e.g., epigraphy, benefactions, public bathing, or the use of Greek), and the impact of the spread of Christianity as imperially sponsored religious ideology. Nor should such a focus be used to level difference in favor of an "average" Palestinian experience. The discussion of upper Galilee and the Golan suggested, in fact, that differential development – in both economic and ethnic terms – was in fact a feature of a regional history. Similarly, urbanization brought with it not only changes to the agricultural production of the countryside, but also possible differentiation between cities and villages in sociability, in bathing practices, and personal (and gendered) comportment.

Another feature that is underscored by such a geographical focus is what I have been calling "provincalization." The term is not entirely satisfactory (for one thing, by the fourth century Palestine had long been "provincial"), but it serves to stress the political economic dimension of a regional history. It is within the context of a Roman empire that Palestine came to have the political and economic landscape that it did, and in which the cities that dominated that landscape came to have their peculiar needs for consumption and display. Northern Palestine is particularly interesting in this respect because it was the the scene of two of the best attested late-antique ethnic resurgences, that of Samaritans and of Jews. And the rabbinic movement – that late-antique Jewish group that we know best, as an urban, literate, movement of men, seems in significant ways to have recapitulated the uneven distribution of literacy and wealth in the provincial context. In this respect, the history of late-antique Palestine, even of groups that stressed their "indigenous" traditions and their difference from "the gentiles," is a history of people who have become "provincial."

Bibliography

Abel, P. F.-M. 1938. *Géographie de la Palestine, Tome II*. Paris: J. Gabalda.

Adams, R. McC. 1981. *Heartland of Cities: Surveys of Ancient Land Use on the Central Floodplain of the Euphrates*. Chicago: University of Chicago.

Adan-Bayewitz, D. 1985. *Ha-rôkēl bě-ʾereṣ yiśrāʾēl: ha-mēʾâ ha-2 ʿad ha-mēʾâ ha-4 la-sěfîrâ*. In N. Gross, ed. *Jews in Economic Life*. Jerusalem: Merkaz Zalman Shazar. Pp. 67–85.

———. 1993. *Common Pottery in Roman Galilee: A Study in Local Trade*. Ramat Gan: Bar Ilan.

———. 1995. "A Lamp Mould from Sepphoris and the Location of Workshops for Lamp and Common Pottery Manufacture in Northern Palestine." *JRA* Supplement 14: 177–82.

Adan-Bayewitz, D., Perlman, I. 1990. "The Local Trade of Sepphoris in the Roman Period." *IEJ* 40: 153–72.

Adriaen, M. 1970, ed. *S. Hieronymi Presbyteri Opera. Pars I, 6: Commentarii in Prophetas Minores*. In *CCSL* 75.

Aharoni, Y. 1993. "Tel Qedesh" In *NEAEHL* 3: 855–6.

Alcock, S. E. 1991. "Urban Survey and the *Polis* of Phlius." *Hesperia* 60: 421–463.

———. 1993. *Graecia Capta: The Landscape of Roman Greece*. Cambridge: Cambridge, 1993.

———. 1997, ed. *The Early Roman Empire in the East*. Oxbow Monographs 97: Oxford: Oxbow.

Alon, G. 1953–57. *Tôldôt ha-yěhûdîm bě-ʾereṣ yiśrāʾēl bi-těqûpat ha-mišnâ wě-ha-talmûd*. Tel Aviv: Hakibutz Hameuchad.

———. 1976. *Studies in Jewish History* [Hebrew]. Tel Aviv: Hakibbutz Hameuchad.

Applebaum, S. 1976. "Economic Life in Palestine" In S. Safrai, ed. *The Jewish People in the First Century*. CRINT 1: Philadelphia: Fortress, 631–700.

———. 1989. *Judaea in Hellenistic and Roman Times*. SJLA 10: Leiden: Brill 1989.

Appleby, G. 1976. "The Role of Urban Food Needs in Regional Development, Puno, Peru". In C. A. Smith 1976a: 147–78.

Arav, R., Freund, R. 1995, eds. *Bethsaida: A City by the North Shore of the Sea of Galilee*. Kirksville: Thomas Jefferson University Press.

Ariel, D. 1996. "A Hoard of Byzantine Folles from Qaẓrin" *ʿAtiqot* 29: 69–76.

Arnold, D. E. 1985. *Ceramic Theory and Cultural Processes*. New Studies in Archaeology: Cambridge: Cambridge University Press.

Asad, T. 1993. *Genealogies of Religion: Discipline and Reasons of Power in Christianity and Islam*. Baltimore: Johns Hopkins University Press.

Aviʿam, M. 1989–90. "Khirbet el-Ghureiyib." *ESI* 9:93.

———. 1991. "Ḥorvat Ḥesheq." In Bottini, Segni, Alliata 1991: 351–77.

———. 1993a. "[Galilee.] The Hellenistic to Byzantine Periods." *NEAEHL* 2: 453–58.

———. 1993b. "Ḥorvat Hesheq: A Church in Upper Galilee." In Tsafrir 1993: 54–65.

———. 1994. *"Ha-yišub ha-nôṣĕrî ba-galîl ha-maᶜarābi ba-tĕqûpâ ha-bîzantît."* MA Thesis. Hebrew University.

———. 1995. "Remains of Churches and Monasteries in Western Galilee [Hebrew]." *Qadmoniot* 28: 47–59.

———. 1999. "Christian Galilee in the Byzantine Period." In E. Meyers 1999: 281–300.

———. Forthcoming. *Jews, Pagans, and Christians in the Galilee: Archaeological Surveys and Excavations.*

Avi Yonah, M. 1940. *Map of Roman Palestine.* Rev. ed. Jerusalem: Oxford University Press.

———. 1946. "Newly Discovered Latin and Greek Inscriptions." *QDAP* 12: 84–102.

———. 1962. *Historical Geography of Palestine from the End of the Babylonian Exile up to the Arab Conquest.* 3 ed. Jerusalem: Bialik.

———. 1975. "The Gaza School of Mosaicists in the Fifth-Sixth Centuries C.E." [Hebrew]. *EI* 12: 191–3.

———. 1976. *The Jews of Palestine: A Political History from the Bar Kokhba War to the Arab Conquest. Blackwell's Classical Studies*: Oxford: Blackwell.

———. 1977. *The Holy Land.* Rev. ed. Grand Rapids: Baker.

Baarda, T. 1969. "Gadarenes, Gerasenes, Gergesenes, and the 'Diatessaron' Traditions." In E. E. Ellis, M. Wilcox, eds. *Neotestamentica et Semitica: Studies in Honor of Matthew Black.* Edinburgh: T & T Clark. Pp. 181–97.

Bagatti, B. 1964–5. *"Le Anichita' di Kh. Qana e di Kefr Kenna in Galilea." LA* 15: 251-292.

Bagnall, R. S. 1976. *The Administration of Ptolemaic Provinces Outside Egypt.* Leiden: E. J. Brill.

———. 1977. "Price in 'Sales on Delivery.'" *GRBS* 18: 85–96.

———. 1992. "Landholding in Roman Egypt: The Distribution of Wealth." *JRS* 82: 128–49.

———. 1993. *Egypt in Late Antiquity.* Princeton: Princeton University Press.

Bagnall, R. S., Frier, B. W. 1994. *The Demography of Roman Egypt.* Cambridge Studies in Population, Economy and Society 23: Cambridge: Cambridge University Press.

Bar Adon, P. 1953. "Bet Yeraḥ." *IEJ* 4: 128–9.

Barag, D. 1988. "Geva and Geva Parashim" [Hebrew]. In Mazar 1988: 4–12.

Baras, Z., Safrai, S., Stern, M., Tsafrir, Y. 1982, eds. *Eretz Israel from the Destruction of the Second Temple to the Muslim Conquest* [Hebrew]. Jerusalem: Yad Izhak ben Zvi.

Ben David, A. 1978. *Talmudische Ökonomie.* Hildesheim: Georg Olms.

Ben David, H. 1998. "Oil Presses and Oil Production in the Golan in the Mishnaic and Talmudic Periods" [Hebrew]. *ᶜAtiqot* 34: 1–61.

Ben-Tor. A., Avissar, M., Portugali, Y. 1996. *Yoqneᶜam I: The Later Periods. Qedem Reports* 3: Jerusalem: Institute for Archaeology.

Ben-Tor, A., Portugali, Y., Avissar, M. 1981. "The First Two Seasons of Excavations at Tel Qashish, 1978–1979: Preliminary Report." *IEJ* 31: 137–64.

Ben-Tor, A., Rosenthal, R. 1978. "The First Season of Excavations at Tel Yoqne'am, 1977: Preliminary Report." *IEJ* 28: 57–82.

Berry, B. J. L. 1961. "City-Size Distributions and Economic Development." *Economic Development and Cultural Change* 9: 573–88.

———. 1967. *Geography of Market Centers and Retail Distribution.* Foundations of Economic Geography: Englewood Cliffs: Prentice Hall.

Biddick, K. 1985. "Medieval English Peasants and Market Involvement." *Journal of Economic History* 45: 823–31.

Bidez, J. *et al.* 1960, eds.. *Sozomenus, Kirchengeschichte. GCS* 50. Berlin: Akademie-Verlag.

Biger, G., Grossman, D. 1993. "Village and Town Populations in Palestine during the 1930s–1940s and their Relevance to Ethnoarchaeology." In A. Biran, J. Aviran, eds. *Biblical Archaeology Today, 1990.* Jerusalem: Israel Exploration Society.

Bijovsky, G. 1998. "The Gush Ḥalav Hoard Reconsidered." *ʿAtiqot* 35: 76–106.

Binns, J. 1994. *Ascetics and Ambassadors of Christ: The Monasteries of Palestine 314–631.* Oxford: Clarendon.

Biran, A. 1993. "Dan." In *NEAEHL* 1: 323–32.

———. 1994. *Biblical Dan.* Jerusalem: IEJ and HUC-JIR.

Blakely, J. A., Brinkman, R., Vitaliano, C. J. 1992. "Roman Mortaria and Basins from a Sequence in Caesarea: Fabrics and Sources." In R. L. Vann, ed., *Caesarea Papers: Straton's Tower, Herod's Harbour, and Roman and Byzantine Caesarea. JRA Suppl.* 5: Ann Arbor. 195–213.

Bloedhorn, H., Hüttenmeister, G. (F.). 1999. "The Synagogue." In Horbury, Davies, Sturdy 1999: 267–297.

Bottini, G. C., Di Segni, L., Alliata, E., eds. 1991. *Christian Excavations in the Holy Land.* Collectio Maior 36: Jerusalem: Studium Biblicum Franciscanum.

Bourdieu, P. 1977. *Outline of a Theory of Practice.* Tr. Richard Nice. Cambridge: Cambridge University Press.

Bowman, A. K. 1984. "Two Notes." *BASP* 21: 32–38.

———. 1985. "Landholding in the Hermopolite Nome in the Fourth Century A.D." *JRS* 75: 137–63.

Bowman, A. K., Rathbone, D. 1992. "Cities and Administration in Roman Egypt." *JRS* 82: 107–27.

Boyarin, D. 1993. *Carnal Israel: Reading Sex in Talmudic Judaism.* Berkeley: University of California.

———. 1999. *Dying for God: Martyrdom and the Making of Christianity and Judaism* Figurae: Stanford: Stanford University Press.

Bradford, M. G., Kent, W. A. 1977. *Human Geography: Theories and Their Applications.* Oxford: Oxford University Press.

Braudel, F. 1982. *The Wheels of Commerce: Civilization and Capitalism, 15th–18th Century, Volume 2.* New York: Harper and Row.

Bromley, R. J. 1976. "Contemporary Market Periodicity in Highland Ecuador." In C. A. Smith 1976: 91–122.

———. 1978. "Traditional and Modern Change in the Growth of Systems of Market Centers in Highland Ecuador." In R. H. T. Smith 1978: 31–47

Broshi, M. 1979. "The Population of Western Palestine in the Roman Byzantine Period." *BASOR* 236: 1–10.

———. 1982. "*ʾOklusyāt ʾereṣ yiśrāʾēl ba-tĕqupâ ha-rômît-bizantît.*" In Baras, Safrai, Stern, Tsafrir 1982: 442–55.

Broshi, M., Gofna, R. 1984. "The Settlements and Population of Palestine during the Early Bronze Age II–III." *BASOR* 253: 41–53.

Brown, P. R. L. 1982. *Society and the Holy in Late Antiquity.* Berkeley: University of California.

Buber, S. 1868, ed. *Pĕsiqtâ, wĕ-hî ʾaggadat ʾereṣ yisrāʾēl mĕyuḥeset le-rab kahanâ.* Lyck [Elk]: Mĕqiṣe nirdāmîm.

———. 1899, ed. *Midrasch Echa Rabbati.* Wilna.

Bunimovitz, S. 1995. "On the Edge of Empires." In T. E. Levy, ed. *The Archaeology of Society in the Holy Land.* New York: Facts on File. Pp. 320–31.

———. 1989. "The Land of Israel in the Late Bronze Age: A Case Study of Socio-Cultural Change in a Complex Society." Diss. Tel Aviv University. Tel Aviv.

Cancian, F. 1989. "Economic Behavior in Peasant Communities." In Plattner 1989: 127–170.

Carlsen, R. S. 1997. *The War for the Heart and Soul of a Highland Maya Town*. Austin: University of Texas Press.

Chiat, M. J. S. C. 1982. *Handbook of Synagogue Architecture*. BJS 29: Chico: Scholars Press.

Christaller, W. 1966. *Central Places in Southern Germany*. Tr. C. W. Baskin. Englewood Cliffs: Prentice Hall.

Cohen, S. J. D. 1981–82. "Epigraphical Rabbis." *JQR* 72: 1–17.

Cohn, J. 1929. "*Die Marktbezeichnung* אטלס *und* יריד *und ihr Verhältnis zueinander.*" *Festschrift zum 75jährige Bestehen des jüdisch-theologischen Seminars, Fraenkelsche Stiftung*. Breslau: Marcus.

Comaroff, J. L. and Comaroff, J. 1997. *Of Revelation and Revolution: The Dialectics of Modernity on a South African Frontier*. Volume II. Chicago: University of Chicago Press.

Conder, C., Kitchener, H. 1881. *The Survey of Western Palestine, 2: Galilee*. London: Palestine Exploration Fund.

Crissman, L. W. 1976. "Specific Central-Place Models for an Evolving System of Market Towns on the Changhua Plain, Taiwan." In C. A. Smith 1976a: 183–218.

Cuno, K. M. 1994. *The Pasha's Peasants: Land, Society, and the Economy in Lower Egypt, 1740–1858*. Cambridge: Cambridge University 1992. Rpt. Cairo: American University in Cairo.

Dar, S. 1986a. *Landscape and Pattern: An Archaeological Survey of Samaria 800 B.C.E.–636 C. E.* BAR International Series 308: Oxford.

———. 1986b. "Agriculture and Agricultural Production in Eretz-Israel in the Roman Byzantine Period" [Hebrew]. In A. Kasher, A. Oppenheimer, U. Rappaport, *Man and Land in Eretz-Israel in Antiquity* [Hebrew]. Jerusalem: Yad Izhak Ben-Zvi. Pp. 142–169.

Dar, S., Safrai, Z. Tepper, Y. 1986. *Um Rihan: A Village of the Mishnah*. Tel Aviv: Hakibbutz Hameuchad.

Dauphin, C. M. 1977. "Shelomi." *IEJ* 27: 256–9.

———. 1979. "A Monastery farm of the Early Byzantine Period at Shelomi" [Hebrew]. *Qadmoniot* 12. 1: 25–9.

———. 1982. "Jewish and Christian Communities in the Roman and Byzantine Gaulanitis: A Study of the Evidence from Archaeological Evidence." *PEQ* 114: 129–42.

———. 1983. "Settlements of the Roman and Byzantine Periods on the Golan Heights." *IEJ* 33: 189–206.

———. 1984. "Golan Survey, 1983." *IEJ* 34: 268–9.

———. 1993a. "A Byzantine Ecclesiastical Farm at Shelomi." In Tsafrir 1993: 43–48.

———. 1993b. "Dora – Dor: A Station for Pilgrims in the Byzantine Period on their Way to Jerusalem." In Tsafrir 1993: 90–97.

———. 1998. *La Palestine Byzantine: Peuplement et Populations*. BAR International Series 726.

Dauphin, C., Gibson, S. 1992–93. "Ancient Settlements in their Landscapes: The Results of Ten Years of Survey on the Golan Height." *Bulletin of the Anglo-Israel Archaeological Society*. 12: 7–31.

———. 1994–95. "The Byzantine City of Dor/Dora Discovered." *Bulletin of the Anglo-Israel Archaeological Society*. 14: 9–38.

Demsky, A. 1979. "The Permitted Villages of Sebaste in the Reḥov Mosaic." *IEJ* 29: 182–193.

Dentzer, J.-M. 1985, ed. *Hauran I: Recherches archéologiques sur la Syrie du sud à l'époque hellenistique et romaine.* Paris: P. Geuther.

Dindorf, G. 1859–62. *Epiphanii Episcopi Constantii Opera* Leipzig: Weigel.

Di Segni, L. 1991. "Ḥorvat Ḥesheq: The Inscriptions." In Bottini, Di Segni, E. Alliatta 1991: 379–90.

———. 1993. "Ḥorvat Ḥesheq: The Inscriptions." In Tsafrir 1993: 66–70.

———. 1995. "The Involvement of Local, Municipal and Provincial Authorities in Urban Building in Late Antique Palestine and Arabia." In Humphrey 1995–1999: 312–32.

———. 1996. "Metropolis and Provincia in Byzantine Palestine." In Raban, Holum 1996: 575–88.

———. 1999. "Epigraphic Documentation on Building in the Provinces of *Palaestina* and *Arabia*, 4th–7th C." In Humphrey 1995–1999: 149–78.

Dolav, M. "*Maṭbēʿôt ḥorbat ʾarbel.*" In Ilan, Izdarachet 1988: 29–34.

Dufraigne, P. 1975. *Aurelius Victor, Livre des Césars*. Paris: Les Belles Lettres.

Duncan-Jones, R. 1990. *Structure and Scale in the Roman Economy*. Cambridge: Cambridge University Press.

———. 1994. *Money and Government in the Roman Empire*. Cambridge: Cambridge University Press.

Eck, W. 1999. "The Bar Kokhba Revolt: The Roman Point of View." *JRS* 88: 76–89.

Edwards, D. R., McCollough, C. T. 1997, eds. *Archaeology and the Galilee: Texts and Contexts in the Graeco-Roman and Byzantine Period.* South Florida Studies in the History of Judaism 143: Atlanta: Scholars Press.

Eliav, Y. Z. 1995. *Sites, Institutions and Daily Life in Tiberias During the Talmudic Period*. Mi'tuv T'veria 10: [Tiberias?:] Municipality of Tiberias and Bar Ilan.

Feldman, L. 1991. "Abba Kolon and the Founding of Rome." *JQR* 81: 239–66.

Feliks, Y. 1980–86. *The Jerusalem Talmud: Talmud Yerushalmi Tractate Shevi'it Critically Edited*. Jerusalem. Ruben Mass.

Finkelstein, L. 1939. *Siphre ad Deuteronomium*. Berlin: Gesellschaft zur Förderung der Wissenschaft des Judentums.

———. 1983. *Sifra on Leviticus*. New York: JTSA.

Finley, M. I. 1985. *The Ancient Economy*. 2 ed. Berkeley: University of California Press.

Fischer, M. L. 1998. *Marble Studies: Roman Palestine and the Marble Trade*. Xenia 40: Konstanz, UVK.

Fischer, M. L., Grossmark, Ts. 1996. "Marble Import and Marmorarii in Eretz Israel during the Roman and Byzantine Period." *EI* 25: 471–83.

Fitzgerald, G. M. 1939. *A Sixth Century Mosaic at Beth-Shean*. Philadelphia.

Foerster, G. 1991. "Beth Shean at the Foot of the Mound." In *NEAEHL* 1: 223–35.

———. 1992. "The Ancient Synagogues of the Galilee." In Levine, ed. 1992: 289–320.

Foerster, R., Richtsteig, E. 1929. *Choricii Gazaei Opera*. Leipzig: Teubner.

Foss, C. 1995. "The Near Eastern Countryside in Late Antiquity: A Review Article." In Humphrey 1995–1999: 213–234.

———. 1997. "Syria in Transition, A.D. 550–750: An Archaeological Approach." *DOP* 51: 189–269.

Foxhall, L., Forbes, H. A. 1982. "*Σιτομητρεία*: The Role of Grain as a Staple Food in Classical Antiquity." *Chiron* 12: 41–90.

Frankel, R. 1986. "*Duaḥ bênayîm ʿal ha-seqer ha-arkēôlôgî bĕ-maʿarābô šel ha-gālîl bĕm 1976–1979.*" In Yedaya 1986: 304–317.

Frankel, R., Getzov, N. 1997. *Map of Akhziv (1); Map of Ḥanita (2)* [Hebrew and English]. Jerusalem: Israel Antiquities Authority, Archaeological Survey of Israel.

Frayn, J. M. 1993. *Markets and Fairs in Roman Italy*. Oxford: Oxford University Press.

Friedland, E. 1999. "Graeco-Roman Sculpture in the Levant: The Marbles from the Sanctuary of Pan at Caesarea Philippi (Banias)." In Humphrey 1995–1999: 7–22

Gabba, E. 1999. "The Social, Economic and Political History of Palestine 63 BCE – CE 70." In Horbury, Davies, Sturdy 1999: 94–167.

Gal, Z. 1990. *The Lower Galilee: Historical Geography in the Biblical Period* [Hebrew]. Tel Aviv: Hakibbutz Hameuchad.

———. 1991. *Map of Gazit* [Hebrew]. Jerusalem: Archaeological Survey of Israel.

———. 1998. *Map of Har Tavor (41); Map of 'En Dor (45)* [Hebrew and English]. Jerusalem: Israel Antiquities Authority, Archaeological Survey of Israel.

Garnsey, P. 1974. "Aspects of the Decline of the Urban Aristocracy in the Empire." *ANRW* II. 1. Pp. 229–52.

Garnsey, P., Saller, R. 1987. *The Roman Empire: Economy, Society and Culture*. Berkeley: University of California.

Gatier, P.-L. 1994. "*Villages du Proche-Orient protobyzantin (4ème–7ème s.). Étude régionale.*" In G. R. D. King, A. Cameron eds. *The Byzantine and Early Islamic Near East II: Land Use and Settlement Patterns*. Princeton: Darwin. Pp. 17–48.

Gelzer, H. 1890. *Georgii Cyprii Descripito Orbis Romani*. Leipzig: Teubner.

Geremek, H. 1969. *Karanis: commaunité rurale de l'Égypte romaine au IIe – IIIe siècle de notre ère*. Wrocław: Zakład Narodowy Imiena Ossoińskich.

Geyer, P., ed. 1965a. *Antonini Placentini Itinerarium*. In *CCSL* 175: 129–53.

———. 1965b. *Theodosii de Situ Terrae Sanctae*. In *CCSL* 175: 114–125.

Geyer, P., Cuntz, O. 1965. *Itinerarium Burdigalense*. In *CCSL* 175: 1–26.

Ginzberg, L. 1909. *Yerushalmi Fragments from the Genizah*. New York: JTSA.

———. 1941–61. *A Commentary on the Palestinian Talmud* [Hebrew]. New York: JTSA.

Goodman, M. 1987. *The Ruling Class of Judaea*. Cambridge: Cambridge University Press.

Goranson, S. 1999. "Joseph of Tiberias Revisited: Orthodoxies and Heresies in Fourth-Century Galilee." In E. Meyers 1999: 335–343.

Grainger, J. D. 1995. "'Village Government' in Roman Syria and Arabia." *Levant* 27: 179–195.

Graser, E. R. 1940. "The Edict of Diocletian on Maximum Prices." In T. Frank, ed. *Economic Survey of Ancient Rome*. Baltimore: Johns Hopkins. [1933–1940.] Vol. 5. Pp. 305–425.

Gregg, R. C., Urman, D. 1996. *Jews, Pagans, and Christians in the Golan Heights: Greek and Other Inscriptions of the Roman and Byzantine Era*. South Florida Studies in the History of Judaism 140: Atlanta: Scholars Press.

Groh, D. E. 1988. "Jews and Christians in Late Roman Palestine: Towards a New Chronology." *BA* 51: 80–96.

Guha, R. 1988. "On Some Aspects of the Historiography of Colonial India." In R. Guha, G. Chakravorty Spivak, eds. *Selected Subaltern Studies*. New York: Oxford University Press. Pp. 36–44.

———. 1997. *Dominance Without Hegemony: History and Power in Colonial India*. Cambridge: Harvard University Press.

Habas, E. 1996. "The Halachic Status of Caesarea as Reflected in the Talmudic Literature." In Raban, Holum 1996: 454–68.

Hachlili, R. 1987. "On the Mosaicists of the 'School of Gaza'" [Hebrew]. *EI* 19: 46-58.

Hamburger, H. 1954. "A Hoard of Syrian Tetradrachms and Tyrian Bronze Coins from Gush Ḥalav." *IEJ* 4: 201–26.

Hanson, R. S. 1980. *Tyrian Influence in Upper Galilee*. Cambridge: ASOR.

Harris, C. D. 1970. *Cities of the Soviet Union: Studies in their Function, Size, Density and Growth*. Monograph Series of the Association of American Geographers 5: Chicago: Rand McNally.

Hayes, C. E. 1997. *Between the Babylonian and the Palestinian Talmuds: Accounting for Halakhic Difference in Selected Sugyot from Tractate Avodah Zarah*. New York: Oxford University Press.

———. 1998. "Displaced Self-Perceptions: The Deployment of Minîm and Romans in b. Sanhedrin 90b–91a." Lapin 1998: 249–289.

Heichelheim, F. M. 1938. *Roman Syria*. In *An Economic Survey of Ancient Rome* IV, ed. T. Frank: Baltimore: Johns Hopkins.

Heikel, J. A. 1902, ed. *Eusebius, Über Constantins Leben. C.'s Rede an die Heilige Versammlung. Tricennatsrede an Constantin. GCS* 7: Leipzig: J. C. Hinrichs.

Hezser, C. 1997. *The Social Structure of the Rabbinic Movement in Roman Palestine*. TSAJ 66: Tübingen: Mohr (Siebeck).

Hilberg, I. 1910–18, ed. *Sancti Eusebii Hieronymi Epistulae*. In *CSEL* 54–56 (1910, 1912, 1918).

Hirschfeld, Y. 1984. "Excavation of a Jewish Dwelling at Khirbet Susiya" [Hebrew]. *EI* 17: 168–80.

———. 1992. *The Judaean Desert Monasteries in the Byzantine Period*. New Haven: Yale University Press.

———. 1993a. *A Guide to Antiquity Sites in Tiberias*. Jerusalem: Israel Antiquities Authority.

———. 1993b. "Monasteries and Churches in the Judean Desert in the Byzantine Period." In Tsafrir 1993: 149–54.

———. 1993c. "Tiberias." *NEAEHL* 4: 1464–70.

———. 1996. "Changes in the Types of Settlement of the Rural Jewish Population before the Revolts against Rome and After." *Cathedra* 80: 3-18.

———. 1997. "Farms and Villages in Byzantine Palestine." *DOP* 51: 33–71.

———. 1999. "Imperial Building Activity during the Reign of Justinian and Pilgrimage to the Holy Land in Light of the Excavations on Mt. Berenike, Tiberias." *RB* 106: 236–49.

Hirshman, M. 1982. *Qohelet Rabbah*. Diss. JTSA.

Hodder, I., Hassall, M. 1971. "The Non-Random Spacing of Romano-British Walled Towns." *Man* 6: 391–407.

Hodges, R. 1988. *Primitive and Peasant Markets*. Oxford: Blackwell.

Hodkinson, S. 1988. "Animal Husbandry in the Greek Polis." In Whittaker 1988: 35–74.

Holl, K. 1915–33, ed. *Epiphanius (Anecdota und Panarion). GCS* 25, 31, 37: Leipzig, Hinrichs.

Holum, K. G. 1996. "The Survival of the Bouleutic Class at Caesarea." In Raban, Holum 1996: 615–27.

Honigman E. 1939, ed. *Le Synekdèmos d'Hieroklès*. Brussels: L'Institute de Philologie et d'Histoire Orientales et Slaves.

Hopkins, I. W. J. 1980. "The City Region in Roman Palestine." *PEQ* 112: 19-32.

Hopkins, K. 1980. "Taxes and Trade in the Roman Empire (200 B.C.–A. D. 400)." *JRS* 70: 101–25.

Horbury, W., Davies, W. D., Sturdy, J. 1999, eds.*Cambridge History of Judaism* III. Cambridge: Cambridge University Press.

Horovitz, H. S. 1917. *Siphre D'be Rab: Fasiculus primus: Siphre ad Numeros adjecto Siphre Zutta*. Leipzig: Gustav Fock.

Horsley, R. A. 1996. *Archaeology, History, and Society in Galilee: The Social Context of Jesus and the Rabbis*. Mount Vernon: Trinity.

Humphrey, J. H. 1995–99, ed. *The Roman and Byzantine Near East. Volume I. Journal of Roman Archaeology* Supplementary Series 14: Ann Arbor, 1995. *Volume II. Journal of Roman Archaeology* Supplementary Series 31: Portsmouth: 1999.

Hunt, E. D. 1982. *Holy Land Pilgrimage in the Later Roman Empire AD 312–460*. Oxford: Clarendon.

Hüttenmeister, F. (G.), Reeg, G. 1977. *Die antiken Synagogen in Israel*. Wiesbaden: Reichert.

IG. Inscriptiones graecae. Berlin: 1873–.

IGR. Inscriptiones graecae ad res romanas pertinentes. R. Cagnat, *et al*. eds. Paris: 1911–1927.

Ilan, Z. 1986. "Ḥorvat Gelil: Its Identification and Finds." [Hebrew]. In Yedaya 1986: 516–20.

———. 1987a. *Bêt ha-kĕnesset u-bêt ha-midrāš bĕ-mērôt*. In Z. Ilan, E. Damati, eds. *Meroth the Ancient Jewish Village* [Hebrew]. Tel Aviv: Society for the Protection of Nature.

———. 1987b. "Survey of Synagogues in Galilee" [Hebrew]. *EI* 19: 169–198.

———. 1988. "*ʾArbel – pĕnê ha-kĕpār he-ʿatîq*." In Ilan, Izdarechet 1988: 35–53.

———. 1989–90. "Eastern Galilee, Survey of Roman Roads." *ESI* 9: 14–5.

———. 1991. *Ancient Synagogues in Israel* [Hebrew]. [Tel Aviv:] State of Israel, Ministry of Defense.

Ilan, Z., Izdarechet, A. 1988, eds. *ʾArbel: yiššûb yĕhûdî bĕ-mizraḥ ha-galîl ha-taḥtôn*. [Tel Aviv?:] *Ha-mādôr li-yĕdîʿat ha-ʾareṣ bi-bĕrît ha-tĕnuʿâ ha-qibbûṣît*.

Isaac, B. 1978. "Milestones in Judaea from Vespasian to Constantine." *PEQ* 110: 47–59.

———. 1992. *The Limits of Empire*. 2 ed. Oxford: Clarendon.

———. 1999. "Inscriptions and Religious Identity On the Golan." In Humphrey: 1995–1999: 179–88.

Isaac, B., Roll, I. 1982. *Roman Roads in Judaea I: The Legio Scythopolis Road*. BAR International Series 141.

Jacob, M. 1995. *Die Institution des jüdischen Patriarchen*. TSAJ 52: Tübingen: Mohr (Siebeck).

Jastrow, M. 1886–1903. *Dictionary of the Targumim, the Talmud Bavli and Yerushalmi, and the Midrashic Literature*. London.

Joffe, A. M. 1996. "Beth Yeraḥ." In *OEANE* 1:312–13.

Johnson, G. A. 1970. "A Test of the Utility of Central Place Theory in Archaeology." In P. J. Ucko, R. Tringham, G. W. Dimbleby, eds. *Man, Settlement, and Urbanism*. Cambridge, MA: Schenkman. Pp. 769–785.

———. 1980. "Rank-Size Convexity and System Integration: A View from Archaeology." *Economic Geography* 56: 234–47.

Jones, A. H. M. 1931. "The Urbanization of Palestine." *JRS*. 22: 18–35.

———. 1940. *The Greek City From Alexander to Justinian*. Oxford: Clarendon.

———. 1960. "Procurators and Prefects in the Early Principate." In *Studies in Roman Goverent and Law*. Oxford: Blackwell. Pp. 115–25.

———. 1964. *The Later Roman Empire*. Oxford: Blackwell.

———. 1971. *The Cities of the Eastern Roman Provinces*. Rev. ed. M. Avi Yonah *et alii*. Oxford: Oxford University Press.

JSG Golan. Epstein, C. Gutman. S. 1972. "The Golan." In *Judaea, Samaria and the Golan – Archaeological Survey 1967–68* [Hebrew]. Ed. M. Kochavi. Jerusalem: Archaeological Survey of Israel and Carta.

Kalmin, R. A. 1999. *The Sage in Jewish Society of Late Antiquity*. London: Routledge.

Kasher, A., Oppenheimer, A., Rappaport, U. 1986, eds. *Man and Land in Eretz Israel in Antiquity*. Jerusalem: Yad Izhak ben Zvi.

Kehoe, D. 1992. *Management and Investment on Estates in Roman Egypt*. Bonn: Habelt.

———. 1997. *Investment, Profit, and Tenancy: The Jurists and the Roman Agrarian Economy*. Ann Arbor: University of Michigan.

Kempinski, A. 1993. "Kabri." In *NEAEHL* 3: 839–41.

Kempinski, A., Niemeier, W. D. 1994, eds. *Excavation at Kabri: Report of the 1992–1993 Seasons: 7–8*. Tel Aviv: Tel Aviv University.

Kindler, A. 1988. "The Coins of Geva." In Mazar 1998: 43–67.

Kleiman, E. 1986. "Were Fairs in Tannaitic and Amoraic Palestine Artificial or Redundant?" [Hebrew] *Zion* 51: 471–84.

Kennedy, D. 1999. "Greek, Roman and Native Cultures in the Roman Near East." In Humphrey 1999: 77–106.

Kohl, H., Watzinger, C. 1916. *Antike Synagogen in Galilaea*. Leipzig: J. C. Hinrichs.

Kohut, A. 1878–92. *Arukh Completum* [Hebrew]. Vienna.

Klostermann, E. 1904, ed. *Eusebius, Onomastikon der Biblischen Ortsnamen*. Leipzig: Hinrichs.

Krauss, S. 1909. "Der Jahrmarkt von Batnan." *ZAW* 29: 294–311.

———. 1914–23. *Qadmôniôt ha-talmûd*. Odessa. Rpt. B. Hartz: Berlin, Vienna.

Lapin, H. 1995. *Early Rabbinic Civil Law and the Social History of Roman Galilee: A Study of Mishnah Tractate* Baba᾽ Meṣiʿa᾽. *Brown Judaic Studies* 307: Atlanta: Scholars Press.

———. 1996a. "Rabbis and Public Prayers for Rain in Later Roman Palestine." In A. Berlin, ed. *Public and Private Religion in the Ancient Near East*. Meyerhoff Series for Jewish Studies 2: Potomac: CDL Press. Pp. 105–129.

———. 1996b. "Jewish and Christian Academies in Roman Palestine: Some Preliminary Observations." In Raban, Holum, 1996: 496–512.

———. 1998, ed. *Religious and Ethnic Communities in Later Roman Palestine*. Bethesda: University Press of Maryland.

———. 1999. "Rabbis and Cities: The Literary Evidence." *JJS* 50: 187–207.

———. 2000. "Rabbis and Cities: Some Aspects of the Rabbinic Movement in its Graeco-Roman Environment." In P. Schäfer, C. Hezser, eds. *The Talmud Yerushalmi and Graeco-Roman Culture II*. Mohr (Siebeck). Pp. 51–80.

———. Forthcoming. "Some observations on Mishnah Megillah 1:1–3."

Lauffer, S. 1971. *Diokletians Preisedikt*. Texte und Kommentare 5: Berlin: De Gruyter.

Lauterbach, J. Z. 1933–35. *Mekilta de-Rabbi Ishmael: A Critical Edition on the Basis of the Manuscripts and Early Editions with an English Translation*. Philadelphia: Jewish Publication Society.

Lentzen, C. J., Lauff, E. A. 1987. "Beit Ras/Capitolias: A Preliminary Evaluation of the Archaeological and Textual Evidence." *Syria* 64: 21–46.

Lerner, M. B. 1971. *The Book of Ruth in Aggadic Literature and Midrash Ruth Rabba* [Hebrew]. Vol. 2. Diss. Hebrew University. Jerusalem.

Levy, J. 1876–1889. *Neuhebräisches und chaldäisches Wörterbuch*. Leipzig: Brockhaus.

Levine, L. I. 1978. "R. Simeon b. Yohai and the Purification of Tiberias." *HUCA* 49: 143-87.

———. 1979. "The Patriarch (Nasi) in Third Century Palestine." *ANRW* 2. 19. 2: 649–88.

———. 1981, ed. *Ancient Synagogues Revealed.* Jerusalem: Israel Exploration Society.

———. 1987. *The Rabbinic Class in Roman Palestine in Late Antiquity.* JTSA: New York and Jerusalem.

———. 1992, ed. *Galilee in Late Antiquity.* New York: JTSA and Havard University Press.

———. 1996. "The Status of the Patriarch in the Third and Fourth Centuries: Sources and Methodology." *JJS* 46: 1–32.

Leyerly, B. 1996. "Landscape as Cartography in Early Christian Pilgrimage Narratives." *JAAR* 64: 119–43.

———. 1999. "Pilgrims to the Land: Early Christian Perceptions of Galilee." In E. Meyers 1999: 345–357.

Lieberman, S. 1929. *On the Yerushalmi* [Hebrew]. Jerusalem: Darom.

———. 1937–9. *Tosefeth Rishonim.* Jerusalem: Bamberger and Wahrman.

———. 1946. "Palestine in the Third and Fourth Centuries" [Part I]. *JQR* 36: 329–70.

———. 1959. *ʿEśer milîn. ʾEškolôt* 3:, 73–89. Rept. in Lieberman 1991: 440–56.

———. 1955–88. *Tosefta Ki-Fshuṭa.* New York: JTSA.

———. 1974. *Midrash Debarim Rabbah.* 3 ed. Jerusalem.

———. 1975–76. "The Halakhic Inscription from the Bet Shean Valley" [Hebrew]. *Tarbiẓ* 45: 54–63. Rept. in Lieberman 1991: 402–411.

———. 1983. *Yerushalmi Neziqin.* [Introduction and commentary; text ed. E. S. Rosenthal.] Jerusalem: Israel Academy of Sciences.

———. *Studies in Palestinian Talmudic Literature* [Hebrew]. Ed. D. Rosenthal. Jerusalem: Magnes.

de Ligt, L. 1993. *Fairs and Markets in the Roman Empire: Economic and Social Aspects of Periodic Trade in a Pre-Industrial Society.* Dutch Monographs on Ancient History and Archaeology XI: Amsterdam: J. C. Gieben.

Linn, M. 1988. "The Location of Geva Parashim." In Mazar 1988: 219–23.

Loffreda, S. 1974. *Cafarnao II: La Ceramica.* Jerusalem: Franciscan Printing Press.

———. 1987. *Recovering Capernaum.* Jerusalem: Terra Sancta.

———. 1997. "Capernaum." *OEANE* 1: 416–19.

Lösch, A. 1954. *The Economics of Location.* Translated from the 2 ed., W. H. Woglom with W. F. Stolper. New Haven, Yale University Press.

Löw, I. 1881. *Aramaeische Pflanzennamen.* Leipzig: Wilhelm Engelmann.

———. 1923–34. *Die Flora der Juden.* Vienna, Leipzig: R. Lowit.

LSJM. Liddell, H. G. and Scott, R 1968, eds. *A Greek English Lexicon.* Rev. ed. with supplement, H. S. Jones, R. McKenzie. Oxford: Clarendon.

MacAdam, H. I. 1986. *Studies in the History of the Roman Province of Arabia: The Northern Sector.* BAR International Series 295: Oxford.

MacMullen, R. 1964. *Roman Social Relations 50 B.C. to A.D. 284.* New Haven: Yale University Press.

———. 1988. *Corruption and the Decline of Rome.* New Haven: Yale University Press.

Mader, E. 1957. *Mambre: Die Ergebnisse der Ausgrabungen im heiligen Bezirk Râmet el Ḫalil in Südpalästina 1926–1928.* Freiburg: Erich Wewel.

Magness, J. 1993. *Jerusalem Ceramic Chronology Circa 200–800.* Sheffield: JSOT Press.

———. 1997. "Synagogue Typology and Earthquake Chronology at Khirbet Shemaʿ, Israel." *Journal of Field Archaeology.* 24:211–20.

———. 2000. "The Question of the Synagogue. The Problem of Typology." In J. Neusner, A. J. Avery-Peck, eds., *Judaism in Late Antiquity III: Where We Stand, Part III.* Leiden: Brill.

Maisler (Mazar), B., Stekelis, M. Avi Yonah, M. 1952. "Excavations at Beth-Yeraḥ (Khirbet el Kerak) 1944–1946." *IEJ* 2:165-73, 218-29.

Mandelbaum, B. 1987, ed. *Pesikta de Rav Kahana.* 2 ed. New York: JTSA.

Ma'oz, Z. U. 1985. "Comments on Jewish and Christian Communities in Byzantine Palestine." *PEQ* 117: 59–67.

———. 1986. *Rāmat ha-gôlān ba-ʿēt ha-ʿattîqâ.* Qasrin.

———. 1993. "[Golan:] Hellenistic Period to the Middle Ages." In *NEAEHL* 1:534–46.

———. 1996. "When Were the Galilean Synagogues first Constructed" [Hebrew]. *EI* 25: 416–26.

Marcus, R. 1943. *Josephus with an English Translation VII. LCL.* Cambridge: Harvard University Press.

Mare, W. H. 1993. "Abila." In *NEAEHL* 1: 1–3.

———. 1996. "The 1994 and 1995 Seasons of Excavation at Abila of the Decapolis." *ADAJ* 40: 259–60.

Margaliot, M. 1953–60, ed. *Midrash Wayyikra Rabbah* [Hebrew]. Jerusalem. Israel Department of Education and Culture.

Marfoe, L. 1979. "The Integrative Transformation: Patterns of Sociopolitical Organization in Southern Syria." *BASOR* 234: 1–42.

Martin, D. 1996. "The Construction of the Ancient Family: Methodological Considerations." *JRS* 86: 40–60.

Marx, E. 1992. "Are there Pastoral Nomads in the Middle East?" In O. Bar Yosef, A. Khazanov, eds. *Pastoralism in the Levant: Archaeological Materials and Anthropological Perspectives.* Monographs in World Archaeology 10: Madison: Prehistory Press.

Mattingly, D. J. 1988a. "Oil for Export? A Comparison of Libyan, Spanish and Tunisian Olive Oil Production in the Roman Empire." *JRA* 1: 33–56.

———. 1988b. "Olea Mediterranea?" *JRA* 1:153–61.

Mazar, B. 1988, ed. *Geva: Archaeological Discoveries at Tel Abu Shusha, Mishmar Ha-ʿEmeq.* Jerusalem: Hakibbutz Hameuchad.

Mayerson, P. 1984. "'Palaestina' vs. 'Arabia' in the Byzantine Sources." *ZPE* 56: 223–230.

———. 1988. "Justinian's Novel 103 and the Reorganization of Palestine." *BASOR* 262: 65–71.

Meier, J. P. 1991–. *A Marginal Jew: Rethinking the Historical Jesus.* New York: Doubleday.

Meshorer, Y. 1973. "Coins from the Excavations at Khorazin" [Hebrew]. *EI* 11: 158–62.

———. 1985. *City Coins of Eretz Israel and the Decapolis in the Roman Period.* Jerusalem: Israel Museum.

———. 1997. *A Treasury of Jewish Coins From the Persian Period to Bar Kochba.* Jerusalem: Yad Izhak Ben-Zvi.

Metzger, B. M. 1971. *Textual Commentary on the Greek New Testament.* Stuttgart: United Bible Society.

Meyers, E. M. 1979. "The Cultural Setting of Galilee: The Case of Regionalism and Early Judaism." *ANRW* 2. 19. 1: 686–702.

———. 1982. "The Byzantine Towns of the Galilee." In R. H. Hohlfelder, ed., *City, Town, and Countryside in the Early Byzantine Period.* Boulder: East European Monographs no. 120. Pp. 115–31.

———. 1985. "Galilean Regionalism. A Reappraisal." In W. S. Green, ed., *Approaches to Ancient Judaism V*. BJS 32: Atlanta: Scholars Press. Pp. 115–31.

———. 1995. "An Archaeological Response to a New Testament Scholar." *BASOR* 297: 17–26.

———. 1997. "Jesus and his Galilean Context." In Edwards, McCollough 1997: 57–66.

———. 1999, ed. *Galilee: Confluence of Cultures*. Winona Lake: Eisenbrauns.

Meyers, E. M., Kraabel, A. T., Strange, J. F. 1976. "Ancient Synagogue Excavations at Khirbet Shema', Upper Galilee, Israel, 1970–2." *AASOR* 42.

Meyers, E. M., Meyers, C. L., Strange, J. F. 1978. "Excavation at Meiron in Upper Galilee – 1974, 1975: Second Preliminary Report." *AASOR* 43: 73–103.

———. 1990. *Excavations at the Ancient Synagogue of Gush Ḥalav*. Winona Lake: Eisenbrauns and ASOR.

Meyers, E. M., Strange, J. F. 1981. *Archaeology, the Rabbis, and Early Christianity*. Knoxville: Abingdon.

Meyers, E. M., Strange, J. F., Groh, D. E. 1978. "The Meiron Excavation Project: Archaeological Survey in Galilee and Golan, 1976." *BASOR* 230: 1–24.

Meyers, E. M., Strange, J. F., Meyers, C. L. 1981. *Excavations at Ancient Meiron, Upper Galilee, Israel, 1971–72, 1974–75, 1977*. Cambridge: AASOR.

Mitchell, S. 1993. *Anatolia: Land, Men and Gods in Asia Minor*. Oxford: Clarendon.

Miller, K. 1916. *Itineraria Romana*. Stuttgart. Strecker and Schröder.

Morley, N. 1996. *Metropolis and Hinterland: The City of Rome and the Italian Economy 200 B.C.–A. D. 200*. Cambridge: Cambridge University Press.

Nagy, R. M., Meyers, C. L., Meyers, E. M., Weiss, Z. 1996. *Sepphoris in Galilee: Cross-currents of Culture*. Winona Lake: Eisenbrauns and North Carolina Museum of Art.

Naveh, J. 1978. *On Stone and Mosaic* [Hebrew]. Jerusalem: Maariv.

NEAEHL. *New Encyclopedia of Archaeological Excavations in the Holy Land*. Ed. E. Stern. Jerusalem: IES and Carta, 1993.

de Neeve, P. W. 1984. *Peasants in Peril: Location and Economy in Italy in the Second Century B.C.* Amsterdam: J. C. Gieben.

Netzer, E. 1996. "Review of the Synagogues at Gush Halav and Khirbet Shemaᶜ" [Hebrew]. *EI* 25: 450–5.

Nollé, J. 1982. *Nundinas instuere et habere*. Hildesheim: Georg Olms.

OEANE. *Oxford Encyclopaedia of Archaeology in the Near East*. Ed. E. M. Meyers. New York: Oxford University Press, 1997.

O'Hanlon, R. 1988. "Recovering the Subject: *Subaltern Studies* and Histories of Resistance in Colonial South Asia." *Modern Asian Studies* 22: 189–224.

OLD. *Oxford Latin Dictionary*. Ed. P. G. W. Glare. Oxford: Oxford University Press, 1982.

Oppenheimer, A. 1977. *The ᶜAm Ha-aretz: A Study in the Social History of the Jewish People in the Hellenistic-Roman Period*. *Arbeiten zur Literatur und Geschichte des hellenistischen Judentums* 8: Leiden: Brill.

———. 1996. "Urbanization and City Territories in Roman Palestine" [Hebrew]. In *The Jews in the Hellenistic-Roman World: Studies in Memory of Menahem Stern*. Jerusalem: Mercaz Zalman Shazar. Pp. 209–26.

Ovadiah, A. 1970. *Corpus of the Byzantine Churches in the Holy Land*. Bonn: Peter Hanstein.

Ovadiah, A., de Silva, G. 1981. "Supplementum to the Corpus of Byzantine Churches in the Holy Land I." *Levant* 13: 200–61.

Ovadiah, A., Fischer, M., Roll, I. 1993. "[Tel Dan] Hellenistic and Roman Period." In *NEAEHL* 3: 857–9

P. Oxy. The Oxyrhynchus Papyri. London: Egypt Exploration Society. 1898–.

P. Yadin. The Documents from the Bar Kokhba Period in the Cave of Letters. Ed. N. Lewis, Y. Yadin, J. C. Greenfield. Jerusalem: IES, 1989.

Parr, J. B. 1980. "Frequency Distribution of Central Places in Southern Germany: A Further Analysis." *Economic Geography* 56: 140–54.

Palumbo, G., ed. 1994. *JADIS: The Jordan Antiquities Database and Information System: A Summary of the Data*. Amman: Department of Antiquities of Jordan and American Center of Oriental Research.

Pastor, J. 1997. "Why were there no Jewish Farmsteads in the Galilee?" [Hebrew]. *Cathedra* 84: 175.

Patrich, J. 1995. *Sabas, Leader of Palestinian Monasticism: A Comparative Study in Eastern Monasticism, Fourth to Seventh Centuries*. Washington: Dumbarton Oaks.

Payne Smith, J. 1903 [1998]. *A Compendious Syriac Dictionary*. Oxford: Clarendon. Rpt. Winona Lake: Eisenbrauns.

Peacock, D. F. 1982. *Pottery in the Roman World: An Ethnoarchaeological Approach*. London: Longman.

Peskowitz, M. 1993. "'Family/ies' in Antiquity: Evidence from Tannaitic Literature and Roman Galilean Architecture." In S. J. D. Cohen, ed. *The Jewish Family in Antiquity*. BJS 289: Atlanta. Pp: 9–36.

Pixner, B. 1985. "Searching for the New Testament Site of Bethsaida." *BA* 48: 207–16.

Plattner, S. 1976. "Periodic Trade in Developing Areas Without Markets." In C. A. Smith 1976a 1, 72–81.

———. 1989, ed. *Economic Anthropology*. Stanford: Stanford University Press.

Polanyi, K. 1944. *The Great Transformation*. New York: Farrar and Rhinehart.

Porat, N., Killebrew, A. E. Forthcoming. "Petrographic Analysis of Late Antique and Islamic Fine and Coarse Wares from Qasrin."

Portugali, Y. 1982. "A Field Methodology for Regional Archaeology (The Jezreel Valley Survey, 1981)." *Tel Aviv* 9:170–88.

———. 1986. "The Settlement Pattern in the Western Jezreel Valley from the 6th Century B.C. E. to the Arab Conquest" [Hebrew]. in Kasher, Oppenheimer, Rappaport 1986: 7–19

Price, P. M. 1987. *Pottery Analysis: A Sourcebook*. Chicago: University of Chicago Press.

Pumain, D. 1997. "City-Size Dynamics in Urban Systems." In J. McGlade, S. E. van der Leeuw, eds. *Time, Process and Structured Transformation in Archaeology*. London: Routledge. Pp. 97–117.

Raban, A. 1982. *Archaeological Survey of Israel: Nahalal Map (28) 16-23* [Hebrew]. Jerusalem: Archaeological Survey of Israel.

Raban, A., Holum, K. G. 1996, eds. *Caesarea Maritima: A Retrospective after Two Millennia*. DMOA 21: Leiden: Brill.

Rathbone, D. W. 1990. "Villages, Land, and Population in Graeco-Roman Egypt." *Proceedings of the Cambridge Philological Society* 36: 103–142.

———. 1991. *Economic Rationalism and Rural Society in Third-Century A.D. Egypt*. Cambridge: Cambridge University Press.

Raynor, J. 1981. "Numismatic Report of Nabratein 1980." In E. M. Meyers, J. F. Strange, C. L. Meyers. "Preliminary Report on the 1980 Excavations at en Nabratein, Israel." *BASOR* 244: 1–25.

Raynor, J., Meshorer, Y. 1988. *The Coins of Ancient Meiron*. Winona Lake: ASOR and Eisenbrauns.

Rea, J. 1982. "P. Lond. Inv. 1562 Verso: Market Taxes in Oxyrhynchus." *ZPE* 48: 191–209.

Reed, J. L. 1999. "Galileans, 'Israelite Village Culture,' and the Sayings Gospel Q." In E. Meyers 1999: 87–108.

———. 2000. *Archaeology and the Galilean Jesus: A Re-examination of the Evidence.* Harrisburg: Trinity Press International.

Rieger, P. 1925–26. "The Foundation of Rome in the Talmud: A Contribution to the Folklore of Antiquity." *JQR* 16: 227–36.

Reiter, S. 1913, ed. *Sancti Eusebii Hieronymi In Hieremiam Prophetam Libri Sex. CSEL* 59.

Roll, I. 1976. "The Roman Road Network in Eretz-Israel" [Hebrew]. *Qadmoniot* 9: 38–50.

———. 1983. "The Roman Road System in Judaea." *Jerusalem Cathedra* 3: 136–61.

Roll, I., Ayalon, E. 1989. *Apollonia and Southern Sharon: Model of a Coastal City and its Hinterland.* [Hebrew.] Tel Aviv: Hakibbutz Hameuchad.

Roseberry, W. 1989. "Peasants and the World." In Plattner 1989: 108–126.

Roseberry, W., O'Brien, J. 1991. "Introduction." In W. Roseberry, J. O'Brien, eds., *Golden Ages, Dark Ages: Imagining the Past in Anthropology and History.* Berkeley: University of California. Pp. 1–18.

Rosenberger, M. 1972–77. *City Coins of Palestine.* (N. P.) Jerusalem.

Rosenthal, E. S. 1963. *Ha-môreh. PAAJR* 31:1–71 (Hebrew section).

Rosenthal, E. S., Lieberman, S. 1983, eds. *Yerushalmi Neziqin.* Jerusalem: Academy of Arts and Sciences.

Rowlandson, J. 1996. *Landowners and Tenants in Roman Egypt: The Social Relations of Agriculture in the Oxyrhynchite Nome.* Oxford: Clarendon.

Rubin, Z. 1983. "Joseph the Comes and the Attempts to Covert the Galilee to Christianity in the Fourth Century CE." *Cathedra* 26: 105–16.

Saarisalo, A. 1927. *The Boundary Between Issachar and Naphthali.* Helsinki.

Safrai, Z. 1977. "Marginal Notes on the Rehob Inscription" [Hebrew]. *Zion* 42:1–23.

———. 1980a. *Gĕbulôt wĕ-šilṭôn bĕ-ʾereṣ yiśrāʾēl bi-tĕqûpat ha-mišnâ wĕ-ha-talmûd.* Tel Aviv: Hakibbutz Hameuchad.

———. 1980b. "Urbanization in Israel in the Greco Roman Period" [Hebrew]. *Meḥqarîm* 5: 105–29.

———. 1983a. "*Ha-kĕpar bi-tĕqûpat ha-mišnâ wĕ-ha-talmûd.*" In M. Stern, ed. *Nation and History* [Hebrew]. Jerusalem: Zalman Shazar Center, 1983. 1: 173–95.

———. 1983b. "*Lĕ-šĕʾēlat ha-mibneh ha-merḥābî šel ha-yiššûb ba-gālîl bi-tĕqûpat ha-mišnâ wĕ-ha-talmûd.*" In *In the Lands of Galilee* [Hebrew]. Ed. A. Shemueli *et al.* Haifa: University of Haifa: 269–88.

———. 1984a. "Fairs in Eretz Israel in the Mishnah and Talmud Period" [Hebrew]. *Zion* 49: 139–58

———. 1984b. "Israel's Borders as Regards Halachic Issues." In S. Israeli, N. Lamm, Y. Raphael, eds. *Jubilee Volume in Honor of Moreinu Hagaon Rabbi Joseph B. Soloveitchik.* Jerusalem and New York: Mosad Harav Kook and Yeshiva University Press. Pp. 1092–1119.

———. 1986a. "*Pirqê galîl bi-tĕqûpat ha-mišnâ wĕ-ha-talmûd.*" 2 ed. Jerusalem: Ma'al-ot.

———. 1986b. "The Influence of Demographic Stratification on the Agricultural and Economic Structure During the Mishnaic and Talmudic Periods" [Hebrew]. In Kasher, Oppenheimer, Rappaport 1986: 20–48.

———. 1994. *Economy of Roman Palestine.* London: Routledge.

———. 1995. *The Jewish Community in the Talmudic Period* [Hebrew]. Jerusalem: Yad Izhak ben Zvi.

Safrai, Z., Linn, M. 1988a. "The Economic Basis of Geva." In Mazar 1988: 120–66.

———. 1988b. "Excavations and Surveys in the Mishmar Ha-'Emeq Area." In Mazar 1988: 167–214.

Sanders, E. P. 1996. "Jesus' Relationship to Sepphoris." In Nagy, C. L. Meyers, E. M. Meyers, Weiss 1996: 75–77.

Sarason, R. S. 1993. *The Talmud of the Land of Israel, A Preliminary Translation and Explanation: Demai.* Chicago: University of Chicago Press.

Sartre, M. 1985. "*Le peuplement et le développement de Ḥawran antique à la lumière des inscriptions grecques et latines.*" In Dentzer 1985: 189–202.

———. 1991. *L'orient romain: provinces et sociétés provinciales en Méditerannée orientale d'Auguste aux Sévères (31 avant J.-C.–235 après J.-C.).* Paris: Éditions du Seuil.

Savage, S. H. 1997. "Assessing Departures from Log-Normality in the Rank-Size Rule." *Journal of Archaeological Science* 24: 233–244.

Sawicki, M. 1997. "Spatial Management of Gender and Labor in Greco-Roman Galilee." In Edwards, McCollough 1997: 7–28.

Schäfer, P., Becker, H.-J. 1991–. *Synopse zum Talmud Yerushalmi.* Mohr (Siebeck).

Schiffman, L. H. 1992. "Was There a Galilean Halakhah?" In Levine 1992: 143–156.

Schumacher, G. 1886. *Die Dscholan.* Leipzig.

———. 1888. *The Jaulan.* London.

Schürer, E., Vermes, G., *et al.* 1973–87. *The History of the Jewish People in the Age of Jesus Christ*, rev. ed. G. Vermes, *et al.* Edinburgh: T. and T. Clark..

Schwartz, E. 1939, ed. *Kyrillos von Scythopolis. Texte und Untersuchungen zur Geschichte der altchristliche Literatur* 49:2: Leipzig.

Schwartz, Seth. Forthcoming. *Imperialism and Jewish Society from 200 BC.E. to 640 C.E.* Princeton: Princeton University Press.

Scott, James C. 1976. *The Moral Economy of the Peasant: Rebellion and Subsistence in Southeast Asia.* New Haven: Yale University Press.

Shaw, B. D. 1979. "Rural Periodic Markets in Roman North Africa as Mechanisms of Social Integration and Control." *Research in Economic Anthropology* 2: 91–117.

———. 1981. "Rural Markets in North Africa and the Political Economy of the Roman Empire." *Antiquitées africaines* 17: 37–83.

Siegelman, A. 1984. "The Identification of Gaba Hippeon." *PEQ* 116: 89–93.

Skinner, G. W. 1964. "Marketing and Social Structure in Rural China, Part I." *Journal of Asian Studies* 24:1–43.

———. 1965. "Marketing and Social Structure in Rural China, Part II." *Journal of Asian Studies* 24:195–228.

———. 1977a. "Regional Urbanization in Nineteenth-Century China." In G. W. Skinner, ed. *The City in Late Imperial China.* Stanford: Stanford University Press. Pp. 211–49.

———. 1977b. "Cities and the Hierarchy of Local Systems." In G. W. Skinner, ed. *The City in Late Imperial China.* Stanford: Stanford University Press. Pp. 275–346.

Skydsgaard, J. E. 1988. "Transhumance in Ancient Greece." In Whittaker 1988: 75–86.

Smith, C. A. 1976a, ed. *Regional Analysis.* New York: Academic Press.

———. 1976b. "Regional Economic Systems: Linking Geographical Models and Socio-Economic Problems." In C. A. Smith 1976a: 1, 1–63.

———. 1976c. "Exchange Systems and the Spatial Distribution of Elites: The Organization of Stratification in Agrarian Societies." In Smith 1976a: 2, 309–74.

———. 1978. "Beyond Dependency Theory." *American Ethnographer* 5: 574–617.

Smith, R. H. 1987. "Trade in the Life of Pella of the Decapolis." *SHAJ* 3: 53–58.

Smith, R. H. T. 1978, ed. *Market-Place Trade: Periodic Markets, Hawkers, and Traders in Africa, Asia, and Latin America.* Vancouver: Centre for Transportation Studies.

Sokoloff, M. 1992. *A Dictionary of Jewish Palestinian Aramaic of the Byzantine Period.* Ramat Gan: Bar Ilan.

Sperber, D. 1978. *Roman Palestine, 200–400: The Land.* Bar Ilan Studies in Near Eastern Languages and Cultures: Ramat Gan: Bar Ilan.

———. 1991. *Roman Palestine, 200–400: Money and Prices.* 2ed. with supplement. Ramat Gan: Bar Ilan.

Spijkerman, A. 1975. *Cafarnao III: Catalogo delle Monete Della Citta'.* Jerusalem: Franciscan Printing Press.

Stepanski, Y. 1992. "Rosh Pinna Map, Survey – 1992." *ESI* 14: 13–5.

Stern, E. 1992. *Dor – The Ruler of the Seas* [Hebrew]. Jerusalem: Bialik Institute and IES.

———. 1995, ed. *Excavations at Dor: Final Report: Volume I A. Qedem Reports* I: Jerusalem: Institute for Archaeology and IES.

Stern, M. 1976–84, ed. *Greek and Latin Authors on Jews and Judaism.* Jerusalem: Israel Academy of Arts and Sciences.

Stobart, J. 1996. "The Spatial Organization of a Regional Economy: Central Places in North-West England in the Early-Eighteenth Century." *Journal of Historical Geography* 22: 147–159.

Strack, H. L., Stemberger, G. 1992. *Introduction to the Talmud and Midrash.* Rev. ed. G. Stemberger. Tr. M. Brockmuehl. Minneapolis: Fortress.

Strange, J. F. 1992. "Nazareth." In *Anchor Bible Dictionary.* Ed. D. N. Freedman. New York: Doubleday. 4: 1050–1051.

———. 1996. "Nazareth." *OEANE* 4: 113–114.

———. 1997. "First Century Galilee from Archaeology and From the Texts." In Edwards, McCollough 1997: 39–48.

Strange, J. F. Groh, D. E., Longstaff, T. R. W. 1995. "Excavations at Sepphoris: The Location and Identification of Shikhin, Part II." *IEJ* 45: 170–87.

Sussman, Y. 1973–74. "A Halakhic Inscription from the Beth Shean Valley" [Hebrew]. *Tarbiẓ* 43: 88–158.

———. 1975–76. The "Boundaries of Eretz-Israel." *Tarbiẓ* 45:213–57.

Taylor, J. E. 1993. *Christians and the Holy Places.* Oxford: Clarendon.

Tate, G. 1992. *Les campagnes de la Syrie du nord du IIe au VIIe siècle, Tome I.* Paris: Librairie Orientaliste Paul Geuthner.

———. 1997. "The Syrian Countryside during the Roman Era." In Alcock 1997: 55–71.

Tchalenko, G. 1953–58. *Villages Antiques de la Syrie du Nord: le Massif du Belus a l'Epoque Romaine.* Paris: P. Geuthner.

Theodor, J., Albeck, Ch. 1912–36. *Bereschit Rabba mit kritischen Apparat und Kommentar.* Berlin.

Thompsen, P. 1917. "*Die römischen Meilensteine der Provinzen Syria, Arabia und Palaestina.*" *ZDPV* 40: 1–103.

Thornton, T. C. G. 1990. "The Stories of Joseph of Tiberias." *VigChr* 44: 54–63.

Thorpe, J. K. 1978. "Periodic Markets in the Caspian Lowlands of Iran." In R. H. T. Smith 1978: Pp. 81–98.

TIR Tabula Imperii Romani. Iudaea. Palaestina. Ed. Y. Tsafrir, L. Di Segni, J. Green. Jerusalem: Israel Academy of Arts and Sciences, 1994.

Tsaferis, V. 1989. *Excavations at Capernaum I.* Eisenbrauns: Winona Lake.

Tsaferis, V., Peleg, M. 1988–89. "Kefar Naḥum." *ESI* 7/8: 108–109.

Tsafrir, Y. 1982. "*Ha-pĕrobinṣiyôt bĕ-ereṣ yiśrāʾēl – šĕmôt, gĕbûlôt, û-tĕḥûmê minhal.*" In Baras, Safrai, Stern, Tsafrir 1982: 350–86.

———. 1989. "The Synagogues at Merot and Capernaum and the Dating of the Galilean Synagogues: A Reconsideration" [Hebrew]. *EI* 20: 337–44.

———. 1993 (ed). *Ancient Churches Revealed.* Jerusalem: Israel Exploration Society.

———. 1995. "On the Source of the Architectural Design of the Ancient Synagogues of Galilee: A New Appraisal." In Urman, Flesher 1995: 1: 75–93.

———. 1996. "Some Notes on the Settlement and Demography of Palestine in the Byzantine Period: The Archaeological Evidence." In J. D. Seger, ed. *Retrieving the Past: Essays on Archaeological Research and Methodology in Honor of Gus W. Van Beek.* Winona Lake: Eisenbrauns. 269–83.

Tsafrir, Y., Foerster, G. 1994. "From Scythopolis to Baysān – Changing Concepts of Urbanism." In G. R. D. King and A. Cameron, eds., *Byzantine and Early Islamic Near East II: Land Use and Settlement Patterns.* Princeton: Darwin Press. 95–115.

Urman, D. 1970–71. "Jewish Inscriptions from Dabura in the Golan" [Hebrew]. *Tarbiz,* 40: 399–408.

———. 1972. "Jewish Inscriptions from Dabura in the Golan." *IEJ* 22: 1–23.

———. 1985. *The Golan: A Profile of a Region during the Roman and Byzantine Periods. BAR International Series* 269.

———. 1995. "Public Structures and Jewish Communities in the Golan Heights." In Urman, Flesher 1995: 2: 375–561.

Urman. D., Flesher, P. V. M. 1995, eds. *Ancient Synagogues: Historical Analysis and Archaeological Discovery.* SPB 47: Leiden: Brill.

Ussishkin, D. 1997. "Jezreel, Tel." *OEANE* 3: 246–7.

Ussishkin, D., Woodhead, J. 1994. "Excavations at Tel Jezreel 1992–1993: Second Preliminary Report." *Levant* 26: 1–48.

Villeneuve, F. 1985. "*L'économie rurale et la vie des campagnes dans le Hauran antique (Ier siècle av. J.-C.–VIIe siècle ap. J.-C.): une approche.*" In Dentzer 1985: 63–129.

Vitto, F. 1981. "The Synagogue at Reḥov." In Levine 1981: 90–94.

———. 1993. "[Tiberias:] Excavation in the South of the City." *NEAEHL* 4: 1470–3.

———. 1996. "Byzantine Monuments from Bet Shearim: New Evidence for the History of the Site." *ʿAtiqot* 28: 115–46.

Wagner-Lux, V. U., Krueger, E. W., Vriezen, K. J. H., Vriezen-van der Flier, T. 1978. "*Bericht über die Oberflächenforschung in Gadara (*Umm Qēs*) in Jordanien in Jahre 1974.*" *ZDPV* 94: 135–44.

Walker, P. W. L. 1990. *Holy City, Holy Places?* Oxford: Clarendon.

Wallerstein, I. 1976. *The Modern World-System I.* New York: Academic Press.

Walmsley, A. G. 1992. "The Social and Economic Region of Fihl (Pella) between the 7th and 9th Centuries." In P. Canivet, J-P. Rey-Coquais, eds. *La Syrie de Byzance à l'Islam.* Damascus: Institut Français de Damas.

———. 1996. "Byzantine Palestine and Arabia: Urban Prosperity in Late Antiquity." In N. Christie, S. Loseby, eds. *Towns in Transition.* Aldershots: Scolar. 126–158.

Warren, C. 1876. *Underground Jerusalem.* London: Richard Bentley and Son.

Weber, M. 1896 [1976]. "The Social Causes of the Decline of Ancient Civilizations." In *The Agrarian Sociology of Ancient Civilizations.* Tr. R. I. Frank. London: NLB.

———. 1906 [1946]. "Capitalism and Rural Society in Germany." In H. H. Gerth, C. W. Mills., eds. *From Max Weber: Essays in Sociology.* New York: Oxford University Press.

Weiss, Z. 1998. "Jewish Infuences on the Art and Architecture of the Jewish City in Roman Palestine." In Lapin 1998: 219–46.

Weiss, Z., Netzer, E. 1996a. "Hellenistic and Roman Sepphoris: The Archaeological Evidence." In Nagy, Meyers, Meyers, Weiss 1996: 75–79.

———. 1996b. "Sepphoris during the Byzantine Period." In Nagy, Meyers, Meyers, Weiss 1996: 81–89.

Wewers, G. A., Hüttenmeister, F. G. 1995. *Demai – Zweifelhaftes. Übersetzung des Talmud Yerushalmi* I/3: Tübingen: Mohr (Siebeck).

Whittaker, C. R. 1988. "Trade and the Aristocracy in the Roman Empire." *Opus* 4: 49–75.

———. 1988, ed. *Pastoral Economies in Classical Antiquity*. Cambridge: Cambridge Philological Society.

———. 1990. "The Consumer City Revisited: The *vicus* and the City." *JRA* 3:110–17.

———. 1993. "Do Theories of the Ancient City Matter?" In T. J. Cornell, H. K. Lomas, eds. *Urban Society in Roman Italy*. London: UCL Press. Pp. 1–20.

Wilken, R. L. 1992. *The Land Called Holy*. New Haven: Yale University Press.

Williams, F. 1987. *The Panarion of Epiphanius of Salamis Book I (Sects 1–46)*. Nag Hamadi Studies 25: Leiden: Brill.

Wolf, E. R. 1957. "Closed Corporate Communities in Mesoamerica and Central Java." *Southwestern Journal of Anthropology* 13: 1–18.

———. 1966. *Peasants*. Englewood Cliffs: Prentice Hall.

———. 1982. *Europe and the People without History*. Berkeley: University of California Press.

Wood, B. G. 1990. *The Sociology of Pottery in Ancient Palestine*. JSOT Supp. 103: Sheffield: Sheffield Academic Press.

Woolf, G. 1988. "World Systems Analysis and the Roman Empire." *JRA* 1: 44–58.

———. 1997. "The Roman Urbanization of the East." In Alcock 1997: 1–14.

———. 1998. *Becoming Roman: The Origins of Provincial Administration in Gaul*. Cambridge: Cambridge University Press.

Yedaya, M., ed. 1986. *The Western Galilee Antiquities* [Hebrew]. Haifa and Tel Aviv.

Yeivin, Z. 1971. *Survey of Settlements in Galilee and the Golan from the Period of the Mishnah in Light of the Sources* [Hebrew]. Diss. Hebrew University.

———. 1973. "Excavations at Khorazin" [Hebrew]. *EI* 11: 144–57.

———. 1993. "Chorazin." In *NEAEHL* 1: 301–304.

Zertal, A. 1992–. *The Manasseh Hill Country Survey*. Tel Aviv: Israel Department of Defense and University of Haifa.

Zipf, G. K. 1949. *Human Behavior and the Principle of Least Effort*. Cambridge: Addison-Wesley.

Zori, N. 1962. "An Archaeological Survey in the Beth-Shean Valley" [Hebrew]. In *The Beth Shean Valley: The Seventeenth Archaeological Convention*. Jerusalem: IES, 135-198.

———. 1977. *The Land of Issachar: An Archaeological Survey* [Hebrew]. Jerusalem: IES.

Zorn, J. 1994. "Estimating the Population Size of Ancient Settlements: Methods, Problems, Solutions and a Case Study." *BASOR* 295: 31–48.

Index of Sources

A. Rabbinic Texts, Hebrew Bible, New Testament

B. Classical and Patristic Texts

C. Papyri and Inscriptions

Index of Authors

Index of Subjects

Texts and Studies in Ancient Judaism

Alphabetical Index

Ipta, Kerstin: see *Schäfer, Peter*
Jacobs, Martin: Die Institution des jüdischen Patriarchen. 1995. *Volume 52.*
Kasher, Aryeh: The Jews in Hellenistic and Roman Egypt. 1985. *Volume 7.*
– Jews, Idumaeans, and Ancient Arabs. 1988. *Volume 18.*
– Jews and Hellenistic Cities in Eretz-Israel. 1990. *Volume 21.*
Krauss, Samuel: The Jewish-Christian Controversy from the earliest times to 1789. Vol.I. Hrsg. von *W. Horbury.* 1996. *Volume 56.*
Kuhn, Peter: Offenbarungsstimmen im Antiken Judentum. 1989. *Volume 20.*
Kuyt, Annelies: The ‚Descent' to the Chariot. 1995. *Volume 45.*
Lange, A.: see *Albani, M.*
Lange, Nicholas de: Greek Jewish Texts from the Cairo Genizah. 1996. *Volume 51.*
Lapin, Hayim: Economy, Geography, and Provincial History in Later Roman Galilee. 2001. *Volume 85.*
Leonhardt, Jutta: Jewish Worship in Philo of Alexandria. 2001. *Volume 84.*
Lohmann, Uta: see *Schäfer, Peter*
Loopik, M. van (Übers. u. komm.): The Ways of the Sages and the Way of the World. 1991. *Volume 26.*
Luttikhuizen, Gerard P.: The Revelation of Elchasai. 1985. *Volume 8.*
Mach, Michael: Entwicklungsstadien des jüdischen Engelglaubens in vorrabbinischer Zeit. 1992. *Volume 34.*
Mendels, Doron: The Land of Israel as a Political Concept in Hasmonean Literature. 1987. *Volume 15.*
Mutins, Georg von: see *Schäfer, Peter*
Necker, Gerold: see *Schäfer, Peter*
Niehoff, Maren: Philo on Jewish Identity and Culture. 2001. *Volume 86.*
Olyan, Saul M.: A Thousand Thousands Served Him. 1993. *Volume 36.*
Otterbach, Rina: see *Schäfer, Peter*
Prigent, Pierre: Le Judaisme et l'image. 1990. *Volume 24.*
Pucci Ben Zeev, Miriam: Jewish Rights in the Roman World. 1998. *Volume 74.*
Reeg, Gottfried (Hrsg.): Die Geschichte von den Zehn Märtyrern. 1985. *Volume 10.*
– see *Schäfer, Peter*
Renner, Lucie: see *Schäfer, Peter*
Reichman, Ronen: Sifra und Mishna. 1998. *Volume 68.*
Rohrbacher-Sticker, Claudia: see *Schäfer, Peter*
Salvesen, A. (Ed.): Origen's Hexapla and Fragments.1998. *Volume 58.*
Samely, Alexander: The Interpretation of Speech in the Pentateuch Targums. 1992. *Volume 27.*
Schäfer, Peter: Der Bar-Kokhba-Aufstand. 1981. *Volume 1.*
– Hekhalot-Studien. 1988. *Volume 19.*
Schäfer, Peter (Hrsg.): Geniza-Fragmente zur Hekhalot-Literatur. 1984. *Volume 6.*
– see *Goldberg, Arnold*
– in Zusammenarbeit mit *Klaus Herrmann, Rina Otterbach, Gottfried Reeg, Claudia Rohrbacher-Sticker, Guido Weyer:* Konkordanz zur Hekhalot-Literatur. Volume 1: 1986. *Volume 12.* – Volume 2: 1988. *Volume 13.*
Schäfer, Peter, Margarete Schlüter, Hans Georg von Mutins (Hrsg.): Synopse zur Hekhalot-Literatur. 1981. *Volume 2.*
Schäfer, Peter (Hrsg.) in Zusammenarbeit mit *Hans-Jürgen Becker, Klaus Herrmann, Ulrike Hirschfelder, Gerold Necker, Lucie Renner, Claudia Rohrbacher-Sticker,*

For a complete catalogue please write to the publisher
Mohr Siebeck ·Postfach 2040 ·D–72010 Tübingen.
Up-to-date information on the internet at http://www.mohr.de.